PENGUIN BOOKS

GRASS ROOTS

Dayton Duncan has been involved in New Hampshire
presidential primaries as a voter, newspaper reporter,
chief of staff to a New Hampshire governor, and adviser
to national campaigns. He is the author of *Out West:
American Journey Along the Lewis and Clark Trail*
(available from Penguin). He and his family live in
Fairway, Kansas.

DAYTON DUNCAN

GRASS ROOTS

ONE YEAR IN THE LIFE OF THE NEW HAMPSHIRE PRESIDENTIAL PRIMARY

PENGUIN BOOKS

PENGUIN BOOKS
Published by the Penguin Group
Viking Penguin, a division of Penguin Books USA Inc.,
375 Hudson Street, New York, New York 10014, U.S.A.
Penguin Books Ltd, 27 Wrights Lane,
London W8 5TZ, England
Penguin Books Australia Ltd, Ringwood,
Victoria, Australia
Penguin Books Canada Ltd, 10 Alcorn Avenue, Suite 300,
Toronto, Ontario, Canada M4V 3B2
Penguin Books (N.Z.) Ltd, 182–190 Wairau Road,
Auckland 10, New Zealand

Penguin Books Ltd, Registered Offices:
Harmondsworth, Middlesex, England

First published in the United States of America
by Viking Penguin, a division of Penguin Books USA Inc., 1991
Published in Penguin Books 1992

1 3 5 7 9 10 8 6 4 2

Grateful acknowledgment is made for permission to reprint material
that first appeared in *The Keene Sentinel.*

THE LIBRARY OF CONGRESS HAS CATALOGUED THE HARDCOVER AS FOLLOWS:
Duncan, Dayton
Grass roots: one year in the life of the New Hampshire
presidential primary / Dayton Duncan.
p. cm.
Includes index.
ISBN 0-670-81851-8 (hc.)
ISBN 0 14 01.0369 4 (pbk.)
1. Primaries—New Hampshire.   2. Electioneering—New Hampshire.
3. Presidents—United States—Election—1988.   I. Title.
JK2075.N42D86   1991
324.5´4—dc20   90–55264

Printed in the United States of America
Set in Primer

THIS BOOK IS DEDICATED TO
THE MEMORY OF THE LATE HUGH GALLEN,
WHO TAUGHT ME THE JOYS AND HEARTACHES,
BUT MOST OF ALL THE HIGHER PURPOSES,
OF POLITICS.

Sometimes it is said that man cannot be trusted with the government of himself. Can he, then, be trusted with the government of others?

—THOMAS JEFFERSON,
First Inaugural Address

CONTENTS

GRASS ROOTS

PROLOGUE

In the beginning were the lists. For the presidential campaigns in early 1987, a year before its crucial primary, New Hampshire existed not as a state of steep granite hills, of black, swift streams and of cold, blue lakes, but as piles of floppy disks, reels of magnetic tape, and sheets of computer printouts. To the campaigns, the state's inhabitants were not one million human beings, each one an individual character with his or her own unique life story filled with nuances of hopes, fears, passions, and quirky complexities. They were just names. Names on lists.

But they were names that could transform a governor, congressman, senator, general, or preacher into president of the United States. The political logic was compellingly straightforward: win New Hampshire or don't win the White House. Since the introduction of its first-in-the-nation preference primary in 1952, no one has won the presidency without first winning in New Hampshire.

If the logic seemed simple, the mathematics weren't much more complicated, merely a matter of subtraction and addition.

Subtraction. Of 1,027,000 people, 767,000 were age eighteen or older and therefore eligible to vote; of those, 586,492 were registered to vote; of those, 214,531 were registered as Republicans, 174,750 as Democrats, and 197,211 as Independents; and of those, about

160,000 Republicans and 125,000 Democrats were expected to cast ballots in the presidential primary on February 16, 1988. Certain victory through a majority vote in New Hampshire was therefore 80,000 votes for the Republicans or 62,500 for the Democrats. But with at least six candidates running in each party, a majority wouldn't be necessary to win. Nearly certain victory through a plurality vote was 55,000 for a Republican or 45,000 for a Democrat.

For someone hoping to be president—and in early 1987 a baker's dozen harbored such dreams—55,000 votes is a tantalizingly small number. About the size of the vote in a single ward in one large city or the vote in one county in an average-size state anywhere else in the United States. If you could count to 55,000 in New Hampshire, however, while you shaved in the morning, you might see a president looking back; you could start rehearsing a convention acceptance speech, perhaps even a draft inaugural address.

Addition. Begin with a small core of New Hampshire supporters—political activists, community leaders, people devoted to a particular issue or ideology or personality. A handful would suffice at the start. Win them over and then, with their help, win over a little larger number that in turn would help with an even larger number. If each one in an initial handful of five supporters found five more, each of whom found five more, 55,000 votes and victory waited at the seventh ring of supporters. Grow by nines and you only needed five expansions. It could be seen as a modestly ambitious chain letter—with a grand prize of becoming leader of the free world. Just count to 55,000.

But to begin the count, a candidate and his campaign had to find people willing to volunteer their time and effort. These volunteers would be the campaign's connection with the rest of the state, the first and critical link in the chain letter. They would be unique (except for their counterparts in the Iowa caucuses) in the long process by which the world's oldest democracy chooses its leaders.

They were ordinary citizens in most respects. If they were different from their next-door neighbors, it was only in their choice, for their own individual and varied reasons, to involve themselves early in a political campaign. If they were different from politically involved citizens in other states, it was only because they lived in New Hampshire, and New Hampshire is small, first to vote by ballot, and, because it's first, disproportionately important in presidential elections.

They were unique in another respect. A candidate running for president gets to know precious few people outside his immediate circle of paid advisers, wealthy fund-raisers, and the reporters covering his campaign. Voters, ordinary citizens, quickly become aggregates of demographic categories lumped together by age, sex, occupation, religion, ethnic heritage, marital status, income, and political party preference. They are faceless statistics, meaningful only by denying their individuality. Conversely, for the overwhelming majority of voters, even in tiny New Hampshire, the candidates are equally disembodied and ethereal: flickering images on the television screen, poster figures, words and pictures on a brochure in the mail, slogans and jingles on the radio.

Grass-roots volunteers at the heart of the presidential campaigns in New Hampshire, however, become acquainted with the candidates, not just as political figures, but as individuals. The candidates, in turn, become acquainted with them. At the same time, they are ordinary citizens who know the voters and whom the voters know, human connections between the soon-to-become-unreachable candidates and the community at large. For a brief moment they are at the pivot point of democracy.

None of New Hampshire's ten counties is entirely representative of the whole state. Some, in the southeastern corner, have been swallowed in the last twenty years by the growth of the megalopolis that stretches along the eastern seaboard from Washington, D.C., to Boston and now spills northward across the New Hampshire border, making New Hampshire the second-fastest-growing state east of the Mississippi River. Towns that were once distinct villages have become vast subdivisions; the old textile mills have been replaced by high-tech firms; shopping malls sit on what once were farms. The northernmost counties, bounded by the White Mountains and Canada, are, on the other hand, still remote, sparsely populated, and less changed—and thus equally unrepresentative of the whole state. The lakes region in central New Hampshire and the seacoast are tourist areas, filled increasingly with second homes of people who live in other states.

Nestled in the southwestern corner of New Hampshire is Cheshire County, bordered by rural western Massachusetts on the south and by the Connecticut River and Vermont on the west. With 67,684 souls living there in 1987, Cheshire County ranked sixth of the ten counties in population. Keene, the county seat and largest of the county's twenty-three towns, was home to 22,800 people. Cheshire County contains equal mixtures of New Hampshire's elements—what the state once was and now is. The region has been growing steadily, but not exponentially, for the last twenty years. The economy is diversified. Some of the old textile and shoe mills still operate, but many have been abandoned; one of them is now an upscale shopping mall. Dairy and sheep farms and apple orchards can still be found, particularly along the Connecticut River, but their numbers are dwindling, giving way to home sites. Industries, health services, a couple of insurance companies, construction, and an increasingly strong retail sector are the major employers. There are three colleges in the county, including a branch of the state university. In recent years New Hampshire has traditionally had the lowest unemployment rate in the nation; the Keene area's is usually one of the lowest within the state—around 2 percent in the late 1980s. At the same time, the median family ($18,454) was slightly lower than the state average, and the percentage of families living below the poverty level (10.2 percent) was slightly higher. The percentages of people with college educations, as well as with no high school diploma, were slightly higher than the state's.

Mount Monadnock, a solitary peak 3,165 feet high, dominates the surrounding topography of hills and lakes; it claims the distinction of being the second most climbed mountain in the world and is the focal point for the area's active but not overwhelming tourism industry. Keene itself boasts of having the widest Main Street in America running through its rejuvenated and picturesque downtown. Several other towns in the county feature eighteenth-century village centers that look like prototypical postcards from New England. Tourist brochures, overlooking some of the grittier towns and the shacks and trailer parks hidden in the backwoods, often refer to the area as the "Currier and Ives" section of New Hampshire. Locals call it the Monadnock Region.

A political operative looking over statistics about Cheshire County would quickly fasten on to three things. First, the county's proportions of Republican voters (36.4 percent), Democrats (29.4), and Independents (34.2) are nearly identical with the state average; in fact, it is the only county that doesn't vary much from the overall norm. Second, despite this statistical normalcy, the county's voting history in presidential primaries is more liberal—or, to be more precise, less conservative—than the rest of the state. Past Democratic candidates like George McGovern, Morris Udall, Birch Bayh, Fred Harris, Jerry Brown, and Jesse Jackson have done better in Cheshire County than in the state as a whole. On the Republican side, Ronald Reagan's percentages in Cheshire County in the 1976 and 1980 primaries were his worst of the ten counties (although Reagan nonetheless won the county in the 1980 race); John Anderson's share of the 1980 county vote was his highest in the state. Finally, as a campaign strategist surveyed the state and began making plans, the fact that Cheshire County represents about 6 percent of the statewide vote would be taken into account. In terms of assigning campaign resources—money, staff, and visits by a candidate—the four more populous counties to the east would get higher priority. That, after all, was where the bulk of the voters lived and the major media outlets were located. Then again, in a tight race 6 percent of the vote is by no means insignificant. Cheshire County was just small enough to be outside the main target of attention, just big enough to avoid being an afterthought in political calculations. On the whole, with the exception of its more moderate tilt, it was just about as average a county as you could find.

As the calendar turned to 1987, the budding presidential campaigns were proceeding along virtually the same tracks in New Hampshire and Cheshire County. All were seeking the magic alchemy that would turn lists into flesh; a disembodied name on a sheet of paper into a living, breathing supporter; a supporter into a worker who could expand the list. The mail, the phones, and personal connections were being mined, panned, and sifted in search of gold nuggets—people willing to meet in small living rooms to hear the same refrains of electoral hope and then commit themselves to the hard work ahead.

At first, of course, even the volunteers were just names. Names on a list—a list of past supporters of some past candidacy, a list of attendees of some past political function, a list of members of some organization, a list of those who had written or called some political office seeking information, an informal list of people who could contact other people. Sometimes potential volunteers were simply people who had their own lists.

1

LISTS

Andi Johnson cradled a small cardboard box in her lap as she sat in the small study of Tom and Valerie Britton's home in Troy, New Hampshire. Outside, a cold winter wind blustered under a cloudless sky, pushing wisps of snow across the frosted windowpane, but the logs crackling in the fireplace made the room drowsily warm. It was February 12, 1987. The primary was one year and four days away. But the seven people arrayed around Britton's wooden desk were talking politics. The first local meeting of a presidential campaign organization in Cheshire County was under way.

The small turnout—only four of them were actually from the Monadnock Region; the other three were campaign staff members who had driven down from state headquarters in Concord—did not bother Andi. *We won last time with small groups*, she thought.

Gary Hart, their candidate, had seemingly come from nowhere in 1984 to upset former Vice President Walter Mondale and win New Hampshire's Democratic primary on the strength, she believed, of the commitment and labor of his small local organizations. The 1984 primary had been the first intensive campaign experience for many of Hart's supporters, like Andi. To them, theirs had been a guerrilla effort of novice yet highly committed idealists against the political establishment, the money and machine of Mondale's campaign. If Hart's eventual demise in later primaries had disappointed her, Andi nevertheless had the sweet memory of the stunning New Hampshire victory. *They* had made the nomination possible; Hart and his campaign in other states had lost it. This time it would be done right—from start to finish. This time they weren't novices. This time they weren't fighting the political establishment, they were part of it. And this time their candidate wasn't a dark horse, he was the presumed Democratic front-runner headed, Andi believed, straight to the White House. The notion, along with memories of her first campaign, warmed her like the fire in the fireplace.

On March 3, 1983—four years later she still remembered the exact date—Andi had attended a Hart reception in Hanover, New Hampshire. She was working at the time at the local hospital, in cost reimbursement, and had become active in a women's crisis center. Besides a general announcement of the visit, the Hart campaign had sought out people involved in various organizations and causes, particularly women's issues. Andi, on the crisis center's board of directors and therefore on a list, received a personal invitation. She went to hear the senator from Colorado out of curiosity.

She was not unaware of politics. Growing up in Massachusetts in the 1960s, she and her father, a Republican, had argued about the Vietnam War over the dinner table. Her mother belonged to the local Republican Women's Club. At New England College in Henniker, New Hampshire, she was a reporter for the college radio station and in 1972 had covered the state Nixon headquarters on election night. She was nineteen at the time and during the school vacation had registered to vote at home as a Democrat without telling her parents. But before 1983 she had never joined any election campaign.

Andi had heard that Hart was "a little bit different" from other politicians, and when he replied "I don't know" to a question of hers about a specific health care cost issue, she decided he was also uncommonly honest for a candidate. A month later (having put her name on a sign-up sheet at the first meeting) she was invited to another reception. This time Hart had a good answer to her question, a sign, she thought, that he did his homework. She volunteered to help.

Long before the end of that campaign, Andi was hooked on politics. Her one-bedroom apartment became unofficial Hart headquarters for the area. Out-of-state college students, sometimes as many as a dozen, would sleep there during weekend blitzes of door-to-door canvassing. She started attending political events in other parts of the state. Increasingly the campaign became the principal focus of her life.

It was a combination of serious political involvement and social activity. It had a purpose, but more than that it was exciting and fun. Andi worked hard and partied hard. Through the campaign she met new people and found a boyfriend. In the flush of Hart's dramatic victory in the 1984 primary, she was sorely tempted by the campaign's request for volunteers to pull up stakes and move on to the next primaries. But other obligations—her job, her cat, her apartment—kept her, reluctantly, in New Hampshire. During weekends, however, she found herself driving long hours to help out in Vermont, Massachusetts, Connecticut, New York, and New Jersey. These weekends were like supercharged rendezvous in a passionate affair. The things she cared the most about—her boyfriend, politics, the sense of crusade and mission within the campaign—were intertwined and packed into those days. She loved it, couldn't get enough of it. Most definitely she was hooked.

Like the others sitting in Britton's house in February 1987, Andi had kept track of "Gary" (all of his early supporters referred to Hart by his first name) in the intervening years through intermittent mailings from his organization. Sue Calegari, the state director, had developed a list of roughly two thousand names—supporters from 1984, Democratic VIPs in the state, and other activists—to receive *Hart Line*, a newsletter with tidbits of information about Hart, the New Hampshire political scene, and the initial stirrings of the 1988 campaign.

Signaling his transformation from insurgent to front-runner, Hart made his first New Hampshire appearance at a state Democratic committee meeting in Concord in mid-January 1987, where he told the large room filled with political activists, reporters, and television cameras that the challenge of the 1988 election would be "to hold candidates to a high standard of character and competence." (Everyone who signed the attendance sheet later received a four-page letter over Hart's signature reiterating his positions on the major issues and outlining his platform "if I run again for the Presidency." They were now on Sue Calegari's growing list; *Hart Line* was soon arriving in their mailboxes.)

After the speech Andi had attended a "Welcome Back Again" reception for Hart and about eighty supporters, all veterans of the volunteer effort in 1984. Her own mood mirrored the feeling palpable in the restaurant's function room. They were confident, almost smug, about their candidate's prospects. Hart was no longer an unknown, he was a national figure, and they had helped make him one. As he mingled among them, Hart was both their leader and their peer. More than that he was their symbol: living proof that, by their collective efforts, they could accomplish anything—win not only a primary, but this time the presidency, and affect the course of a nation. Most of them, like Andi, were young, in their twenties and thirties, and the reception had the aura of a college mixer at the start of classes for sophomores, who could still enjoy the tinglings of excitement that school was back in session, but already knew the ropes and therefore lacked first-year jitters.

Andi was itching to get started and was the first to arrive at the Britton home a month later. The Cheshire County meeting was similar to the local organizational meetings that would follow, not just for the Hart campaign, but for those of other candidates. Despite a short agenda and the small number of participants, it was a long meeting—nearly three hours.

The discussion alternated between specific organizational issues (Andi wanted to know when a Keene office would open), rambling discourses on national politics (would Joe Biden run? Mario Cuomo? Andi proudly reported that she had recently called a Boston radio talk show to complain about coverage of Massachusetts Governor Michael Dukakis; he didn't have the foreign policy experience to be president, she had complained), local gossip (which activists were supporting other candidates), and critiques of their own candidate.

"People say Gary's too cold and aloof," Andi offered. "He ought to be seen in more casual clothes. And he's *got* to smile more." She herself was anything but cold and aloof. She was impulsive and outspoken, and her most distinctive facial characteristic was a wide, toothy smile, which she flashed to demonstrate what she believed her candidate needed to do.

Sue Calegari, the state director, listened patiently to the advice and then gently steered the conversation to the two items of particular interest to her: an upcoming visit to Keene by the candidate himself and what she called "list management."

Hart was scheduled to be the keynote speaker at the annual dinner of the Cheshire County Democrats in March, and his campaign wanted to use the event as a tool for building a larger local organizational base. Details needed attending to, and many of them revolved around lists.

The county party would be mailing an announcement of the speech and dinner to the 450 Democrats on its own list, but Calegari wanted a more strenuous effort. A good turnout would be doubly beneficial to Hart's interests: it would demonstrate to people, particularly the media, his drawing power as a candidate; and by exposing Hart to more Democrats locally, it would provide an excuse for them to be reached by follow-up contacts to seek their support.

Lists were essential to augment the turnout. Andi and the others agreed to call likely Democrats to reinforce the invitations (and gauge their initial opinions toward Hart). The list of those who actually showed up would be the basis for follow-up calls and letters. From those, it was hoped, some would join the campaign and help during the rest of the year as more people were contacted and added to the lists. Subtraction and addition.

The cardboard box had rested on Andi's lap throughout the meeting. As the discussion focused on lists, she patted and stroked it like a friendly cat she was particularly proud of. It contained nearly 800 three-by-five index cards, each one with a name, address, telephone number, and other notations about a voter in the Keene area. They represented the distilled essence of the multitude of campaigns in which she had participated since moving to Cheshire County from the Hanover area in 1984—names of supporters of state and local Democratic candidates, names of activists who had fought against a proposed nuclear waste dump and the Seabrook nuclear power plant. They were, in effect, Andi's credentials, demonstrating who she was now versus who she had been when she went to her first campaign event four years earlier.

The names were to be entered into the computer at state headquarters. The box of names was her gift, and not an inconsequential one, to Gary.

"Well, if we did it last time [won the primary] from behind, we should be able to do it now," said Tom Britton, partly out of confidence and partly seeking reassurance from the others as the meeting ended.

They nodded. "We're gonna win," he repeated.

Andi gave him a big grin, patted her cardboard box one more time, and handed it over.

"We'll win," she said.

Lists have other uses.

In early March 1987 the Republican parties of the Northeast convened a "leadership conference" in Nashua, New Hampshire, ostensibly to discuss a range of national and regional issues. Mainly, however, the conference was an excuse for the budding presidential campaigns to display their candidates in the state of the first primary. Whether they were already committed to a campaign or still shopping, party activists saw it as a chance to gather in one place for two days to appraise the field of contenders in the flesh and, of course, handicap the race ahead.

All of the likely GOP candidates attended: Vice President George

Bush, Senator Robert Dole of Kansas, Congressman Jack Kemp of New York, former Delaware Governor Pierre S. ("Pete") du Pont, televangelist Reverend Pat Robertson, former Secretary of State Al Haig, and former Congressman Donald Rumsfeld (who would later drop out before formally declaring his candidacy). Bush's campaign arranged for him to skip a joint dinner appearance with the other contenders and appear alone to address the luncheon—a maneuver that prompted a buzz of resentment from the other camps and became the conversational and media focus of the conference. The primary was still eleven months distant, and even in New Hampshire most people were unaware of the proceedings, but for the small coterie of political junkies the internal competitive tactics of the conference took on an importance that far exceeded whatever the candidates said during two days. Such is the nature of these things that speculation was rampant whether Bush had already crippled his chances for the presidency by not appearing side by side with his competitors.

Collections of candidates, campaign strategists, and political activists attract political reporters as magnets attract iron filings. That this conference was being held roughly a year before the all-important primary made it a major media event, a curtain raiser for the quadrennial drama of American politics. Press badges nearly outnumbered conferees' nametags. Reporters roamed the hotel corridors, stopping to talk to campaign staffers, to recognizable political figures, or, just as often, to themselves. If one reporter was seen jotting in his notebook while he talked with someone, soon a few more journalists would gather and open theirs, sometimes before determining who was being quoted. The cluster would grow geometrically like a cancer cell, until hallway traffic was momentarily clogged. Television crews, still photographers, reporters, and a clutch of serious-looking aides surrounded each candidate as he walked from one room to another, every movement brightly lit and recorded on film.

Knowing that the conference would draw so many national political reporters, the Kemp campaign had devised a strategy to impress them. For nearly a month the campaign had contacted New Hampshire Republicans who were willing to be named publicly as Kemp supporters. The point of gathering the names was not so much to build their organization as to publicize their list with the press. By showing a large number of supporters, the campaign hoped to convince reporters that, in a race with a sitting vice president and Senate minority leader, both of whom had run for president before in 1980, Kemp was making progress in New Hampshire and should be accorded the attention of a major contender. Early in the campaign season underdog campaigns are caught in a vicious circle as they struggle to prove their legitimacy. Without serious mention in the press they have trouble raising money or registering well in public opinion polls; without the money and the poll ratings, they have even further trouble being considered viable by reporters. Campaigns that break out of this downward spiral are the historical exception rather than the rule.

So the Kemp forces had labored for weeks on their secret list strategy. On the two days of the leadership conference, they unveiled full-page advertisements in the Nashua and Manchester newspapers. Under the headline WE BACK JACK was a brief endorsement and the names of five hundred people, grouped by their towns in New Hampshire. The two newspapers have combined circulations of about one hundred thousand people, but the real target for the ads was much smaller: the collection of a hundred-plus political reporters gathered in Nashua, who, it was hoped, would peruse the local papers over morning coffee.

The same newspapers carried a smaller advertisement from the Haig campaign, aimed at New Hampshire residents but noticed by reporters. It announced that Haig would be appearing at a Manchester shopping center after the leadership conference. As an added attraction to entice a crowd, he would appear with Fuzzy the Kop, Happy the Clown, and Uncle Sam on stilts. A Dixieland band would play. Hot dogs and balloons would be free.

Much to the chagrin of the Kemp campaign, which had spent considerable time and money for their newspaper ads, the list strategy fizzled. News reports of the conference concentrated on Bush's refusal to appear with his competitors. If any reporters had noticed the Kemp list, they kept it to themselves and didn't mention it. A few stories, however, made passing reference to the fact that Haig— the former supreme commander of Allied NATO forces, former White House chief of staff, and former secretary of state—was last seen campaigning in the company of clowns.

At least one person, however, noticed the Kemp list. Kendall Lane clipped out the ad, took it to his office in Keene, and pored over it with intense interest. Kendall was already well versed in the importance campaigns place on lists. It seemed to him, in fact, that about all the Bush campaign did was collect them, talk about them, go over them, and refine them. To be honest, he was getting a little sick of it, and there was still nearly a year to go. He had volunteered for the Bush campaign at its very start to be an inside player, someone who participated in shaping political strategy, who knew what was going on *before* he read it in the newspapers. Instead, from the moment a small group first met in early 1986 to map initial plans for Bush in New Hampshire—long before they had even named themselves "Freedom Fighters" as the self-designation of an elite corps—the principal topic of their weekly meetings was lists.

Bush's young campaign director in New Hampshire, Will Abbott, believed that "the whole key to winning an election is knowing who your voters are and getting them to the polls." That meant compiling lists, and two full years before the primary Abbott started his first. By the spring of 1987 it had four thousand names—supporters of Bush's 1980 campaign, members of the state Republican committee, the New Hampshire Federation of Republican Women, and any Republican who had held elective office in the previous eight years. During the state elections of 1986, Bush's political action committee had donated money to every Republican candidate for every elective office in New Hampshire—$50 each to the 267 house and 66 county office candidates, $200 to $1,000 to 16 state senate hopefuls, $500 to $3,000 to all 5 executive councillors, and various large sums to Governor John Sununu and the two congressmen. Some already publicly supported Bush's competitors. Abbott gave them money anyway. It buttressed the public explanation that Bush was helping the entire party rather than buying support, and it provided a deposit of goodwill that might come in handy if any of the other presidential campaigns collapsed before the primary. As local politicians started endorsing Bush in early 1987, Abbott reaped a rich harvest of lists. From sheriffs to the governor, all of them had names—some on index cards, some on computer disks—of their supporters, people with a proven interest and some experience in politics. These were merged with Abbott's growing target list.

His grand plan called for Bush's core supporters to contact each of the four thousand target Republicans, personally and repeatedly, and try to enlist them for the campaign. Abbott hoped eventually to have an organization in virtually all of New Hampshire's 298 voting precincts, even if the organization was just one person who could be counted on to help when the time came. His dream was a network of local volunteers broad and deep enough to call 175,000 potential Republican voters, determine how many and which ones liked Bush, and then contact those again just before the voting day.

Such a mathematical, almost mechanical approach to electioneering was not a new concept for Kendall. When he was in sixth grade and junior high school in the late 1950s and early 1960s, he had helped his father, chairman of the Cheshire County Republican party, keep file cards on all the registered voters in the county. After every election they would drive to each town clerk's office (often the clerk's home). While the elder Lane talked politics with the clerk, Kendall would go through the checklist recording new voters, registration changes, and who among the registered voters had bothered to show up to cast ballots. Election nights during high school and college were special nights. Kendall would stay up late entering election returns onto a handmade chart, much like other boys might keep a box score of a baseball game heard on the radio.

As a student at the University of New Hampshire, he spent more than a few idle hours in the library looking up returns and statistics from past elections simply, he would explain later, "because that part of politics always had a certain fascination for me."

From his own experiences running for the state legislature, the constitutional convention, and the city council, and from his wife Jane's race for county commissioner, Kendall had developed a further appreciation for the importance of grass-roots groundwork. To a certain extent he felt that one thing that separated the political dilettantes from the real insiders was an understanding of the mechanics of an election. Being clued in to Abbott's grand plan from the very beginning also reassured Kendall's methodical nature. He liked plans and strategies.

Yet he was somewhat surprised, even a little disappointed, that so far his first involvement on a presidential campaign was remarkably similar to a Ward 4 council race, only for higher stakes and on a higher scale. As a "Freedom Fighter" he had envisioned more discussion of what the vice president should be doing—where he should campaign, what he should be saying—rather than the mundane topic of whether Abbott's master list was growing on schedule. More than that, in these formative stages of the campaign, Kendall was actually *compiling* his region's portion of the lists, and deep down, even despite his lifelong "fascination," he now felt he had a lot more to offer a campaign than the grunt work. The gap between his early expectations of what he would be doing and what was actually happening reminded him a little of the difference between what most people thought lawyers did versus the reality of a general practice like his. There wasn't the constant courtroom drama of *Perry Mason* or any of the other television lawyers, merely a lot of painstaking time reading the fine print of contracts, deeds, and wills.

Building the list was not particularly easy, either. Kendall may have been committed to his candidate for a full year by this point, but in March 1987, as he talked to other people whom he wanted to join the Bush effort, he found most of them, even though they

had a record of involvement in campaigns, either unwilling to give
it much thought so far before the primary or ambivalent toward
Bush. Even some people who had supported Bush in the 1980 New
Hampshire primary seemed reluctant. Questions about Bush's real
role in the disastrous sale of arms to Iran and questions about
whether the vice president was capable of being "his own man"
hung over the campaign and occasionally seeped into the conversations Kendall would initiate to feel out people on his target list.
Preferring an informal approach, he would look for another excuse
to contact someone and then try to steer the talk to the upcoming
presidential race. "Have you decided who you're going to support
yet?" he asked the woman behind the counter at the motor vehicle
registry. (He wanted her to lead the campaign in her small town,
and when Jane's car needed its yearly license plate tag, he'd gone
there himself specifically to take advantage of the opportunity.)
When she said no, he had explained why he liked "the vice president" (as all of Bush's supporters called him), said he hoped she
might consider helping in the future, finished getting his tag, and
left. The work was slow, and for every success there seemed to be
ten disappointments. Meanwhile, Will Abbott would call him in the
evenings to talk about lists.

When the Kemp list of five hundred supporters appeared in the
newspaper, Kendall read it closely—out of both competitive interest
and sheer habit. Most of the twenty-three names from the Keene
region didn't surprise him. He already knew they favored Kemp
over Bush. But a few jolted him. Two fellow city councillors were
on the list. Neither had given him any indication of their preference.
How did Kemp get them? Could Kendall have gotten them by
working harder or earlier on them? One name on the Kemp list
was also on Kendall's Bush list. Which list was wrong, theirs
or his?

And where was Al Rubega's name? Why wasn't it on the list? Al
and Mary Rubega had sat with Kemp at the leadership conference
dinner in Nashua; they had worn Kemp buttons during both days;
Al had distributed Kemp folders (along with bumper stickers that

proclaimed "I'M THE NRA . . . AND I VOTE") during Bush's luncheon address. But Al's name wasn't on the list. Kendall couldn't figure it out. What were they up to? Were they holding back even more names for another announcement? Maybe Al wouldn't let them use his name publicly. In his own contacts Kendall had found people who assured him they supported Bush but didn't want it announced. Yet Al seemed very visible with his buttons and folders. Maybe, Kendall thought, Al was backing Kemp at the moment but wasn't wholeheartedly committed. Maybe, at the right moment, he could be brought over and put on a Bush list.

The oversight that resulted in his not being listed in the Kemp newspaper endorsement didn't disturb Al Rubega. He shrugged it off and kept on working. There were others on the list who would have created a ruckus at state headquarters if their name had been forgotten on a public announcement. Every campaign has its share of "high maintenance" supporters, people who are always making demands to meet privately with the candidate, always elbowing their way forward to be seen near him at the podium, always complaining that they aren't being consulted enough for political advice, and always passing on gossip to reporters (often inaccurate and often to the detriment of the campaign) simply to see their name in the paper. The amount of attention they require is usually in indirect proportion to the actual work they perform. They are the political equivalents of the black holes in outer space: they consume all the campaign energy in their immediate vicinity for no discernible result.

Al was not like that. His value to the Kemp campaign and the high regard they had for him, in fact, was due in part to their realization that Al would knock himself out for Kemp without a lot of ego stroking. "If I only had ten Al Rubegas [one for each county], no one could beat us in New Hampshire," Paul Young, the state director for Kemp, said in early 1987. Al considered himself a "foot soldier" and even as he took on more leadership responsibility for the campaign in Cheshire County would never think of asking other

volunteers to do some task he wasn't willing to do himself. Mary
Rubega sometimes wondered whether her husband took it a little
too far: it often seemed he just did the work himself when he could
have asked others to help.

Al brought something extra to the Kemp table beyond his boundless enthusiasm and self-effacing willingness for hard work. As
president of Gun Owners of New Hampshire, he had access to
an important mailing list. Few interest groups in America were better organized politically than gun owners through the National
Rifle Association, with which GO:NH was affiliated. An appeal in
their newsletter that the legislature was considering a new law re-
stricting the sale or ownership of firearms could turn people who
otherwise might pay little attention to politics into letter-writing,
check-writing, representative-calling activists.

Like many conservative Republicans, Kemp's New Hampshire
strategists placed a high premium on direct-mail tactics. Letters to
targeted audiences served several purposes: bringing Kemp's name
to their attention, identifying him with issues important to them,
and eliciting enough donations to at least cover the cost of the
mailings. Most of Kemp's rivals for the Republican nomination had,
at one time or another, voted against the gun lobby. Kemp never
had. Pointing that out through Al's mailing list could be a valuable
tool in the late stages of the campaign.

By early 1987 their campaign was already the most active in its
use of direct mail, sending out about three thousand pieces a month
in New Hampshire. Their list included names from single-issue
groups (gun owners, right-to-life organizations, an antitax foundation) and identified conservatives (supporters of a conservative
U.S. senator and representative, the former town chairmen from
Ronald Reagan's previous campaigns), as well as the rolls of the
state Republican committee and Republican elected officials. They
viewed the mailings like seeds broadcast loosely over several fields
at the same time. Some would take root and blossom with responses.
Lists, in other words, would cross-pollinate and help breed a confirmed Kemp list.

Because of its more liberal voting history, Cheshire County was not considered the Kemp campaign's most fertile field. Nevertheless, by late April the mailings were able to produce nine people willing to meet at the home of Dr. David Ridge, a Keene chiropractor active in the antiabortion movement and previous conservative Republican campaigns, for their first organizational meeting. Al and Mary Rubega, already firmly committed to Kemp, were there, serving as unofficial lieutenants to Paul Young, who arrived to give the group an overview of the campaign and start things moving on the local level.

List development was Young's foremost objective, but building morale among these core supporters quickly became the meeting's focus. Kemp was languishing in single digits in national and state polls, far behind Bush and Dole. Rumors were rampant that the campaign was having financial troubles. And the political news was filled with reports that other conservatives, from Senator Paul Laxalt to former Ambassador Jeane Kirkpatrick, might enter the race because Kemp was not galvanizing the right wing of the Republican party. Young realized that before he could energize these troops to do the work he wanted of them, they needed some encouragement that the effort would pay off. One by one he answered their concerns, Al often weighing in with his own anecdotal tales of good news. The polls showed weak commitment to Bush and Dole, Young said, reminding them that this far ahead of the New Hampshire primary in past campaigns, Ronald Reagan, George Mc-Govern, Jimmy Carter, and Gary Hart had all suffered even lower poll standings and gone on to success. Laxalt, he told them, would have image problems because he had been governor of Nevada, a state with legalized gambling and prostitution; Kirkpatrick was Kemp's choice for secretary of state and would probably not run. The campaign was solvent, he assured them. He expected Pat Robertson to drop out of the race before New Hampshire, which would leave the conservative field to Kemp alone. Dole would beat Bush in Iowa, he predicted, and then collapse in New Hampshire.

Al had attended Kemp's formal announcement in Manchester

earlier in the month and reported enthusiastically on the large media turnout and the excitement of the crowd's response to their candidate. "All of us can name people supporting the vice president," he said, "but who can name one person in the county who's with Dole?" Their silence made his point: it was going to be between Bush and Kemp.

The cumulative message of the pep talk was that, despite the disappointing press coverage at the moment, a Kemp victory was not only possible but nearly inevitable. These nine citizens could play a part in putting another true conservative in the White House and taking the "Reagan revolution" into its next phase.

Now Young could focus their attention on the task at hand. He handed out sheets of paper under the title "The Cotton System." Named for a former New Hampshire senator who had used it in all his campaigns, it was merely a form with spaces for ten names, addresses, and phone numbers. Each person was to find ten other people who supported Kemp, enter the information, and send it to the state headquarters, then ideally get each of the ten to take a form as well and get ten more supporters. The nine here tonight would become ninety, the ninety would become nine hundred, and on to victory.

Al was already filling in some names on his sheet when the coffee and cookies were served. Simple addition to the presidency. This didn't seem hard at all.

2

LIVING ROOMS

The nine people sitting around the breakfast table at Dan Burnham's house chatted amiably as they passed around platters of sausage and bacon, croissants and English muffins, jars of homemade preserves, and a large pitcher of orange juice. The discussion was lively, eclectic, spiced with occasional humor—the kind of informed discourse you might expect from well-educated members of the professional class. These were people who read avidly—books, magazines, more than one daily newspaper—both to keep abreast of the latest developments in the news and to satisfy a well-honed curiosity in the world of ideas. All had traveled extensively in their lives, which, added to their educations and their involvement in numerous community and state organizations, from the arts to commerce, made them able to converse intelligently on a diverse range of topics: the balance of trade, the new leadership asserting itself in the Soviet Union, environmental issues from the depletion of the ozone layer to nuclear power, domestic politics, and the nature of leadership. It had the tone of a conversation among peers. Everyone participated.

They tried fairly successfully to carry on a *normal* conversation, though this wasn't exactly easy. Two reporters were taking notes from nearby chairs. A photographer from a local paper leaned in occasionally and popped a flash picture, making them self-conscious enough not to emphasize a point by gesturing forcefully when a sausage was on the end of their fork. A television crew from Cable News Network circled behind their chairs, shooting footage. Two young men in business suits hovered at the edges, hanging on everyone's words and studying their body language for signs of discord. Their group included a banker, the owner of a small woolen mill, the director of a charitable foundation, an environmental activist, a woman involved in the local United Way and arts council . . . and a candidate for president of the United States. Dan Burnham had invited friends over for breakfast with Bruce Babbitt.

March of 1987 was not yet a week old. New Hampshire's citizens, the first Americans to cast ballots for a presidential candidate, still had eleven months to make up their minds. Most of them were as yet unaware of the field of candidates, let alone concerned about the choice they would ultimately have to make in the primary. The general election, when the next president would finally be chosen, lay even farther over time's horizon: twenty months away. By the time the election came, a child could be conceived, carried to term, and born, could learn to walk and master enough words to thrill its parents. But Bruce Babbitt, the former Democratic governor of Arizona, had already been campaigning for president for roughly a year and a half.

He had been in New Hampshire enough times by now to know the state's geography, its political demography, and its various idiosyncrasies. Since June of 1986 he had been making two excursions into the state a month. He already knew the names of every Democratic mayor in the state and had met privately with each one more than once. The same for a host of state legislators, party officials, environmental activists, day care advocates, and editorial writers and political reporters of most of the state's small daily and weekly newspapers. Two of his aides had already lived through a complete cycle of New Hampshire's four seasons; to study the political atmosphere firsthand, they had moved to the state in 1986, one to volunteer at the state party headquarters and the other to help in the elections of local Democratic candidates. His state headquarters had held its official opening in January 1987 (although it had been set up a good month earlier). Babbitt himself had already climbed Mount Washington, New Hampshire's highest peak. (As interested in history and government as in the outdoors, he had also used his hike to learn more about the Weeks Act and the formation of the White Mountains National Forest than 99.9 percent of New Hampshire's population knew.) He knew that people who lived in Milan and Berlin, two small towns in the remote North Country that were closer to Montreal than to Boston, pronounced their town names "MY'lan" and "BER'lin" and considered anyone who said "MehLAN' " or "BerLIN' " unintelligent. He had attended a pancake feast at the home of a state representative in the mountain region, a clambake hosted by a state senator on the seacoast, a hot dog barbecue with the county chairman along the upper reaches of the Connecticut River, and a meal at a Greek restaurant in Manchester, where one of the walls now displayed a picture of Babbitt and the state senator, who owned the place—next to pictures of the restaurateur and other Democratic presidential hopefuls.

Sharing a meal with a small number of New Hampshire voters was, therefore, nothing new to Babbitt when he sat down to breakfast at the Burnham household. Nor was the fact that, as he had been driven in "Babbitt One," the customized van owned by one of his aides, from the Boston airport to Cheshire County last night, a potential supporter had been put in the van with him for the two-hour ride. Neither was his spending the night in a private home, Burnham's, rather than in a hotel; nor was his schedule for the rest of the day: an interview with *The Keene Sentinel* editorial board, a meeting with some more local environmentalists, an interview with a weekly paper in nearby Peterborough, then on to another part of New Hampshire for more small gatherings, meals, interviews, and meetings before going to sleep in someone else's house.

None of it was new. All were rituals of the New Hampshire primary, and Babbitt had them down pat.

Presidential campaigns once began and ended in the same calendar year. In fact, well into the twentieth century candidates did not actually stump for votes prior to the conventions. Primaries existed, but these were held to elect convention delegates, most of whom were affiliated with their state or region's political leaders—a governor, mayor, senator, party chairman—rather than a national candidate. At the conventions party leaders haggled, argued, bargained, and eventually anointed the nominees they thought had the best chance of capturing the White House. Campaigning as we now know it—traveling to a state, making speeches, asking for voters' support—rarely began until after Labor Day. Less than three months later a president was elected.

When the New Hampshire preference primary was inaugurated in 1952, half of the candidates didn't bother to show up. Dwight Eisenhower, then the head of NATO forces in Europe, allowed his name to be placed on the Republican ballot but stayed at his post on the other side of the Atlantic Ocean while surrogates, mostly prominent state officials, campaigned on his behalf. Ohio Senator Robert Taft also wanted the Republican nomination but originally thought it better to sit out the New Hampshire primary and wait for more favorable political terrain in midwestern primaries. Late in the game Taft was talked into contesting New Hampshire, and in the final weekend before the vote, in early March, he came to the state for a three-day, twenty-eight-town campaign tour. Large crowds—1,500 in Manchester, 300 in Peterborough—turned out to hear him speak at every stop. The absentee Eisenhower still won handily.

President Harry Truman initially disdained participating in the 1952 Democratic primary, bluntly calling it and other primaries "eyewash," beneath the concern of a sitting president and irrelevant to the way parties nominated candidates. He, too, finally succumbed to pleas from his supporters, and his name was placed on the ballot.

But Truman steadfastly refused to do any personal campaigning in New Hampshire. Like Ike, he relied on the leaders of his party's organization. Truman's challenger was Estes Kefauver, a young senator from Tennessee who had risen to national attention during televised Senate hearings on organized crime. Kefauver made two campaign trips to New Hampshire, both within a month of the primary, and he adopted a personal approach, often jumping out of his car to grab a citizen's hand and exclaim, "I'm Estes Kefauver, running for president—how'm I doin' here?" He met with people in their homes, on the main streets, on the factory lines, on the ice of frozen lakes as they fished, wherever he could find them. Even his set speaking appearances took on a more personal, intimate cast, as much because of disappointingly small turnouts of thirty or forty people as out of a conscious strategy. Every political reporter was predicting a Truman victory. Yet to everyone's surprise, including Kefauver's, Truman lost the primary and shortly afterward withdrew entirely from the presidential race.

Those first Republican and Democratic primaries of 1952 were actually mirror images of the same political picture. Both pitted a candidate who campaigned actively in the state against one who didn't; a candidate who staked his own presence against the party establishment aligned with his absent opponent; a senator of modest national repute against a truly national figure; a candidate who the prevailing political wisdom believed couldn't win against someone who couldn't lose. Faced with identical options, however, the two parties made opposite choices. The Republicans selected Eisenhower, who had stayed in Paris, content to bank on his popular appeal while New Hampshire's governor and other local officials did all the campaigning. The Democrats, on the other hand, preferred Kefauver, the barnstorming, handshaking, insurgent senator.

A maverick bucking the establishment, a David toppling a Goliath, an underdog taking his case directly to the people in spite of the smug opinion of "insiders" and experts, a candidate for the nation's highest office answering ordinary citizens' questions and

listening to their concerns in a small town hall or private home—
these are the fundamental elements of America's idealized con-
ception of itself, how we prefer to think our democracy works: *Mr.
Smith Goes to Washington* applied to the presidential race. It is
not surprising, therefore, that of the contradictory results in 1952,
the one that was remembered and that fathered the rituals and
popular notion of future New Hampshire primaries was that of the
Democrats.

In the primaries that followed, more often than not the early
favorite would win as expected. Well-known, established candidates
would usually defeat lesser-known insurgents. Instances of candidates prevailing without even setting foot across the state's borders would outnumber those in which the winner had been in New
Hampshire significantly more often than his opponents. But those
didn't fit the mythic, more dramatic mold. The few instances that
did conform became the memorable primaries, further reinforcing
the rituals. In 1968 Senator Eugene McCarthy invaded the state
with an army of college kids, who went door to door for their antiwar
candidate. President Lyndon Johnson did not campaign and in fact
did not even allow his name to be on the ballot. A write-in effort
mounted by the Democratic party establishment brought LBJ 49.6
percent of the vote to McCarthy's 41.9 percent. Nevertheless the
results were portrayed as a stinging "defeat" for Johnson, an impression that was solidified when he, like Truman before him, decided
to withdraw from the impending battle for reelection. Four years
earlier Henry Cabot Lodge had easily won the 1964 Republican
primary, also on write-in ballots, also without campaigning in person (he was U.S. ambassador to South Vietnam). Lodge's 35.5
percent overwhelmed Senator Barry Goldwater (with 22.3 percent),
who had spent twenty-one days touring the state, and Governor
Nelson Rockefeller (with 21 percent), who had campaigned twenty-
eight days.

By 1970 New Hampshire had hosted five presidential primaries.
Out of ten races (five Republican, five Democratic), only four had
been seriously contested. Candidates who remained in Paris, Sai-

gon, and Washington had won three of them—two without being on the ballot. Kefauver was still the only victor who had taken his case directly to the people. Regardless, New Hampshire was already seen as a state inhabited by a bucolic and flinty folk who insisted on making would-be presidents look them in the eye and ask for their vote and who liked nothing better than giving a self-important politician who ignored them his comeuppance.

The two primaries of the 1970s, with three of the four matches hotly contested, further enhanced New Hampshire's political profile as a maker and breaker of presidents. Equally significant, the start of campaigning moved irretrievably forward into the year, and eventually the *years*, preceding the actual voting year. The political folklore of what it took to win in New Hampshire hardened into unquestioned rituals of a state religion.

George McGovern had decided that as an unknown senator from the remote state of South Dakota, his chance of victory in 1972 relied on an earlier start in New Hampshire. He announced his candidacy in January 1971 and was soon touring the Granite State trying to build support. Edmund Muskie, a senator from the neighboring state of Maine—and, according to the public opinion polls, the overwhelming favorite for the Democratic nomination—waited until the next January to officially kick off his own campaign. Even though Muskie (with 46.4 percent) outpolled McGovern (with 37.1 percent) in the 1972 primary, the result was reported as a major setback for Muskie. The "expectations" had been that the Man from Maine should amass a clear majority. When Muskie fell short, McGovern—the candidate who fought the party establishment and campaigned longer and more personally—was, in effect, declared the "winner." New Hampshire's image as a mine field for frontrunners was now accepted political faith.

The calendar moved forward again prior to the 1976 primary. Responding to moves by other states to also hold primaries on the second Tuesday in March, New Hampshire legislators, jealously guarding their pole position, moved theirs to the last Tuesday in February. As early as December 1973 potential candidates could be discovered addressing Republican or Democratic party functions. By the end of March 1974 California Governor Ronald Reagan, Illinois Senator Charles Percy, Minnesota Senator Walter Mondale, and Texas Senator Lloyd Bentsen had all tested New Hampshire's waters. (The last three later decided against running.) Before the end of December two Democrats—Arizona Congressman Morris Udall and Oklahoma Senator Fred Harris—had already officially announced their candidacies and were attending kaffee-klatsches in homes across the state. Jimmy Carter, a nationally obscure former governor of Georgia, entered the race in February 1975. For the remainder of the year he and his large family swarmed across the Yankee state, staying in people's homes, strolling into newspaper offices and tiny radio stations for interviews, prowling Main Streets to shake hands and distribute their brochures, greeting workers at factory gates during shift changes, and personally answering the political question surrounding his candidacy: "Jimmy who?" Only Henry "Scoop" Jackson, a senator from Washington widely viewed as one of the most serious contenders for the Democratic nomination, decided to bypass New Hampshire.

Carter won the crowded primary, the nomination, and then the White House. His dramatic climb from obscurity to the presidency wrote the book that became bedside reading for virtually all those who dreamed to the tune of "Hail to the Chief." Jackson was the last candidate to save the filing fee for New Hampshire's primary.

Gerald Ford, the sitting president, narrowly held off Ronald Reagan's challenge, 50.1 to 48.6 percent, in the Republican contest in 1976. But he had learned how to play the "expectations" game that Muskie and Johnson had ignored in previous primaries. He was the winner of the actual tally and, more important, the winner in the eyes of the media's political handicappers.

The 1980 primary featured donnybrooks in both parties. Carter was opposed by California Governor Jerry Brown and Massachusetts Senator Ted Kennedy. Reagan was back, facing a field of six serious challengers, including George Bush. Neither Carter nor Reagan spent nearly as much time campaigning in the state as did their opponents. Ironically Carter, whose tireless scouring of New Hampshire prior to his 1976 victory was now the universally accepted model, remained in self-imposed exile in the White House because of the Iran hostage crisis. He never campaigned personally. Reagan's appearances were restricted chiefly to speeches before large audiences, designed as much for the television cameras as for reaching voters face to face. Their victories, however, did nothing to impede the conventional theories about the first-in-the-nation primary. The myths had too much momentum by now.

Gary Hart's startling defeat of Mondale in 1984 seemed to confirm all the popular beliefs about New Hampshire: that it loved mavericks versus established front-runners, that a grass-roots network of volunteers could accomplish anything, and that in such a small state the key to victory was in "retail" campaigning of direct candidate-to-voter salesmanship. In fact, Hart's was the first true upset since Kefauver's in the initial primary of 1952, bracketing a thirty-two-year period in which those who had their party establishment's blessing or were well ahead going into the election year usually got the most votes in New Hampshire's primary. And in truth, Hart's rivals had also devoted lavish personal attention to New Hampshire and had built extensive grass-roots organizations—as had innumerable other candidates who had lost in previous primaries.

But the historical text of the New Hampshire primary is like the Bible. It is filled with enough contradictions to supply endlessly different interpretations, yet an orthodoxy has ossified around the elements that simultaneously reaffirm our democratic beliefs and provide the grist of popular drama: the chance for virtually anyone to compete on equal footing for the nation's highest office, the active participation of citizens seeking to affect the direction of the nation, and the considered verdict of voters who have taken a face-to-face measurement of those who would lead them.

Overarching it all stood two hard facts. Since 1952 no one had won the presidency who hadn't won his party's primary in New Hampshire at the start of the year. And in a political environment

increasingly reliant on media images and costly campaign commercials, the overwhelmingly disproportionate media attention paid
to the outcome in this small but kickoff vote made winning New
Hampshire worth untold millions of dollars in free advertising.

With that in mind, no candidate for president in 1988 was going
to take any chances with New Hampshire. Even Vice President
Bush, according to Governor John Sununu, his principal New
Hampshire supporter, was going to conduct a "see me, touch me,
feel me" campaign. If you were an unknown dark horse like Bruce
Babbitt, the political exigencies were even clearer: without a victory
or at least a surprisingly strong showing in New Hampshire, the
race would be over after the first ballots were counted in February.
You came to the state and went through its quadrennial rituals.

Serious candidates for the presidency, whether they are considered
long shots or sure bets, are normally from the highest ranks of
prestige and power in our society. Many either are, or have been,
United States senators or governors of their states (early handicappers often dismiss "mere" congressmen as lacking the *gravitas*
for the job); and most have held various political, legal, or business
posts of some prominence on their way to the Senate or state house.
They are accustomed to the exercise of power, and they have embarked on a quest for the most powerful position on earth. They
are used to considerable public attention through the media, and
the path they have chosen can lead them to the most highly publicized and scrutinized existence imaginable. They have already
held jobs of weighty responsibility in which there are far more
demands on their time than there is time to meet those demands;
and as they work toward a job in which the demands explode
exponentially so that virtually every waking minute of life is tightly
scheduled, they gather about them a staff and organization to weed
out the requests and demands so that they can concentrate their
limited time on those things that are most essential.

Inviting one of them over for an informal breakfast at your home
with just a few of your personal friends is not something that would

come to mind to many people in America. Intriguing as the prospect might be, the idea just wouldn't pop up. Nor would it be entertained seriously by any presidential campaign, unless the host was someone of considerable political influence—someone who could raise several hundred thousand dollars in contributions, for instance, or the owner of a television station, or perhaps an important elected official. Or, in one of the years leading up to the presidential caucuses and primaries, someone who happens to live in Iowa or New Hampshire.

The idea came to Dan Burnham in early 1987: what better way to learn about the Democratic presidential hopefuls and take their measure than to sit them down in his house and have a long talk with them? Having spent a good portion of his life in the news and public relations fields, Dan knew the difference between reading about an event or a personality and actually attending the event or meeting the person. It isn't that things are necessarily distorted by the media, although that sometimes happens; it's just that so much is left out—a lot of the nuance, the context, even a lot of the basic information is sacrificed to the rigid space limitations of a newspaper or magazine account. Why rely on someone else to interview a candidate and then present a highly condensed, edited version of the experience when Dan, a former reporter himself, could be interviewer, reporter, editor, and reader in one stroke?

Dan had already decided to involve himself with one of the Democratic campaigns; he just needed to decide which one. He was curious about how they worked, about learning from the inside the answers to what he called "the tantalizing questions of what it takes to win the New Hampshire primary." The initial impulse was almost academic, a detached interest in the process more than any concern for the outcome. Perhaps his attitude was a vestige of his early years as a reporter for *The Wall Street Journal* or later as editor and publisher of the *New Hampshire Times*. A journalist's tools are a curiosity about the way the world works, the intelligence to gather the necessary facts and opinions, and the objectivity not to allow his own prejudices to skew his story unfairly. Dan prided himself

on his ability to remain journalistically neutral. Covering West
Coast politics in the early 1960s—particularly Richard Nixon—he
thought he had developed the skill of putting aside his personal
feelings, like his distaste for Nixon, and figuring out what other
people were thinking and feeling, even if he did not agree with
them. His instincts, he believed, were disconnected from his own
biases. It wasn't that Dan didn't have political beliefs. He did—
probably best described as moderately liberal, although certainly
not as liberal as those of his father, a vice president for a major
book publisher, whom Dan remembered as always being "indignant
at the state of the world, from injustices toward blacks to the introduction of Muzak at Grand Central Station, a *real* liberal." His
father was active in local Connecticut issues; his mother was a
selectman for the town of New Canaan. Politics, particularly as part
of the world of ideas, was part of Dan's upbringing. He grew up in
the midst of a kind of rural sophistication. New Canaan was un-
developed enough in the 1930s and early 1940s that Dan spent
many happy boyhood summers helping a neighboring farmer, but
life was actually already oriented toward the urbane center of New
York City, where his father worked.

He learned his journalism working on *Stars and Stripes* with
the peacetime army, after graduating from Harvard in 1952 with
a degree in English history. Then for eight years as a reporter for
The Wall Street Journal, he had the time of his life. After three
years in New York on the media-as-business beat, he moved to the
Dallas bureau, where he was free to travel the South to write fea-
tures and news stories for the front page, and then on to San
Francisco, where one of the continuing stories he covered was
Nixon, the defeated presidential candidate returning to California
to run (and lose) the race for governor.

Through the bulk of the 1960s and 1970s, he was back in New
York, rising the corporate ranks of IBM to become director of press
relations. He had married Moira, and their three children were born;
his job was a good one, but it began to seem dull and routine. He
would find himself gazing out the window of his corporate office,

daydreaming about the pleasure and sense of accomplishment he had felt as a boy after scything a row of millet in his neighbor's field or thinking about a beautiful hilltop he and Moira had discovered in Dublin, New Hampshire, during weekend visits to her family's summer home. He constructed a theory that within every person is an innate sense of association with the land, that by working a farm and attuning themselves with the cycle of the seasons, people could find a truer set of values and a simpler, happier life.

In 1978, restless, middle-aged, with the career ladder seemingly closed above him, Dan retired early, moved his family to New Hampshire, built a house on the hilltop he and his wife had admired, and started a farm raising Holsteins as breeder stock for dairy herds. It was as much a romantic notion as a hardheaded business decision, a search to replicate his boyhood for his children—and himself. New Hampshire was, in effect, the new New Canaan: just far enough beyond the modern urban sprawl to allow a truly rural lifestyle, yet close to the cultural ambience of Boston and the rest of the eastern megalopolis. Dan's farming venture was great fun, but never much of a financial success. America already had too much milk and too many dairy farms; it didn't need Dan's. Much as he didn't regret his move to the farm—he found satisfaction, if not serenity and simplicity (or much profit) working with animals—he concluded that his notion of a desire by everyone to return to the land was a "truism that turned out not to be a truism." He sold off his herd of 150 Holsteins and became editor and then publisher of the *New Hampshire Times*, a weekly statewide paper that was a progressive alternative to the arch-conservative *Manchester Union-Leader*, until financial difficulties forced the sale of the weekly.

By 1986 Dan was keeping himself busy with projects. His herd was gone, but he'd saved a few heifers because he enjoyed them. He was no longer associated with a newspaper, but he still wrote on occasion, usually about the issues of growth and development. He became chairman of the local chapter of the Sierra Club and a member of the Society for the Protection of New Hampshire For-

ests. He joined efforts to improve public education in Dublin's
school district and kept involved with the local Farm Bureau and
Soil Conservation District. His abiding project, however, was the
struggle against a new highway bypass of Dublin. Like many people
in Cheshire County, particularly those who had moved to the area
from urban centers, Dan was troubled by New Hampshire's rapid
population growth. In his eyes the quality of life that had attracted
him here was being challenged by the waves of people moving
across the state border. New Hampshire was the second-fastest-
growing state east of the Mississippi River (after Florida), and parts
of it were already ruined in his eyes. Towns due east of Dublin—
Nashua, Milford, Wilton—had been engulfed by development. They
were now mere extensions of Boston's suburbs with condominiums
and tract housing sitting in former farm meadows and with shopping malls and fast-food franchises lining once scenic highways.
The sprawl seemed to be creeping his way. A proposal by the state
highway department to build a bypass around Dublin and ease east-
west traffic was viewed by many people in the region as a threat to
bring such growth into an as yet unspoiled section of New Hampshire. There was something extra in the issue for Dan, something
that made the bypass proposal more visceral than the abstraction
of whether it would increase the population growth of the area
several percentage points. Under the most likely plan, the western
end of the bypass would slice across about 25 acres of his 150-acre
farm.

The bypass battle was both a fight of the most elemental sort for
Dan—it involved his own land and what might be done to it against
his wishes—and an education in politics and government from the
viewpoint of a participant instead of a detached observer. He and
other opponents hired lawyers and fought the highway department
in court over arcane provisions of highway planning regulations.
They sought favorable coverage of their point of view of the issues
in the local newspapers. They met with candidates for the state
legislature, executive council, and governor's office, pleaded their
case, and often contributed to those who agreed with them. They

hired a lobbyist in the state Capitol. Dan mastered enough of the intricacies of federal highway law and historic preservation law to start an application for designating part of the route as a "rural historic district," which could derail the federal funding of the bypass. He ushered it through the state bureaucracy and into the upper reaches of the federal warrens of Washington. But he kept butting up against the hard political fact that the governor, who was philosophically progrowth and whose election campaigns had been financially supported by the area's bypass proponents, wanted the highway built. And, although the battle was far from over, the governor was winning.

Dan Burnham is the kind of man who enjoys mulling over the larger implications of things. He likes to develop theories, tinker with them in his mind, and he likes having discussions that challenge them. He is as apt to draw conclusions from his actions as he is to act on his conclusions. Which is a way of saying that, deeply as he felt about whether the state and federal government were going to bulldoze across some of his beloved farmland for the purposes of a highway he believed was not only unnecessary, but might unalterably despoil the rural region he called home, Dan could go through the long, frustrating, and sometimes bitter struggle and still find the experience intellectually fascinating.

From his bypass fight he drew an appreciation for the interplays of bureaucratic power, for the way influence can be targeted and brought to bear at strategic pressure points, for how politics and policy can sometimes intersect and sometimes collide—and he learned a graphic lesson about the practical consequences of who wins an election. It also moved him for the first time from the periphery of reportorial detachment toward the center of the action. He had crossed a line. He was involved this time. He was trying to make things happen rather than observing and reporting on what happened. "There's a place for someone who can write, has a lot of energy, can get to the nitty-gritty details of an issue, and have an impact," he said of the experience. He was still capable of observation; that was part of his intellectual makeup as well as his career history. But this time he was part of the actions he was observing. And he liked that.

So he decided to try electoral politics as a participant rather than as an observer, and he started at the very top: the race for president. First he had to choose a candidate to support. A close reader of the newspapers to begin with, he started paying closer attention to the early political stories. He watched for opportunities to learn more about the campaigns. The forest society to which he belonged launched a series of meetings with the candidates to discuss environmental issues. Babbitt appeared in the fall of 1986. Dan went, signed an attendance list, and soon afterward was getting calls from Babbitt aides asking if he wanted to meet Babbitt privately, perhaps ride with him in "Babbitt One" so they could talk at length. Dan said he wasn't interested at the moment. He attended a statewide conference on child abuse. Babbitt was one of the speakers. Dan was impressed that a presidential candidate would be there and that Babbitt seemed so conversant on the issue.

Babbitt had piqued his interest, but with all of 1987 still ahead, Dan wanted to get a closer look at all the Democrats before he committed himself to helping a campaign. Having them all over, one at a time, for breakfast seemed like a reasonable way to proceed.

One of the popular views about the New Hampshire primary's role in selecting presidents is that it makes politicians a little more humble. Forcing someone who would lead the nation to begin his campaign by, in effect, running for a city council seat—listening to people's complaints, answering their questions, asking them personally for their vote—can have a bracing and healthy effect before the candidate virtually disappears forever behind the wall of Secret Service, aides, sycophants, and media horde that separates him from normal contact with normal people. It can remind him that, in a democracy, a president is both leader and servant, but certainly not ruler, of the people. It can serve as a simple lesson that government policies are not abstractions but instruments with real consequences on real people; that a position paper on, for instance, catastrophic health coverage is more than an academic theory to the couple he just met who sold their house to pay their medical bills. Or it can provide an astute politician with visceral information on what issues are on voters' minds; that, perhaps, his speech on Third World debt is thoughtful and interesting, but the crowd wants to hear what he's going to do about drugs in their children's schools. Above all else, our idealized notion of democracy demands that our elected officials not get too big for their britches, and one appealing function of the New Hampshire primary is that, in theory, at least, it requires the candidates to present themselves, whether they like it or not, for a personal inspection by the common folk. At the close range of a small room in winter, any whiffs of inflated self-importance will wrinkle all noses.

This could be described as the Norman Rockwell view of the primary. Quaintly humorous, yet endearing and reassuring, it is a gallery of quintessentially democratic tableaus: overheated candidate stands near a woodstove, sweating and gesturing, as plump Yankee ladies knit while they listen from the couch and their angular husbands huddle near an open window, smoking pipes and maybe trying to sneak a peek at the basketball game playing on the television in the next room; befuddled politician is cornered on a Main Street by two housewives who are clearly angered about the price of the groceries in their bags, and meanwhile the ice-cream cone of one of their kids drips slowly on the big shot's polished shoes; leaning against the limousines of a parked motorcade, worried aides and bored cops glance at their wristwatches while a man in an expensive suit is clearly having the time of his life skating across a roadside pond in a pickup game of hockey; twenty Rotarians in a tiny cafe have their hands raised to ask a question of the dignified man behind the podium who is obviously responding to a query from the cook standing next to the kitchen door with his arms folded.

In recent campaigns a countervision of the primary has developed. As the campaigns have started earlier and earlier, the organizational stage has gotten longer, further increasing the disproportionate political solicitude already being paid to a relatively tiny circle of potential activists. Too much attention can warp anyone's sense of self-importance, candidate or average citizen. And political leverage can be used in many ways—to raise an issue, for instance, or simply to raise some money. In 1984 one New Hampshire city's Chamber of Commerce decided to charge the candidates if they wanted to address the group on the issues facing the nation. The state Democratic party chairman also came under fire for, in effect, seeking an admission fee to a press conference. Tales circulated then and again in 1988 of noted political figures holding off decisions on which campaign to join until donations were made to their own election funds or until they were assured to be hired as "consultants" or legal counsels.

At another level some activists demanded handling that bordered on a demeaning obsequiousness from the candidates before they would sign up—or even, sometimes, stay on board. Personal calls and notes, private meetings, lunches with relatives, car rides to places where they could be seen emerging with a smiling candidate—for some of them, such things were no longer special touches, called "stroking," that might swing them over into one campaign; it was a requirement, the price of admission every candidate was expected to pay for consideration. The campaigns were hostages. Any public complaint might be construed as an attack on the virtue of the state and its people as a whole and jeopardize their chances in the all-important voting; but terms like "prima donnas" and "shakedown" and "highway robbery" arose frequently whenever out-of-state campaign operatives spoke privately. There was a sense that more than a few people in New Hampshire had begun to consider their unique role in American politics not as a privilege, but as a right to be flaunted. (Similar complaints were surfacing about the Iowa caucuses.) Political leaders from other states, already envious of New Hampshire's special place in the national spotlight, had new evidence to buttress their arguments that the existing system was seriously flawed. In this version the people in New Hampshire were no longer civic-minded surrogates for the population at large; they were a spoiled and greedy tribe taking unfair advantage of their strategic position on the political map to extort various forms of ransom from candidates and campaigns. This is the Strait of Hormuz view of the primary.

Exaggerated though both versions might be, either one contained enough factual and anecdotal evidence to support a point of view. Either one would also explain why the Babbitt campaign in Concord could receive an invitation for its candidate to have breakfast with fewer than ten people in the tiny town of Dublin. And, since in March 1987 virtually all of the campaigns (with the possible exception of the vice president's) were eager for any opportunity to put their candidate in front of potential members of their incipient organizations, regardless of the host's motives, either one would also explain why the Babbitt schedule for March 3 and 4 included an overnight stay and breakfast at the home of Dan Burnham.

Luckily for the Babbitt team, Dan turned out to be from the Norman Rockwell mold. His invitation arose from curiosity, not arrogance. He was genuinely interested in what Babbitt was like and what he stood for, not in putting a candidate through the paces in front of some friends. He wanted to help out, not help himself, once he settled on which candidate to support. To any campaign he would be considered worth the effort—not only an "opinion leader" in his community, but also fresh blood, someone who might give back more political energy than he consumed.

Babbitt One was late arriving in Dublin the night of March 3. Babbitt's commercial flight to Boston had been delayed, and a serious ice storm had added more than an hour to the normal two-hour drive. The highway Dan Burnham didn't want to see made into a major corridor from the east had played its part: its twists and turns and occasional steep grades were all the more tortuous with a slick coating of ice.

The time, however, wasn't wasted. Babbitt's New Hampshire campaign staff aggressively booked every moment they had their candidate in their clutches. His ride was spent in deep discussion with Bruce Anderson, a prominent Democrat from Harrisville, a town neighboring Dublin. (Anderson had been driven down to Boston solely for the purpose of being driven back with Babbitt.) Babbitt One's equipment included two comfortable seats in the middle section, swivel seats that faced one another expressly for this purpose: one-on-one courtship.

Bruce Anderson was a rising star in the state's Democratic party. A young entrepreneur in the alternative energy field, he had helped organize a grass-roots effort to oppose federal plans to place a high-level nuclear waste repository in the region in early 1986 and then sought his party's gubernatorial nomination that fall. He had lost (although he carried Cheshire County), but the recognition and respect he had earned made him one of the most sought-after Democratic activists in western New Hampshire for the presidential campaigns. They were all anxious to have him on their side. He was young, good-looking, articulate, energetic, and, within one part of New Hampshire, at least, he had something of an organizational following.

During his own campaign in 1986, he had met most of the presidential candidates more than once. Coming into New Hampshire for the ostensible purpose of helping the state party and its candidates was a good way for a presidential hopeful to make contacts with party activists, get a feel for the state, and keep his name in the press. By March 1987 Bruce had already been to events with Hart and with Hart's wife; he had gone to a meeting of Hart partisans who were trying to expand their base of supporters. Congressman Dick Gephardt had led a training seminar for new local candidates that Bruce had attended; the two had met again in late 1986 at a small gathering. Bruce had been in the audience when Senator Joe Biden addressed the state party's annual dinner in early 1986; the two had been to several political picnics together (including the Cheshire County Democratic picnic in the fall of 1986); Bruce had been one of thirty-five people at a Biden reception only a week before his car ride with Babbitt; he and Biden had exchanged letters and Christmas cards. Also, he had already spent a good deal of time with Babbitt. During Babbitt's first trip to New Hampshire in June 1986, when Babbitt had toured to a series of small Jefferson-Jackson Day celebrations across the state and Anderson was still running for governor, they had both spoken to the crowds, even traveled together to a few of the events. Bruce was there when Babbitt met with the group that had fought the nuclear waste dump and had gone to a Babbitt reception the same evening. They had later held two lengthy talks about the Seabrook nuclear power plant and the nuclear waste issue, had traded letters following up the conversations, and had shared a private breakfast in December 1986. By the time Babbitt climbed into Babbitt One for the ride to New Hampshire, he knew almost as much about Bruce Anderson as Bruce knew about him.

There were three criteria Bruce was using to decide which candidate to support: 1) Is he capable; 2) Does he agree with me on the major issues; and 3) Is he electable? During their ride he told Babbitt he was "increasingly comfortable" with Babbitt's positions and that the former governor had "as good a background as any of the candidates" to be an effective president.

"But," he said as the van moved on into the stormy dark, "do you have that quality that's hard to define, that turns people on and can get you elected?"

Before Babbitt could respond, Bruce answered his own question: "I'm not sure you do."

Babbitt had heard these "buts" before. The "charisma problem" had haunted his campaign from the outset. He said he recognized that a "chemistry" with the voters was something you couldn't create or necessarily do anything about, but, after all, he *had* been elected governor in a traditionally Republican state. He hoped Bruce would remember that. He was edging to the moment of making his real sales pitch—"closing the deal," it's called—which was why Babbitt's staff had arranged the car ride; they thought the courtship and political dating had proceeded to the point where Bruce should be asked to go steady.

Bruce beat him to the punch. "I'm not ready to make any commitment," he said. "I'm quite a long ways away from any decision."

They stopped at a small college, where a group of students had been waiting several hours to hear Babbitt speak. It was ten o'clock. Another aide drove Bruce home. Babbitt talked with the students and headed toward Dublin. It was nearing midnight when he reached Burnham's house, tired from his long day.

Late as it was, Babbitt stayed up a while with the Burnhams, getting acquainted and unwinding with a beer. Dan and Moira liked him immediately. Babbitt was remarkably intelligent, honest, and unpretentious. They kept a pile of current books on the living room coffee table, and in their chat it turned out that Babbitt had already read many of them. They discovered that, like Moira, Babbitt had been studying the countries of Africa—Moira out of curiosity, Babbitt for that reason and also because it was the kind of thing a presidential candidate was expected to know. They shared an enthusiasm for the out-of-doors and a concern for environmental issues. He answered their many questions with an honest appraisal of himself and his chances. He said he enjoyed campaigning—meeting new people, being involved in the important issues of the day, and, yes, being the center of attention. He admitted he was a long-shot candidate, but by focusing principally on the Iowa caucuses and New Hampshire primary, he could conduct a campaign at a relatively low cost; his fund-raising was going well at the moment; he had a chance to break through the pack and win. They showed him his guest room, and before he went to bed he grabbed one of the books from the table. They were impressed—and pleased that they had thought of inviting their first presidential candidate into their home.

The next day dawned bright and clear. The Burnham house was a contemporary structure on the crest of a pasture hill. In the vaulted-roof living room, a fire burned in the huge stone fireplace. The opposite wall was a large picture window, looking south toward Mount Monadnock. The previous night's storm had coated everything with a veneer of ice, and a maple tree in the foreground of the dramatic view from the living room glistened in the sun like an oversize piece of heirloom crystal. Having subjected a candidate to one of its darker moods the night before, New Hampshire was showing off for Babbitt this morning. He and everyone else who showed up for breakfast seemed infected by the cheery sunshine.

Besides Babbitt, the Burnhams' guests were all close friends from the Dublin area, plus a woman they knew only slightly who had asked if she could attend. The friends, like the Burnhams, were interested in meeting presidential candidates as a way of educating themselves about the field of contenders. Shelley Nelkens, on the other hand, wanted personal meetings as a way of educating the candidates. She was on a crusade to convert them all.

After moving to Antrim, New Hampshire, from New York in the mid-1970s, Shelley had gotten peripherally involved in the opposition to the Seabrook nuclear power plant, until the birth and raising of her children preoccupied her time for nearly ten years. The proposal to site a nuclear waste dump within a few miles of her town brought her back out of her house with a vengeance. "Nothing," she said, "is as dangerous as a cornered mother." She threw herself into the fight to stop the dump, and when the plans were finally withdrawn in 1986, she moved on to try to stop the entire nuclear power industry. Her target was the Price-Anderson Act, a federal law that limited the financial liability of nuclear plants in the case of meltdowns. If the federal government removed the protective limits, she believed (as did the nuclear power industry), no company could afford to maintain or build a nuclear plant.

With so many would-be presidents in the state—many of them important members of Congress, regardless of whether they won the White House—the New Hampshire primary presented her with a personal lobbying opportunity people in everyday Washington would kill for. "Sometimes I feel like I'm being very manipulative, and I don't like it," she said in early 1987. "It's very calculated on my part, but I want to have some power and influence." She had already talked to the staff members of the Democratic campaigns about the importance of the Price-Anderson issue, had even talked

to the state director of Republican Jack Kemp's campaign, and told
them she wanted to meet their candidates. At a conference with
antinuclear activists in January, Gary Hart had lost his temper with
her for suggesting he wasn't doing enough, but later he promised
to talk about the Price-Anderson issue more often in his speeches.
When a *New York Times* article appeared later that month about
Hart's campaign, with no mention of her issue, she tracked down
the reporter by telephone to see if Hart was keeping his word.
Fortunately for Hart, the reporter told her Hart talked about Price-
Anderson all the time, but he hadn't thought it was worth putting
in his story—so she harangued the *reporter* about the evils of nuclear power. At an event in 1986 she chewed Babbitt's ear on the
issue, then followed him to another event where, she felt, "he got
it all wrong." Shelley Nelkens is both persistent and intense. The
Burnham breakfast was a chance to see if Babbitt had learned his
lesson.

Once everyone was seated Babbitt began a short monologue
about the prime importance of economic issues in the 1988 election
and the nation's future. As a governor, he said, he had learned that
without economic growth, the progressive legislation he favored for
dealing with various social problems simply didn't have a chance
for passage; unless a new president dealt effectively with the deficit
and America's declining competitiveness in world markets, the
same would apply on the national level, and many social causes
important to Democrats would wither because of the country's financial straits. From that launching point the discussion wheeled
freely, with questions and comments from the group ranging from
the most basic ("Why would anyone want to be president after
Ronald Reagan?" and "Isn't the way presidential campaigns are
conducted now too long, too trivial, and too demeaning—I mean,
do you *enjoy* this?") to the more arcane (the banker wanted his
opinion about the effect of current European interest rates on America's economy).

The polite, almost genteel atmosphere was only punctured a few
times, always by Shelley. She challenged Babbitt on his entire prem-

ise of expanding the economic pie. Industrial pollution is killing the Black Forest in Germany, she said, and the ozone layer is being depleted, so "maybe it's time you politicians talked about survival instead of economic progress." A little later she accused him of inaction while radium from Arizona mines worked their way into the air and endangered people as far away as Pennsylvania. As he was trying to wrap up the breakfast discussion, she interjected again. She had read reports in the newspaper that the first draft of the commission on the Three Mile Island nuclear plant accident (Babbitt had been a member) was "sanitized" to downplay the real health dangers. Was he willing to propose a reopening of the whole investigation? Babbitt was shaking his head throughout her speech, looking somewhat exasperated; the Burnhams appeared a little pained and embarrassed.

Then Babbitt smiled. "Shelley," he said, "every time I come, you've got a new hurdle for me."

"That's okay," she answered. "We're here to teach you."

Dan Burnham thought the initial session of his planned series of breakfasts with Democratic candidates was a success. His project was going well. He had gotten a good feel of Babbitt in their late night talk and during the breakfast, including how he responded to Shelley's pointed nudging. Babbitt dealt with her firmly but politely, even with some humor, showing admirable restraint, Dan thought. (Shelley thought just the opposite. "God, that man frustrates me," she confided afterward. "He seems to weigh every word before he speaks, like he's chicken about what will be reported. I'm not sure I could support anyone who doesn't have a stronger personality than me. If he has trouble handling me . . ." She let the implication speak for itself.)

Dan spent the rest of the day with the Babbitt campaign, driving some extra aides to the other events in the region. He accompanied the entourage in a walking tour of a mall in Keene, sat in during an interview with *The Keene Sentinel,* and stood in the back of the room at the Harris Center, a conservation organization in

nearby Hancock, while Babbitt addressed fifteen environmentalists. The bulk of questions were about environmental issues, but
one of them echoed Bruce Anderson's comments the night before
in Babbitt One.

"How can you win without any charisma?" one person asked.

Babbitt smiled wanly. "I'm tryin'," he said. "In the wake of what's
going on in Washington, I think the American people are looking
for substance this time around. I offer the charisma of competence."

Dan liked that answer, although he had the same reservations
about Babbitt's chances. He knew enough about Babbitt's background and record as governor to feel sure that Babbitt was well
qualified for the job. (Earlier, he had called his brother, a reporter
for *The New York Times* who had covered the Three Mile Island
investigation, and checked out Babbitt's environmental bona fides
from an objective source.) His exposure to the personal side of
Babbitt had left him genuinely liking the man. Yet, as he had sat
across the breakfast table from Babbitt, Dan had found it difficult
to see him as president. Something—maybe the old instincts from
his reporting days—made him doubt that Babbitt was going to make
it. Moira shared the same doubts.

A week later Babbitt's state director called Dan on the telephone.
They were compiling a list of people in New Hampshire who supported Babbitt. They wanted to release the names to the media to
prove he was making progress. (It was also an excuse to see if they
could move some potential supporters off the dime and into the
committed column.) Could they include Dan's name? It was the
first time they had actually asked him for a decision.

Dan thought about it for a few days. He weighed his doubts and
pondered his plans for breakfast meetings with the other candidates. He considered what he knew about Babbitt the governor and
Babbitt the man. Then he called the state director.

He wasn't exactly sure what it was that had made up his mind,
but he had reached a decision. "Yeah," he said, "put me on the
list."

3

A TALE
OF TWO VISITS

Kendall Lane was ticked off. Nothing was going right. In just two
days Vice President Bush would be in Cheshire County for a series
of campaign appearances. Kendall was happy about that fact.
Southwestern New Hampshire had been neglected for too long
already, he thought. Here it was April 1987, and the vice president
had been to every other region of the state at least once, but not
Cheshire County. One of Kendall's self-imposed missions as a
"Freedom Fighter" was that, when the core group of Bush supporters met each Monday morning, he tried to make sure his less
populated corner of the state wasn't forgotten. It was as if he were
the equivalent of a congressman representing his district in the
halls of the state campaign: he felt a certain subtle duty—and
pressure—to "deliver the pork" back home; in this case that meant
bringing the vice president into the Monadnock Region. The pressure worked the other way as well. If the campaign expected Kendall to "deliver" Cheshire County on primary day, he wanted them
to provide him what he needed, and in Kendall's mind one of the
most important things he needed was the physical presence of his
candidate. This was the New Hampshire primary, after all. No
candidate, no campaign.

When the state headquarters told him the last week of March

that Bush would be in the Keene area on the afternoon and evening of April 16 and asked for some ideas for events, Kendall's first reaction was excitement, tempered by a wish that they could have given him more than three weeks' notice to put things together properly. "This is the fun part of the campaign," he said the day he heard the news. "When we finish this, we've got to get back to checklists, voter lists, lists of town chairmen for the next six months—things that no one likes to do and I always seem to end up doing."

From the very start of his involvement in 1986, he had envisioned how Bush should campaign in Keene. The scenes played like film footage in his mind. In his first visit Bush would hold a huge reception, where he would mingle informally with up to six hundred Republicans the local campaign had targeted as prospective volunteers. Kendall would guide the vice president through the crowd—or perhaps stand next to him in a receiving line—to make sure Bush was introduced personally to each voter as they shook hands and had their picture taken. Bush was effective at this, Kendall believed; he had witnessed it firsthand in the summer of 1986 when he and Jane had been invited along with a group of select New Hampshire Republicans to the Bush compound at Kennebunkport, Maine, for a cookout. A framed autographed picture of Bush standing with the Lanes on his summer home's porch now hung as proof on the wall in their family room. The personal handshake, the photographs, maybe a note from the vice president as a follow-up—these things would make it a lot easier for Kendall to call up people later and ask them to be a town chairman or work on a phone bank.

But a trip to Keene shouldn't be confined to organizational matters, important as those were at this juncture, Kendall thought. His mental filmstrip showed Bush on a plant tour of a local industry, mixing amiably with working people, identifying with their lives, and countering his image as the candidate of the country club set. Kendall could close his eyes and see Bush out of the limousine and walking down Keene's Main Street, from City Hall south for two blocks, spontaneously meeting average people on the sidewalk, chatting with them, asking for their vote, and showing that, despite his lofty position, he did not take New Hampshire's voters for granted.

Halfway down Main Street Bush would turn and walk a quarter block, past the bus station to Lindy's Diner, where he would enter, greet each patron briefly, and sit down at the counter for a cup of coffee. Just as there are generic candidate rituals for the primary— addressing a small group in a living room, the "town meeting" event in a school or church, the photo with a small child, the stroll along a sidewalk (preferably during a snowstorm)—there are certain ritualistic places in many communities to which campaigns traditionally bring their candidates. Lindy's Diner is Keene's. Partly because of its strategic position at the city's heart, partly because it serves good food quickly and at reasonable prices, it is virtually always full, with a clientele ranging from loggers heading out for a hard day's work to the city manager on a coffee break, from carpenters sitting beside bankers at the counter for lunch to families having supper at one of the booths. Campaigns go there because it, in effect, symbolizes being in Keene as much as a picture of the city's signature Central Square. On a more practical level, since it's always busy Lindy's provides a guaranteed crowd, a good "photo opportunity," and a good piece of pie in one quick stop. For Kendall, having Bush drop by at Lindy's was essential for his dream visit. It would be the perfect touch. His plan had an added benefit. George and Arietta Rigopoulos, the owners, probably saw more Keene voters in a day's time than anyone else in the city. Getting them firmly behind the Bush effort—perhaps convincing them to wear Bush buttons every day—was high on Kendall's organizational priority list for Keene. A visit by the vice president of the United States would be a mighty weapon in Kendall's battle plan.

Within hours of receiving the good news that Bush would be coming to his area, Kendall saw his dream start to unravel. And it got worse with each day. This was his first experience at setting up a presidential campaign appearance. He had attended events before, stood in the crowd or gone to a reception, but now he was finally where he had always wanted to be: "in the loop" of decision making and behind the scenes of getting things done. The problem was that part of the price of being in the loop was witnessing firsthand the swirl of petty infighting, bureaucratic tangling, and occasional chaos and indecision that bubbles just under the surface of any campaign; and part of the price of being behind the scenes meant, as it had with list management, that he was often left with the task of carrying out decisions rather than making them. Kendall quickly got very frustrated.

His first job was finding a place for Bush to meet prospective supporters. He called the hotel in Keene with the biggest function rooms. They didn't want the vice president's business—they had one room already booked, and frankly they weren't interested in all the commotion and disruption of letting the Bush campaign use the other room. Kendall was stunned. He had expected them to be honored by the request, probably even willing to kick out any club meeting or convention that might compete with having a vice president and his entourage in their midst. One other hotel, the Ramada Inn, had some function rooms, although they were smaller. Kendall called them. They said they'd get back to him. *What if they say no, too?* The thought made Kendall nervous—and a little angry that he had been given such short notice. The country club had a spacious dining room that often catered to large events. As a member, Kendall knew he could probably reserve it easily. *No, we don't want the country club*, he decided. *That's the image we don't want any part of.*

Two days later the Ramada Inn was reserved, but Kendall had new, more aggravating problems. His suggestion for Bush's block of time in Keene—from 2:30 to 7:30 P.M.—had been for the walk down Main Street and Lindy's visit, a tour of a local plant, some local media interviews, and then a reception whose goal would be for Bush and his wife to shake as many hands as humanly possible in an hour and a half. The answer from Washington was "no" to all four ideas.

The Secret Service assigned to the vice president was vetoing any walk through town; they thought it would leave Bush too exposed and vulnerable for adequate security. (The other presidential candidates would not be offered Secret Service protection for nine months, until January 1988; even then their security precautions would normally be much less extensive than those for a vice president.) A plant tour was out, ostensibly for the same security reasons, although Kendall learned that Bush's staff wanted the public focus of his day to be farm issues and therefore they weren't interested in any event that might run counter to those images. Setting aside time for individual interviews with the local paper and radio stations was also ruled out; they would just distract from coverage of his events—but the staff agreed to invite a reporter from *The Keene Sentinel* to a group interview Bush was hosting at Kennebunkport the weekend before his trip. As far as a large reception was concerned, the Washington staff preferred a sit-down dinner with perhaps a hundred guests. Bush would eat, speak briefly, maybe "work the tables," and leave.

"I'm so sick of arguing with people in Washington, I could scream," Kendall said later in the week. "We make suggestions and they just say, 'No, you can't do that.' They don't know anything about campaigning in New Hampshire—it's a foreign country."

Kendall had made his case to the state campaign director, the New England director, and the northeast director. Each one said he was on Kendall's side. They said they had talked with headquarters in Washington, which in turn talked with people in the vice president's White House office, where scheduling was discussed. The whole process seemed so cumbersome to Kendall, he sometimes wondered whether the problem was that his arguments weren't getting through to the people who made the decisions or that there simply wasn't anyone actually making decisions.

He spent the next week traveling back and forth to the Concord headquarters—four trips in five days—to work on the trip details. When he wasn't in Concord he was on the phone with Concord or meeting with a small group of Keene supporters about the trip. The battles—and confusion—over virtually everything continued. Washington clung to the notion of a smaller dinner instead of a larger reception and wanted to charge ticket prices of at least $15 per person. The Secret Service insisted that invitations include RSVPs that also asked for a respondent's Social Security number and date of birth (which would permit security checks to be run on each person who intended to show up).

Kendall was sputtering. "Screwing around with money when you're trying to get people to see the vice president doesn't make any sense," he said. "This isn't a fund-raiser, it's a campaign stop." If the event were limited to one hundred guests, the number of people who would be angry at not being invited would exceed by far those who were happy at getting in—and they would be angry at both the campaign in general and Kendall in particular; it would deliver his grass-roots organizational work a setback instead of a boost. He asked Governor Sununu and Congressman Judd Gregg to intercede. They called Washington and won a partial victory: a reception instead of dinner, no ticket prices, but the detailed RSVPs were still a requirement. A Main Street walk was definitely out; the Secret Service wouldn't budge. And the White House staff now wanted the three hours between two and five o'clock reserved for "vice presidential time" in Bush's suite at the Ramada Inn.

"Does he want to be vice president for the rest of his life, or does he want to be president?" Kendall exploded. He believed Bush was being ill served by the people around him. "The bureaucracy around the vice president doesn't want to run a campaign," he said. "They're not at all interested in it and are doing their damnedest to block anything. I get the impression they see primary campaigning as basically an intrusion on his time. They're already thinking after the nomination [Bush was far ahead of every other Republican in the polls in New Hampshire] while the rest of us are running around trying to get him nominated. The only way we can get through is with the governor or Judd; otherwise we go through the staff, and everything goes into this morass down there and nothing comes out."

His time was consumed with developing the invitations. He drafted a letter to go out over the governor's and congressman's signatures. He pored over various lists—his own from Cheshire County, former campaign supporters of Sununu's and Gregg's, party officials—to cull out the names of 500 couples. He and Jane and a few others from Keene stuffed envelopes and attached mailing labels. The staff in Concord told him to expect a 30 percent response from the invitations—about 150 couples, or 300 people—which seemed overly pessimistic to Kendall. "This is not just a political event," Kendall replied. "He *is* the vice president." His principal concern was not the turnout. He was worried about likely supporters being inadvertently left off the list and feeling snubbed. His personal expectation was for 500 to 600 people to show up.

Other aggravations arose the week before the event. Heavy spring rains flooded the highways on Monday, forcing Kendall to leave even earlier for the weekly "Freedom Fighters" meeting. He took a series of back roads to Concord; the trip took two and a half hours. But when he arrived he found the group of seven was now thirty, and it seemed that the larger the group, the longer the meeting and the less that actually got accomplished. Kendall made another pitch for a Main Street walk and an "impromptu" stop at Lindy's. It wouldn't take that much time, he argued. Maybe the governor, who would be riding in the limousine with the vice president, could just have them turn off the motorcade route and get Bush to climb out without telling the Secret Service in advance. The answer was still "no."

The turnout itself became troublesome. Responses weren't coming in. By Thursday, April 9, with only seven days before the reception, fewer than a hundred people had accepted. Worried that the event would be a complete flop, Kendall gathered nine people at an insurance and real estate office that night to use their phones and call people on the invitation list to urge them to attend. Some said they objected to divulging their age and Social Security number; some simply hadn't gotten around to replying; others weren't

all that interested at the moment. Slowly the expected crowd built
to three hundred.

The advance team (staff people whose job it was to oversee all
the details of a trip) and some Secret Service agents arrived over
the weekend, and Kendall showed them the Ramada Inn room and
helped them set up their trip headquarters in the hotel. When they
asked for someone to help staff the headquarters, Jane quickly
volunteered. "I hate to put a spy in the vice president's advance
team office," Kendall confided, "but we've got to do something to
protect ourselves, so they don't get any bright ideas about changing
more things at the last minute." Complicating things, his home
phone went on the blink that weekend, but he convinced the phone
company, which was installing phones for the Secret Service, to
work on his as well. "I suppose I got *something* out of all this," he
said bitterly. "I got my phone fixed a day early."

Tuesday, April 14, put Kendall in a foul mood. He was in the
midst of a court case—"I still have to earn a living," he complained—
that demanded a lot of his time. Despite the work of the phone
bank, he remained worried about the turnout for the reception. A
news notice in *The Keene Sentinel* had announced the impending
visit, pointing out that the reception was restricted to people with
invitations. "How come you're running an exclusive event for the
vice president?" some neighbors had needled Kendall. (A few local
Republicans who supported other candidates had contacted Kendall
wondering if they could attend; he admitted that informing them
that the reception was confined to people either already committed
to Bush or still undecided gave him one of his few pleasures in
days.) To cap off the day he got some bad news. The state's executive councillor from Keene, a member of the Bush steering
committee, had refused to let Kendall see his list of supporters for
invitations, insisting instead that he be allowed to send out his own
letter inviting people to meet the vice president. As if that weren't
nettlesome enough, Kendall was informed Tuesday night that the
executive councillor, not Kendall, would make the formal introduction before Bush spoke to the reception. Kendall was expected

to do the bulk of the work—he learned he was also now in charge of making sure the room at the Ramada Inn was properly decorated—but not share in the limelight of the evening.

"It was just going to be me and the vice president on the podium," he said about the original plan. "I was going to get to speak for five minutes, make some introductions, and then turn it over to him.

"Now . . ." His voice trailed off in disappointment. "Well, I'm kind of ticked off."

Not all candidate trips to Cheshire County required preparations as elaborate as Bush's. A vice president, only a heartbeat away from being president, travels with a permanent entourage of Secret Service, aides, and media—regardless of whether he is a candidate for president. The sheer logistics of his movements are complicated and intricately planned, from provisions for emergency medical care and quick communications with the White House to painstaking reconnaissance of his motorcade route (even the hallways he will walk from one room to another) and background checks of anyone expected to come near him.

As the clear front-runner for the Republican nomination, Bush was also under closer political scrutiny by national reporters. Any slip of the tongue would be broadcast to the nation on the nightly news. Foul-ups and mistakes in a campaign event would become the grist of endless columns and speculation in the press. The aura of his high office was a powerful political tool, bringing with it advantages in fund-raising, name recognition, and public attention, but it also carried with it the baggage of higher expectations for him, his staff, and his campaign. Such a campaign is normally uptight—there is less room for mistakes and thus less room for spontaneity.

Compared with Bush, the other candidates traveled light. Unless they managed to appear before existing organizations, their events were normally small, often attracting only a reporter from *The Keene Sentinel* for press coverage. Gary Hart had spoken to the annual dinner of the Cheshire County Democrats. Even with the extensive calling from Andi Johnson and the other Hart supporters, only 150 people came, many of them already committed to or leaning toward other candidates. Congressman Richard Gephardt of Missouri had toured a Senior Meals site, thrusting pamphlets into the hands of elderly people as they looked up, bewildered, from their soup; he spoke to forty-five people at the Westmoreland Town Hall, west of Keene; and, after spending the night at a supporter's home, he went to a sugar house where maple syrup was being made to have his picture taken (he wore a red plaid jacket loaned from his host) in an identifiably New Hampshire setting. Senator Joe Biden had met with thirty-five people—including Andi Johnson and the other Hart supporters from Tom Britton's meeting (all of whom had been invited to help swell the crowd)—in the living room of Pat Russell, a Keene Democrat who was on the Democratic National Committee. Senator Bob Dole had made a two-day swing through the county, speaking to the Republican Women's Club and the Keene Rotary. Babbitt had been to the Burnhams' and the conservation center, seeing a grand total of twenty-three voters.

All the visits were variations of the same New Hampshire ritual: concentrate on meeting people the campaign organizations hoped would become volunteers; try to establish some "presence" and public image through interviews and press coverage; follow up the trip with letters and phone calls to expand the circle of support. The Bush plan was the same, but because of his position as vice president and front-runner, it was just the most complicated and elaborate—at the extreme end of the scale in terms of the number of people and the number of details required to carry it out.

The other extreme occurred on April 15, the day before Bush arrived, when Pete du Pont came to town.

"Good morning, I'm Pete du Pont, and you're on *Open Mike*. What's your question?" The voice came across any radio tuned in to radio station WKBK early in the morning. Du Pont, the former congressman and governor of Delaware, scion of the fabulously wealthy chemical company family, candidate for the Republican nomination for president, was sitting in a small booth in the station's studio in downtown Keene, announcing his visit by being the guest on the daily talk show.

Du Pont had no organization at all in Cheshire County. Early as it was in the campaign cycle, virtually every other campaign in the state could name at least four to twenty people in the region already committed to their candidate and probably doing some sort of preliminary organization work. Du Pont's—and Al Haig's—had no one. (Du Pont had been to the outskirts of the Monadnock Region in January. Ending a day devoted to agricultural issues, he had attended a reception in Temple, in neighboring Hillsborough County. The campaign had promoted the reception site as a local farm. It turned out, in fact, to be a private hunting reserve. The thirty-five guests included a few Democrats and some federal employees—prohibited by law from doing any real campaign work—who had shown up as a favor to the host, a family friend of du Pont's whose principal concern was turning out a decent-size crowd.) Lacking any local contacts, du Pont's campaign brought him to Keene without much planning and apparently without any clear objective other than to move him randomly around the city, get some "free" media, and attempt to reach voters directly, even though in April the voters were more focused on the first balmy spring day than on politics.

After the radio show—during which du Pont fielded questions about the war in Central America (he supported the Reagan policy), Social Security (he wanted to make some radical changes in it), and the price of tomatoes (he couldn't explain to the angry caller why they were so expensive)—he went to Keene High School, where he told a hundred students and five teachers during study hall that his presidential platform was "a little different." He proposed forcing anyone on welfare to work for local governments, eliminating all farm subsidies, and testing and searching teenagers for drugs and punishing offenders by taking away their driver's licenses until age eighteen. The general consensus of the group,

95 percent of whom were old enough to drive but too young to vote, was that du Pont was indeed "different," perhaps even a little weird. Their questions were uniformly hostile.

Du Pont's next stop was Yankee Lanes, a bowling alley not far from the high school. Sixty women were startled when a tall, patrician-looking man in a business suit, trailed by two aides, disrupted their morning bowling league to introduce himself, press some brochures into their hands, and leave. After lunch at Lindy's Diner, where he spent most of his time talking with Will Fay, a reporter from *The Keene Sentinel* and the only person in Keene whose face he recognized, du Pont headed out the door for a stroll up Main Street.

Had Kendall Lane been along, he might have reconsidered his desire for George Bush to do the same thing. For an hour du Pont searched in vain for anyone to talk with for more than a few seconds. People he encountered on the street were polite, some a little bemused, when he would stop them, give them a brochure, and start to recount the reception at the high school to his drug proposal. "I don't think those kids liked it," he told them. (Which of course was the point; he wanted the *adults* to like it.) At the City Hall the mayor and most of the top officials were gone. His chat with the dispatcher at police headquarters was interrupted by radio calls. Outside the district courtroom, three people were sitting. "Pete du Pont, running for president," he exclaimed cheerfully. "How're you all doing today?"

"Just terrific," one answered sarcastically—he was waiting to be arraigned.

The candidate spied the local Social Security office across the street and marched in, figuring to engage them in debate over his own proposals. "I'm sorry, sir, but I really would appreciate it if you didn't disrupt things," said the woman at the reception desk. "We're trying to get some work done here."

"Can't I just go back to the desks and say hello?" du Pont asked.

"No. I really would rather that you just left." (Had du Pont gone on to win the White House, regardless of whether Congress would have gone along with his Social Security reforms, Keene would undoubtedly have had its office closed.)

At the fire station around the corner, he figured he'd finally found some people with time on their hands. But the fire chief was on his way to a meeting with the Secret Service for Bush's visit, and after du Pont sat down with five firemen and had just enough time to explain his driver's license drug program, the alarm went off. Someone had overdosed and needed help. "There you go," a fireman said as they climbed into the ambulance. "That guy just lost his driver's license."

Wandering into the local senior center, du Pont discovered twenty people getting ready for a talent show. He listened to a ninety-two-year-old woman do an impersonation of George Burns. He ordered an aide to find three cue balls for him, and after summoning a drumroll from the band ("What for?" asked the drummer. "To introduce me properly," he said), he amused them with a demonstration of his juggling abilities.

Back down Main Street, he entered Timoleon's, another restaurant, and went to the kitchen to meet Lindy Chakalos, the cook-owner.

"How ya' doin? I'm Pete du Pont, running for president. Here's some literature for you."

"President of what?"

"The United States."

"What party?"

"Republican."

"Who against?"

DuPont named his opponents.

"Let me tell you something," the cook told him. "My father came to this country and went through Ellis Island. But my son is at *Dartmouth*. This is a great country, and don't forget it." (Du Pont didn't. The story became a standard refrain in his stump speeches for the rest of his short-lived campaign, offered as proof that even though it was far from his own personal history of privileged upbringing, he understood the promise of America.)

At the Keene Chamber of Commerce offices in the city's bus station, du Pont borrowed a telephone for an hour to make fund-raising calls. He made more calls from a pay phone at Peter Christian's, yet another restaurant, had a glass of iced tea, and then shaved in their restroom. His final stop of the day was at Keene State College, where, after an interview on the college radio station, a political science class verbally tore apart his positions on Central America, the Strategic Defense Initiative, and drug testing. The weather, at least, had been sunny and warm.

The day had proceeded as if du Pont and his campaign had studied the campaign of Jimmy Carter in 1976 but only understood part of it. Du Pont had just spent more consecutive time in Keene than any of the other candidates before him (or after, with the exception of Gary Hart, who in late January 1988 would also devote an entire day—and evening—campaigning within the city limits). Like Carter, he had taken his campaign to the streets. He had managed to appear on two radio shows, and the *Sentinel* devoted two stories to his visit. Missing, however, was any attempt to make real connection with someone who might carry on his campaign locally in his absence, the kind of meticulous organizational work that was another hallmark of Carter's model. Du Pont was observing some of New Hampshire's primary rituals, but without comprehending their purpose.

His encounters left more of an impression on him—he was still retelling the Ellis Island story the next February—than he left on the city. To a great extent the primary campaign at this juncture was confined to the small universe of activists, and at least in Cheshire County du Pont wasn't participating in that campaign. The twenty people at the senior center might remember that someone running for president had juggled for them, but on the whole his trip to Keene in April would be forgotten by the month's end, let alone by primary day ten months later. He came and went without leaving much of a trace.

As his car pulled out of Keene State College, an air force C-141 transport plane was landing at Keene's Dillant-Hopkins Airport to deliver a specially equipped limousine. The vice president of the United States was expected the next day.

Kendall Lane's great-grandfather, the first Lane in Keene when he moved to the city in 1860, quickly became active in Republican politics, running for and winning the office of sheriff of Cheshire County. Kendall's grandfather was a Teddy Roosevelt Republican, bolting the GOP in 1912 when his hero formed the progressive Bull Moose party. Howard Lane, Kendall's father, returned the family firmly to the Republican fold. He served on the Keene school board in the 1940s but after a loss in 1949 chose not to seek office again, preferring instead to be a behind-the-scenes political power broker. Candidates for governor and senator would often stay at the huge family house at the south end of Main Street; Howard was city chairman of the party, and his wife was president of the county's Republican Women's Club. (One governor gave Howard a two-digit license plate, a symbol of powerful connections in New Hampshire; another governor awarded Mrs. Lane with a three-digit number.)

Politics was one part of Kendall's heritage. After graduating from the University of New Hampshire in 1969 (where he served in the student senate and took part in some counterdemonstrations against the campus turmoil of the late sixties), a stint with the army's recruiting center in Washington, D.C., and law school (Boston University, 1975), he returned to Keene and his father's law practice, which he and his older brother, Howard Lane, Jr., bought and carried on in partnership. In 1980 he "got the itch to run for office myself" and ran successfully for the state legislature. He loved it. Kendall enjoyed "making things happen" and threw himself into both the procedural work and the social whirl of the Capitol in Concord, rising simultaneously in the committee structure and state party. But when the legislature switched to yearly, versus biennial, sessions, the demands on his time were too great. Reluctantly he left after two terms. Instead he ran for and won a seat on the city council (his brother had previously been a councillor)—a duty added to his roles on the regional planning commission and on the boards of the YMCA, local hospital, Masonic Temple, the Keene Academy Fund, and the appellate division of the New Hampshire Department of Employment Security. Jane, his wife, was also immersed in political and civic groups. She was one of three elected Cheshire County commissioners, an officer in the state's Federation of Republican Women, and an appointed member of the New Hampshire Commission on the Status of Women. Community leadership was another part of Kendall's heritage.

Passed along from one Lane to another over the generations, as a sort of family political talisman, was a giant American flag, more than fifteen feet long and ten feet wide. It first belonged to Kendall's great-grandfather and had only forty-five stars in its faded blue corner, reflecting the number of states in the 1890s. Teddy Roosevelt himself, during a campaign stop in Keene in 1912, had stood in front of it when he spoke to an outdoor rally on Central Square. In 1976, after a rally at the high school and at the start of an all-day motorcade across the southern base of New Hampshire, from Keene to the seacoast, President Gerald Ford had stopped his limousine to shake hands with people gathered in front of the Lane homestead on Main Street. The giant flag, unfurled from the balcony, was a perfect backdrop for the photographers. As he and a friend worked to hang the flag across the front wall of the Ramada Inn function room the night before Bush's arrival, Kendall was, therefore, carrying out an honored family tradition.

"Will it hold?" Kendall looked up nervously as John Croteau stapled the top of the flag to the wall. The crew of seven volunteers Kendall and Jane had assembled to decorate the hall had already inflated hundreds of red, white, and blue balloons and arrayed them along the ceiling and other walls. Kendall had attached "George Bush for President" bumper stickers to each balloon; Jane had cut and curled ribbons to tie the balloon clusters. The work had taken more than two hours. Putting up Old Glory was the finishing touch.

The flag was nearly a hundred years old, and the fabric was weakened from age. Kendall was eager for yet another presidential candidate—another *president*, he told himself hopefully—to stand before the Lane flag at a Keene function. Explaining its history would have been part of his remarks in introducing the vice president, if he hadn't have been "big-footed" off the podium by the executive councillor. Instead Kendall intended to brief Bush privately before the event; he was sure Bush would appreciate the flag's connections with Republican history. But as he held the flag taut for Croteau to apply the staple gun, he could see the strain in the fabric, and he was a little worried that unless they were careful he'd be the last Lane with a whole flag to display.

"Are you sure it'll hold?" Kendall asked again.

Croteau, knowing his friend's anxiety, rammed home another staple. "Oh, it'll hold all right," he said playfully. "The problem's going to be when you try to take it down."

Bush's day in western New Hampshire began in Claremont, a city forty miles north of Keene in Sullivan County, with an "Ask George Bush" forum at the high school. He spoke to a crowd packed into the auditorium, answered some students' questions, and then began a motorcade south toward Keene. In Walpole, a small town on the Connecticut River, he stopped briefly at a farm implement dealership and posed for photographs on a tractor. Then he made a fifteen-minute tour of Hubbard Farms, a company that breeds chickens for the domestic and foreign poultry industry. The cameras recorded the vice president holding a small chick in his hands while a hatchery official explained the company's business. (Several days before the visit, Secret Service agents had combed through the company's buildings, inspecting 350 boxes containing one hundred chicks each and running every employee's Social Security number through a Washington computer for security clearance.) With the two "visuals" in Walpole completed, the entourage of vice president, governor, congressman, Secret Service, state police, emergency vehicles, staff, and media motored on to the Ramada Inn, arriving at two-thirty. Bush and his wife were ushered quickly to a secured wing of the hotel for the rest of the afternoon.

When Kendall walked into the Ramada Inn a little after four

o'clock, the lobby was a quasi-armed camp: nearly half the people milling around were police, fire officials, or Secret Service with guns and walkie-talkies bulging under their coats. People either stood, waiting quietly and watchfully, or they conversed in hushed tones. Aides wearing special security pins in their lapels occasionally emerged officiously from the guarded door to the corridor leading to the vice president's suite of rooms. There was an air of anticipation in the room, an atmosphere that someone of powerful importance was nearby. Loud noises or sudden movements would have seemed inappropriate, perhaps even threatening.

Kendall's first mission was to get a security pin. Without it he could not move freely around the hotel. To compensate for taking him off the speaking program, the campaign had told Kendall he would accompany Bush and Governor Sununu through the reception as sort of a local guide while they mingled. Jane would be with Mrs. Bush and the wife of Congressman Gregg as they worked the other part of the function room. Kendall also needed the pin to allow him into the sanctum of the suites, where, just before the reception, he and Jane were to have their pictures taken with the Bushes. After hunting down a member of the advance team for his pin, he settled into more pressing business: making sure his people got into the reception.

To a large degree this was Kendall's event. Its success or failure would reflect on his standing within the ranks of the campaign. At the same time most of the guests would be, if not his close friends, at least his acquaintances in the community. How they were treated, how good a time they had, would affect not only his chances of bringing them into the organization, but also their view of him. The names of the governor, congressman, and executive councillor might be on the invitations, but Kendall was shouldering the real responsibilities of host. And in his eyes there was this *bureaucracy* to deal with: all these people with their own intricate procedures and seemingly irrelevant internal concerns, and yet authority, who could really foul things up.

Kendall was worried that prospective organizational workers

would be stopped at the reception table that blocked the entry to the reception room. Some of the people he had invited still had not responded or been contacted by telephone. Others who had at first declined might just change their minds and decide at the last minute to go hear the vice president. His worst fear was that they would come to the event, not be on the confirmed list, and be turned away haughtily. Kendall knew about injured feelings. His had already been wounded in the changed orders of who would introduce Bush. But he called himself "an Indian, not a chief, and the Indians are the ones who get the real work done." His commitment was mature and strong enough to withstand the petty slights of politics. Others, he worried, might not respond the same way. His objective was to include, not exclude, as many people as possible for the Bush effort.

He negotiated at length with the head of the advance team so that he could stand at the reception table and vouch for anyone whose name wasn't on the approved list. As people began arriving at four-thirty (it is standard procedure in campaigns to tell people the event will start an hour or more earlier than it is actually intended to begin; no campaign wants its candidate to walk into a room that isn't already full), Kendall greeted them personally and waved them through, whether they were on the list or not. His friendly bravado masked a lingering unease that the room wouldn't be packed.

When Bush walked in at five forty-five, there were about 350 people in the room. It was full enough, although not jammed to the walls. A wall of flesh—several Secret Service agents, an aide, the governor—surrounded the vice president as he waded into the crowd. They formed a three-quarter circle, with Bush in the center and whomever he was greeting at the open end. Kendall, who was supposed to be leading Bush and making personal introductions, found himself behind the wall instead of in front of it. This wasn't the way it was supposed to happen. Kendall peered over the shoulders of two husky agents and kept trying to slip into the circle. They kept blocking him.

"One of us is going to have to move," he finally told an agent in exasperation.

"It's you," said the agent, keeping the vice president in the protective near cocoon. *What am I doing here?* Kendall thought, trailing the clot of bodies as it worked slowly across the floor. At last he wiggled around the group and stationed himself where it was headed. When it arrived he took on his role of guide for the last third of the handshaking. He would join Bush with a guest, say a few words about the local person to the vice president, wait while they chatted about thirty seconds, and then move Bush to the next waiting person. Slowly they circled back to the riser in front of the Lane family flag.

Kendall stood near the exit as the speaking began. He rose on his tiptoes to scan the crowd, searching the faces and paying little attention to what was being said at the microphone. (He did, however, perk up annoyedly when the executive councillor said words to the effect that he hoped the vice president was pleased at the crowd he—the executive councillor—had gathered. And he noted that the riser held a small crowd of people, mostly elected officials, rather than just Bush and his introducer.) As Bush spoke, Kendall tuned out. He was more intent on finding two people who hadn't yet shaken Bush's hand. He had high hopes of getting the two on the Bush bandwagon and did not want the evening to end without them meeting the vice president. When he caught their eye, he motioned them to work their way to the door and began jostling with another Secret Service agent to get them into position.

Bush concluded his brief remarks and moved briskly toward the door, enveloped instantly in another shield of agents and aides. Kendall lunged across their outspread arms and directed Bush to his two prospects for a hurried handshake.

Then the entourage swept out the door. Two agents blocked the exit for everyone else, to give Bush time to leave and get into his limousine. Kendall waited with the crowd. His event was over. It was six-twenty.

In the days that followed, Kendall would settle back into his organizational routine. He would compose a follow-up letter to be sent from Bush to the attendees, then another letter from state headquarters asking the guests to join the campaign. Using the event and the letters as a topic to call them, he would begin contacting people to see if they would serve as town chairmen and ask them to a meeting at his house. A few prominent Republicans who had been overlooked in the invitations would be incensed at the slight, and Kendall would have the governor call to calm them down. At the next "Freedom Fighters" meeting, when the group reviewed the western New Hampshire trip, he would make the point as forcefully as he could that "you don't do your local organization any good if it's just the elected folks around the vice president; he's not being briefed about local people doing the work so he's aware of them and can say something to make it easier to recruit people."

He would complain to the *Sentinel* reporter about their coverage—he thought they made too big a point over the event being closed to the press and, despite his own feelings along the same lines, over the fact that Bush spent most of his time in Keene huddled in a hotel room. He also thought du Pont got more coverage than the incumbent vice president. And he would have some pictures developed, taken by a friend, of Bush standing in front of the Lane flag. Even without Kendall in the pictures, they would become valued mementos. (Nearly a year later, when the primary was over and the worries and frustrations of the days leading up to the reception had long receded, he would even point to the event as his personal highlight of the campaign.)

But in the immediate aftermath of the reception, mainly he was just relieved that it was over. By six forty-five the balloons were gone, and Kendall and John Croteau had carefully taken down the flag without rending its fabric. He wished he had gotten to tell its history to the vice president, but between his duties at the reception table and the tussles with the Secret Service, the chance had never arrived.

Kendall made arrangements with Jane and some friends to meet at the country club for a late dinner. At seven o'clock, with the flag properly folded and tucked safely under his arm, he walked out through the empty hotel lobby. He had a city council meeting to attend.

4

BREAKING UP IS
HARD TO DO

The news about Gary Hart and Donna Rice reached Andi Johnson via her television set. The Sunday night network news on May 3 told her that the morning's edition of the *Miami Herald* had reported on a liaison between the senator and the model at Hart's home in Georgetown. Andi's first reaction was that it wasn't very important. It was just another minor aggravation in a month of such annoyances—bad news, but nothing disastrous.

From the time he had officially announced his candidacy in April, Hart had been off to a slow, sometimes rocky, start. To Andi's chagrin, most of the news reports about the Hart campaign had centered on either rumors of his "womanizing" (on his first trip as an official candidate, Hart had accused rival campaigns of spreading the rumors; the accusation brought the rumors out into public and attracted more media coverage than his substantive speeches) or the debts lingering from his 1984 campaign (some small vendors in New Hampshire who were still owed money from the primary four years earlier were being particularly vocal with the press). The press focus on money and sex peeved her: *Why don't they print Gary's position on the issues?*

Locally—and much more of a concern to Andi at the moment— a second organizational meeting had flopped. Everyone who had attended Hart's speech to the county Democrats in March had been mailed an invitation to the meeting, and between Andi, Tom Britton, and the state headquarters, each one had thought someone else was making phone calls to follow up the mailing. As a result, no calls were made. When the night arrived only eight people had showed up—the original four supporters from the meeting at the Britton home in February, plus four more. Everyone agreed they had learned a valuable lesson about assigning specific responsibility for specific tasks. Next time important details wouldn't fall through the cracks.

Still, two months' time and a high-profile appearance in Keene had been squandered without making any real organizational progress. Hart was due back in Cheshire County for a visit in June. Lee Hart, his wife, was scheduled for May 16 and 17. Andi and the others were confident the trips would get them back on track locally. Hart was leading his Democratic rivals in national opinion polls and in Iowa; in New Hampshire only Michael Dukakis, well known because of his position as governor of neighboring Massachusetts, seemed potentially capable of challenging the front-runner. *If we're going to make mistakes or get some bad publicity, better now than later*, Andi thought. Her attention was focused on preparing for Lee Hart's upcoming trip and on trying to convince the state director to hire her boyfriend, now living in Massachusetts, as Cheshire County campaign coordinator, the role he had played in 1984. Hart himself would be in New Hampshire Friday to officially open his campaign headquarters in Manchester, then attend a party for the faithful. Andi planned to attend both events. The news item Sunday about Donna Rice seemed too remote and much too trivial to concern her.

When she got out of work Monday and saw the headline on the front page of that afternoon's *Keene Sentinel* (HART DENIES WEEKEND AFFAIR), she reached a different conclusion. *Hey*, she told herself, *this is serious*. She hurried home and started working the phone. She called state headquarters and her friends on the campaign to find out what was going on. She was an insider now and wanted the inside story. But no one could tell her anything more than what was in the paper and on television. Like everyone else in America, longtime Hart supporters or not, she would have to get all her information from news coverage.

Over the next four days there was plenty of news coverage to follow. Glued to her TV every morning and evening and poring through each day's newspapers, Andi watched in horror as the incident mushroomed into a media explosion of atomic proportions. Before her eyes Hart's suspected trysts with Rice (he denied that anything improper had occurred between them) quickly became the top political story and then the top national and international story. On Tuesday afternoon he addressed the annual meeting of newspaper publishers in Washington, denying having done anything wrong and angrily attacking the press for staking out the bushes outside his home. At least one network interrupted its programming to carry his remarks live. On Wednesday, in Hanover, New Hampshire, the town where Andi had first met him in 1983 and asked him about health care costs, Hart held a press conference in which a reporter asked him something quite different: "Have you ever committed adultery?" This moment—the question being asked in the open, the long pause of silence as Hart appeared to be simultaneously absorbing the body-blow implications of the question and mentally processing the myriad possible responses, then his refusal to answer—seemed to be playing on television every time Andi turned on the tube or changed channels, like the constant replays of the *Discovery* explosion for days after the shuttle disaster. Thursday's *Boston Globe* carried eight stories, two cartoons, one editorial, and two op-ed columns about the Hart-Rice imbroglio. Hart canceled the remainder of his New Hampshire trip and fled to his home in Colorado, where a swarm of television satellite transmitters stood sentry over his front yard. On Friday afternoon, again on live network television, he dropped out of the race for president.

The week was a swirling nightmare for Andi. No matter what she did or where she went, the subject of Gary Hart and Donna Rice kept popping up.

On Tuesday morning Will Fay, a reporter from *The Keene Sentinel*, called her at work for a story he was writing about how local activists, particularly Hart supporters, were reacting to the ballooning controversy. The top of that afternoon's front page carried the headline HART, RICE DENY SEXUAL RELATIONSHIP; CAMPAIGN IMPACT EYED. In a separate story on the local reaction, Andi was quoted as saying, "I think it's a setup. Gary is too honest, and I just think the whole thing is ridiculous." Knowing her connection with the campaign, her co-workers at the Beech Hill Hospital, a drug and alcohol rehabilitation center, kept raising the topic, either by commiserating with her disgust at the media or by making snide jokes.

Bruce Babbitt was in Cheshire County on Tuesday evening, attending two small receptions in private homes. The second was at Bruce Anderson's. Just as she had already attended local receptions for Biden and Gephardt, despite her commitment to Hart, Andi went to hear Babbitt. Going to other campaigns' events satisfied her craving to mingle with other people steeped in politics—and to take her own measure of Hart's competitors as well as to scope out how well they might be doing locally. It wasn't as if she were spying. Anderson, still uncommitted to any presidential candidate and planning a series of such receptions, was a friend of hers. He had invited her. Like many hosts of such events, the imperatives of assuring a good-size crowd and of not alienating friends in the area often outweighed the narrower organizational interests of the candidate-guest. Nonetheless, four years ago, involved in her first campaign, she wouldn't have done this. Her devotion was totally and personally to Hart. (During the general election of 1984, Andi had taken a bumper sticker for the Democratic ticket that read "Mondale/Ferraro" and cut off the "Mondale" before putting it on her car. When she voted that fall, she wrote in "Hart for President.") Whether she realized it or not, her presence at other candidates' receptions this time around was further evidence of her transformation since 1984: now she was a political activist first, a Hart partisan second.

Hart's entanglement being the principal and unavoidable topic of conversation in America at the moment, Babbitt addressed it briefly at the start of his remarks. "Gary Hart is a friend of mine," he told the twenty-five people gathered in Anderson's living room. "I like and admire him. But when you step across the threshold to run for president, *everything* about you is relevant. I'm not saying it's fair, but that's the way it is. New Hampshire allows us to rub against people so you can figure out who we are. None of us are plaster saints, because all of us are mortal beings, but we can't afford to make another mistake in selecting our leader." He then moved on to talk about the congressional hearings on "Irangate," greed running rampant on Wall Street, the need for better day care and health care, and his commitment to the environment.

The second question from the audience was what kind of family life he had. After Babbitt said he had been married happily for seventeen years and had two children, the questioner, an elderly woman, interjected: "Don't get caught with some other woman now." Andi, standing at the perimeter of the crowd gathered around Babbitt, turned crimson at the twitter of laughter that spread through the room. After a question and answer about Central America, she raised her hand and Babbitt motioned to her.

"Your brochure," she said, holding it up, "says there should be no new nuclear waste dump in the Northeast." There was a challenge in her voice, as if she were a prosecutor about to pin down a defendant on the stand. "But haven't you also proposed creating a new waste site in the West?" She crossed her arms as Babbitt responded, explaining his position in detail. Then he moved on to other people's questions. When she went home that night, Andi was the only one from the crowd who thought Bruce Babbitt had been exposed for having an indefensibly contradictory position on nuclear waste.

Thursday night, when the news hit that Hart had hurried home to Colorado with his wife and that there was speculation he might quit the race, Andi was on the phone all evening. She called the state headquarters several times. No answer. She called the state director's home several times. No answer. She called her boyfriend.

She talked with Tom and Valerie Britton, and with Jo Robinson, the other people who had attended that first local organizational meeting. Finally she tracked down Sue Calegari, the state director, at another supporter's home in Concord and was told that yes, it was very likely, though not official, that Hart would pull out on Friday; the current media environment made continuing impossible. She hung up the phone, poured herself a drink, and then called the other Hart supporters to give them the news, as if she were notifying members of her own family that their older brother, the favorite among the siblings, was terminally ill and not expected to survive the night: Gary would probably be gone by tomorrow afternoon.

She was emotionally exhausted. "I've watched too much news, and I'm tired of explaining away Gary Hart all week at work," she said. She was angry at the press ("If they really wanted to know what's going on inside [Hart's Georgetown home], they should have gone to the windows like any other peeping Tom"), angry at the entire topic ("That part of his life never bothered me. Who cares? I mean, look at Kennedy. Look at FDR. It didn't affect their ability to govern"), and angry at the snickering that so often accompanied its discussion. She was also angry because she didn't want Hart to end his campaign. It wasn't solely his campaign; it was hers and a lot of other people's. She, like so many of them, had a lot invested in it—time, work, emotions, dreams, personal history. They had helped give the campaign its life, but now they weren't participating in the decision to end it. It was all so . . . unfair. It was like being informed by your first serious boyfriend that you and he were breaking up. It wasn't that he loved someone else or even no longer loved you, it was just over, that's all. Just plain unfair.

Andi wasn't angry at Hart personally. She preferred not to believe the worst about him and Donna Rice. Even if something had happened between them, she didn't think it was relevant to Hart's qualifications to be president. Unlike some of Hart's other supporters, she didn't even blame him for allowing himself to be put in this position, for being careless with appearances and foolishly jeopardizing what they all had been working toward for more than four years. Her support was too heavily tinged with devotion to allow that. The farthest she could go at the moment was disappointment, if he indeed had decided to quit.

She understood the political situation. That evening an acquaintance had called her to say that after the Donna Rice incident he could never consider voting for Hart. "Why?" she asked him. "Because he cheated on his wife," was the answer. "*This* was from a guy who I knew was cheating on his own wife," she would recall later. "I knew at that point there was no hope for the campaign." But, she thought, couldn't Hart simply suspend campaigning for a while, take some time off to be with his family and regroup, and then pick it back up? Ending the campaign seemed so final, so extreme. What about all the work that had already gone into it? If the Hart campaign was gone, what would take its place? *What will I do now?* she wondered. *What will I tell people?*

Will Fay called her again later that night, working on a story for Friday about how local Hart supporters were dealing with the whole controversy. Even though Hart's decision was still unofficial, Andi had prepared a formal statement and read it to the reporter:

I'm very angry with the press. The press has been bombarding Senator Hart with questions about his so-called campaign debt and his personal life, suggesting they influence his ability to run the country. They have not in any way focused on his knowledge and solutions on the issues of nuclear war, Central America, the Middle East, the economy, education, or social issues.

I believe Senator Hart would have been one of the best presidents ever elected by this country, and I personally would have preferred that he keep on fighting and stay in the race. But Gary Hart cares deeply for his family, and I'm sure he feels his decision is in their best interest. I personally feel let down by his decision.

Thursday night was a night without sleep. The telephone, the television, the extreme emotions, took her through to the morning. At work the next day the television in a patient lounge was tuned in to watch Hart's noontime announcement. Wearing the Hart campaign button that had been part of her everyday attire for months, Andi waited nervously among the group of patients gathered to watch. Before Hart appeared, as the television anchorman recounted the swift avalanche of remarkable events that in the course of five days were about to culminate in the withdrawal of the leading Democratic candidate, Andi could feel herself starting to fall apart. *I can't handle this*, she thought. *I can't handle this, and I'm not going to start crying in front of the patients.* She bolted from the room and was in her office, trying to compose herself, when Hart told the world his campaign for president was over.

Friday night more than a hundred Hart partisans met at a supporter's home in Manchester for the reception that originally was to have followed the opening of the Manchester headquarters. Andi, Jo Robinson, and Tom and Valerie Britton attended from Cheshire County. What had been planned as a festive reunion of the candidate and activists who had pulled off the great upset of 1984 turned instead into a wake for the unexpected death of their hopes for 1988.

The mood at first was quiet and somber, a little awkward since nobody knew quite what to say to each other. After a few beers or drinks, however, everyone loosened up and started releasing their pent-up frustration, anger, profound sadness, and collective tension. They hugged one another. They traded various conspiracy theories over whether Hart had been "set up" by Donna Rice as part of a plot to end his candidacy and whether the press had been out to "get Gary." They exchanged gallows humor and laughed too hard at their own jokes. ("One reporter called me up and asked if I had ever noticed any improper behavior by Gary," Andi recounted to a fellow Hart worker. "The only thing I could think to say was: 'Do you mean, did he ever make a pass at me? No, he didn't.' ")

They turned up the music and danced. Late in the evening they posed for a group photograph. One picture, of them smiling, was to be sent to Hart in Colorado to let him know they were still behind him. Another one, of them extending their middle fingers, was for the *Miami Herald.*

They reminisced about the 1984 New Hampshire primary and talked about their own future plans for the upcoming contest, now that they no longer had a candidate.

"We'll never have a candidate again like Gary Hart," Andi said, summarizing everyone's feelings. "We'll never have the same caliber of people working for a candidate. We'll never have the same level of commitment. It'll never be the same."

What she didn't mention during the evening was that earlier in the afternoon, not long after Hart made his announcement of withdrawal, she had come to a conclusion about herself: *I'm a diehard political junkie. I've got to be working for somebody, so I'm not going to wallow in pity.* She had then called a friend of hers on the staff of the Simon campaign in Washington, asked for some issues papers, and arranged to meet him for lunch in a week.

5

BROTHER PAT AND BROTHER DOUG

Doug Kidd pulled his aging Toyota Corolla into the parking lot of Kingsbury Machine Tool Corporation, one of Keene's largest employers, found an open space for visitors, and parked. This would have been a perfect day for painting his house: the mid-June weather was warm but not hot, the forecast called for several more clear days without rain, and the yearly late spring onslaught of black flies, the multitudinous pests that discouraged any outdoor activities in rural places near bodies of water like Doug's home in nearby Stoddard, New Hampshire, had finally passed.

Instead Doug was making another business call. The house could wait. It would be there all summer. He reached across to the front passenger seat and rummaged through the material strewn on it—some glossy campaign brochures, the day's newspaper, a stack of one-page fliers announcing the upcoming visit of Pat Robertson to Keene, and an annotated volume of the Bible. He grabbed one of the fliers and walked out into the bright sunshine. At the front desk he smiled politely, gave the name of the middle-level manager he wished to see, and sat down to wait, appearing for all the world like the other salesmen in the reception area.

At age thirty-six Doug might easily be mistaken as someone still in his twenties. He was trim, his smallish frame exhibiting none of the droops or bulges that normally developed on other men his age unless they worked constantly at keeping in shape. (In Doug's case it wasn't from physical exercise—although he was an accomplished skier—it was from eating properly and not smoking or drinking.) He might make a good male model. Even in a coat and tie he looked casually comfortable. A thick mop of dark hair, always immaculately in place, swept back fashionably from his forehead. If, as the saying goes, by age forty you're responsible for your own face, Doug was headed toward a smiling middle age. His entire demeanor—affable, outgoing without any trace of pushiness, an easy sense of intelligence and competence—gave a first impression of gentle friendliness that was only reinforced the more you got to know him.

Robertson was due in three days for his first appearances in Cheshire County—a public reception and press conference at the Ramada Inn during lunch hour, some media interviews, a house party, an evening speech at a church, an overnight stay, and a breakfast restricted to women. Doug, who for nearly two months now had been assigned by the campaign to build an organization in western New Hampshire, was concentrating on the public reception in the closing days. Weeks earlier he had set preparations in motion for the other events. Using the church service announcements in *The Keene Sentinel* as a guide, he had contacted the ministers of twelve area churches to talk about Robertson's candidacy and see if one of them might want Robertson to speak to their congregation. The minister of Doug's church, the Trinity Evangelical Church, had finally agreed to issue an invitation. A fellow church member had offered his home for the house party and was taking care of its turnout. Three women from Doug's weekly Wednesday night prayer and Bible study group were organizing the breakfast.

The public reception—the only event outside the circle of Doug's church affiliations—was the only remaining part of the schedule somewhat in doubt: Doug simply had no idea how many people, if any, would show up, and he was trying everything he could think

of to get people there. He had printed up the fliers and spent a day
going from store to store on Main Street in Keene to ask if he could
put them in the windows. The response had not been encouraging.
Although some allowed him to put up his poster, most of the shop-
keepers were coldly indifferent, if not antagonistic, about a television evangelist running for president. (As one result, however, a
woman who had seen a flier tracked Doug down and offered to put
up more posters on grocery store bulletin boards and to invite some
of her friends to the women's breakfast.) Only a little discouraged,
Doug had changed tactics and was now doing his notification person to person, calling on acquaintances of his whom he thought
might be even remotely interested in meeting his candidate.

A young woman emerged from the Kingsbury offices into the
reception area. Doug stood to greet her. She had been a student of
his at a management course he taught in the evenings at Keene
State College. They chatted briefly about her job, the weather, and
Doug's new class of students.

"Listen," he finally said, the time having come to close his sale.
"My man's coming to town, and I thought you might like to come
hear him." He handed her the flier. "I'm just contacting some folks
to let them know."

She looked at the flier awkwardly. "How's the response been?"

He shrugged his shoulders. "Some good, some . . ." He made
the sign of the cross with his fingers, like someone in the movies
recoiling and trying to ward off a vampire, and laughed.

Laughing with him, she thanked him for the flier and said good-
bye. It was clear, though unspoken, that, much as she liked Doug,
she wouldn't be in the crowd at the Ramada Inn.

Back in the parking lot, Doug looked up at the clear blue sky.
"Good day for painting," he said, and then got back into his car
and went to another call.

Doug Kidd spent the first thirty-six years of his life paying almost
no attention to politics. While he was growing up in New Jersey
in the 1950s and 1960s, it was never the topic of discussion in his

family, although the influence of his parents and the times led him to the vague desire of wanting, in his words, to "please others, help people—to serve." After graduating from Hope College in Holland, Michigan, in 1976, where he majored in psychology, he married immediately, traveled for six months, and ended up in New Hampshire, where he and his wife decided to spend the winter skiing while they supported themselves working in bars and restaurants. When their child was born Doug decided he needed a steadier job. He took evening courses at Keene State College to earn his teacher's certification for special education and began work at a workshop for physically and mentally handicapped people in Keene. Rising in responsibility at the workshop, he went on to get a master's degree in management from Antioch New England graduate school in Keene. In the meantime his marriage collapsed; he was separated in 1979 and divorced in 1981.

Those were dismal years. Living in a tiny apartment on Central Square, Doug lost himself in "alcohol, drugs, rock and roll, and women." He became an unreliable employee and was fired from three jobs, most of them as a bartender. Like the rest of his existence at the time, his finances disintegrated. He was not yet thirty, but he felt his life, or at least his worth as a human being, was already wasted and over.

Then he met and fell in love with Allison, a stunningly beautiful woman who was also a born-again Christian. Her explanation of her belief struck a chord within Doug: the values of loving others, self-sacrifice, and trust hearkened to his childhood Sunday school classes and offered him hope of deliverance from the pit of his current desolation. After a weekend spent without sleep, talking and thinking about the meaning of Christ, he told Allison: "I accept Him. Now I'm going to learn in my walk with the Lord what it means." They married in 1982. He got back on track professionally, first as a management consultant, then with a state job-training program and teaching a college course in the evenings. By the mid-1980s they had bought and tastefully redecorated an old house in the small town of Stoddard, where Doug was now a solid citizen.

Finding Allison and Jesus, which he linked in his mind as two "gifts from God," had transformed his life. He was grateful for them both.

Doug and Allison consider themselves charismatic Christians. They believe the Holy Spirit is still present on earth and still evidences itself when fellow worshipers "speak in tongues" or when ailing people are healed by a laying on of hands. Allison claimed a chronic bad back had been cured this way; two days after being "born again," Doug had spoken in tongues during a prayer meeting. They believe in miracles, things that cannot be rationally explained except by faith.

If there is a national stereotype of Christian fundamentalists, reinforced by media treatment of them, it is probably this: unsophisticated, poorly educated (and suspicious of any academic training beyond the basics), primarily rural folk of the working classes—rubes of society's backwaters trapped economically and culturally by generations of strict upbringing and blind faith, making them easy prey for any leader promising simple answers or salvation from the complications of life. In everything except their religious belief, Doug and Allison Kidd (and in fact virtually all of the friends they have made through their church connections) seemed cut from a totally different stereotype. College-educated, upwardly mobile in the managerial and entrepreneurial strata, wearing the latest fashions, driving foreign cars (Doug was about to trade in his Toyota for a Saab), owning expensive houses and taking yearly vacations in places from which they return with winter tans—and even in their concentration on their personal lives to the exclusion of politics—they more closely fit the "yuppie" mold.

Although Doug and Allison were worshiping at the Trinity Evangelical Church in the spring of 1987, actual membership in a church is not important to them. (One happy by-product for Doug of his work for Robertson was that it brought him into contact with another church in southern New Hampshire, where the services were more charismatic; by the end of the campaign he and Allison had begun attending services there.) "I've come to see how many

Christians have almost kept their Christianity separate from the
rest of their lives," Doug said. "They keep what they know for
Sundays and Wednesday nights, and confined to the group that
goes to that building, as if they're leading two different lives." For
him, church is "more a time of celebration, like the Super Bowl."
Disciple of organization that he may be because of his professional
training, Doug does not apply it to his religion, except to refer to a
church as a "network of resources" for the individual Christian. Of
more emphasis is the "daily walk" of faith: reading the Scriptures,
personal prayer, and trying to live his life according to the example
of Jesus.

In 1986 he was interested in finding work that would "blend
business management with Christian values, the principles of leadership with the principles of love." It was from that perspective—
management and Christianity, not politics and Christianity—that
he accepted an offer to join the Robertson campaign.

An acquaintance of Allison's family, Kerry Moody, approached
him in the fall of 1986. Moody, though still in his thirties, was
already a veteran of the New Right fusion of Christian fundamentalism and conservative politics. The son of a minister in Dublin,
New Hampshire, Moody had worked in the gubernatorial campaigns of Meldrim Thomson, Jr., and the 1976, 1980, and 1984
presidential campaigns of Ronald Reagan. He had left a job in the
Reagan White House to join Robertson when the televangelist set
up a committee to explore a presidential bid. When he told Doug
he was working for Pat Robertson, Doug didn't even know much
about the man, let alone that he was considering a switch from
being the head of the Christian Broadcast Network to president of
the United States.

Moody asked whether Doug thought his expertise in management techniques could be applied to building a grass-roots political
organization. The notion intrigued Doug. He didn't know anything
about campaigning or politics. In the few elections he had even
bothered to vote, he had made last-minute decisions, casting his
ballot for someone whose name he'd recognized rather than making

a choice based on any ideology or study of the issues. A job with Robertson seemed like both a great learning experience and a chance to put his beliefs, professional and religious, into action.

In May 1987 Doug Kidd became a political operative, although he would never call himself by the term. It was, in his excitement and euphoria after his first month at the task, "the first job in my career where I come home without any stress"—a job description no one deeply involved in a political campaign, particularly at the high stakes of the presidential level, probably had ever used before, and one that Doug himself would reassess before the primary finally arrived.

The candidacy of the Reverend Marion "Pat" Robertson was literally a political phenomenon. No one in the established political community—the professional campaign operatives, reporters and commentators, elected officials, and the "junkies" for whom political speculation is a never-ending enterprise, whether a campaign is already under way or years in the future—knew exactly what to make of it. Candidates with religious backgrounds had run for the presidency before (the final three contenders for the 1984 Democratic nomination were Walter Mondale, the son and son-in-law of ministers; Gary Hart, who had attended divinity school; and Jesse Jackson, an ordained minister), but Robertson was nonetheless unique as a serious candidate for the presidency. He was certainly no stranger to politics: his father had been a prominent United States senator from Virginia, and, as the host of the *700 Club* on his own television network, Robertson had been discussing the major international and domestic issues for years. Still, the reason he was well known by millions of people (in fact, the only reason he was thought to have a potential base of support large enough to be considered seriously, despite the fact that he had never run for any political office in the past) was his celebrity as a religious leader.

In the horse race handicapping that preoccupies campaign discussion, especially in the long months before anybody actually casts

ballots in the initial primaries, Robertson represented a new breed
of animal. No one was certain how to gauge his chances and place
their bets. Would his religious affiliation be a political advantage or
disadvantage?

On the one hand, he might energize a whole new group of people
who heretofore had never participated in the electoral process, particularly in the caucuses and primaries in which relatively small
numbers of voters can have a dramatic impact. Most campaign
strategies are predicated on the fact that the voters in the early
contests are essentially the same, easily identifiable people who
have habitually voted in past primaries and caucuses. The key to
victory is seen as ignoring those who haven't previously shown
such inclinations and instead concentrating the campaign's efforts
on persuading a plurality of the smaller number of targeted "likely"
voters to support your candidate. Nothing is more unsettling to the
manager of a traditional campaign than the prospect of huge numbers of unexpected voters suddenly taking their franchise seriously
and turning out on election day. In theory, at least, Robertson had
the potential of transferring a bloc of citizens' religious zeal into a
political crusade and therefore rearranging the normal mathematics
of a presidential race.

On the other hand, the American people, religious though they
might be in comparison with citizens of other democracies, have a
historic aversion toward too overt a mixture of religion and politics,
of any direct link between church and state. They might expect
their president to be a moral leader in the larger sense of the word,
but not their national preacher. Teddy Roosevelt's description of
the presidency as a "bully pulpit" was not to be taken too literally.
Even among fundamentalist Christians (by no means a monolithic
group in the first place), there were concerns that in pursuing the
presidency, Robertson was stepping across an invisible yet profoundly important line. For some of those who didn't share his
religious beliefs, once the inevitable news stories started appearing
about various pronouncements he had made in his television ministry, Robertson's candidacy was simply frightening. Nobody had

ever run for president before who had claimed to have healed terminal illnesses or diverted a hurricane from the Atlantic shore by
the power of prayer.

Robertson's campaign was aware of this dichotomy between the
simultaneous opportunities and the severe limitations inherent in
his candidacy, and his appearances in the Keene area clearly dem-
onstrated it. At his public reception/press conference (attended by
thirty people, half of them reporters and campaign aides), he spoke
about the trade deficit, the national debt, the crisis in education
and literacy, and his proposal to provide child care tax deductions
for families with mothers who stayed at home. In asking for their
support, he told the audience that "fifty thousand people here in
New Hampshire can choose the Republican nominee; the publicity
of winning here alone is worth fifty million dollars." It was a political
speech that could have been made by any conservative Republican,
and in talking informally with the few voters there, his campaign
staff was more likely to stress Robertson's background as a business
executive than minister.

The audiences at the house party and the breakfast further exemplified the untested waters Robertson had set sail upon. One of
the sixteen people at the house party told him, "God called me and
guided me to this [event]," and pledged her support, then asked
which party's nomination, Republican or Democrat, he was seeking. At the breakfast, in which virtually all sixty women were attending their first political gathering, a woman rose during the
question-and-answer period to say that she was troubled that Robertson might be ignoring the Scriptures' injunction to "render unto
Caesar what is Caesar's" and that he could be more effective remaining as a leader of Christians rather than as a Christian trying
to be leader of the nation. Robertson replied that he had prayed for
several years about the issue. "But in America," he said, "*we* are
Caesar. To render unto Caesar is to be good citizens. If we are to
obey the command of Christ, we *must* be involved. If we want to
become a persecuted, hunted minority, then we can stay out of
politics. If we stay out, then those who are not Judeo-Christians

will be ruling us." Another woman, prefacing her question by telling Robertson, "May the peace of the Lord be upon you," asked whether, as president, he would "acknowledge the Lord." He said he would, pointing out that even on the campaign trail he set aside two hours each morning for prayer and Bible study, but as president it would "not be appropriate to promote Christianity as such." He would "create a level playing field" for all sects but acknowledge God in office. His other questions were about nuclear power (he favored it, including the controversial Seabrook plant in New Hampshire), the environment (he wouldn't have vetoed the Clean Water Act, as President Reagan had just done), and terrorism (he wanted a special strike force for retaliations).

The crowd at the Trinity Evangelical Church was large—nearly two hundred people—and the proceedings had an air of pageantry about them. The local minister, waving an American flag, led the group in singing the "Battle Hymn of the Republic" and "God Bless America" before introducing Robertson: "We know him as a man and a believer; we come tonight to know him as a political figure. Pat believes God has called him in his ministry to heal America." Robertson, at ease and beaming at the turnout, gave a half-hour speech that mingled ardent conservative rhetoric ("Containment of communism is the wrong goal," he said. "Our goal should be to roll back communism and eliminate it, including in the Soviet Union"), social issues associated with fundamentalism (permitting prayer in schools, outlawing abortion), and populist themes ("I'm dreaming tonight of a time when there are no more bankers and industrialists financing communist dictatorships . . . when our streets are safe to live in and criminals are punished and there is an end to mob-supported pornography and drug trade . . . when the phrase 'Made in America' is again synonymous with the best in the world").

The campaign added a new wrinkle to its standard procedures that night. Following Robertson, a young campaign aide took the microphone. He explained that he was Jewish, had worked for Ronald Reagan since 1976, but like many other people he had quit his job (in his case, in the White House) to work for Robertson. He talked about the success the campaign was experiencing in other states by focusing on "people like you" instead of Republican party endorsements. As Doug Kidd and other workers passed pre-printed envelopes down the pews, he urged them to sign the envelopes, enclose a donation or a pledge to make future payments and to volunteer their time, and pointed out that there were tables at the rear of the hall offering Robertson books, videotapes, and copies of a petition urging "Pat" to officially announce for the presidency (at this point Robertson was technically still "exploring" the possibility). He said Robertson would stay to answer their questions, but first he needed them to fill out the envelopes. Then he simply stood silently at the podium for ten minutes so that nothing could distract them from the task.

This technique killed several political and organizational birds with one stone. The aide's speech simultaneously answered two of the unspoken concerns in the audience: Robertson's support was not restricted to fundamentalist Christians (the aide was Jewish), and Robertson's political goal was attainable (the aide was a Reagan operative and therefore knowledgeable in these things; the campaign was going well in other states). It provided a brief electoral tutorial for people uninitiated in political matters, and by inserting the sales pitch into the middle of the event and waiting for them to fill out their envelopes—like passing the collection plate well before the end of the service—it both caught the audience when the spirit to participate was the strongest and created a communal sense (and, perhaps, subtle pressure) to pitch in. Robertson then returned to the microphone and answered a half hour's worth of questions, all dealing with nonreligious issues, from "Aren't you tired of campaigning?" to what he would do about mismanagement of the Pentagon.

Doug Kidd, whose normal demeanor was one of generous goodwill anyway, was overjoyed by this first visit of his candidate to his home region. With the exception of the Ramada Inn reception, the crowds had been good and, more important, receptive. Nearly three hundred people had met Robertson personally. Most of them had signed the petition for his candidacy, and a number had offered to host home parties at which the campaign video would be shown to their friends. At the church event alone several thousand dollars had been put into the envelopes, with pledges for more; eleven of the twelve videocassettes (at $5 each) at the rear tables had been sold, as well as several books. Doug said he had learned a valuable organizing lesson—if you "empowered" people, put them rather than the campaign in charge of an event, the responsibility resulted in getting them more deeply committed to the cause.

On a more personal level, Allison seemed to be getting excited about the campaign. She had attended the church meeting, sitting with her arm locked in Doug's during the speech, and the women's breakfast, where she smiled proudly as Doug introduced Robertson and then, after the candidate's remarks, enlisted the audience to fill out pledge envelopes and sign the petition. With only a little more than a month's experience on the job, Doug was already realizing that the campaign would be taking him away from home for long periods of time in the year ahead. If Allison could feel she was part of the effort, it would mean a lot to them both and mitigate his absences.

Robertson's other events in western New Hampshire, north of Cheshire County but still within Doug's region of responsibility, were also successful. The crowds were uniformly larger than expected. "It was," Doug said later, "as if the Lord stepped in and said, 'Let me help.' " Several Democrats, enthused by the notion of a Christian leader seeking office, offered to switch party affiliation to help the campaign. Doug, reflecting the management perspective that had been as much of the reason for his involvement as his religious beliefs, summarized it this way: "The Christian bloc is a market segment that gives us a lot of room to move around in." A meeting held to woo former Governor Meldrim Thomson seemed promising. Robertson himself, joking and praising in his informal talks with Doug, was obviously pleased with his two days.

They had good reason to be satisfied. Doug had no way of knowing it at the time, but from a strictly political, organizational point
of view, Robertson's trip to Cheshire County had been the best of
any campaign's thus far in the year. They had reached more people
directly, signed up more names for the computer data base they
were compiling, raised more money, and prompted more offers of
future assistance than any of the established candidates' campaigns, including the vice president's.

The questions of campaign arithmetic for Robertson, however,
were still open. Would the people who had been enlisted in the
visits, nearly all of them new to politics, be willing and able to bring
in more of their kind, expanding the organizational circle? Or were
they, perhaps, the outer edge of the circle itself, circumscribed by
the constraints implied in the concerns even some of his most likely
supporters had voiced about a man of the cloth trying on the suit
of a politician? At this point there was no way of knowing. But you
didn't have to believe in miracles to recognize that Robertson was
indeed a political phenomenon, and his staff seemed skilled enough
in the traditional campaign tactics of signing people up, creating a
network for the phones and mails, and getting people to donate
time and money—*making lists*—to push the circle to its organizational limits.

Doug recognized the daunting tasks ahead. In the weeks immediately following Robertson's visit, a number of the people who
had offered to host home video parties were coming up with various
excuses why they hadn't actually held them. Some were clearly ill
at ease about calling their friends for political purposes. And press
reports about Robertson's candidacy all seemed to treat him as a
religious zealot who threatened to impose a national religion upon
the Republic. But Doug, as was his wont, looked ahead and saw
mainly possibilities. Whatever happened, the Lord's will would be
done.

As a staff person in his first political job, Doug also now cherished
the kind of fond personal memory from his close contact with Rob-

ertson that can fuel any worker for any candidate. At the end of the second day of the western New Hampshire campaign swing, as they were walking into their last event, Robertson had turned to Doug and smiled.

"Brother," he had said, "this has been a blessed day."

6

COURTSHIP

The swift collapse of Gary Hart's candidacy in May 1987 not only removed the Democratic front-runner from competition, it also created a large pool of volunteers and campaign workers with proven political experience who no longer had someone to support for president. In New Hampshire, where Hart had won so dramatically in the 1984 primary and where he had seemed organizationally months ahead of the other Democrats when the Donna Rice bombshell exploded, the traditional political courtship rituals assumed some new forms as the scramble began to fill the void created by his disappearance.

The other campaigns quickly began reaching out to the Hart partisans, gingerly at first, conscious that a kind of mourning was taking place and therefore careful not to appear like crass opportunists at a funeral. With varying speeds virtually all of Hart's supporters went through the grievance cycle of shock, denial, anger, acceptance, and then continuance. As deeply and personally committed as they had been to Hart, few of them ultimately decided to sit out the New Hampshire primary simply because the political figure who had triggered their initial interest was now, for all political purposes, dead and buried. It was as if fate had unfairly and prematurely made them young widows: they wanted their grief acknowledged and respected, but they hoped their youth and sudden eligibility wasn't entirely overlooked, nor the fact that they had become so committed to the institution of marriage that they would entertain the notion of a second husband. For some the memory of Hart and his campaign, like that of a first true love, would still be on their minds even as they took new nuptial vows. Others gradually grew to view him quite differently, deciding that his demise was the result of his own selfish recklessness and that he had, in effect, betrayed their trust. Some reacted like Scarlett O'Hara in *Gone with the Wind* after the death of her first husband. They went to charity balls dressed in black but started tapping their toes when the band struck up the Virginia reel and waited impatiently for someone to ask them to dance.

A week after Hart dropped out of the race, Governor Michael Dukakis made his first visit to Keene. Among the 150 people who came to the Keene Junior High School cafeteria to hear him on a Saturday afternoon was Andi Johnson. From the first moment it appeared that Hart might quit the race, Andi's choice had been not whether she would join another campaign, but which one. She had even written a letter to *The Keene Sentinel*, publicly announcing her disgust with the press treatment of Hart and signaling her desire to find another candidate who would carry on "Gary's" issue agenda, particularly in foreign policy. Friends on the Babbitt, Gore, and Gephardt campaigns had contacted Andi, commiserating with her about the media coverage of Hart and then suggesting she consider their candidates. She appreciated their attention and didn't entirely dissuade them from hoping she would join them, but privately she was leaning toward Paul Simon or Joe Biden. Like Hart, both were senators—"I have this thing about governors becoming president," she said—and on her own initiative she was already talking with their campaigns about their organizational plans and reading the issues papers she had requested from them. Dukakis, being a governor, was not high on her list. In fact, partly because of her competitive instincts (Dukakis had been seen as Hart's principal rival in New Hampshire) and partly because she saw his campaign as essentially the same group that had supported Walter Mondale in 1984 (she still begrudged Mondale's ultimate victory over Hart for the last Democratic nomination), Andi didn't like Dukakis at all.

Nonetheless she showed up at the public reception to hear Dukakis speak and to check out the large crowd. After his opening remarks, hers was the first question, and it was pointed, almost hostile. She quoted a recent newspaper article that said Massachusetts's economic boom had been fueled principally by President Reagan's defense spending. "Is that what you mean by the 'Massachusetts miracle'?" she asked. After the event a Dukakis aide, an acquaintance of hers, came up to her. Apparently giving more weight to her presence than her question, he invited her to help the campaign in Cheshire County. Andi looked at him as if he were crazy. "No way," she said curtly. *"Ever."*

For the rest of May Andi weighed a decision between Biden and Simon. She had reservations about each of them. She had heard Simon speak at a Democratic gathering in 1986 and found him very boring. On the other hand, she had friends on the campaign, and since Simon was just now organizing in New Hampshire, they could see to it that she played a more enhanced role with Simon in Cheshire County than she had played with Hart. Biden already had the support of many Democratic leaders in the state, including Pat Russell of Keene, a member of the Democratic National Committee, and several other political veterans in southwestern New Hampshire. Andi thought they were building the only remaining organization that could rival Dukakis's and was attracted to the notion of being part of another campaign based around the candidacy of a young senator making broadly thematic generational appeals, one that might topple another establishment candidate. It wouldn't be exactly the same as 1984—as far as she was concerned, nothing could ever equal that exhilarating experience—but it might come as close as possible under the circumstances. Yet she didn't know much about Biden himself. She had seen and heard him in person several times, as recently as February at the small gathering at Pat Russell's house, but hadn't paid all that much attention to him. Being firmly in Hart's corner at the time, she had attended the functions more for the sociability of being with fellow political "junkies" than to scrutinize the candidate. To the extent that she occasionally listened intently to Hart's opponents, it had been during remarks that she thought might be exposing political vulnerabilities.

Andi's concern about Biden, now that she was thinking about supporting him, was what she described as "questions about his temperament." Earlier in the year she had gone to a Hart event in Claremont, New Hampshire. It was some distance north of Cheshire County, but she had made the journey "to see if Gary was as good as he used to be." A man at the reception had pestered Hart with questions about his educational background and which historical figures Hart respected the most. Andi didn't think they were necessarily bad questions, but the man's tone had been needling and impertinent. She had been encouraged that Hart handled the situation with patience and even a trace of humor. Afterward several people told her that the same man had been to a Biden reception the night before, where Biden had responded to his questions by "throwing a real temper tantrum." At the time Andi had enjoyed this bit of gossip and passed it along several times in the next days to show Hart to advantage by comparison. Now, however, she wondered if it should affect her selection of Gary's replacement. When a former congressman (Andi had been a volunteer in his unsuccessful race for the Senate in 1986) called to urge her to support Biden, she raised the incident. He said he had been there when it happened and wasn't concerned about it, so she dropped the topic.

By early June she was favoring Biden. Simon had announced officially as a candidate and concluded his announcement swing (after stops in Illinois and Iowa) with a listless and poorly attended event in Manchester that drew bad reviews in the press. More important to Andi, she had met with several Simon aides and asked a series of questions about how they planned to organize their New

Hampshire effort, but they didn't get back to her with answers. Was the lack of response meant to signal Andi that they weren't very interested in her support, or was it simply organizational disarray? For someone who considered herself an emerging political professional, either reason was sufficient to look elsewhere. She gladly accepted Pat Russell's invitation to attend a small home party to watch Biden being interviewed on the CBS television show *West 57th Street* and see a videotape of Biden's speech to the California Democratic convention. (The Biden campaign, which considered the CBS interview a good excuse to hold many such home parties and build local organizations, supplied the videotapes as well as copies of other Biden speeches.) Andi found the California speech particularly stirring but was even more impressed by the home parties themselves: it seemed to her that the Biden people knew how to run a campaign, as did Pat Russell's news that they would be opening a Keene office in July, months before any other campaign.

A few days later she made up her mind. Less than a month had passed since the Hart debacle, but the weeks had seemed endless to Andi. She was anxious to get them behind her and move on. The campaign for president was proceeding with or without Gary Hart, and she didn't want the same thing to happen to her. She had no way of knowing that two of the incidents that played a role in her decision—Joe Biden's flash of temper in Claremont and his California speech—would also contribute to the demise of her second campaign three months later. All she knew and felt at the moment was that the only thing worse than being part of a disintegrating campaign was being part of no campaign at all. Even if it meant choosing between what she considered two lesser candidates, choosing was preferable to not choosing and therefore sitting on the sidelines.

Andi reached Pat Russell on the telephone. "I'm with you," she said. Then she called Biden's state headquarters in Manchester to arrange to bring over her box of voter cards, which she had rescued from the Hart headquarters just before it closed.

———

Tom and Valerie Britton were not as anxious to join another campaign. The circumstances of Hart's departure left Tom especially embittered. He believed that, solely because of being the early front-runner, Hart had been singled out by the press for unreasonable scrutiny. For weeks afterward the topic was a sore one for Tom. "This is a lousy way to lose," he would say. "Getting beat head to head by somebody is one thing; getting beat this way is hard to swallow. The more I've thought about it, the more pissed off I get."

Like so many other Hart volunteers, Tom and Valerie, both in their mid-thirties, had become active in politics because of their personal devotion to Hart in the 1984 primary, and in four years they had been transformed from political outsiders to members of the party establishment. Tom came from a Republican family in the Keene area, had become a liberal Democrat during the anti-Vietnam fervor of his college years, and then moderated in his views somewhat after he married, started a family, and moved up in responsibility working in technical support and marketing for a high-tech firm in nearby Massachusetts. Within the Hart campaign in the 1984 primary he had found a way to put his emerging political philosophy—which he described as liberal on social issues, tempered by a realism on the way the world works and a belief that traditional Democrats were no longer electable—into practice. Now he was a member of his town school board and chairman of the Cheshire County Democrats. Prior to 1984 Valerie had never voted. But politics was now such a part of their family life that Corinne, their third-grader, could name all the candidates for president and would tell people they'd be crazy to be Republicans. Whenever the name of New Hampshire's Republican governor was mentioned, Allyson, their four-year-old, would say, "Sununu makes me puke."

As county Democratic chairman, Tom was the kind of activist any presidential campaign in New Hampshire would want on its side. He began getting calls the night Hart withdrew from the race but wasn't in the mood even to talk about other candidates. "The only time I've spent thinking of them," he said, "was in comparing them negatively to Hart. I can't see myself supporting any of the candidates in the field right now." Because of his party position, he also attended the Dukakis reception in mid-May, even though, like Andi Johnson, he didn't care for Dukakis. "I'm still having trouble turning my head around from thinking Hart is the best and the rest are so inferior, to a point of thinking one of them is now the best," he said afterward. "I guess I keep waiting for a white knight to ride in."

At the end of May he was still wishing that "Gary would come back and tell them all to kiss off," and a month later his view was that Hart should not have dropped out of the race. "He got a bum rap, the country got a bum rap," Tom said. "They knocked out the best candidate for less than significant reasons."

June was an active but bizarre month for Tom. He was contacted by several Gephardt supporters, including a Minnesota congress-man who extolled Gephardt's record in the House. Gephardt himself telephoned, asked for Tom's help, and offered to answer any ques-tions or have his staff supply any information Tom wanted. Pat Russell called to talk about Biden. Babbitt's staff inundated him with material—copies of speeches, position papers, videotapes of a campaign commercial and a debate in Iowa between Babbitt and Republican Pete du Pont. Babbitt called him at work, hoping to meet him personally. Tom was uncomfortable with it all. He didn't dislike Babbitt or Gephardt, and their positions on the issues were essentially his own, but he kept hoping in vain for the kind of inspiration he had felt for Hart. (Dukakis and Biden were different cases; he ruled them out entirely, making predictions about them both. On Dukakis: "If his message is 'Let me do for you what I've done for Massachusetts,' he's going to eat that message." On Biden: "I think he's going to do some suffering. There's something about him that seems insincere to people.")

He was also uncomfortable about becoming part of a group of activists who, he thought, were beginning to act like political "prima donnas," one of the very things he disliked most about politics. Shortly after Hart's withdrawal, the group—mostly but not exclusively former Hart supporters—had gathered secretly in Concord to talk about the presidential race. Tom was among the twenty-five people who listened as the group organizer explained that they all were now uncommitted activists who shared many of the same ideals and who liked to work together. If all or most of them decided as a bloc to support a single candidate, it "would be good for the candidate and good for us." They were broken into teams to research each of the Democratic candidates and report on their findings at the next meeting. Then they were asked to vote for their top two picks at the moment, as well as to mark a separate ballot for the candidate they liked the least.

Given his doubts about the current list of candidates, Tom offered to research the record of Bill Clinton, the governor of Arkansas who reportedly was considering a presidential bid. Tom had heard him speak once, had been impressed by Clinton's style, and had kept track of him through the papers ever since.

At the next meeting, in early June, the group had grown to forty people. Tom hadn't yet received the information he had requested from Clinton's office, so he couldn't make a detailed report when they discussed the strengths and weaknesses of each candidate before balloting again, this time on a weighted, ranked system for their top three preferences and again for their least favorite. Babbitt won the sweepstakes that day; Biden received the most blackballs. Tom, who by now felt the whole procedure was taking on the aura of a "smoke-filled room," cast only one ballot, for Clinton, and decided this was his last meeting. A week later, when the group interviewed Senator Albert Gore, Jr., of Tennessee—one of the bottom finishers in the two straw polls—Tom declined to attend, and he was not among the twenty-two who publicly endorsed Gore on June 29.

As June ended, no white knight having arrived, Tom fastened on the next best thing. Clinton, he decided, was his white knight, if only the young governor would saddle up. By this time he had studied Clinton's record and, on his own initiative, called the governor's office in Arkansas to say he'd support Clinton, could probably even swing over some other Democrats as well, but they needed a clear signal of a candidacy. "Time's running out," Tom told Clinton's political aide. "People are dropping [to other campaigns] like flies, and it's costing him each day he waits."

Meanwhile the courtship calls from other campaigns continued. At least now Tom could tell them that he was waiting for Clinton. The thought of an insurgent, late-starting (even though the primary was still eight months away) campaign gave Tom an occasional thrill. Maybe he could recapture the sense of mission he had felt for Hart's candidacy. Still, when he thought about the last two months, his principal emotion was displeasure. If Clinton opted against running, Tom had decided somewhat resignedly, he'd support Babbitt or perhaps Gephardt. They were nice enough guys, and he liked their staffs, particularly Babbitt's. It was as if he had become somehow obligated to get involved in a campaign. "It's kind of a pain in the neck, because I can't see myself killing myself to elect any of these guys president," he said. "But I'd feel like a jerk if I go only halfway. Once I commit myself, they're going to expect me to do the things that need to be done. I'd rather not have it feel like such a chore."

About the only effect Gary Hart's withdrawal from the race had on Bruce Anderson's political life was that it reduced by one the number of Democratic campaigns wooing him for his support. Still uncommitted to any candidate, he had devoted a lot of time over the winter and spring to studying the entire Democratic field. He had purposefully set out to see as much as he could of them and was on friendly terms with them all. (Whether he admitted it or not, moving around to the myriad campaign functions could have the side effect of making personal contacts that might be beneficial to his own political future.) The campaigns, in turn, expended considerable energy trying to enlist him in their own ranks. Because of his standing in the party—derived from his run for governor in 1986, his deep involvement in party activities over the next two years, and his identification as a rising young star on the political scene—and because of his obvious interest in the presidential primary, Bruce would be a good "catch" for any campaign. If a social columnist were covering the various political courtships taking place among the pool of activists, Bruce Anderson would probably have been described at the top of southwestern New Hampshire's "most eligible" list.

In the three months since his ride in Babbitt One, every Democratic campaign (except Jesse Jackson's, which at this stage was not organizationally mobilized in the state) had continued to come calling. Senator Biden had sent him letters with personal notes written at the bottom. Bruce had attended Pat Russell's home party to watch Biden's television appearance on CBS and to see a videotape of the senator's fiery California speech; and he had traveled to Biden's official announcement of candidacy. Prior to the Donna Rice debacle, the Hart organization had invited him to Colorado for the official kickoff of the campaign (he couldn't make it) and sent him *Hart Line*, letters, and position papers. He had taken an afternoon off from work to go to Manchester to hear Paul Simon declare for president. Albert Gore's supporters were trying to arrange a meeting between Bruce and the Tennessee senator. He and Dick Gephardt had spent an hour-long lunch talking about trade policy and the presidency. Bruce had later sent Gephardt some magazine articles he thought were particularly interesting ("I remembered from my own campaign how little reading I got done unless someone pointed them out," he explained) and received a handwritten thank-you from the congressman. Governor Dukakis had telephoned for a short chat, and some high-ranking supporters in the state had taken Bruce aside to intimate that, win or lose, Dukakis's extensive organization and fund-raising apparatus in nearby Massachusetts would "remember their friends" long after the primary.

None of the campaigns, however, was as inventively aggressive as Babbitt's in its pursuit. The long ride in Babbitt One in March (itself the culmination of months of wooing) had not ended the way Babbitt's staff had hoped. Bruce had, in effect, dodged Babbitt's embrace in the backseat. But the staff still considered Bruce a likely

supporter and continued their contacts. He was sent videotapes of
some Babbitt commercials and asked for his comments; a tape of
the Babbitt-du Pont debate in Iowa also arrived in the mail. A list
of top prospects in Iowa and New Hampshire was circulated around
Babbitt's national headquarters in Arizona, asking people there if
they knew anyone on the list. As a result, an old friend of Bruce's
wrote him, saying she was working on Babbitt's energy positions,
and solicited his opinions. Reading in the paper that Richard Lamm,
the former governor of Colorado, was teaching for a year at Dartmouth College in Hanover, New Hampshire, Bruce had arranged
to meet with Lamm, whom he had admired from afar for several
years. When the discussion turned to presidential politics, Lamm
had expressed his own admiration for his fellow former governor
from the West. An avid outdoorsman and skier, Babbitt had planned
a late spring climb of Mount Washington, in northern New Hampshire, to ski the famous and difficult Tuckerman's Ravine during
a political swing through the North Country. Bruce was among a
handful of New Hampshire activists invited to come along. At the
end of the hike avalanche dangers prevented any actual skiing, but
the two nevertheless spent a lot of time together during the weekend. And, at the staff's request, Bruce had hosted a reception for
Babbitt at his home in Harrisville. He explained that he planned
to do the same for some other candidates (Gore would eventually
be at one in July, Gephardt in September), but his introduction of
Babbitt in May was full of praise about the governor's qualifications
to be president. Following a Babbitt reception in Concord, which
Bruce had attended (Tom Britton had also been invited from Cheshire County but declined), the staff's hopes rose again when Bruce
told them Babbitt had "significantly improved in his delivery, much
more energetic and loosened up" and was at the top of his list.

By the start of July, however, he was still unwilling to commit
himself. "It's getting harder to choose, the more I see of them all,"
he said. "It's almost as if familiarity breeds a kind of contempt. I
like them all intellectually—they're all good on the issues—but they
lack pizzazz and inspiration. I'm beginning to think that's more

important, the ability to lead people through inspiration and personality, to get people to say, 'I like that guy.' " His personal ranking of the candidates was Babbitt first, then Biden, then Dukakis, but he wasn't operating on any timetable for making a final decision. The first nationally televised debate among the Democrats was coming up in a few days. Bruce planned to watch. Maybe that would help him decide.

Traditionally, discussion of the primary and the disproportionate notice paid to it by the national media has focused mostly on the influence of New Hampshire's primary coverage upon the primaries that follow in other states. (According to one study, although Iowa and New Hampshire comprise only 3 percent of the total vote in the primaries and caucuses, they receive more than 30 percent of the media coverage during the nominating process.) A win in New Hampshire could land a candidate's picture on the cover of *Time* and *Newsweek*, prompt reams of stories in the nation's newspapers, and, most important, grab the attention of the television networks and therefore the viewing public. The tidal wave of national exposure would simultaneously make a candidate better known to the voters in the next primaries and make it much easier to raise campaign funds—two of the most important elements for winning more primaries. Realizing this potential public relations bonanza, the candidates over the years began devoting more and more time and energy to New Hampshire's primary and the early caucus in Iowa. The increased political effort, of course, only spurred increased press coverage, which in turn made an early win that much more valuable. Coverage followed effort, as effort chased coverage up a spiral staircase. When Pat Robertson told crowds in 1987 that a victory in New Hampshire was now worth fifty million dollars in free national publicity, no serious political observer disputed his arithmetic.

From the beginnings of the presidential primary, however, the impact of media coverage of the campaign upon *New Hampshire* has been profound—more profound than that suggested by the popular image (which itself is partly a media image) of how the whole thing works. Certainly, because of its small size and its traditional place at the start of presidential race, New Hampshire offers a candidate both the scale and the time to reach citizens directly, person to person, face to face. As Estes Kefauver proved in the first preference primary in 1952—and Jimmy Carter confirmed in 1976—it provides someone lacking national stature, huge financing, or the support of the party establishment the chance to circumvent those obstacles by taking his case personally to the voters. But the primary has never taken place in a media vacuum. Unless they had served in World War II and had met Dwight Eisenhower when he reviewed the troops, the only things the voters who gave Eisenhower his majority in the 1952 Republican primary knew about their candidate was what they had read in the newspapers, seen on newsreels and their new television sets, or heard on the radio. Henry Cabot Lodge, Lyndon Johnson, Gerald Ford, and even Carter (when he ran for president again in 1980) all prevailed in their primaries with voters who had to base their decisions virtually exclusively on information provided through the mass media. The fact is, despite the opportunities to do so and contrary to the myths, the great preponderance of New Hampshire's primary voters never meet a candidate for president. The "retail" campaign of candidate to citizen is waged principally within the smaller universe of activists and potential volunteers—a universe impossible to quantify precisely, but probably not much larger than several thousand Granite State Republicans and an equal number of Democrats.

Even this proportionately tiny fraction of New Hampshire people actively involved in the campaigns, however, is not immune to the media's reach and impact. Far from it. In the early months of a campaign, when the bulk of citizens are uninterested in politics, these activists (and their counterparts across the country) are pretty much the *only* people—other than political professionals and the reporting corps itself—following the campaign coverage with regularity and any intensity.

The activists differ from the rest of the voting public in two significant respects in regards to press coverage. Because of their interest and involvement, they pay much closer attention, starting much earlier. At the same time, unlike virtually everyone else, they are not totally reliant on the press for their information. The image of the candidate they see on their TV or in their paper is not the only image they have, because they've actually met, heard, seen, and even touched the candidates in the flesh, perhaps several times and certainly for longer segments of exposure than is possible on the nightly news. They have other information and images to factor into their final assessment of a would-be president—information unfiltered and unedited by the process of journalism.

Uniquely among one hundred million Americans who eventually register their choice on the presidency, these several thousand activists (with their counterparts in Iowa and significantly smaller numbers in several other states) possess a more intimate and much more exhaustive inventory of impressions and information upon which to form their image of the candidates. Nevertheless, as the Democratic debate on July 1 would prove, the media image could be just as powerful as personal contact in swaying the grass-roots activists.

The debate, hosted in Houston by conservative Republican columnist William F. Buckley, was not the first time the Democratic contenders had been on the same stage together, nor would it be the last. But it marked a milestone of sorts. It was the first such encounter to be televised nationally and thus was the first exposure many of the viewers had to most of the Democrats. (In comparison with the Republican field—which included a vice president, a nationally prominent Senate leader, a former secretary of state, and a televangelist with his own network—the Democrats were not as well known individually and were often referred to as "the Seven Dwarfs.") With an estimated 2.3 million households watching, it was an important event.

Presidential campaigns approach televised debates with four audiences in mind. The first is the live audience in the debating hall.

Small in number and normally comprised of partisans in the first place, this is by far the least important audience. Next is the viewing audience, which, depending on when the debate takes place and who is televising it, can range from the thousands in a small, local TV market in an early primary to more than eighty million Americans during the general election when all the national networks simultaneously broadcast the encounter between the two parties' nominees. Obviously the larger this audience, the greater importance it holds for the campaigns—but it is always significantly, sometimes astronomically, larger than the audience in the hall. The third audience is the group of political reporters and commentators, smallest in number and yet crucial for two reasons: they will be publicizing their verdicts on which candidates did well and which ones didn't, who made mistakes and who "won"; and in their news reports following the debate, theirs will be the only version of what happened available to the fourth and largest audience. This last audience is the population at large, or at least those who watch television news and read the morning papers—and it includes not only all three of the audiences who witnessed the entire debate, but the even greater number of people who didn't bother to tune in.

The Houston debate had a special significance to the New Hampshire activists, too. By this point they had seen most of the candidates both individually and in a group (all but Babbitt had appeared at a fund-raiser for the likely gubernatorial nominee in May). But this would be the first opportunity to see the seven of them together, in the sustained, combat format of debate, on television. Whether already committed to one of the candidates or still deciding, the activists were an especially attentive, and politically important, part of the total electronic audience. Having already encountered the candidates standing in their living rooms, they would now see the candidates' images on the television screens in those same living rooms.

From the dawn of televised debates in 1960, it has been clear that people's perceptions of what takes place is profoundly influenced by the medium through which they witness it. Someone relying on a written transcript derives a different impression of the event from that of someone who watches or hears it. The audience listening in 1960 to the Kennedy-Nixon debate on the radio, for instance, was more likely to think Nixon had prevailed; the television audience was more likely to tilt toward Kennedy. Similarly, watching from the debate hall is not the same as watching a television screen—so much so, in fact, that most political reporters, anxious to have the same "experience" as the bulk of the debate's audience, prefer to sit in a hall adjacent to the debate site and view the event on TV monitors.

This potential for the filter of television to create its own "reality" was never more dramatically proven than in the case of Bruce Babbitt and the Houston debate. Like every person, Babbitt had his own characteristic idiosyncracies in body movements and speaking style. When he talked, he tended to throw his shoulders back rigidly, tuck in—almost bury—his chin into his neck, creating folded jowls in his lower face, and turn his entire upper body sharply from one side to another to dramatize his points. His voice was deep (and often compared with Nixon's) and he spoke in a flawlessly articulate, yet structurally complex English, often in herky-jerky bursts punctuated by quick licks of his lips. Even in encountering him personally in the informal settings of small groups, these traits could be initially disconcerting, although over time they receded from perception to become a minor, hardly noticeable quirk of an impressively articulate, confident, and humorously thoughtful public figure. The unwavering, unblinking, intensely close and intimate gaze of the camera lens, however, highlighted these traits to the point of painful, unavoidable exaggeration.

Partly because the Houston debate was uneventful in the traditional sense of political news—the candidates avoided direct attacks on one another, no one made any major factual blunders, there were few memorable and quotable lines or exchanges—Babbitt's "performance" received even more attention in the postdebate coverage and commentary than it otherwise might have. The press pundits declared no one the "winner." Unanimously, however, Babbitt was declared the "loser" of the evening, his style dissected and criticized to such a degree that even the kindest review pointed out his "distracting gestures and mannerisms that interfered with his message."

For the overwhelming majority of viewers, who were encountering the Democratic field for the first time, the Babbitt they saw was the only Babbitt they could know. Even his own campaign recognized that Babbitt's introduction to the public had not established a good image of him—worse, even, than the obscurity he had suffered previously. But what his staff would soon realize, to their dismay, was that within the small universe of activists who already knew the "real" Bruce Babbitt, particularly those who had been moving gradually toward supporting him, this first exposure to the televised Babbitt had just as profound an effect. The gains he had been making among the New Hampshire activists—through his own personal contacts and the hand-to-hand work of his organization—hit a brick wall and even recoiled somewhat, all because of the way he came across on their living room television sets.

Tom Britton watched the debate in his home in Troy, wishing all the while that Governor Clinton, his potential "white knight," had announced for president to join the other candidates on the stage. When the debate was over he had favorable things to say about six of the seven Democrats. Biden had given a good response to a question about Cuba and communism; Gephardt looked "good and relaxed" and addressed the issues directly; Simon seemed like a "straight-shooting political maverick, willing to say the things that need to be said"; Jackson was both folksy and eloquent; even Dukakis, though Tom still ruled him out for support, was strong on domestic issues and "didn't hurt himself." Gore, whom Tom had never met because of dropping out of the Concord bloc, was particularly impressive. (Based on the debate, Valerie now liked Gore best of all.) Only an official candidate for a few days at this point, Gore had made a "credible showing, worth a lot" in making up for lost time, Tom believed—just what he thought Clinton could have done.

And Babbitt? "Whew!" He expelled the word like someone who had just witnessed an unfortunate but gory accident. "He's got so many good people in this state," Tom said as if they were surviving next of kin. "He's strong on the issues, and I suppose if you shut your eyes it wouldn't be so bad, but he looked lousy on TV."

The debate altered Tom's ranking of the candidates. Clinton, if he would run, was still at the top. Gephardt had inched up a little, although Tom harbored reservations about his trade policies. The Brittons had already agreed to host a breakfast for Gephardt; the campaign had requested it, and as county chairman and uncommitted to any candidate, Tom thought it only right to accede. Now he was happier that he had. Babbitt, once just behind Clinton, had dropped from serious consideration. "Electability"—the political handicapping assessment often applied to a candidate as if it were a personal trait—was not a prime criterion for Tom (though it was for a good number of other activists), but if he had to choose someone who didn't fit his "white knight" category, it certainly figured in his calculations. With the television persona Babbitt had displayed that night, "I don't think he can capture the imagination of people, even if he's good on other things," Tom concluded. "He can't meet *everyone* face to face." Babbitt was scheduled to be in the Keene area in a few weeks, and Sue Calegari (a friend of Tom's, the former New Hampshire director for Hart, now on Babbitt's staff) wanted Tom to meet the candidate privately. Tom no longer saw much reason to do so.

Gore, however, was now a possibility, had even taken Babbitt's place in Tom's internal pecking order. A reporter from *USA Today* called immediately after the debate, seeking comment from uncommitted New Hampshire activists on their opinions of the event. Tom told him he thought Gore had done the best. Proving that the media can affect the organizations as much as it affects the activists, a Gore aide was on the phone to Tom within hours of the paper coming out the next morning. Gore was coming to Keene soon and wanted to meet Tom in person.

When Dick Gephardt showed up for breakfast at the Britton home on a sunny Saturday morning in July, about twenty-five people were there to hear him. Tom and Valerie's cars still proclaimed "Take Hart New Hampshire '88" on their bumpers, as did Andi Johnson's, although hers now also sported a Biden bumper sticker. The congressman, standing by the pool in the Brittons' backyard, spoke for fifteen minutes ("The real challenge to America is whether we can hold our economic strength in the world," he said), answered a dozen questions (Andi asked about funding to treat drug addicts and alcoholics), mingled with the crowd, and then prepared to leave. On his way to his car, Gephardt took Tom aside for a brief talk.

"Tom," he said, munching the doughnut that was his breakfast for the day, "I need your help, and I *want* it."

Tom had given a praiseworthy introduction of Gephardt to the guests he had assembled and had been favorably impressed by both Gephardt's demeanor and his explanation of his views on foreign trade. But Clinton was still mulling over a decision whether to run, and Tom, who by now was talking regularly with the Arkansas governor's staff about the campaign, was still waiting for a clear signal. He told Gephardt he had enjoyed the Houston debate and based on it believed Gephardt could make a good president.

"I feel stupid saying it," he told the candidate, "but I'm still hanging out."

Gephardt and his entourage—including his wife, three children, and his brother, plus ten aides—departed for a residential section of Keene, where the candidate was scheduled to campaign door to door for the rest of the morning.

Presidential candidates knocking on the doors of New Hampshire homes is not entirely unprecedented, although it happens rarely, and when it does, it's usually for appearance' sake. Campaigns realize that, compared to other ways of having their candidates reach voters—from small groups to rallies, from highly targeted telephone calls to appearances through media interviews—it is not the most effective use of a would-be president's time. In fact, the principal reason Gephardt was in a quiet Keene neighborhood that morning was not to reach those people who answered his knock, listened to his short spiel, and accepted the brochure he presented them. The real reason could be seen standing a few feet away: a television crew and a clutch of reporters and photographers, including a campaign staff photographer.

The voters the campaign hoped to reach were not the owners of the twenty homes Gephardt and his family visited, but the voters who, in the papers and newscasts, would see a mythic ritual of the New Hampshire primary being reenacted and therefore reaffirmed. Obviously the press was there because the candidate was there—a candidate for the nation's highest office going door to door, like someone running for neighborhood council, appeals to our most basic, yet romantic, notions of democracy; it makes a good story, or at least a good picture. What is less obvious is that the candidate was there only because the press was there. If the campaign had been told that no reporters, photographers, or television crews could make it, the event undoubtedly would have been canceled.

The campaign's staff photographer was along as a protection against just such an eventuality, as a guarantee to make the neighborhood walk worthwhile regardless of who else showed up. She was compiling pictures for a direct-mail brochure, targeted specifically to thousands of New Hampshire Democrats, that would make much of the fact that Dick Gephardt took the time and effort to meet the state's voters—*even if it meant coming to their homes*—and listen to their concerns. One of the several pictures in the brochure from that morning would be of Gephardt and his family knocking on a house door. No one was home, which permitted more time to pose the shot.

At the second-to-last house Gephardt visited, an elderly woman was standing by her front gate. Eleanor Labrie, a retired schoolteacher, had never been involved in a political campaign in her life. But she had just read that day's *Keene Sentinel*, which carried a story quoting Gephardt, at a reception in Cheshire County the night before, that Ollie North, the former member of the White House staff who had masterminded the Iran-contra affair, should be thrown in jail. Now the candidate himself was reaching out his hand to introduce himself.

"Hi, I'm Dick Gephardt, running for president," he said.

"I saw your remarks about Ollie North," she replied as they shook hands and he gave her a brochure. "It's about time somebody said that."

The exchange was brief, hardly long enough for the photographers to get into position for a good picture, and after introducing his family, Gephardt was quickly on his way down the street. Eleanor gave her name to an aide who trailed behind, collecting information for the campaign to use to follow up the candidate's encounters.

Designed as it was to be a "media event" more than a technique to sway the handful of voters he met personally, Gephardt's street walk was a success. Over the next days pictures and stories appeared everywhere showing him as a humble "candidate of the people." The brochure, filled with shots portraying him in a mythic New Hampshire vignette, including two of the Gephardts and Eleanor, would arrive in the mails of Democrats across the state several months later. "Last summer," it proclaimed, "Dick Gephardt wanted to find out what the first-in-the-nation voters up here in New Hampshire were thinking. No, he didn't call up a political pollster. Or listen to the media pundits. He did it the hard way. *He asked us.* Himself. In person. One to one."

But the event also had a totally unintended consequence. Based on that scant encounter—one of the shortest "courtships" imaginable—Eleanor Labrie decided on the spot that Dick Gephardt should be the next president of the United States. She would become one of his hardest-working volunteers in New Hampshire.

Bruce Babbitt was in town four days later. In the two weeks since the Houston debate, as virtually all political discussion about his campaign centered on the damage sustained by Babbitt's television presence, both he and his staff had been extremely public in recognizing the problem. They referred to it as a bad "performance" that, luckily, had occurred early in the season, leaving plenty of time for improvement. Aides toting video cameras recorded every event and then went over it at night with the candidate. Babbitt began consulting a television and debate coach, even invited the press in to watch one session. (It resulted in one scene that could symbolize both the power of television as well as the resulting "What is reality?" quality in modern campaigns: as Babbitt sat with his media coach to watch himself on a TV monitor, television crews circled him to record the moment for the news; meanwhile a documentary film crew shot footage of the television cameras getting footage of Babbitt watching footage of himself.)

Dan Burnham hosted another small breakfast reception for his candidate. Babbitt, at his best in these settings, led the freewheeling discussion in a Socratic way, drawing out the views of the six participants as much as telling them his own thoughts on subjects ranging from naval strategy to public apathy. Several of the people were won over to his candidacy, and as he left Babbitt told Dan: "There was some magic here this morning. I feel refreshed by it— it'll help me slog through another day's handshaking and speeches. Thanks for arranging this."

Dan was reinvigorated, too. The debate had aroused his old reporter's instincts, worrying him that the campaign he had taken on as a project was headed nowhere. Unlike the others in the campaign, he found it hard, almost impossible, to put Babbitt's debate performance in the best light. It wasn't that he thought less of Babbitt; the morning's session had only reaffirmed his choice. He had been encouraged to overhear one of his friends, chatting with the candidate before the breakfast, kindly reassure Babbitt that "it [the debate] wasn't as bad as you thought." Still, he confided after Babbitt departed, this candidacy might be "doomed" because of Babbitt's "presence on the tube." The dichotomy intrigued him intellectually but saddened him somewhat.

At an evening reception in the backyard of a Keene supporter, a Babbitt aide stood in the small circle of voters with a video recorder, shooting material for the nightly review. Even though they were Republicans who already supported Jack Kemp, Al and Mary Rubega were there at the invitation of the host, a fellow lawyer. When Babbitt mocked President Reagan's reference to Ollie North as a "national hero," most of the crowd laughed. "No hero fans of Ollie's in the audience?" Babbitt asked. Al and Mary, alone in the crowd, raised their hands. During the question-and-answer portion of the evening, Al asked Babbitt his position on gun control (Babbitt said he opposed it), and as the event broke up Al went up to shake his hand and pat his back.

Sue Calegari had persisted in trying to arrange for Babbitt to meet Tom Britton, her friend and colleague from the now defunct Hart campaign. Out of loyalty to her, Tom finally relented. It had not been a good day for him. The morning paper had contained a story about an enthusiastic response to Governor Clinton's speech to a national conference of county government officials, which Tom had clipped out and was reading at work when Clinton's political aide called. The governor had finally made a final decision, Tom was told. Clinton wasn't running. As they talked Tom crumpled up the clipping and tossed it in the wastebasket.

"I'm 0 for two," he said after the call. His co-workers, who knew of his previous support for Hart and his yearnings for a Clinton candidacy, had ribbed him about being a campaign jinx. "Since you don't like Dukakis, maybe you should join *his* campaign," one of them joked. *Maybe it's just not my year*, Tom thought.

A staff member of Albert Gore's campaign had called, wanting Tom to meet with the candidate when he came to Keene in a week and seeking help in identifying Cheshire County activists who were not yet committed to other candidates. Tom had agreed to help. In his mind it was now between Gore and Gephardt (Valerie was now leaning to Gephardt, following the breakfast they had hosted), and he looked forward to meeting the young senator from Tennessee before making a decision.

The same evening the state Democratic party's executive committee, of which Tom was a member, met in Keene. Babbitt stopped by for a brief talk, as did Kitty Dukakis, who was also in Keene campaigning for her husband. Most of the people Tom talked to mentioned Babbitt's horrible debate performance. Pat Russell approached him again about supporting Joe Biden; a Dukakis staffer made a pitch, which Tom cut short.

His meeting with Babbitt took place at a quiet table in a Keene restaurant/bar late that night. They talked about the campaign in general, and Babbitt admitted he had been "flat" during the debate but was working on his technique. When he asked Tom to join the campaign, Tom changed the subject.

"He's a very sincere, very impressive guy," Tom told Sue Calegari afterward. "I can see why so many good people are supporting him. If I hadn't seen him in the debate, maybe I'd be more impressed." Then he left to meet Gore's campaign worker.

More than forty people showed up for breakfast with Al Gore on July 21 during his first visit to Cheshire County. Tom Britton, still uncommitted to any campaign, had been scheduled to be in North Carolina on a business trip, but he delayed his departure by half a day for the chance to see Gore. After the morning reception (held in the same restaurant where Babbitt and Tom had met the week before), Gore and Tom walked the half block to Lindy's Diner for a private breakfast.

For forty-five minutes they talked about politics and policies. Dating back to his Hart days, when he had measured other candidates against "Gary's" positions, Tom was aware that Gore differed with his fellow senator from Colorado on several issues. One in particular, Gore's vote supporting development of an MX missile, bothered Tom—it symbolized his concern that Gore was too conservative for his tastes—and he pressed Gore on it. The senator explained his reasoning on the issue and then looked Tom in the eye and said he'd vote the same again under similar circumstances. Although Tom still disagreed with the vote, Gore's directness impressed him. "If he's willing to take that kind of stand, whether it's popular or not, because he thinks it's in the best interest of the country, I like that," Tom said later. "It's an indication of his character."

Tom also liked Gore's response to one of the people in the diner, who stopped briefly to shake the candidate's hand and tell him, "Good luck to you, but since you're so young if you don't get it this time, there's always the next election."

"*This* is the time," Gore answered. He also assured Tom that, though he was a southerner and starting his campaign late, he planned to make an all-out effort in New Hampshire.

Throughout the breakfast Tom found it a little strange, yet exciting, to be talking with a candidate for president who, at thirty-nine, was only two years older than he. "Well," Gore told him as they left Lindy's, "I think you ought to support the candidate closest to your own age."

During his drive to Boston and flight to Raleigh, Tom thought about the primary. Weighing Gore against Gephardt was still a tough choice. Both, particularly Gore, were more conservative politically than Tom, and yet he liked them both. Gephardt, he decided, was solid—he had a good campaign building in New Hampshire (and Iowa), was already a candidate with more than a year's experience behind him, and seemed like he would be a good president. Gore was more of a gamble. He was young, new to presidential politics, and, in Tom's mind, would turn out to be either very, very good or not good at all in the Oval Office. But he had more guts and more style.

When he arrived at his hotel in North Carolina, Tom was told by the desk clerk a package had been brought over for him. It was a bottle of Jack Daniel's whiskey (the sour mash made in Tennessee) and included a note from Gore's North Carolina campaign director, who had delivered it after a call from the candidate. (During their breakfast Tom had mentioned his trip to Raleigh and had been surprised when Gore asked him where he was staying.) *He certainly has more style*, Tom thought that night when he had his first sip.

Two weeks later, back home, sitting in the hot tub with Valerie and discussing the presidential race, Tom reached his decision. He had just finished a book about politics that makes the point that what makes the difference in national leadership was often "intangibles"—a hard-to-define element of a leader's character, a *style*, that separated and distinguished him from others. Babbitt's campaign was filled with Tom's favorite activists, followed by Gephardt's. If anything, the Concord group he had joined briefly before becoming uncomfortable with their attitudes and who now supported Gore, was more of a negative than positive factor to consider. But there was something about Gore, the person, that he liked. Maybe it was his youth, or the way he stuck to his guns on the MX vote, or even the flourish of remembering Tom's hotel and sending the bottle of Jack Daniel's. They were "intangibles," but they were the reason he now supported Gore.

Bruce Anderson was disappointed by Al Gore. Hosting a reception for the senator the evening of Gore's campaign day in Cheshire County, Bruce had been hoping that perhaps this last candidate for him to meet would make it easier for him to decide whom to support. The Houston debate had reshuffled things in his mind. Nearly every impression he had formed of the candidates through his personal contacts with them had been contradicted by what he saw on his TV screen.

Babbitt, whom he still regarded as "such a solid, solid individual," had not seemed on television like the same person Bruce had seen standing his living room, hiking Mount Washington, or riding in the backseat of Babbitt One. Dukakis, who was "strong and crisp" in the debate, had, as a result, switched places with Babbitt in Bruce's ranking—third to first, first to third. Gephardt, who in person seemed so down to earth, sort of a friendly midwesterner, had come across in the debate as "too smooth, almost contrived, and totally packaged." Biden seemed to talk without really saying anything and, especially compared to the magnetism Bruce had sensed in his announcement speech, his talk at Pat Russell's, and the videos his campaign had provided, was overly reserved in the debate. The listless Paul Simon he had met at Simon's campaign kickoff in Manchester was still hard to imagine as president but in the debate had exuded a "refreshing sense of integrity and honesty." Only Jackson, the one candidate he had never seen in person, had been the same in the debate as Bruce had expected.

Gore—at ease, articulate, and forceful in his debate performance despite his young age and recent candidacy; second only to Dukakis that evening—had impressed Bruce, and he had passed along this opinion to the senator's staff. He believed the Democratic race might well come down to a contest between Dukakis and Gore. But after the reception at his house, Bruce's initial regard was lessened. "We in New Hampshire take the primary seriously," he said, introducing Gore to the sixty people crowded into the living room (mosquitoes had forced the event indoors). "We look at these characters belly button to belly button on behalf of the 250 million Americans before the 'media wars' begin." Gore handled the questions of the evening well, Bruce thought, but there was something disconcerting about him. "He seemed more cool and aloof than I expected," Bruce said later, trying to put his finger on it. "He has a strength of conviction that sometimes turns people on, but sometimes it's those convictions that turn people off."

All the various Democratic campaigns were still avidly pursuing Bruce. Calls from staff members, invitations to receptions, letters, and position papers kept pouring in. The Babbitt campaign in particular was making a strong pitch for him to lead the Cheshire County effort. The longer the courtships went on, however, the harder it was for him to make a choice. It was becoming agonizing for everyone involved.

Shelley Nelkens went through the spring and summer and also emerged without a candidate to support. But, unlike Bruce Anderson, Shelley had come to a firm decision: she didn't like *any* of the Democrats. Most of her encounters with the candidates mirrored the breakfast with Bruce Babbitt at Dan Burnham's in the winter— she held them up to her uncompromising standards on her pet issue, and on the more intangible standard of leadership, and found each one wanting.

None of the would-be presidents was as fiercely opposed to nuclear power as Shelley. Watching the Houston debate (she taped it so she could go over it in detail), she fumed when the topic of energy was raised and no one turned the discussion toward exposing the dangers of nuclear power and nuclear waste. Her reaction to the debate had little to do with the candidates' performances, although she thought Gephardt and Dukakis appeared "comfortable" and Babbitt had come off badly. "That lip licking isn't helping him," she said.

She pursued every opportunity to meet the candidates, as much to further her personal crusade against the Price-Anderson Act as to search for someone to support. Gephardt, a co-sponsor of the bill she favored, sent her a draft of a "Dear Colleague" letter he was sending to others in the House seeking more co-sponsors. After talks with Biden and Simon, she kept in contact with their staffs to keep up the pressure; she even called the campaign of Jack Kemp, a Republican, to argue for him to join the cause.

Part of Al Gore's visit to the Monadnock Region included a meeting with the group that had opposed the proposal for a federal nuclear waste repository in the area, and Shelley was prominent among the forty people there to question him. "There are two things I'd like to see you do to prove to us that you're as concerned as you say," she told the senator, and asked him to call for reopening the investigation into the Three Mile Island accident and to lead the fight in the Senate for her Price-Anderson bill. As Gore responded, she interrupted constantly to correct him on some specifics, creating a slight aura of tension in the event until Gore joked: "I'm disappointed that you all haven't looked into this in any detail." Shelley was the only one who didn't laugh. "Would you be willing to learn all the details that *I* know so you can lead the debate on this?" she interjected.

Near the end of the meeting, which, as Gore had been fore-warned, concentrated exclusively on environmental and nuclear topics, one person complained to him, "You know, if you want to be president, you need to talk about some other issues, too." As he began, relievedly, to make a short stump speech, Shelley piped in again: "I want to hear more about low-level radioactive waste."

Nonetheless Shelley was somewhat impressed by Gore, particularly after following him to Bruce Anderson's reception, where he had faced a set of withering questions on his position against federal funding for abortions. Even though she also disagreed with his position, the way he stood up for his beliefs at least briefly prompted her to think she had at last found a candidate with a stronger personality than her own (the test that Babbitt had failed at Dan Burnham's). "I still think he needs a lot of educating," she said afterward, "but he's willing to be educated."

At a reception for Joe Biden the next week, she posed the same two challenges to Biden that she had to Gore, adding a third: stopping the expansion of nuclear power in Third World countries, including food irradiation plants. "I've forgotten more about these issues than some of my opponents have learned," Biden replied. "I'm with you." She later cornered him near the kitchen refrigerator to press harder for his support of the Price-Anderson bill. Afterward, bothered by his flip answer, she checked more deeply into Biden's record on nuclear power, decided he had misrepresented it, and ruled him out of consideration.

At a conference of environmentalists across the state in Portsmouth, she gave Gore a book about nuclear waste and reminded him that she expected him to follow up on his promises. She met Dukakis at an event near the Seabrook nuclear power plant (Dukakis opposed its opening) and asked him his position on closing nuclear plants that were already operating. His answer—"Only if they're unsafe"—infuriated her by its implication that some might not be unsafe; Dukakis was out.

After a lengthy *Boston Globe* article appeared comparing the candidates' campaign positions on the environment to their records, she threw up her hands. None of them had the purity she sought. "I've come to the conclusion they're *all* hopeless," she said. "I'm not going to support any of them. Now I'm going to focus on educating the field—one of them, after all, will be the nominee."

Having chosen her candidate, Andi Johnson was happy. The Biden campaign opened a Keene office in late June, the only one in Cheshire County for another two months, and she immediately began spending her evenings and weekends there. She went to Manchester to watch the Houston debate with other Biden supporters. "Joe was more relaxed than I expected him to be," she said afterward. Her concerns about his temper and lack of substance had eased. Biden was preparing to lead the Senate fight against President Reagan's nomination of Robert Bork to the U.S. Supreme Court and therefore would be getting a lot of national press attention. The New Hampshire campaign was growing steadily. Andi felt things were going well. When she attended Bruce Anderson's reception for Al Gore, she didn't even ask a question.

The reception for Biden in late July gave her both a focus for organizational work and her first chance to meet her new candidate in person. She put up signs to direct people to the home where the reception was to take place, helped welcome and sign in the guests, and stood in the background, chatting with the national staff, while Biden talked. As he left there was time only for a brief handshake and introduction to the senator. Biden was running behind schedule and in a rush. Besides, Andi was in a bit of a hurry, too. She was busy collecting the sign-up sheets and wanted to get back to the headquarters to add the names to the cards in her file box. It was, in effect, the dowry for her new political marriage.

7

DOG DAYS

Al and Mary Rubega arrived early for the Cheshire County Republican picnic in late June. More than any of the other leaders of local campaigns, Al viewed the picnic, held in the backyard of the county chairman, as an important test of organizational strength, a way to prove that Jack Kemp's supporters were avid and innovative—and unwilling to take a backseat to any other campaign for president. For Al the picnic was like friendly combat, a kind of war game to prepare his troops for the real contest next February by honing their team spirit and measuring them against the competition.

At a Kemp meeting in the Rubega home a month earlier, plans for the picnic had been the first item on the agenda. "What we want there are a lot of Jack Kemp buttons and a lot of Jack Kemp hats, a table to sway the uncommitted people there, to show a Jack Kemp presence," Al told the eight people who attended. He handed out tickets (he was a member of the county committee) for them to sell to boost turnout. Mary added a sense of urgency to the ticket sales. Most of the county committee consisted of Bush supporters, she said, so most of the tickets were in their hands. "That's why we called this meeting, so Kemp will make a good showing, too," she told them. "It's critical to get the word out."

Prior to the picnic, Al and Mary had spent their nights silkscreening the Kemp campaign logo on the crowns of a batch of baseball caps they had purchased with their own money. Each was wearing a cap when they showed up for the event, and they handed one out to each Kemp supporter who arrived. Near midnight earlier in the week, after a Gun Owners of New Hampshire meeting in Concord, they had rousted the Kemp state director from his home to open the state headquarters so they could fill their car trunk with pamphlets, speeches, and buttons; these were now covering a table at the picnic.

But their prize possession—their coup de grace for establishing the Kemp presence—was a pair of huge canvas banners, each one about six feet by nine feet, with "JACK KEMP for President" emblazoned in giant blue letters next to a stylized American flag's red stripes. Al and Mary had traced the Kemp logo onto a transparency, then used an overhead projector to shine it onto the canvas sheets and retraced its oversize outline. Al had filled in the outline, with blue and red paint, by hand.

Al strapped the banners to the sides of the picnic tent and stepped back to admire their effect. No one else had anything remotely comparable.

As the picnic progressed, Al was even more pleased with his campaign's effort. Of the sixty people attending, there were no representatives of the Robertson or du Pont campaigns. The Dole campaign was barely evident: just two women, whom hardly anyone knew, with a few brochures and buttons. A man and wife from Manchester—*They're not even from Cheshire County*, Al thought, almost scornfully—arrived wearing blue golf shirts that bore Al Haig's logo. (The man said that when he stopped at a gas station to get directions to the picnic site, the pump jockey noticed the shirt and said, "You seem to be pretty much behind him. What's he running for?") A majority of the people, including Kendall and Jane Lane, were wearing Bush buttons, but not that many more than those who had Kemp buttons on their shirts and blouses. And, Al noticed with pride, his was the only group that had hats, not to mention the two banners that dominated the picnic tent. Chuck

Douglas, a former state supreme court justice and chairman of Kemp's New Hampshire campaign, had even driven over from Concord to mingle with the crowd and, by his presence, show that the Kemp campaign took Cheshire County seriously.

Kendall Lane took special note of the Kemp effort. As competitive in nature as Al (Kendall had given up tickets to a Red Sox game in order to attend the picnic), he had his own little victories to savor. The Bush campaign could clearly claim the largest number of people at the picnic, the result of the work he and Jane had undertaken among the party leadership in the county. Even the county chairman, host of the event and prohibited by Republican party rules from active support of any primary candidate, had quietly assured Kendall that he wanted Bush to win and would help as much as he could, within the party's restrictions. Ken Lysitt, the popular county sheriff, had just committed himself to the campaign. Kendall took personal satisfaction in pinning a Bush button on Lysitt's lapel when the sheriff arrived.

The Kemp hats and banners were visible proof to him that, in Cheshire County, at least, the only two campaigns with any real organizations were Bush's and Kemp's—a conclusion Al was making on the same evidence. A month earlier at a Bush meeting at the Lane's house, as they went through the names of party activists in the Keene area and discussed which ones might be enlisted for Bush, Kendall had remarked that he thought Al Rubega liked Kemp but (based on Al's absence from the published Kemp list) might be "twistable." Now he realized his mistake. Al was the main spark plug for what Kendall now considered the Bush campaign's principal rival in the area, and as such, he was Kendall's principal rival.

Chuck Douglas's arrival put Kendall on edge. It was as if the presence of Kemp's state chairman dramatically upped the ante of the picnic. Some staff members from the Bush headquarters in Concord were there, but no one with a public standing comparable to Douglas's. Governor Sununu's top political aide had agreed to attend but wasn't there yet. As Kendall watched Douglas make the rounds of the picnickers, he got more nervous, muttering several times to the Bush staffers that the Sununu aide "better get here soon." In the meantime he tried to carry the Bush campaign presence on his own shoulders. A state senator from the region, wearing a Kemp hat, mentioned loudly to him that a recent poll "looked pretty bad" for Bush. "I can't remember," Kendall replied sarcastically, even though he knew the numbers by heart, "was Kemp in double digits yet?" He breathed a sigh of relief when Sununu's aide finally showed up.

Virtually all of the people at the event were already committed to a campaign. At the tables displaying buttons, brochures, and other information, only two names were written onto the sign-up sheets available for people who wanted to be put on mailing lists for more material—and they were the same two names on each sheet. Most of the literature was left untaken. Haig buttons disappeared quickly. People pocketed them, not to wear or because they preferred the former general, but because everyone figured the buttons would be collector's items someday. Very little of the discussion at the tables, where people sat eating hot dogs and drinking beer or soda, focused on politics. It was a warm summer day, and even for these party activists the primary seemed remote and totally secondary to their social pleasures. The representatives from the Bush and Kemp state headquarters seemed the only ones with the campaign primarily on their minds. Douglas spread the rumor that he had heard a major publication was about to publish a "Gary Hart–type story" about Bush; the Bush people said they had heard that damaging rumors about Kemp were about to be made public.

When Kendall and Al gathered with a few others near the beer keg as the picnic was breaking up, the two avoided any direct comparisons of their campaigns' performance. Instead they exchanged their amazement that the Robertson and du Pont campaigns hadn't even shown up. Most of all, neither could figure out why there didn't seem to be any Dole campaign to speak of in Cheshire County. Dole was doing well in the national polls, even leading Bush in Iowa, but at least in terms of grass-roots organization in New Hampshire he was nowhere to be found at this point.

For Al and Kendall, both of whom had already devoted enormous amounts of time and energy to their local organizations, such an obvious gap was inexplicable. Was it a deliberate strategy of the Dole campaign or an abject failure to build grass-roots support? Either way the stark comparison with the Bush and Kemp local efforts pleased Al and Kendall immensely, implicitly making them compatriots in their derisive dismissal of Dole's feeble showing.

Al, always eager to talk about the right to bear arms, mentioned that, in appearing at a court in another county, his Swiss army knife had been confiscated at the court door—another example, he thought, of a misguided trend in America diluting the Second Amendment. "People forget that this country was established because those wearing uniforms were trying to confiscate guns from those who didn't wear uniforms," he said.

Kendall kept the discussion on Al's favorite topic, relating an anecdote from Bush's visit to Keene. Chatting with a Secret Service agent, Kendall had asked, "Is your gun loaded?"

"Does your car have gas in its tank?" Al repeated the punch line at the same time as Kendall, and they both laughed like old friends.

Al Rubega was as different from Kendall Lane as his homemade banner was from Kendall's heirloom flag. Kendall represented more than a century of Lanes in Keene (and Jane was from a longtime Cheshire County family as well); Al and Mary had moved to New Hampshire in the early 1980s and to Cheshire County as recently as 1985. Growing up as he did in a family intertwined in the social and political leadership of his community, Kendall's political philosophy was more pragmatic than ideological, tinged with tradition and exercised almost indistinguishably from the normal, but extensive contacts he had established over a lifetime and which he renewed in the course of everyday work and friendship. Al's political involvement was initiated and driven by his conservative ideology, something he'd developed in college independently from his family, for whom politics was not of much interest. Most of the people he knew in the area he had met *because* of his activism, whether in the gun owners' group, the right-to-life movement, or Republican party events. Both men were lawyers, but Kendall, a graduate of Boston University law school, was a partner with his brother in the successful, well-established firm they had taken over from their father. Al, with a degree from the New England School of Law, had moved through several legal jobs before coming to the Keene area as assistant county prosecutor. The Lanes vacationed more than once a year in places like Florida and Hawaii; the Rubegas used their time off to attend NRA conventions, visit relatives in southern New England, participate in mock Revolutionary War celebrations; and, this summer, to man a Kemp table at the county fair.

The Lane family homestead, an imposing nineteenth-century structure at the south end of Main Street, had been sold and converted to an insurance and real estate office after the death of Kendall's father. But Kendall and Jane lived in a home nearly as old and spacious—a rambling house that they had painstakingly renovated on Keene's west side, the section of the city that included most of the local executives and professionals. They entertained frequently, and an attached barn had been modernized specifically to accommodate large gatherings. The large double lot had space for Jane's neatly kept garden, a back patio, and the private swimming pool they were planning to add in a year. The country club was a short distance away. Their house pet was a pedigreed dog.

Al and Mary's house had been built in the 1970s deep in the woods of Sullivan, a small town northeast of Keene. "Keep Out" and "Beware of Dog" signs were posted where the dirt driveway emerged from the pines to join a winding blacktop road. The house itself, guarded by two large dogs on long chains attached to a doghouse, sat in a small, sidehill clearing, invisible from the road. One part of the yard was filled with tree-length logs, waiting to be cut into firewood; a target range, with a human profile outlined in black on a large sheet, was in another corner. Inside, on the walls of the living room, were old muskets, sabers, antique pistols, a tomahawk, a bugle and drum, and two replicas of the black, fuzzy hats worn

by the Royal Grenadiers—props Al used in his mock battles. Lith-
ographs of war batttles and heroic prints depicting a town meeting
and freedom of religion decorated some of the other walls. Al's major
upcoming house project was a deck from the second story, which
he was building himself.

Both men were tall—six feet or over—and energetic, articulate,
and friendly, with a healthy sense of humor they often employed
in self-deprecation. Kendall favored good suits or tweed jackets and
wool slacks, and his hair, though not long or shaggy, was full and
modern-styled; he sported a trim mustache. Al's build was more
angular, like a teenager going through a growth spurt, and some
of his suits fit him oddly; his thick-soled black shoes made him
even taller. With his close-cropped black hair, he appeared, as an
acquaintance at the courthouse once described him, somewhat like
a paramilitary Ichabod Crane. Kendall was capable of occasional
cynicism; Al came across more as a Boy Scout leader.

Al was born in 1955 in Connecticut, the oldest of eight children.
His father, an electrical engineer, was a civilian employee of the
navy, working on sonar. He and Mary met at Southern Connecticut
State College, where Al was majoring in physical education and
Mary was training to become a physical science teacher. His three
years of law school in Boston formed his political leanings, as well
as his belief that politics—the making of laws by elected leaders—
was the most critical endeavor of democracy. Already a member of
the National Rifle Association and a disciple of its unyielding inter-
pretation of the Constitution and conservative political bent, he
found himself increasingly at odds with what he perceived as the
"strong liberal bias" of his fellow students and the faculty. In his
constitutional law class, his professor "said things that were quite
obviously wrong about gun ownership" and wouldn't listen to Al's
opposing view. Notices of "left wing" causes, like those opposing
U.S. involvement in Nicaragua, remained unmolested on the school
bulletin boards; fliers from the Young Americans for Freedom were
routinely torn down. Al sensed an intellectual dishonesty in it all
and resented it deeply. When American hostages were taken in

Iran and nothing effective seemed to be done to free them, it represented to him what was wrong with the country. Al looked at a magazine cover showing Iranians burning an American flag and, as a personal statement, made red and blue signs for both sides of his briefcase. In blue was "GOD BLESS AMERICA" and in red was "TO HELL WITH IRAN." His classmates ridiculed him for it. Near graduation, a fellow student noticed the signs still on the briefcase. "Al, the hostages are released," the student said.

"Yeah, but the sentiment's still there," Al replied.

"All the rules we live by and the direction we take as society depend on what happens in politics," Al decided. "That's the bottom line. Therefore, I said to myself, if I don't like what's going on, the way to do something about it is to get into politics. You can *do* something about it in politics." When the 1980 presidential campaign started, Al became politically active for the first time in his life. He studied the Republican field, particularly the candidates' positions on gun issues, and found Ronald Reagan and Congressman Phil Crane the most consistently conservative. Consistency and conservatism were the two attributes Al admired the most. Crane, much younger than Reagan, seemed the "most salable politically," so he and Mary, now married, went to Crane's Boston headquarters and volunteered. They stuffed envelopes and made phone calls two or three nights a week. Al took advantage of his height and posted Crane posters on the school bulletin board high enough to prevent them from being torn down. After Reagan won the New Hampshire primary, they switched their allegiance and voted for him in the Massachusetts primary a few weeks later, even though Crane was still on the ballot. Reagan was now the conservative alternative to Bush (who won in Massachusetts) and needed their votes more than Crane.

The Rubegas decided on New Hampshire during his first year at law school. Southern New England, where they both were raised, was "too crowded, too flat, too defoliated, and too left wing politically." Maine was too remote. Vermont was prettier, but New Hampshire had more variety, a healthier economy, and a political

climate more compatible with Al's conservatism. Finding summer
jobs wasn't easy. "My grades were okay," he recalled, "but I wasn't
at a big, rootsy-tootsy law school." He contacted fifty firms before
landing a job, ironically with a firm full of Ted Kennedy Democrats.
(Al had a Crane bumper sticker on his car and backed it up against
the trees in the parking lot each day so the partners wouldn't see
it, and "I had to hold my tongue when they'd talk about Kennedy.")
After graduation, despite contacting more than a hundred firms in
the state, Al couldn't find work in the law. Mary took a teaching
position; Al poured concrete for a contractor and was a substitute
teacher. Their finances were so tight that he even let his membership in the NRA lapse momentarily for lack of the fifteen-dollar
annual fee. A year later he became an assistant county attorney in
eastern New Hampshire, a position he later held in a central county
of the state before moving to Cheshire County. His reputation in
Cheshire County was one of a gung ho prosecutor, fiercely loyal,
perhaps even deferential, to the law enforcement community, a
hard worker who saw his role as a mission, not just a job.

In the meantime Al quickly rose in the ranks of GO:NH. His
boundless energy, his willingness to do even the most tedious organizational tasks, and his single-minded devotion to the cause of
"honest, law-abiding owners of firearms" (a phrase he spoke like
one word) were quickly recognized by the group's leaders. In spite
of being relative newcomers to the state, he and Mary were elected
to the board of directors. By 1987 Al was president of the organization. His penchant for writing letters to publicize his views on
gun policies had landed him on the NRA's national legislative policy
committee. As easygoing and friendly as he was in person, Al could
become cuttingly sarcastic and strident with a pen in his hand. Any
editorial in *The Keene Sentinel* questioning the political power of
the NRA or suggesting even the slightest measures toward gun
registration or restrictions on certain ammunition and guns was
sure to be followed in a few days by a biting reply from Al Rubega
in the letters-to-the-editor column. "Why does the *Sentinel* have
such a horrible bigotry against honest, law-abiding NRA mem-

bers?" he asked in one such letter. "Ask a 120-pound female victim of a rape by a 210-pound male, who *she* thinks is more 'dangerous'— the NRA, which defends her right to choose to own a handgun (so as to discourage another such experience) or media people who seem to think themselves morally superior to her because they choose not to own one (perhaps because they have never experienced the need for one, 'up close and personal'). No contest, folks, and that's why the NRA has three million members, and is signing up more all the time." (Al had launched his letter-writing career in law school, placing pieces defending the NRA positions in the school paper after the murder of John Lennon and the attempted assassination of Ronald Reagan had prompted renewed calls for gun control. Reagan, he wrote while the president was still hospitalized, would surely not want the assassination attempt—and the wounding of his press secretary—to be turned against the rights of gun owners.)

His relatively new devotion to political action also found fertile ground in his adopted state. There was no shortage of candidates for state and local offices who shared Al's beliefs, and, being a small state now half-full of nonnatives, New Hampshire also provided the chance for someone interested in helping campaigns to play a relatively larger role more quickly than might be possible in bigger states with more entrenched party structures. (The state's governor, two senators, and one of the two congressmen, for instance, were all transplants from other states.) Every two years Al could be counted on to hold placards or make phone calls for conservative candidates. Coupled with his growing prominence in GO:NH, this brought him to the attention of the Republican party's leadership. By the time the 1988 presidential primary campaign was first stirring, Al was a member of the Cheshire County Republican committee and on a first-name basis with many of the state's top political figures, including the governor. Though not by conscious design— his political and issue activism was motivated by his ideological fervor, not by a desire to move in the higher circles of the state's leadership—Al was now what political insiders would call a "player" and was a logical prospect to take on a larger campaign role than ever before.

Kemp had spoken to the gun group's annual banquet in 1985, where Al had been impressed by the young congressman's charisma and true conservatism. When Kemp called personally in 1986 and sought Al's help on his presidential campaign, Al had been flattered and surprised by the attention. His response had been firm and immediate. Paul Young, the state campaign director, made the follow-up contact.

"You were described to me as the resident gun . . . person," Young said.

Al had caught the pause. "Oh," he said. "I suspect what I was really described to you was as the 'resident gun *nut*.' "

"You noticed that hesitation, huh?" Young laughed. "I was being diplomatic."

"It's not gun nut," Al corrected amiably. "It's firearms enthusiast." They liked each other and worked well together from that point on.

As president of GO:NH in 1987, Al arranged for Kemp to return as the keynote speaker in May and glowingly introduced the candidate. "In 1970, when a young visionary named Jack Kemp was first elected to the United States Congress," Al told the crowd, "antigun sentiment ran awful high, and there were a lot of unfair consequences for anyone who presumed to stand up for the law-abiding gun owner. But because of men like him, this country has been turned around on our issue and many other issues." Kemp had given a strong progun speech and pointed out that in 1968 Congressman Bush had supported a gun control bill. Al, who had opened the banquet by introducing Kemp to Nackey Loeb, publisher of the arch-conservative *Manchester Union-Leader*, book-ended the event with a second personal pleasure: giving Kemp a .50-caliber Hawken rifle.

Al was buoyed by the county picnic. The other campaigns, even Bush's, seemed either nonexistent or lackadaisical compared with his own cadre of committed Kemp supporters. The only fly in the ointment was that none of the area media had been there; the only people aware of the strong Kemp presence were the activists who showed up. Chuck Douglas, the congressman's state chairman, however, had been impressed and said so to Al, asking him to assume the role of regional coordinator for western New Hampshire and to attend a statewide meeting to tell the other counties what he was doing in Cheshire County. "You send us the ammunition— the buttons and bumper stickers—and we'll take care of the rest," Al replied.

When the Keene downtown merchants held their annual street fair in mid-July, Al pulled off what he considered another coup. He had secured a permit for a Kemp table on Main Street—a tactical move he'd conceived before the county picnic and sworn his troops to secrecy about, for fear other campaigns would counter if they heard about his plan. For two days, as thousands of people strolled up Main Street, browsing for bargains, one of the displays they encountered featured three tables of Kemp campaign literature and paraphernalia in front of Al's huge homemade banner. It was the only campaign display—Republican or Democrat—to be seen. Once again, the effort received no press attention. Al decided to complain to the *Sentinel* and called one of the political reporters. "We dominated the county picnic, even the Bush people said so," he told her, and at the street fair "we blew everyone else away." The only coverage that seemed to get in the paper, he said, was when a candidate was in the area, but "if you can get people involved when the candidate *isn't* around, that's when you've got a strong campaign."

Kendall Lane, of course, noticed the Kemp booth at the street fair and blamed himself for not having any Bush effort, although, he said, "I'm not sure how effective it is except maybe to get some attention." The summer campaign was proceeding on two tracks for Kendall. Will Abbott, the state director, was relentlessly pushing his people to get town chairmen named and to then have the local chairmen pore over computerized voting lists to add the correct

telephone numbers and addresses. Neither was a particularly pleasant task. Kendall preferred the indirect approach—engaging a prospect in social banter before sliding into the subject of committing
them to Bush and the list work. Jane, now the Bush county chairman, got right to the point with the people on her list. Because
Bush was the front-runner, and because he had the support of both
the governor and the area's congressman, finding local leaders was
simultaneously easier and yet more delicate a task than for other
candidates. People were more willing to support an incumbent vice
president and, by most accounts, the most probable nominee than,
say, a relatively unknown congressman. But, especially with two
strong state political organizations involved, the Bush campaign
had to be careful that in naming one person town chairman it didn't
alienate several others who might feel slighted if they didn't have
a title. Virtually every name had to be checked and double-checked
with the state headquarters before a person could even be offered
a chairmanship. The Lanes kept a list on the kitchen wall, near
the phone, for the constant conference calls involved. It was painstaking, slow-moving work. The phone bill skyrocketed. By mid-
summer most of the towns had chairmen, but Kendall and Jane
still found themselves sitting in the sun in the backyard on weekends, with a phone book and pile of computer paper on their laps,
filling in the gaps.

The other campaign track was more fun. "Sometimes," Kendall
said at the time, "the social part of the campaign is busier than the
work." Invitations to campaign-related cookouts, cocktail parties,
and golf games crowded their schedule. At a cocktail party/fund-
raiser in Nashua, Kendall was as excited about talking with Ted
Williams as with the vice president. ("How do you feel about the
events in D.C.?" Kendall asked Bush. The Iran-contra hearings
were in progress, and former National Security Adviser John Poin-
dexter had testified that neither President Reagan nor Bush had
known of the diversion of arms profits to Nicaragua. "I'm in seventh
heaven," Bush replied. "It's been a glorious day all around.") Kendall spent a summer Sunday at a Red Sox game with some Bush

staffers from the state headquarters. At yet another campaign picnic, near Concord, Jane and Kendall were chosen from among the three hundred supporters to sit at the vice president's lunch table. The campaign had staged a contest to see who signed up the most people for a list of Bush supporters that was to be made public in the fall. The Lanes, with eighteen people signed up, had come in second in the state; the winner, also awarded a seat at the table, had put sixty-eight names on the list in the Hanover area. Surrounded by Secret Service and photographers, they ate their lunch and chatted amiably. Bush was upbeat and not as tired as Kendall had expected. With the memory of the Keene visit and its logistical complications very much in mind, Kendall broached the topic of the need for a candidate in the New Hampshire primary to be out among the people. Security precautions made it difficult, the vice president admitted. "It's not like 1980," he said, "when I could come up, stay at someone's house, and circulate at cocktail parties."

The Merrimack County Republican party held its own picnic in early August. The likelihood of a straw poll being conducted spurred the campaigns to bolster the turnout from all parts of the state. Al and Mary Rubega drove over from Cheshire County (bringing their banners), as did the Lanes. Bush won the straw poll (94 votes) over Kemp (78), with Dole a distant third (33), barely ahead of Al Haig (31); Robertson (13) and du Pont (7) were hardly represented. Both Al and Kendall were encouraged by the results, which further confirmed their beliefs that New Hampshire was a Bush-Kemp contest. "Without the governor's staff [to vote for Bush], Jack would have won by ten," Al kidded Kendall when the totals were announced. A statewide list of Dole supporters, released the same weekend, only heightened Kendall's euphoria when he obtained a copy and read through it. *Very thin*, he thought, looking at the few names from the Keene area.

Summer was far from smooth sailing, however. Virtually all the campaigns, in both parties, discovered that few people were particularly interested in politics—not just the voting public, for whom the upcoming primary was the farthest thing from their minds, but even most of the political regulars responded indifferently to the proddings of the organizational zealots. Meetings were poorly attended, and few people wanted to commit themselves so early to any candidate. Following Babbitt's trip to Cheshire County in July, more than one hundred invitations to an organizational meeting were mailed. Other than the host and two staff members, only one person showed up, and she was an hour late. Other campaigns were only slightly more successful in attracting volunteers.

Riding high from the county picnic and street fair, Al Rubega attended a statewide Kemp meeting. He and Mary represented a third of the turnout. The "Cotton system" of list development was not proceeding well, they were told. (Even Al, one of the few who had filled in the required ten names on his sheets, found it hard to approach people for a commitment.) New orders were given. The headquarters had a backlog of Kemp tabloids and wanted them distributed before Labor Day. When Al passed out the stacks of papers at his next local meeting—where fewer people were present than at the first gathering in the spring—it "didn't go over with a lot of enthusiasm," he reported back. Having sold phone directories in college ("God, it was hard," he remembered), Al understood his troops' feelings. He and Dr. David Ridge were the only ones to actually attempt hand-to-hand distribution, standing for an hour and a half outside Keene grocery stores. The rest of the supply ended up being stacked in public places and forgotten.

As inveterate a reader as he was a writer of letters to the editor, Al began watching *The Keene Sentinel* columns for letters from others who expressed views he thought might imply a political bent favorable toward his candidate. He would then write these prospects personal letters, inviting them to join the Kemp campaign. No one replied.

After devoting his summer vacation time to manning a Kemp table at the annual Cheshire Fair, Al had his own summer duties to attend to, other than the campaign's. A couple of weekends were spent building the new deck on his house—a welcome excuse to avoid the pile of tabloids. The town of Sullivan celebrated its bicentennial, and Al, a member of the celebration committee, was in charge of staging a reenactment of a Revolutionary War battle. During the nation's bicentennial he had joined a mock regiment of British grenadiers who dressed in the high fur caps and uniforms of the eighteenth-century English army and marched in the constant parades and battle reenactments taking place all over New England. Now, besides organizing Sullivan's battle and encampment of military and history buffs, he was the commander of the irregular troops. Dressed in homespun and carrying old muzzleloaders, he and his troop of patriots marched over a hillside rise and "won" a fight for liberty. He and Mary camped with the group in historically authentic tents, roasted a pig on a spit over a large campfire, participated in a hatchet-throwing contest, and relaxed in the ambience of conversation about flintlocks and gunpowder. When the weekend encampment ended, he reluctantly turned down the requests to meet at the next reenactments. He needed to get back to "Kemping."

The campaign staged an evening of statewide "Making of a President" home parties, where a Kemp video was shown at each local gathering. The state headquarters called in the afternoon. A *USA Today* reporter and photographer were in New Hampshire to cover the event, and they were being directed to Al, who the campaign figured could be counted on to host a successful party. He had to scramble on the telephone to assure a turnout of ten people. They posed for a picture around Al's television set, ate some sandwiches, watched the video politely, and dispersed. Al kept the reporter around after the crowd left and taught him how to shoot skeet off the front deck.

The *USA Today* story two days later carried a Sullivan, New Hampshire, dateline and mentioned the Rubega home (but no picture)—a bit of national publicity that only made Al more unhappy about the lack of local coverage he felt his organizational efforts had been unfairly given. He wrote a press release outlining the Kemp campaign activities of the summer, gave it to the *Sentinel*, and waited in vain for a story to appear.

Kendall Lane was having his own campaign headaches, despite his soaring confidence that Bush was headed for certain victory. The night of the Kemp video party, Kendall hosted a meeting of the Bush town chairmen in the county. Will Abbott was there and outlined the organizational plan for the rest of the year: lists and more lists. By Labor Day all the town checklists were to be handed in, with the telephone numbers added; new registrations and changes were to be added (something that would require going to each town clerk's office). By mid-September, a month before Bush would officially announce his candidacy, the campaign wanted a firm list, ready for release to the media, of five thousand New Hampshire Republicans who publicly supported the vice president. Cheshire County's quota was five hundred names for this steering committee—a number that made Kendall wince, it seemed so high. Abbott wanted each county to devise its own primary day plan by the first of November—how many people would stand at the polls with placards, who would provide phone banks to reach supporters and urge them to vote, whether to have rides to the polls, and so on. By mid-January all the Republican voters in the state were to have been called and polled to see if they liked Bush. Next the supporters, leaners, and undecideds would be called again before the vote in February; then came the final get-out-the-vote calls. Listening to Abbott's recitation and watching the faces of his chairmen, Kendall had a sobering thought: *Jane and I are going to end up doing a lot of this.* Sure enough, as August progressed, only eleven of the twenty-two towns' checklists had been turned in with the voters' phone numbers. Jane and Kendall retrieved some of the unfinished lists, got out their phone book, and went to work.

At a weekly "Freedom Fighters" meeting in August, news was relayed from the Washington headquarters that the endorsement list was way behind schedule; most of the counties had only reached 25 percent of their quotas. The Lanes had 150 signed up from

Cheshire County, but with a month to go, 500 seemed out of the question. "We'll come fairly close to our target, but not in their time frame," Kendall complained afterward. "It's an overly ambitious project for the summer—with vacations and apathy. I'm having trouble getting excited about it myself. We don't really need it until October, so why the rush?" The aggravation was heightened by the news that the headquarters' computer had "lost" a significant number of steering committee names—thirty-eight names on two entire sheets from Cheshire County alone; sixty-eight from another. Distrustful of the large campaign bureaucracy, Kendall had fortunately kept a copy of his lists, but the other county didn't have a backup list and had to start from scratch.

Kendall didn't object to the elaborate organizational plans and the heavy emphasis on list management—in fact, they coincided with his own views on the importance of identifying and pulling out your vote in any election and with his personal style of leaving nothing to chance—but he felt the national staff was unrealistic in its demanding schedule. They didn't understand how much labor was involved and how hard it was to motivate volunteers this soon before the primary.

"There's a constant tug-of-war between the local people and the national people," he said. "We're very capable. We've been through the New Hampshire primaries before. We know how to run them. But they think they're the only ones who know how to do it."

The same applied to scheduling Bush's events, he believed. The national staff always thought it knew best, and local ideas were discounted. Kendall's defeats in arranging "spontaneous" and public appearances during the vice president's one trip to Keene still stung. At another "Freedom Fighters" meeting, the group decided to make a video of the core supporters to send to Bush—a direct message from New Hampshire. The mood was upbeat: the Iran-contra hearings had left Bush unscathed; Dole, the principal challenger, still had no visible organization in the state; Bush was building a list of volunteers in every county. Kendall seized the opportunity, nonetheless, to repeat his well-worn refrain, as pleasantly as possible, that the vice president still needed to hold more appearances with the general public, not just the organizational or tightly controlled media events. "I'm catching on," he said later. "There are ways to short-circuit the bureaucracy." With the video, "at least I didn't have to go through ten layers of staff to get my message through."

Summer for Doug Kidd on the Robertson campaign had the same starts and stops as it did for Kendall and Al—only Doug's extremes were more pronounced. The summer sluggishness that struck all of the campaigns like a political cold from June to August seemed to grip Doug's organizational efforts and keep them bedridden. While Al and Kendall were alternating between aggravation and optimism, Doug went through the depths of two crises—one more spiritual than political, the other organizational—and rose to epiphanies.

Like the other core campaign activists, Doug discovered that the volunteers he had been grooming through the spring were reluctant to set aside their normal summer activities for a presidential campaign. The result was devoting more of his own time at an even greater expense to his personal plans. His house in Stoddard probably would have remained unpainted, had his wife, Allison, not shouldered the bulk of the work to get it done. Responsible for all of western New Hampshire, Doug was busy trying to set up home video parties (much like the ones organized by the Kemp campaign), phone banks,, and petition drives. But it seemed that for every ten parties he would arrange, when he checked on their results a week later, eight or nine had been canceled for reasons varying from sickness in the family to low response to "we decided to wait until fall." His volunteers, unaccustomed to and still uncomfortable with political work, found it difficult to call total strangers from a phone bank and ask them to support a candidate. Many didn't return after their first experience. "It's like moving through molasses," Doug said of his organizational progress in July.

The setbacks only fed into the self-doubts already nagging Doug for his decision to join the campaign. Increasingly, he felt, the campaign staff was concentrating on presenting Pat Robertson as a businessman-political leader, almost to the total exclusion of what Doug referred to as the "spiritual man" he had once seen in the same person. Doug began each small meeting he called—even a gathering in a shopping center parking lot held in preparation for a door-to-door canvass—with a short prayer. But it seemed that others on the headquarters staff were consciously trying to downplay the religious roots of Robertson's quest for the White House. Even listening to Robertson at several events, Doug thought he heard fewer and fewer references to Pat's "calling." He felt confused and became uncharacteristically gloomy. "Is this a personality or characteristic of Pat I've never seen before and now I'm seeing it and don't like it?" he wondered. "Or is it just a part of the campaign that's painting him that way?"

Then, even though it took place in Manchester, outside of his own assigned territory, Doug attended Robertson's speech to the Full Gospel Businessmen's Fellowship in late July. It was as if the Lord had heard Doug's private questions and directed him to the place to hear the answers. Robertson delivered his "testimony"—recounting the times before he accepted Jesus and was born again and explaining what his religious conversion had meant to his life. To be sure, he included many of his business achievements and his political positions in his story, but they were woven into the greater fabric of his faith.

Robertson was a "whole man" again in Doug's eyes. Reassured and reinvigorated by witnessing what he referred to as "not a political event, [but] a spiritual event," Doug now saw things in a different light. Robertson was unchanged; it was the campaign— the political entity around him—that had been going in the wrong direction. "I don't believe that Jesus Christ would want to come into anything riding the coattails of something else—He's got to be first," Doug said afterward. "It's very obvious that Pat serves Christ. *Everyone* has to recognize that and move with that. It doesn't mean that he's going to try to convert America, it doesn't mean that he's

going to lead Bible studies from the Oval Office, and it doesn't mean
that he's only going to hire Christians. It doesn't mean all those
things that people constantly fear. But *that* has to be his banner.
He can't make it secondary. He can't hide it or apologize for it—
and I don't think he is. But I think there's part of the campaign
that would really like to downplay that because of the fear that it
doesn't sell."

Doug's attitude toward the campaign would never be the same.
Witnessing Robertson's testimony had reaffirmed his faltering faith
in the reasons he had joined his first political campaign: a desire to integrate his organizational and spiritual selves for a civic
cause, to be a "whole man" himself. He no longer questioned his
decision to enlist in the campaign. At the same time, however,
Doug's renewed confidence in his own instincts now allowed him
to question the campaign's (and, to a certain extent, even Robertson's) political and organizational decisions from this point onward.
As deeply immersed in the campaign as his life had become, his
sense of himself and his worth in this strange new environment
were no longer tied to the fortunes of the campaign or even to the
candidate to which he was committed. He was no less devoted to
his task. If anything, he was ready to proceed with even greater
energy. But compared with some of his activist counterparts on
other campaigns, he was now absorbed in his work without being
swallowed by it. His religious faith was total, but his political faith
was not blind.

His new perspective also affected Doug's organizational strategy.
In his view the campaign had concentrated on "going after the
people who drove the right car or lived in the right neighborhood—
if you approach them they are turned off, or they won't commit, or
they can't perform—instead of those whose hearts have been prepared by the Lord." From now on he would be "as sensitive as I
can to the Holy Spirit leading me to the right people."

He found a prepared heart in Helen Bouchie, an older working-
class woman in the small town of Hinsdale in southern Cheshire
County. She had attended Robertson's first public reception in

Keene in June, and Doug had kept in touch with her throughout the summer. Any task he asked of her, she accomplished and then exceeded. No excuses, no complaints—"a real hurricane," Doug called her. She organized Robertson events in her fundamentalist church, made phone calls, canvassed the town door to door, distributed petitions and fliers at flea markets. Her home video party not only took place, it attracted more people than her small house could hold, so she moved it to the town hall. (*The Keene Sentinel* even covered the event, a fact that Al Rubega noticed with both irritation and suspicion.) As Doug prepared for Robertson's return trip to the county in late August, he tacked on a small reception at Helen's as a personal and heartfelt reward for her efforts.

Near midnight three days before the visit, Kerry Moody, the young Christian political activist who had first recruited Doug and was the New Hampshire campaign's principal connection with Robertson's national headquarters, called with bad news. The trip was off. Robertson wasn't coming, and Doug should start contacting the people in his area to cancel the events on the schedule. Moody didn't offer any explanation for the change.

Doug was crushed. He had put together a full day of campaigning in Cheshire County: an interview with a local weekly newspaper whose owner seemed friendly to Robertson's candidacy, a visit to the *Sentinel*'s editorial board, a speech to the Keene Rotary, a home reception in Keene, a small rally in Winchester, and, finally, Helen Bouchie's reception. The volunteers he had organized to hold or work on the events would be particularly disappointed. Seeing the candidate in person was the principal payoff for all the other unheralded tasks they were asked to perform. From his business management background, Doug also had learned that "dissatisfied customers say more than satisfied customers." Canceling the trip at this late date, he believed, would be disastrous to his efforts in the area, possibly amounting to "writing off the county."

The next day he contacted the people involved, but rather than canceling the events as he had been directed to do, he told them instead that the day was "on hold." Pat might not be able to make

it. He'd get back to them with more details. Something inside him—
Doug called it the "inner voice" his faith had taught him to obey—
wouldn't allow him to cancel the trip until he had more answers.
He suspected that Robertson had made a decision without being
told its consequences. It just didn't make any sense otherwise; it
was so unlike Brother Pat. *I need to talk to him*, Doug decided. *I
need to hear it directly from him.* A little after ten P.M. Doug picked
up the phone, took a deep breath, and dialed Robertson's private
number.

The candidate was in a good mood. He had been told that day
that his goal of collecting three million signatures on petitions for
him to mount an official campaign was in sight, and he had started
making plans for his announcement tour in the fall. Doug's news
was a double blow. Robertson said this was the first he had heard
that a New Hampshire trip had even been considered for that day.
His schedule from the national headquarters called for him to be
in Virginia, conducting some press interviews. Obviously, Doug
said, there had been a breakdown in communications between the
New Hampshire office and the headquarters; he had been told a
month ago to set up a day's worth of events. Doug outlined the
schedule and tried to impress upon his candidate how much damage the cancellation could cause to the organization in southwestern New Hampshire. "Brother Pat," he said, "it's very, very
important for you to be here." Robertson, his euphoria gone, said
he'd think about it.

When he hung up the phone, Doug was both relieved and nervous. His suspicions had been confirmed. Robertson had not only
been uninvolved in the decision to blow off the Cheshire County
visit, he hadn't even been told about the foul-up. By going around
the campaign's chain of command to call Robertson directly, Doug
knew, there could be trouble within the staff. Someone had slipped
up, and now the candidate knew it.

By chance, Kerry Moody called a few minutes later to make sure
everything had been canceled.

"I think he might still come," Doug answered.

"No, he won't," Moody said.

"Well, I just talked to him about it."

There was dead silence at the other end.

Doug prayed that night, even more fervently than usual. Sometime after midnight the telephone rang again. It was Robertson's private security agent, who said he had been awakened himself by a call. "I just talked to Brother Pat—he's not very happy," the man said. But Robertson was coming to Keene, and the security agent wanted to make arrangements to meet Doug later in the day to go over the schedule and sites.

"Hallelujah!" Doug exclaimed. He set a time and place for them to meet and asked the agent to repeat his name.

"Miracle," the man said. "Dave Miracle."

Robertson's campaign day was a success—a mixture of large public and more intimate organizational events across the county that, once again, made maximal use of the candidate's time, furthering the campaign's nuts-and-bolts objectives while bringing Robertson into contact with hundreds of voters personally, not to mention the broader visibility the media coverage made possible. Even the most veteran political operative would have had trouble improving on what Doug, the novice, had accomplished.

Throughout the day there was an air of tension between Doug and some of the other staff members, especially Kerry Moody. But Robertson appeared relaxed and increasingly ebullient with each event. At the rally in Winchester, attended by more than one hundred people—the largest crowd that small town would turn out through the entire primary campaign—Robertson was asked if he had decided definitely to run. "I'm very close," he said to wild applause. "If people like you keep working, there may be some very good news in a couple of weeks." He reiterated his stock phrases about how well things were looking in Iowa and in Michigan, where a preliminary caucus would be the first test of Republican strength, and how crucial New Hampshire would be in deciding who would be the next president. "Do me one favor," he concluded. "Give me the satisfaction of looking at Dan Rather's face when he announces that Pat Robertson won New Hampshire."

Helen Bouchie's house was crammed with people when Robertson arrived. She presented him with a carrot cake, decorated with the message "GO FOR IT, PAT," and when the candidate gave her a kiss of thanks, she said, "I'll never wash that cheek."

Doug had not had a chance to talk with his candidate during the day—Kerry Moody and another national staff member had ridden with Robertson in his limo to every event—but as he climbed into his car after the Bouchie reception to ride back to the Keene airport and depart for Virginia, Robertson summoned Doug to the open back door. With Moody sitting next to him silently, Robertson motioned Doug to lean in. "I want you to know that I'm really pleased that you called me," he said. "Obviously it was the Lord that moved you and the Lord that brought me. Otherwise the ball would have been dropped."

Doug and Moody met later that evening to talk about the entire incident. Kerry was friendlier than he had been earlier. The day had gone well, and he wanted to move forward rather than dwell on the mistakes that had led to the trip almost being canceled—no one person was to blame, he said, it was just an oversight on everyone's part. Doug suggested that the entire New Hampshire staff meet to review what had gone wrong in order to prevent any more foul-ups. When he got home near midnight, the phone rang.

"Brother, did I wake you up?" It was Robertson. They talked about the trip and the organizational problem that preceded it. Robertson wanted an honest view of how things looked in New Hampshire—the first time he had ever talked about numbers with Doug—and said he was going to send his top man to the state to look over the operation.

Mark Nuttle, the national campaign director, arrived from headquarters two days later. The New Hampshire staff had already confronted Moody about the contradictions between his and Robertson's versions of the problems with the Keene trip, and he had agreed to delegate more authority to them. The incident, though still hanging in the air, was behind them. Nuttle's assessment was more sobering. Their computer list contained twelve thousand names of New Hampshire residents the campaign considered possible Robertson voters; the goal was more than fifty thousand. "You've put a lot of time and effort into this," Nuttle told them. "Now you've got less time to get more people. I don't see how it's going to happen." The group looked at each other silently. "Neither do we," one said dejectedly, "unless we get Pat up here fifteen days a month." Nuttle said they could count on a candidate maybe four times a month, at most, through the fall. He suggested they come up with some better ideas and left.

Doug went home to Stoddard for the Labor Day weekend with the national director's command for a new approach much on his mind. He found what he considered the solution in the two important facets of his life: business and the Bible. In the Old Testament, in Exodus, was the counsel Moses received from his father-in-law, Jethro, as the people of Israel were about to enter the Sinai wilderness on their flight from Egypt. Jethro, noticing that Moses' day was consumed with handling all of the questions and details of his people, remarked: "Thou wilt surely wear away, both thou, and this people that is with thee: for this thing is too heavy for thee; thou art not able to perform it thyself alone." He advised Moses, in effect, to delegate responsibility and organize differently, "and Moses chose able men out of all Israel, and made them heads over the people, rulers of thousands, rulers of hundreds, rulers of fifties, and rulers of tens." It reminded Doug of the way Amway operated its business. The salesmen "networked" with their neighbors and friends, building a pyramid that broadened as it reached downward.

Within two weeks the New Hampshire campaign had dropped its emphasis on phone banks, home parties, and canvasses and replaced it with "Pat's Pyramid: 8 × 8 in '88." At the top of each pyramid would be a supervisor, one of the best volunteers, whose responsibility would be to find eight organizers willing to commit themselves not only to voting for Robertson, but also to finding eight more supporters each among their friends at work or church. Each pyramid—or family, as Doug called them—would therefore constitute seventy-three voters. The heads of each "family" would make sure the members registered to vote, were kept informed about the campaign, had their names entered into the campaign's computerized data base, and on primary day got to the polls. "It helps push down other tasks to the level where it needs to be," Doug said. "Using neighborhood and personal networks is not as threatening or stressful as making cold calls." The campaign staff's new focus would be on sifting through the twelve thousand names already on its list to cull out potential organizers to start this chain reaction. In theory, at least, if only a tenth of them became organizers and filled their pyramids, the goal of fifty thousand Robertson voters would be met and surpassed.

"God has blessed us with this simple model to work with," Doug told Helen Bouchie when he visited her house to explain the new plan to her. He wanted her to be a supervisor. Helen asked how many people she would be expected to get. Eight, Doug said. She thought for a second, sitting on a chair near some framed pictures of Robertson, one of them showing him and her carrot cake.

"Oh, I can do more than that," she replied.

Al Rubega arrived late for the local Kemp campaign meeting in mid-August and was disappointed with what he saw: only four other people. Al believed in holding regular meetings. It helped keep the troops focused on the campaign—"I want them thinking, Jack Kemp, Jack Kemp, Jack Kemp," he said—even if there weren't any particular tasks the headquarters wanted accomplished. But tonight he had an unpleasant chore to ask of them, and he wished that summer hadn't siphoned off so many of his core group to things like vacations, outdoor barbecues, and housework, or a heat-induced attitude that February and its primary were a *mañana* that would never arrive.

He carried with him a thick pile of computer sheets listing the names and addresses of Republican voters in every town of Cheshire County. The state headquarters wanted the local volunteers to go through the lists, double-check the addresses and phone numbers, and make any corrections or additions (many of the names had no phone numbers) by early September. "It's something nobody likes doing," Al had said before the meeting. "There's no glory or anything else to it, but it's one of the most important things to get done." Mary (who was at a summer school course she was taking) was already dropping pointed hints that she and Al and only a few others seemed to end up doing the bulk of the work; she wouldn't be very happy with his report from this night.

"First, I have some good news," Al told the small group. Kemp was coming to Keene in a week, and one event on the schedule was a reception for the "faithful." It would be his first visit to Cheshire County in 1987 (he had attended a dinner held by the county's Republican Women's Club in the fall of 1986) and therefore the first chance for some of the volunteers to meet the man they supported. Al listed some other Kemp events coming up in New Hampshire—a debate between Kemp and Democrat Richard Gephardt and a cookout for campaign workers in Concord—and suggested they all attend. He handed out some plastic trash bags for people's cars, emblazoned with "SHAPE TOMORROW TOGETHER" and the Kemp logo, as well as a new supply of buttons for them to distribute. Finally he turned to the stack of computer paper.

Each person took his or her own town's list (hardly making a dent in the pile) and leafed through it as Al explained the chore ahead. A groan went up from one of the volunteers. He was looking at his own name on the list. Both the address and phone number were wrong, even though he hadn't changed either in years. This was not going to be easy.

A week later Kemp arrived in Keene by private plane with three national staff members, a photographer, and three reporters. Al, the organizer and lead car driver of a three-car motorcade (Kemp would not have Secret Service protection until early 1988), was there to greet him. The schedule was filled primarily with press interviews—visits to all three local radio stations and to *The Keene*

Sentinel's editorial board—plus the reception for volunteers and a luncheon address to the Keene Lions Club. Al, a Lions member, introduced Kemp as "someone I admire for his consistency and his courage, an individual you can trust to do what he says and say what he means." One of Al's homemade banners hung on the back wall.

Prior to the *Sentinel* interview, Al gave Kemp a memo outlining the newspaper's editorial positions, which basically were the opposite of the candidate's on virtually all of the major presidential issues. With Al standing in a corner of the interview room, feeling a little like Daniel in the lions' den, the newspaper's editors pressed Kemp on how he would have handled the situation of Ollie North, whom President Reagan had called a "national hero" yet contended had carried out foreign policy without Reagan's knowledge or approval. Kemp wouldn't be drawn into the trap; he supported both North and Reagan. The editors tried another tack.

"Well, what if you're president," one ventured, "and Al Rubega is on your staff and he—"

"He wouldn't be," Kemp interrupted jokingly. "He's too liberal."

"Thanks for the plug." Al laughed.

The campaign day had Al in a mood as sunny and warm as the weather. The chance to be so close to his candidate as he led Kemp from stop to stop—even penetrating the walls of the newspaper with whom he had exchanged so many caustic letters and meeting his editorial adversaries face to face for the first time—made him expansive. He told the national reporters that the New Hampshire Republican race was between Kemp and Bush, with Kemp poised, like Gary Hart in 1984, to surge to victory. Standing next to his motorcade, waiting for Kemp after one of the interviews, he confided: "I wish there was a way to do this full time. I *love* it."

The reception, the last stop in Keene and in Al's plans the pinnacle of the visit—when he could both show off his candidate to his volunteers and display his local organization to Kemp and the national staff—turned out instead to end in a personal embarrassment. The crowd was big enough. All of the county's core Kemp group, about fifteen people, were there, plus an equal number of other interested voters. (One couple from the town of Winchester appeared wearing Kemp buttons. They had assured Al they supported Kemp and had even attended a few organizational meetings. A week earlier their names had been included on the Dole campaign's list of committed activists and they had attended a Dole event, where they asked the candidate to pose for a picture with them. Less than a week after Kemp's visit, when Robertson made his nearly canceled trip to the area, they helped Doug Kidd organize his Winchester rally and told a reporter from the *Los Angeles Times* that Robertson was their candidate. They kept up their secret multiple commitments—a kind of political triple bet—for the remainder of the primary campaign.)

As Al accompanied Kemp around the living room, introducing him to the guests, he came across Jean and Errol Sowers. Al had never seen them before, but their nametags struck an alarm bell in his mind. Their letters appeared as regularly in the *Sentinel* as Al's, but from a totally different political perspective. Members of an organization called Beyond War, which promoted a "peace curriculum" in local schools and called for nuclear disarmament, they were not, Al suspected, here to consider backing Kemp. He knew they had not been invited. Al politely introduced them to his candidate, thinking at the same time, *As long as they behave themselves, I suppose it's okay for them to be here. But if all they want is to engage him in debate, grab some media attention, and that kind of garbage, not on our time. There are too many supporters here who've worked to earn the right to his attention.*

Sure enough, after Kemp's opening remarks, Errol Sowers asked the first question, posed as a long statement against the "Star Wars" defense system, which Kemp wanted not only developed, but deployed as soon as possible. Al, standing next to Kemp in the corner of the living room, tried to interrupt. "Please make your questions short," he said, reddening. "We only have a few minutes." Kemp started to address the issue, and Sowers interjected several times, until Al, tense and nervous at the direction his reception was headed, broke in again.

"There are a lot of people here who've worked tables in the hot sun," he said, "and should get the chance—"

"Al," Kemp said heatedly. "Let me handle the questions. You can't pull me out of something like this."

In the brief hush following the exchange, Al reddened even more. After a few more questions from the audience, Jean Sowers asked where and how the arms race could end. Al kept his silence. Kemp turned his answer into an impassioned call for antisatellite and antimissile weaponry as a way to prevent, not inflict, war and its human destruction. "Is it moral to develop and use such weapons?" he asked rhetorically, answering it himself. "Yes. It [Star Wars] is a legitimate, profoundly moral system. And as president I will build it." The crowd burst into sustained applause.

Kemp was running late, and his staff wanted to move him quickly to his motorcade. But Al delayed him to make sure he had shaken hands with all of his volunteers. "It's not fair that someone who has worked hard for this guy doesn't even get to shake his hand because Mr. Sanctimonious over there wanted to debate him," he complained.

Once they were in the car (Al was driving them to another reception in the next county north), Al apologized to Kemp for the incident. "Forget it," he was told, and they drove on—Al in silence, Kemp with a national reporter interviewing him in the backseat.

For a few days afterward the exchange clouded Al's memory of the campaign swing through his county. He still seethed when he thought about the Sowers's crashing "my little tea party," and he considered writing a letter to the *Sentinel* to call them to task for what he considered their rudeness and the personal humiliation he felt they had caused him. "I had a lot of myself invested in the fact that I wanted things to go smoothly," he said. "I wanted to make sure everything stayed on schedule and to show these guys from Washington and Concord that everything goes right here and for everybody to be happy. It never occurred to me that maybe the candidate himself would want to take this guy on in front of a friendly audience."

Gradually his natural optimism prevailed in his recollections. Kemp had "batted home runs" with the Sowers's questions, impressing the rest of the crowd with his command of the facts and the situation, even if it was, to a certain extent, at Al's expense as much as the Sowers's. "It energized the troops, *and* I still had the chance to introduce him to those who needed it—so I accomplished what I wanted," he said. "On balance, I guess it was a plus."

By the time of the Kemp-Gephardt debate in Nashua several days later, Al was back in stride. Conceived by the two campaigns as a good "media event"—Kemp and Gephardt, after all, were not running against each other—the debate attracted a crowd comprised of more reporters than supporters or voters. Ten television cameras lined the back of the hall, and once the debate was over and the hall emptied, the two candidates sat next to each other for half an hour of point-counterpoint interviews with television stations in other parts of the country, hooked to Nashua by satellite. In the midst of this high-tech media environment, Al was conspicuous with his hand-held video camera, moving around the proceedings like a happy father at his child's birthday party to capture the moment for later viewing on his home television set. (He showed the tape at his next local organizational meeting.) The Kemp entourage of national and state staff members included him into the inner sanctum of Kemp's holding room before and after the event and sent him to Gephardt's postdebate press conference (preceding Kemp's) in case something was said that the candidate should be forewarned about—a clear sign that they recognized his hard work and appreciated his loyalty.

At a supporters' picnic following the debate, Kemp gave what Al described as "one of the best speeches we ever heard." Some of his troops were there, and at one poignant point in the speech Al looked over to see one of them—a woman he had recruited at his street fair booth—crying from deep emotion. As a little bonus of personal

satisfaction, Al's banner was fluttering in the breeze behind his
candidate. The headquarters staff had commandeered one of them
for use outside Cheshire County.

With summer ending, both Al and Kendall Lane were feeling essentially the same. Each was confident of his campaign's position,
still pleased but baffled at the absence of any evidence of a major
Dole grass-roots organization in the area, somewhat daunted by
the list work still unfinished, and harried by the quotas their headquarters were pressing upon them. But they were hopeful that,
with the first tinges of fall in the air—New England's signal for its
residents to snap out of any lingering lethargy and start preparing
for the long winter—there would be more help as the campaign
pace quickened.

Independently both thought they smelled something of a conspiracy in the way *The Keene Sentinel* was covering the Republican
race. Robertson seemed to get more ink than their two candidates.
"Is the paper trying to encourage someone likely to be beaten?"
Kendall wondered. "I can't explain it otherwise." Al was even more
suspicious. He had emerged from Kemp's interview personally liking the people at the paper, even though they obviously saw the
world through entirely different eyes. But the day after the visit,
an editorial castigated Kemp's position on the contra war in Nicaragua, and the coverage of Robertson's trip a few days later fueled
the kind of acerbity Al normally confined to his letters. The editorial
was a "cheap shot," he said, and Robertson got a longer article and
more pictures from his tour than they had accorded Kemp's visit
—not to mention that Robertson's video parties got covered while
Kemp's organizational triumphs of the summer had gone unre-
corded. "They're scared silly of Jack, trying to downplay him," Al
concluded. Since Kemp would be the Robertson supporters' natural
second choice if the televangelist's campaign folded, he thought,
it was clear what the paper was up to.

Despite his continued annoyance about the obstacles of the Bush
campaign's ponderous bureaucracy, Kendall was almost cocky

when he contemplated Bush's prospects in the state. Forty-five to fifty percent of the primary vote didn't seem out of the question to him. Cheshire County looked particularly good, especially if the only real challenge was coming from Kemp. He had received a complete report of Kemp's reception from one of his web of political informants (he had also sent one to Robertson's rally in Winchester), knew the names of who had attended, and considered both the size of the crowd and the number of committed Kemp partisans "nothing to get excited about."

Al saw things in equally rosy terms. Paul Laxalt, the former senator from and governor of Nevada, had ruled out a presidential bid, avoiding a further split of the conservative vote. New Hampshire Senator Gordon Humphrey, the most conservative elected official in the state, had finally endorsed Kemp. Bush had an extensive organization, filled with the party's state and local leadership, but Kemp's was "the only campaign with any life in it." Regardless of what the local paper might be doing, Al predicted Robertson wouldn't make it to the primary.

"I defy any other campaign in the area—even Bush's—to do what we've been doing," he boasted. He remembered his wrestling coach's axiom: "You don't win the match on the mat, you win it in practice months and months before." In the heat of the summer he and his team had sweated off some pounds and were getting ready to pin the opposition.

8

THE NOVICE AND
THE PRO

Molly Kelly was up before seven o'clock on September 4, a Friday. It was going to be a busy day. Kitty Dukakis was coming to Keene on behalf of her husband's campaign for a series of events that would culminate in the official opening of the Dukakis for President headquarters for Cheshire County. As the campaign's principal local organizer (and part-time employee), Molly had taken a day off from her job as assistant director of admissions for Franklin Pierce College in nearby Rindge. There was a lot to do.

First, her three kids—Zach, 15; Justin, 14; and Rachel, 11—needed to be fed and sent off to school. Her clothes dryer broke down, and she hurried from her Keene apartment to a self-service laundry to finish the chore. By midmorning she was at the headquarters, a small second-story office on a corner overlooking Keene's Central Square that she had located, liked for its convenient location and "visibility" in the city's heart, and secured only a few weeks earlier. She decorated the walls with colorful crepe, arranged a few flowers she had picked on the way, and tidied things up. Mike Cook, a young political organizer who had just arrived from Texas to be the full-time Cheshire County coordinator for Dukakis, was busy making posters that listed the office supplies he hoped volunteers would donate. Molly called the Keene Police Department:

if too many people showed up for the office opening, could it be moved to the town common? Then she hurried home, showered, changed her clothes, and headed to meet Mrs. Dukakis at the first event.

The next several hours were a blur. Kitty Dukakis spoke to a small group at Keene State College's Holocaust Center, met with members of the college's committee on the status of women, toured a former woolen mill that had been converted into a shopping mall, and had a brief meal with seven other politically active women. Molly's tasks were not glamorous. She made sure the two-car motorcade found parking spaces at the college, peeked in to make sure there was a decent-size crowd, ran after coffee for Mrs. Dukakis during the second event, led the caravan to the mill, secured a table for the meal—and in every spare moment was on the telephone with people she had invited to the office opening or with the office itself to make sure things were ready. ("I need to go get a haircut, but this office list isn't done and seems more important," Mike Cook said in one phone conversation, looking for advice. "Finish the list," she said.)

Forty people turned out for the office opening—including Andi Johnson, who dropped in from the Biden office next door to check things out; Zach, Justin, and Rachel were there as well—which jammed the space but didn't necessitate moving outside. When Mrs. Dukakis and the crowd departed shortly after six P.M., Molly finally had a chance to relax and think about the day.

An ice-cream cone at the mill, she realized, had been her only meal. But the events had gone well, and as she cleaned up the office she was pleased, particularly with the turnout at the opening. As she'd talked with one potential supporter that afternoon on the phone, the woman had asked, "Can I bring my children?"

"Can you bring your children?" Molly had answered, incredulous. "Of course. What is this about, if not our children?"

In her thirty-nine years Molly Kelly had rarely been far from the circle of children and family. The second of eleven children and the oldest daughter, she lived with her parents and siblings in Fort Wayne, Indiana, until she got married at age twenty-one. Her father, once a member of the Young Republicans in town, was transformed in the early 1960s into a liberal Democrat. He became involved in the Christian Family Movement, the social action arm of the liberalization trend within the Catholic church. He led civil rights marches, helped reopen a church to serve the inner city, rewrote the church's liturgy, and hosted the Berrigan brothers and other Catholic social activists at the dinner table.

Molly, in her teens, was deeply influenced by it all. She stayed up late at night discussing modern theology with her father and participated in his causes. She cut out pictures of starving children in Biafra and put them on the family refrigerator. When Martin Luther King (one her heroes, along with Gandhi and Robert Kennedy) was assassinated in 1968, she marched alongside her dad in public mourning. "We were all out to save the world, to do things for other people," she remembers. While she worked on an associate's degree in mental health technology, she worked five nights a week with retarded children at the state hospital.

At a summer camp for retarded people in Connecticut, where she was working, she met her husband, a Wesleyan College student involved in mental health issues. They married in 1970 and moved through a series of his jobs and locations—a state mental hospital in Connecticut, a psychiatric halfway house for boys and a group home for multiply handicapped youths in Pennsylvania, a group home in Massachusetts, and, in 1977, a therapist's job with the area's mental health service in Keene. With the first of their three children born a few years after their marriage, Molly was busy raising a family but deeply involved in her husband's work and her own causes. In Pennsylvania she helped form a La Leche League, a group committed to natural childbirth and breast-feeding, and for two months nursed the infant of a mother who had been seriously injured in a car accident. She drove to Washington to join her father in a march against the Vietnam War.

When her marriage broke up in 1978, sheer economic survival

became her top concern. She enrolled at Keene State College, moved herself and her three children to family housing (which she paid for by being the complex's manager), worked several jobs at a time—waitressing at Papa Gino's restaurant, delivering *The Keene Sentinel* with her aging Datsun pickup—and, surviving one semester at a time, eventually earned a degree in philosophy and history. Politics was still an avid interest, but it was confined to long discussions with her fellow students and friends; she didn't have time for much else. (In the 1980 primary she liked California Governor Jerry Brown, a Democratic candidate, and when he came to speak at the college, she was scheduled to drive him from the airport to the event. But his plane was delayed, and Rachel needed to be picked up from her day care. Someone else met the candidate.) Her studies were "like falling in love," and after graduation Molly decided to get a law degree, as much for the study of the social order as for a career. She received her law degree from Franklin Pierce Law Center in 1985, practiced with a firm in Keene for a year, but failed her bar exams and joined Franklin Pierce's admissions department in 1986.

That same year she participated in peaceful demonstrations against the Seabrook nuclear power plant in New Hampshire and the Vermont Yankee nuclear plant just across the Connecticut River in Vermont. Paul McEachern, the Democratic candidate for New Hampshire governor in 1986, was running on a platform that called for stopping the Seabrook plant (which was completed but not licensed to operate). Molly volunteered and was soon organizing the Keene area for the campaign. Her first real foray into electoral politics was simultaneously exciting and frustrating. Molly—a shortish, bouncy, dark-haired woman with a dazzling smile and vivacious spirit—forged into the campaign with fervor and bright-eyed energy, but was constantly filled with doubts that she didn't know what she was doing. After the Democratic primary in September, some of the county's party regulars—Andi Johnson, Tom Britton, Pat Russell, and others, many of whom had supported Bruce Anderson for the nomination—suddenly started showing up at McEachern campaign meetings, confidently asserting themselves. Deliberately or not, they made Molly feel like a novice and an interloper on the local party's territory.

Her work, however, did not go unnoticed. As the presidential campaigns began organizing, the Dukakis staff sought her out and offered her the job of full-time coordinator for Cheshire County. Molly had already decided to support Dukakis—as governor of Massachusetts he had taken actions that were preventing Seabrook (on the New Hampshire-Massachusetts border) from being licensed, and his state programs for day care and helping mothers get jobs and off welfare appealed to her. "I couldn't *not* get involved," she said afterward. "I feel a sense of responsibility for something more than just my family, the house I live in, or my job. It has to feel connected with a bigger picture. And there's nothing bigger than being a part of electing the next leader of the government—that's what you're doing. I wanted to do something good. It's not enough that it's good in my kitchen, not enough that it's good for my children." But with three children to support, a campaign job, however tempting it might be, was neither lucrative nor secure enough for Molly to abandon her position with the college. Instead she worked out an agreement for a part-time responsibility with the campaign: nights, weekends, and days off, a hybrid between being a local volunteer and a staff member, a role she accepted only after talking it over with her family.

"What did you always tell us your dream was as a little girl?" Rachel, her eleven-year-old, asked.

"To do something that made a difference," Molly answered.

"You're still doing it," said her daughter.

Joe Biden's presidential campaign crashed and burned in mid-September, following a pattern hauntingly similar to that set by Gary Hart in May.

First came the news stories that in a number of public appearances Biden's closing statements were virtually word-for-word cribbings of a speech by Neil Kinnock, a British politician. Sometimes

Biden attributed the phrases to Kinnock (as he did at a picnic reception in Keene in late August), but sometimes he didn't, leaving the impression that the thoughts and words were his own. Within days, as it seemed that the entire American press corps had turned its sights on Biden, more damaging stories appeared. In several other prominent speeches Biden had borrowed phrases from other political figures—Robert Kennedy, John Kennedy, Hubert Humphrey—without giving them credit. (One of the prime examples was his speech to the California Democrats—the one his campaign had videotaped and distributed for its home parties in the spring and that had impressed Andi Johnson and Bruce Anderson with its soaring rhetoric.) In college he had committed plagiarism in one of his papers. And—the most damaging story of all—during the reception in the Claremont area earlier in the year, when a man had pestered him on his intellectual qualifications for president, Biden had not only lost his temper (as Andi had been told), but, on closer inspection, had fabricated and exaggerated major portions of his academic record.

For the second time in a year, Andi Johnson watched press coverage about the candidate she supported build from flak to a sustained aerial bombardment and in one week's time bring down his high-flying campaign. This time, however, she parachuted to emotional and political safety more quickly.

The troubles started unfolding as Andi was immersed in organizational details. With posters declaring, "COME HEAR JOE BIDEN . . . on videotape," she had convened a recruitment meeting at Franklin Pierce College, hoping to find some student volunteers. Only five showed up to watch the tape of the California speech and hear Andi explain what the Biden campaign was doing and "why it's exciting to be in a campaign—getting a candidate elected and having fun." Plans were afoot for an initial door-to-door canvass in October, and Andi was appalled at how little the staff from the national headquarters seemed to know about conducting one. The necessary materials weren't ready, and there were problems scheduling the importation of volunteers from Delaware and Washington and college campuses to provide the manpower. *I'm going to have to teach this campaign how to canvass,* she decided, and began work on a manual for the volunteers based on the one she had saved from the Hart campaign in 1984, when she had gone on her first canvass. Four years ago she had been wide-eyed and eager to learn about politics; now she considered herself a campaign veteran, as knowledgeable as anyone on the national staff about how to organize New Hampshire.

Memories, many of them fond, of her two Hart campaigns were already much on her mind before Biden's problems began stirring more unpleasant recollections. Hart's New Hampshire campaign in 1984 didn't have many conflicts with the national campaign, she said, "because there really wasn't a national campaign—we were it." Biden's staff was only beginning to "learn that they have to listen to people in New Hampshire," she said. "We're first and we're bratty and we're spoiled. We want to do what *we* want to do."

Nonetheless Andi thought things were going well. A Biden reception in late August in Keene had drawn two hundred people. (Jean Sowers, as part of her self-designated role for Beyond War, attended and asked the same question she had posed to Kemp and some other candidates, eliciting an answer much more in line with her own thinking.) The Keene office had opened in June, far earlier than any other campaign's, and Andi hurried there after work each day. The crowd at the Dukakis office opening had not impressed or concerned her. As far as she could tell, the "other campaigns have practically conceded Cheshire County."

Hart emerged from public exile to appear on ABC's *Nightline* and, although not saying it unequivocally, seemed to Andi to close the door on reentering the race. She was relieved. In her mind Hart was still superior to the other Democrats. "None of them have any specific plans for anything," she said after the broadcast. "Just ideas—including Biden. All of them have good records and good ideas, but no plans, that one step further that Gary had taken. That's why I liked him in the first place." Rumors had circulated that Hart was thinking of jumping back in. Andi had burned the phone lines talking about them with other former Hart supporters but agreed that he wouldn't do it—it would be "stupid." Besides, she didn't want to back out of her commitment to Biden and her position in the campaign.

Her response to the initial stories about Biden's borrowing of speech material was that it would blow over. A call from the Manchester headquarters the afternoon of September 21, however, signaled otherwise. *Newsweek* had hit the stands with a story about Biden's exaggeration of his college record in Claremont; the networks were expected to show a tape of the incident on the evening news; an important message, perhaps a withdrawal announcement, was expected to be faxed from Washington to the New Hampshire headquarters—she ought to drive over after work. *Such minor, minor offenses*, Andi thought on her way to Manchester. *I don't think he should drop out because of them.* At most, she thought, Biden should put things on idle for a few months and let the flap blow over. He was opening the hearings on the nomination of Robert Bork for the Supreme Court; he could legitimately suspend campaigning until the nomination fight was over. *If Gary had only put his campaign on hold, instead of abruptly terminating it, coming back would be possible, not stupid.* She had been angry that Hart had buckled to the media uproar and would feel the same way if Biden copied him. Still, the decision wasn't hers to make, and if Biden withdrew, she thought as she drove, she'd have to choose again from the leftovers. Gore was a possibility—he had attracted a cluster of former Hart volunteers to his New Hampshire campaign, and she might have a good time working with them again. Pat Schroeder, a congresswoman from Colorado was talking about running for president—a woman candidate would be exciting, and in many ways, besides coming from the same state, she seemed to share many of Hart's issues. And there was Paul Simon—she had seriously considered him when Hart departed, even though, as she put it, "he kind of puts me to sleep."

By the time she reached Manchester Andi was almost fatalistically detached from the scene of despair and panic she encountered at the headquarters. Her commitment to Biden had never been freighted with the same emotional intensity she had felt toward Hart and his campaign, anyway. "I've been through this before," she told some of her co-workers. "Hey, I can handle it." When the evening news came on, and everyone else was glued to the television set showing the damaging piece about Biden, Andi was addressing envelopes. The fax came in from Washington, outlining what the top staff considered were Biden's political options: drop out now, hold on until January to collect federal matching funds and withdraw, or stay in the race and lose. Andi still favored fighting on but privately came to another conclusion: *It's hard for us to work a campaign when the national staff has given up.*

No decision had been made by the time Andi reported at the Keene office the next evening. Pat Russell, one of Biden's first and most ardent supporters, wanted him to fight back. She, Andi, and a young coordinator from Connecticut who had been assigned to Cheshire County conducted their own informal telephone poll of people who had attended the reception in August: most thought he should stay in, only one thought the news was so troubling that he ought to withdraw; quite a few were totally unaware of any controversy. Pat called in the results to Washington, hoping it might affect the staff's recommendation.

Andi, meanwhile, had changed her mind. The night before she had called the friend who had convinced her to join the Biden campaign, and the more she talked to him, the more she thought Biden should quit—and he only had himself to blame for it. The Claremont event was looming larger in her mind. Her assessment of it had come full circle. "I was very happy to hear about it the day after it happened [when she supported Hart], because I knew that Joe Biden had a tendency to be arrogant and to blow his cool," she said. "And then when I got involved in his campaign, I could turn that around to say, 'Well, that's just because he's so concerned and passionate.' But the more I think about it, the angrier I get about all the exaggerations that occurred up there." She now saw it as crumbling under pressure and "if he were to become president, how would he react under the pressure of the Oval Office? That's a big question, and I have sincere doubts about that." If Biden did decide to stay in the race, he might have to do it without Andi: "I'm not sure I still back him."

She didn't care much for the other candidates. "I'm disillusioned with them all," she said. Simon was a "snore"; Gore was too green; Gephardt had "flip-flopped on so many issues, I don't trust him"; Jackson she liked, but "not as president, not as president—I'm sorry"; governors (Babbitt and Dukakis) lacked foreign policy experience, and beyond that, she firmly disliked Dukakis. At least, from what she knew about Pat Schroeder, "I think she's clean, I don't think she's done anything outrageous or trivial—but we'll find out, right?" While she conducted the Biden phone poll, she asked a few people what they thought about Schroeder. And before she left the office that night, she called the congresswoman's office and told them she'd be willing to help, if Biden dropped out.

He withdrew the next day, Wednesday, September 23. Andi was at work when Biden's announcement was broadcast in the afternoon, so she didn't see it. Pat Russell and the coordinator, sitting in the Keene office, alone except for a reporter and photographer from the *Sentinel*, watched silently from chairs a local funeral home had loaned the campaign. The television cable had been installed just the day before. Boxes of brochures for the upcoming canvass were stacked in the corners. The office lease was paid up through February.

Andi came in that night and from the wreckage of another campaign reclaimed a small table, a chair, a typewriter, and some other supplies of hers. Her box of voter cards was at the Manchester headquarters, waiting to be entered into the computer.

On Thursday Biden did what Hart had not: he came to New Hampshire to meet and personally thank the volunteers on the campaign he had just terminated. As she drove to the event in Manchester, wearing both Biden and Hart buttons on her dress and bumper stickers from both defunct campaigns on her car, Andi said, "I don't feel right—I'm not torn up." This was a different

experience from the emotional wrenching of Hart's demise. She
was ready to join another campaign immediately. "I've got to go
with *someone*," she said. "I've got too many lists, too many names,
too many contacts." But the night before, she had come to a decision
reflecting a calculated pragmatism. She was joining Simon's campaign, even if he was a little boring. "I'm tired of defending records,"
she said. "I'm tired of defending why someone is running—like
'Pat Schroeder's a woman, and she can't win.' I can't deal with
that. I'd go with Gore, but I'm tired of the abortion issue and I'm
tired of the MX vote. I can't defend that. Paul Simon is *safe*. I think
I'm ready for safe."

Biden's New Hampshire farewell was held in the law office of
one of his principal supporters. When Andi arrived, the building
was surrounded by hundreds of reporters and television crews and
by satellite trucks parked like siege machines around a fortress.
Biden spoke privately to about fifty supporters in a conference room,
appearing upbeat, making a few jokes about his temper and his
reputation as an eloquent speaker, urging them to join other campaigns and stay committed to politics, and promising that New
Hampshire might see him as a candidate in some future primary.
Before emerging to face the press encampment, he shook hands
with each volunteer. "Good luck," Andi told him. "And get Bork."

On her way out of town she stopped at Simon's campaign headquarters, a few blocks away. She had called his state director the
night before to offer her help, and when she arrived he gave her
some pamphlets, issue papers, and a pile of Simon buttons. She
put one on, next to her Hart and Biden buttons. As soon as she
retrieved her voter cards, she told him, she'd have a good list of
Cheshire County Democrats for them to work on.

In the week following Biden's departure, Molly Kelly organized her
first extensive political canvass, attended her first big political fund-
raiser, and, when reports surfaced that it had been the top staff of
the Dukakis campaign who had first directed reporters to Biden's
cribbing from Neil Kinnock's speeches, experienced her first po-

litical crisis. She was learning more about politics more quickly than she had expected.

An often overlooked fact about the New Hampshire primary is that, despite the intensive efforts the candidates and the campaigns make to enlist local people in their activities, despite the premium accorded the tradition of grass-roots organization, and despite the virtually unique opportunity that exists for the citizens to participate in the highest-stakes political poker game in the nation, much of the work that gets done relies on out-of-state volunteers. To be sure, most campaigns attract their own core body of local volunteers. In Cheshire County in the early fall of 1987, this ranged from perhaps a handful of activists (or fewer) organized for the campaigns of Gore, Gephardt, Simon, Jackson, and Dole to roughly twenty-five for Dukakis and Bush. The campaigns of Babbitt, Kemp, and Robertson could claim a number of active, local volunteers somewhere in between; if Haig and du Pont had any citizens of the county expending any serious effort, they were doing it so quietly that even the campaigns' state headquarters were unaware of it. When a particularly sustained or concentrated task needed to be done, however, even within those camps with the largest pool of committed supporters, only several people could be counted upon. By the time the primary was more imminent, this would change, of course—but not dramatically.

As governor of a neighboring state, Dukakis therefore held a tremendous organizational advantage over his opponents: thousands of volunteers from his past campaigns, all within a short drive of politically crucial New Hampshire. The door-to-door canvass staged the last weekend of September was logistically complex. In Cheshire County alone, two hundred Massachusetts volunteers were expected. The objective was to reach voters at their front door, find out what they thought about the Democratic race (particularly whether they already were favorably inclined toward Dukakis) and what issues were of concern to them, give them some campaign literature, make a pitch for Dukakis, and keep a record of it all. Some residents would receive follow-up letters from the person who

contacted them or material about Dukakis's position on the issues
that interested them. Eventually a list of likely Dukakis voters would
emerge for use in getting out the vote on primary day. It was a
massive, volunteer-intensive effort, and something each of the
Democrat campaigns would mount at least once before the primary
day. For the Dukakis campaign—which, as the Democratic favorite
in New Hampshire, was even more cautious about leaving little to
chance than Vice President Bush's on the Republican side—the
October canvass, however, was the first of *four* it had planned.
(Mike Cook, the young coordinator from Texas assigned to Cheshire
County, wondered whether the first couple of canvasses, coming
so far before the primary, weren't simply scheduled to give the
Massachusetts volunteers something to do.) In the conventional
warfare of door-to-door politics, with its seemingly endless wave
after wave of volunteers massed at New Hampshire's southern
border, the Dukakis campaign was the political equivalent of Chi-
na's Red Army—and roughly as popular with its more meagerly
supplied competitors.

Molly and Mike's job was to prepare for the influx of volunteers
and see that things went smoothly. The campaign provided com-
puter-originated cards listing the names and addresses of every
Democrat in Keene and ten other towns. These had to be arranged
in packets that included maps, walking or driving routes, and instructions for each team of canvassers. Free housing for Saturday
night needed to be found for as many as possible. Some teams
would need local drivers to take the volunteers to their canvass
areas. A central site for everyone to gather for their materials and
instructions, and to return their completed cards, needed to be
found. And the horde would need to be fed two lunches, one dinner,
and a breakfast. Merely getting things ready for the weekend consumed three weeks of the local group's time.

Although he had been in the area only a few weeks, Mike Cook
concentrated on the canvass routes. He pored over street maps,
trying to figure how much one team could be expected to cover in

a day and which paths got the most done with the least amount of travel. Working late into the night, he once became confused on a proper route in Keene, so he got in his car and drove through the area. It was three A.M. By the time of the canvass he knew his county's geography as well as a native. Molly assumed the other chores. As the campaign's principal local representative, she contacted people who had attended the office opening and Dukakis's spring visit, enlisting them as drivers, one-night landlords, and coordinators of specific canvass areas. "It sounds like a lot of work," she told one gathering of potential helpers, "but I think it will be a lot of fun." She arranged the use of a large hall at Keene State College to serve as the canvass headquarters. She visited some local bakeries and restaurants, soliciting donations of doughnuts, bread, and sandwiches, and found other volunteers to help with more food and large amounts of coffee. "It's important that they know *you* will pick the food up, that the favor is for *you*," she explained to Mike when he suggested that she send someone other than herself. She was learning fast.

With the flush of a successful canvass still in their minds, Molly and Mike drove to Boston on Tuesday night for a gala fund-raiser— a glittering event at which the campaign announced it had already raised eight million dollars in the primary, a record for Democrats. Dukakis played the trumpet and danced with his wife. *Hey, we're on the move*, Molly said to herself at the party. *Maybe we're going to win—it's been so long since I supported a winner.* The staff held its own postparty celebration, and she didn't get back to Keene until the early hours of the morning.

The state headquarters called her at work before noon. There was a big . . . problem. John Sasso, the national campaign manager, had been the person who'd leaked videotapes of Biden and Kinnock to the press, showing Biden's verbatim and unattributed copying. Only two days before, Dukakis—who earlier in the campaign had complained that Gephardt was conducting too "negative" a campaign—had told reporters he would be "astonished" and "very, very angry" if someone from his campaign had been involved. Sasso was now leaving the campaign, as was the national political director, who had also been involved in the incident, Molly was told.

She was stunned, and a little frightened. *If John Sasso, a political professional, can make this kind of mistake*, she wondered, *what about someone inexperienced like me?* Recent memories flooded her mind. Dukakis insisted on personally meeting everyone who worked for him, and when Molly and some other New Hampshire staffers had their group interview, he had stressed that things can get competitively intense in a political race, but he wanted them to focus on running a clean, positive campaign. At a state staff meeting in the summer, the workers had been warned to be particularly careful about things like driving while intoxicated; it could reflect on the campaign. *That's something I wouldn't do anyway*, she had thought, *but now it would have an effect on more than just me and my family.* The notion seemed overwhelming. Molly had always enjoyed freewheeling political discussions in which she offered her own opinions openly. Now, she realized, her friends and colleagues at work saw her not just as Molly Kelly, but as a representative of Michael Dukakis, candidate for president. She would have to be more careful. "There's no such thing as an off-the-cuff remark to anyone—but especially to reporters," the state director had told his staff. Exceedingly cautious to begin with, the campaign was now hunkering down even farther.

When Will Fay, a political reporter for *The Keene Sentinel*, reached her for his story on the local reaction to the Sasso flap, she declined to comment. The headquarters called again. They were holding a statewide staff meeting in Manchester that evening to go over the troubles and how to respond, and she should attend. Molly was torn. She would come if it was required, she finally answered, but after the canvass and the fund-raiser, she felt she had neglected her children the last few days and thought she should spend the evening with them. The state director summarized the "party line"—Dukakis wasn't personally involved; it was a mistake; but the campaign was going to push ahead—and allowed her to skip the meeting. She passed the night worried, but at least in the warmer comfort of her family.

Each fall the Cheshire County Democratic party holds its annual Octoberfest, an event that gives the party regulars the chance to assemble, drink some beer, eat some hot dogs, talk politics, and, with luck, raise a little money. With a presidential primary under way, the 1987 Octoberfest took on the added element of intraparty competition. Beneath the veneer of friendliness ran a minor undercurrent of stress—like a high school reunion in which the classmates check nervously to see who has been the most successful since graduation, or like a gathering of an extended family when an estate is about to be divided.

A steady, chill rain was falling, washing out any chance of a celebratory air. The year that had started so hopefully, almost overconfidently for the Democrats, had turned dark with political clouds. Donna Rice and Gary Hart; Joe Biden and Neil Kinnock; Mike Dukakis and John Sasso; even Bruce Babbitt and his television persona—trouble seemed to touch everyone. Al Gore, who in recent debates had tried to separate himself from the Democratic pack by talking a harder line on defense and foreign policy issues, was chasing to correct a news article that mistakenly reported he had changed his policy and now supported military aid to the contras in Nicaragua. Gore was also encountering considerable disgruntlement from some of the liberal Concord group who had endorsed him en masse earlier in the year. Only Simon seemed to be on a bit of a roll.

Of the fifty Democrats who huddled to eat under a sodden tent and then moved inside a small lodge near a lake in Swanzey to hear each campaign make a brief presentation, virtually all were already committed to a candidate. Bruce Anderson—still undecided and much courted—was about the only one there whose mind might be swayed.

Tom Britton, county chairman and therefore the emcee of the speaking schedule, opened by saying, "I think we owe a debt of

gratitude to Joe Biden" for defeating the Bork nomination. Hattie
Babbitt, wife of the candidate, spoke for the Babbitt campaign,
prompting a few murmurs by advocates of other contenders in the
back of the room that she would be a more formidable opponent
than her husband. Andi Johnson, now the head of the Simon campaign in the county, introduced a Dartmouth College professor to
present her candidate's case. Dick Gephardt's top supporter in the
region (the one who had loaned Gephardt a plaid lumberjack coat
during his late winter visit to a maple syrup shack—so Gephardt
would "*look* like New Hampshire") called his man a "Democrats'
Democrat" and added his regrets that Biden had been forced to
withdraw from the race.

Molly Kelly stood near the rear. The constant references to Biden's demise seemed partially aimed as subtle digs at her campaign
and sometimes as if they were directed toward her personally. *Wait
a minute*, she felt like saying, *Mike Dukakis didn't do it; I didn't
do it.* Her planning for the Octoberfest showed that, inexperienced
or not, political calculation was part of her makeup. Conscious that
the Dukakis campaign was now viewed not only as the front-runner
in New Hampshire, but also, at least for the moment, as the bad
boy on the block, she deliberately held back from making the same
kind of show of organizational strength at the event that the other
campaigns had mounted. Some had arrived early to put up posters
and display buttons or literature; the Dukakis "visibility" was comparatively understated.

At the same time, since Al Gore himself was scheduled to attend,
Molly rejected the headquarters request that she represent the
campaign in the speaking program. She was shy about such things
to begin with, and her lingering sensitivity from the gubernatorial
campaign of 1986, when she had felt that the party regulars viewed
her as a bit of an upstart, made her think a high public posture
might seem presumptuous. So she demanded a speaker from the
state committee—someone whose presence might be a better coun-
terweight to Senator Gore's and would show that the Dukakis campaign cared enough about the county event to dispatch a surrogate.

Gore was the center of attention, once Valerie Britton delivered him from the airport. Tom had a written speech for his introduction, as he had for Hart at the party's dinner in the spring. Although Tom harbored his own doubts about a couple of Gore's recent harder-line statements on foreign policy and defense matters, he made it a virtue in his introduction. "We [Democrats] seem to have lost our ability to focus our compassion on individuals and still be perceived as strong on national security," he said, noting that Harry Truman and John Kennedy had done both. Gore, he promised, was "poised to return us to this forgotten tradition."

Gore picked up on the same theme in his remarks, saying that to win, the Democrats needed a candidate who could appeal to independent voters rather than nominating someone "who can do the most beautiful swan dive through the hoops of every interest group." He corrected the record on Nicaragua—he opposed military aid to the contras—and asked for their support. "The difference between involvement and commitment is found in a breakfast of ham and eggs," he said. "Those chickens were involved, but those hogs were *committed*." Like many of the other speakers, Gore also had a special comment for the former Biden supporters in the crowd. "Let me express my condolences," he said. "It was a terrific campaign, and Senator Biden is a distinguished national leader."

Pat Russell came up to Molly Kelly when the speaking was over. "Why so many condolences?" she said. "Who died? Who died?" And then she laughed. Molly took it as a sign that Pat didn't blame her.

Andi Johnson wasn't as ready to forget and forgive. From the beginnings of the campaign, when Hart was still a candidate, she had reserved a separate niche in her judgment of the Democratic field for Dukakis (whom she disliked profoundly and considered unqualified, especially compared with the senators in the race) and his campaign (toward which she had an even stronger distaste; it constantly reminded her of 1984 and the Mondale organization). The news that Dukakis's top staff had played a role in Biden's demise only hardened her antipathy. "I had a feeling it was that campaign," she said at the time. "They're such a machine-type group. I'm ashamed of them." She considered the leak of the Biden-Kinnock tapes a dirty trick and felt vindicated by its exposure. At the Octoberfest—where, like Pat Russell, she thought the repeated professions of regret for Biden's withdrawal were overdone and disingenuous—she perceived Molly Kelly's quiet attitude as a snub. She mentioned to some friends that a couple of Dukakis supporters had left in the midst of Gore's speech and claimed she overheard them talking about how the other campaigns didn't stand a chance. "That's typical of what the Dukakis campaign is doing—running down other candidates," she said. "I hate that in a campaign."

Her work for Simon, however, quickly preoccupied her. She wrote a letter to the *Sentinel*, bemoaning the press coverage that seemed "intent on destroying each next best and most viable candidate with its version of Trivial Pursuit" and declaring herself for Simon. A longer version of the letter, with more detailed praise for her new candidate, was mailed from Simon headquarters to two hundred Democrats on her voter list, and she followed it up with personal calls to invite them to an organizational meeting. Finding a Keene headquarters was a task to which she accorded great importance. Once a vacant space was located (on a second story across the corner from the Dukakis office), she waited impatiently for the day that she and the newly hired coordinator could move in, get phones installed, and start calling people in the evenings.

In her assessment, Gore had moved too far to the right, Gephardt and Babbitt weren't going anywhere, and with Hart and Biden gone (and Pat Schroeder deciding against running), the choice for Democrats she had talked to had narrowed to being between Simon and Jackson. As for Dukakis, "they're not forgetting what he did to Biden—and I'm not talking about just Biden people, either."

One weekend she drove to Newport, about an hour north of Keene, to attend a Simon reception. Her original purpose was to see her candidate in person for the first time, but she ended up manning the sign-up table at the door while she was there. To her pleasant surprise, she found Simon "anything *but* lackluster; I was really impressed: it's nice to be impressed with the candidate you support." Simon really had been boring in the past, she insisted, but he must have worked on his delivery, because he was now much improved: "I was totally amazed, totally surprised at the way he came across. I like him."

In late October Simon came to Keene for a speech at Keene State College. Andi took off the morning to work the event she had helped organize. With her car washed and cleaned, she drove to the airport to pick up the candidate.

"Andi," Simon said as he climbed into the front seat next to her, "we met in . . ."

"Newport," she offered.

"Newport. That's right. I'm told you're a very hard worker. Tell me about yourself. Where were you born?"

As she related a brief biography, Simon's aide worked on several notecards in the backseat—reminders to announce the opening of the Keene office and to publicly thank Andi for her efforts.

"What should I say to this crowd?" Simon asked the two of them. "The standard pitch?"

"The standard pitch," the aide said. "Education—this is a state college—arms control, Central America." Andi agreed.

The crowd was large—several hundred people, most of them students, but a scattering of people Andi had called—and Andi stood contentedly by the side door as Simon spoke, smiling and nodding when he mentioned her name. After the speech she hovered at a near distance with the aide as Simon mingled and chatted with the audience.

At her car she took Simon aside quickly to tell him that Pat Russell would be riding with them, that Pat was a national committee-woman and former Biden stalwart and would be a valuable addition to the local campaign.

"Is she ready to come over?" Simon asked.

"Not yet," Andi answered. She felt she had finally moved up the ladder of campaign jobs: a candidate had asked for her advice on a speech, had mentioned her name publicly, and now had relied on her personal political judgment.

They all climbed in, and Andi drove them off. On her rear bumper was a shiny new Simon sticker. Just before arriving at the airport earlier in the morning, Andi had remembered to stop and slap it on over a faded Hart decal. The Biden sticker had pulled off easily.

Dukakis was in Keene the same week, also for a speech at Keene State College. The state director would later refer to this event as part of a "turnaround": an overflow crowd created an air of infectious excitement that seemed to touch everyone, including the candidate, and to lift the dark fog of uncertainty and lethargy that had haunted the campaign since Sasso's departure. It was something of a turnaround period for Molly, as well. She had been feeling her way tentatively up to now—testing but not entirely trusting her political instincts and searching for a balance in her life among the familiar demands of work and motherhood and the new, alluring, but seemingly unending demands of the campaign. "Sometimes I'll be ironing or doing the dishes, thinking about the campaign," she said, "and suddenly it will hit me: Hey, this is the presidency of the United States we're talking about. Then it's back to ironing and dishes."

With the success of Dukakis's appearance, Molly became more confident of her political abilities. And, though the tug of competing demands would be a constant throughout the primary, she came to grips with it by clearly recognizing each strand's place in her life and acknowledging her own limits.

"I have to remind myself I can only do so much," she said in the days leading up to Dukakis's speech. "A campaign isn't something where you can say, 'Everything's done,' because there's always more to do. All you can hope to say is, 'We've done all we could do.' " Her role on the campaign was bringing her more into the public, with occasional duties of speaking at small gatherings such as local meetings of NOW (the National Organization of Women), League of Women Voters, or an association of university women, in addition to leading organizational meetings of Dukakis volunteers. She was slowly becoming more comfortable with it—her children were her best critics when she practiced—and the notion that people saw her as a representative of a presidential campaign was no longer quite so disconcerting.

The campaign was pushing to expand its base of support, but Molly intuitively felt it necessary not only to recruit volunteers, but to keep them engaged and interested. They needed to have some fun and to feel important as they were expected to take on more tasks. In that respect it was a lot like raising children. She noticed, for instance, that many of the volunteers didn't get their call lists completed if they were asked to do it from their home—even though that might seem to be easier. They did better if they were brought to the local headquarters and made their calls among other volunteers doing the same thing. "So much of my energy is already spent with the people we have," she said of the push for more supporters. "Encouraging them, making sure they're called, thanked, and rewarded. There's a lot of 'stroking' in this."

The multitude of projects—list management, organizing for statewide caucuses to elect delegates to a party convention, planning for the next canvass, and preparing for visits by Dukakis and campaign surrogates—and the intense, tunnel vision atmosphere emanating from state headquarters that methodically concentrated on accomplishing things according to schedule threatened constantly to overwhelm the rest of her life. "Sometimes," she said, "I have to step back and say, 'Wait. Is this me? Is this coming from me?' It's easy to let them and their tasks and my own focus on success and winning take over and define me."

In the days before Dukakis's visit, the desire to assure a big crowd and a successful evening consumed her thoughts. She lost sleep worrying about it. (Mike Cook had the same anxieties. The night before Dukakis arrived, he had three nightmares. In the first, no one showed up. In the second, too many people arrived and a lot of them couldn't get in. The third surrealistically combined the first two: not enough and too many at the same time.) "I want to pack that speech," Molly said. "I want them spilling into the streets."

The speech was actually sponsored by a group lobbying for greater federal assistance to long-term health care, part of a series of forums it was holding in New Hampshire with a different presidential candidate at each. It was a dry topic, one not normally expected to draw many people. Molly and Mike decided to have their volunteers call everyone on their lists of potential supporters and simply say that Dukakis was speaking at the college and invite them to attend, without mentioning the principal topic. They distributed fliers in the college community to the same effect.

A half hour before the event, the small library room the health group had reserved was jammed with one hundred people, and twice that number was standing outside. Molly's hope and Mike's second nightmare seemed to be unfolding. They scurried to bring in more chairs but quickly realized the futility of trying to squeeze the growing crowd into the room they had. Molly conferred with a college official and soon announced that the speech was being moved to a larger lecture hall down the street. She and Mike supervised the migration. The move seemed to heighten a sense of suspense and excitement in the proceedings. As most political advance men know, there is nothing like the sight of people clamoring to get into an event—even if it is the result of a hall that's too small to begin with—to intensify a feeling of political energy and generate a mood of momentum.

When Dukakis appeared, four hundred people were waiting. He gave a prepared speech on the need for the federal government to expand its coverage of long-term health costs, answered a few questions about the issue, and, realizing that a large part of the audience was there for other reasons, opened up for questions on other topics. The crowd responded enthusiastically.

Molly stood by the door, constantly scanning the audience for affirmation that things were going smoothly and searching for faces she recognized from her lists. (Afterward she wouldn't be able to summarize or remember anything her candidate had said; she had been too intent on the crowd.) Her attention was also riveted on the front row, where a line of elderly people sat in wheelchairs listening to Dukakis. They represented a "pet project" of Molly's, an idea she had come up with on her own and had spent considerable time planning.

In the month and a half since he had arrived as coordinator, Mike Cook had developed a friendly, ongoing debate with Molly about the role of "issues" and grass-roots organizing in politics, a kind of repartee the two engaged in and kidded each other about during long hours at the local headquarters. Molly might start it by discussing the need to keep the volunteers happy or the importance of the personal touch in reaching voters. Mike would say things like "I come from Texas, and the way we campaign there is raise money and spend it on commercials." If Molly tried to start a bull session about, say, the Democratic candidates' positions on day care, Mike would revert to his role as the hardened, cynical operative. "You're an issues person," he would say. "But politics isn't about issues."

As they had set about work on attracting the largest-possible crowd to Dukakis's speech, partly by downplaying or even totally ignoring its proposed topic, Molly had decided to contact a nursing home near the college. There were elderly people there who would enjoy getting out for an evening, she decided, and who would have an obvious personal interest in the issue being discussed. It would be a nice gesture, and if the older people's appreciation extended to Dukakis and his campaign, so much the better. Then she added an additional touch to her plan: she put her three children in charge of executing the project. This would bring them into the campaign, develop in them a sense of responsibility, and show them that politics had a purpose—all in one stroke. "I like the challenge and the puzzle of the campaign," she said at the time, "but it's important that you try to succeed for something with meaning."

Zach, Justin, and Rachel—with some friends they recruited— showed up at the nursing home the night of the speech and led a caravan of wheelchairs, one helper per old person, down the street and into the space Molly had reserved for them. When the event was moved, the caravan moved with it. As she watched her children sitting attentively next to the people they had wheeled to the speech, Molly felt a warm rush of satisfaction. She was proud of them—and pleased with herself for thinking of the project. When Dukakis finished speaking she rushed to the podium and directed him to the line of wheelchairs so he could shake each person's hand (including the children's) before the rest of the audience crowded in.

Before Dukakis left she got another burst of gratification. On his way to his limousine—Pat Russell was waiting in the backseat; the campaign hoped Dukakis could sway her for support—he turned to his state director, who had driven over from Manchester for the event.

"Who was responsible for this great crowd?" he asked, clearly energized himself from the audience's size and enthusiasm. For a campaign not noted for excitement, this had been a big night.

The state director pointed at Molly, who was standing nearby, and, as Dukakis turned to follow the pointing finger, said one word: "Her."

9

STALLED

As if they were all following photocopies of the same organizational manual, the presidential campaigns moved through the final third of 1987 in virtual lockstep. The sluggish political pace of summer gave way to a quicker tempo as the leaves turned gold and crimson and then dropped to earth, and New Hampshire descended into the chill of winter. Candidates showed up in the Monadnock Region with greater frequency, the most visible signal that the campaigns were turning up the heat several notches. In the four months between Labor Day and New Year's Eve, the field of twelve candidates running for their parties' nominations made a total of nineteen trips to Cheshire County—only four less than they had made during the first eight months of the year. The primary was just around the corner, not yet within sight. But in the mental calendar of each activist, February 16, 1988, loomed like a larger and larger presence that they could now feel, if not see, awaiting them just beyond the turn of the year.

In Cheshire County most of the campaigns ripened to organizational maturity in early autumn. There were a few exceptions. Although each made appearances in the region, Haig and du Pont still lacked any local effort, an absence that would persist right through the day of voting. Dole and Jackson, whose campaigns had been locally dormant throughout most of 1987, finally showed signs of life. Jackson's campaign held its first organizational meeting in Keene in early September, drawing a handful of supporters; two weeks later, after a mailing of 250 invitations, eight people showed up for the second. Several busloads of Jackson volunteers, most from campuses in Massachusetts, arrived on a Saturday in mid-November for a door-to-door canvass. Dole's first Cheshire County campaign meeting, in late October, drew forty people, but to the dismay of the few avid Dole partisans in the region, the campaign seemed unable to follow up this tardy, yet initially promising, start. Like a late planting in soil already hardening for winter and then neglected instead of carefully nurtured, the organizational seed did not take root.

The other campaigns, however, were already in full gear by the end of September. Whether they used a pyramid structure (Doug Kidd's model for Robertson), the Cotton system (Kemp), a quota for a steering committee (Bush), or an elaborate mix of canvassing and phoning (Dukakis), all of them had the identical objective: expand from the small circle of core supporters toward the magic number of 55,000 votes. And regardless of what names they gave to their techniques, all of them employed the same tools: the lists, the mail, the phones, the candidate appearances, but most of all the personal contacts by the campaigns' local partisans. Six campaigns dispatched paid coordinators to Cheshire County in September to augment their local organizations, and several of the Democrats opened Keene headquarters. A block-and-a-half walk up Main Street to Central Square in the fall would encounter offices for Gephardt, Dukakis, Simon, and Gore—and then Jackson in December.

But as they all strove to move forward, all of them encountered the same, frustrating roadblock. The ready supply of activists was exhausted. Both parties had some strays—like Bruce Anderson, still undecided; or Pat Russell, abruptly available with the disappearance of Biden—not yet committed to a candidate. Little room for dramatic expansion existed, however, within the population of activists, and the traditional courtship rituals that had dominated the earlier phase were quietly abandoned. With their organizations so firmly in place, the natural imperative, therefore, was to forge into the next phase: reaching out beyond the confines of the small population of the politically attuned toward the voters at large.

The problem was that the voters seemed singularly resistant to being reached. Their own calendars told them it was still 1987, not yet an election year, and they saw little reason to pay much attention yet to the campaign, let alone be rushed into choosing a candidate. This race for president may have begun earlier than ever before (the first local headquarters in the previous primary didn't open until January 1984), and the political community of candidates, aides, fund-raisers, reporters, and activists may have adjusted their organizational clocks several months forward, like some sort of political daylight savings time taken to absurd lengths. But, as the campaigns would gradually realize, the voters wouldn't be budged from following their traditional timetable, which called for beginning serious deliberations only when the actual day to cast their ballots was imminent. If the two timetables were now months out of sync, that was the campaigns' problem, not the voters'. It was as if two parallel universes—the campaigns' and the public's—were existing without intersecting in Cheshire County, the latter one blithely oblivious to the other one struggling vainly to break through and make contact.

The campaign staffs and volunteers were busier than ever before. They tried to engage more people and infect them with the same political fever the hard-core activists had been running for some time. In truth, however, during this time they had little to show for all their efforts. Despite repeated exposure, the voters were seemingly immune.

Unintentionally, the activists' energy therefore focused once again on themselves: minor competitions, political plots, and anxieties whose victories and defeats consumed their thoughts and were occasionally the grist of political pundits in the press but were little noticed by the larger community around them. The campaign engines were running at higher RPMs now, and to the volunteers and workers behind the wheel and locked inside, it seemed as if the race were picking up speed. To everyone else, it was clear that they were just spinning their wheels.

The six campaign coordinators assigned to Cheshire County not only arrived at about the same time, around Labor Day, but seemed so similar in age, background, circumstances, and temperament as to have been cast from a single mold. They were all in their early twenties, not long out of college, housed by volunteers and paid equivalent amounts (from $500 to $800 a month, depending on whether their gasoline expenses were covered), energetic and keenly competitive, at least slightly experienced in politics and government (both in and outside of college), and initially committed more to the excitement of being involved in the race for president than to the candidate for whom they worked.

The local volunteers uniformly welcomed the coordinators' arrival. A full-time staff member in the area was a sign that the state headquarters considered Cheshire County—although it represented only 6 percent of the statewide vote in either party—seriously and, by implication, recognized the volunteers' own importance in the presidential sweepstakes. Even though a coordinator answered directly to the headquarters staff, not the local organization, he or she quickly became viewed not as the campaign's emissary to supervise the locals, but as *their* staff person and *their* representative to the statewide effort and its decision making.

The campaigns, of course, saw it a little differently. Unlike a volunteer, a paid staff member could be ordered, rather than requested, to do something and could be counted on to devote his or her every minute, not just spare time, to completing the myriad campaign tasks. As an outsider the coordinator was required to fit in well with the pool of local volunteers but was also expected to provide a political judgment independent of whatever parochial or personal biases might skew those of the community members.

The common interest—that the candidate get the most votes

possible from the county—overarched the two viewpoints, however, and the locals appreciated having a coordinator in their midst as much as the state headquarters wanted one there. Besides, for the volunteers who had already expended so much exertion in the cause, the arrival of a coordinator provided not only some relief from the load of work, but also another person—so unlike the voters at this point—whose waking moments were immersed in the campaign.

Mike Haas, twenty-three, had graduated in January from Harvard University, where he had studied government and economics and been the backup quarterback on the football team. In the fall of his senior year, when many of his classmates were interviewing for jobs on Wall Street, Haas seemed headed in the same direction and went through the recruiting process with investment and commercial banks. But he had decided instead on a taste of politics. A career could wait. He had served as an intern in the governor's office in his home state of Wisconsin one summer and enjoyed the variety of tasks and people he met. A presidential campaign would be the same, he figured, only on a larger scale. The Dukakis campaign, his first contact, was looking for volunteers instead of staff members at the time, so he tried Gephardt's Washington office. He had loans to pay off and needed at least minimal pay. Gephardt hired him but couldn't use him until fall. He went home, painted and roofed houses for the summer, bought a 1972 Buick LeSabre for $500, and headed toward New Hampshire, surviving flat tires and failed brakes on the way. Within the campaign he found the variety and competitive excitement he had sought, although it sometimes seemed he was carrying part of the Gephardt campaign's debt on his Visa card, where his gas expenses mounted without prompt reimbursement. When he talked to the friends who had gone to Wall Street, they uniformly complained of long working days without enjoyment—but the money was great. "Now," he joked in late fall in the Gephardt office, where he was putting in fifteen-hour days, "I not only don't have time to relax, I don't have the money." But he didn't regret his decision.

Jon Meyer, the Gore coordinator, was another Harvard graduate—1986, with a degree in social studies. Active in student government and politics in his high school in Cincinnati and in college,
he had gone to work for his hometown congressman in Washington,
D.C., which he considered an interlude before pursuing a career
in the law. As the presidential campaigns began, he decided first
that he wanted to join one; and later he set about finding which
one. He interviewed with the Simon and Gore campaigns. Simon's
was in the midst of a hiring freeze, so when Gore's offered him the
Keene job he took it and then asked, "Where's Keene?" Campaign
work, he discovered, was a big change from Capitol Hill. The pay
was worse, the hours longer, and the resources backing him up
were scantier, but the responsibilities and challenges seemed
greater, and he had freer rein to make his own decisions. "It's scary
sometimes," he said. "There's a lot of weight on my shoulders. It's
up to me to get them [the volunteers and the voters] to like Al Gore."
The emotional swings connected with his work were also more
extreme: from depression and complete frustration to near ecstasy.
The family that gave him a room to sleep in actually supported
Simon. Their high school–aged daughter said she liked Jack Kemp
the best but ended up helping Jon many evenings in the Gore office.

Lisa Babish was sent to Cheshire County by the Babbitt campaign
when the young coordinator it originally planned to assign to the
region didn't work out. She had been out of Cornell, where she'd
studied public policy, for two years and had held jobs in private
industry ("which convinced me I didn't want a career in business,"
she said) near her home in Rochester, New York, and then in
government with a Pennsylvania congressman. Her political interests had been honed as a college intern with the Justice Department. "It just seemed like it was time to put some action behind
my espoused views to make a difference," she said of her decision
to join a campaign. She planned to attend law school and eventually
become a civil rights lawyer once the campaign ended. Biden attracted her originally—she went to his announcement of candidacy
and was moved by his oratory—but when she watched the Houston

debate on television, she found herself thinking of Babbitt: "I like what he says. It's too bad [from his performance] he'll never get elected. Then I said, 'That's the attitude I detest.' You should never say 'can't.' If you like him and what he says, you should go with him. We're not electing an actor." That argument—and her bubbly personality—became her principal weapons in fighting for Babbitt.

For Pete Kujawski, a twenty-two-year-old from Long Island, the intensity of a political campaign was its principal attraction. As a student at New England College in Henniker, New Hampshire, he had been drawn to politics through a summer job with a citizen action group and was head of the college's political awareness committee. During his last semester, in the spring of 1987, he had been named the Hart campaign's campus representative and was scheduled to take on a paid job in the summer. Then Hart dropped out. When summer arrived he set out in his car to travel the country, but from phone booths along the way he kept contacting the remaining campaigns. In California, where he learned that Biden had also dropped out, he was finally hired on the phone by the Simon campaign and headed back east. His reason for staying involved seemed to make him perfectly suited to join Andi Johnson, with whom he would work through the primary: "I don't think I *couldn't* do it. I thrive on Dracula hours. I live for the intensity of a campaign."

Mike Cook's first choice of a candidate had also been Gary Hart. Growing up near Dallas, Texas, he had always looked on politics as something of a hobby. He read Teddy White's *Making of a President* series in junior high school and was fascinated by the process; it "seemed like a chess game," he said. He entered Texas A&M in 1982 as a free-market, anticommunist political conservative, but the young Republicans he encountered there seemed to him to define their conservatism as protecting social and economic privilege and denying it to others. He became instead a populist Democrat and ran several classmates' campaigns for student office against the campus establishment. After graduating in 1986 in economics, he worked on a congressional campaign and then the

mayoral race in Dallas, where, after watching a campaign commercial being shot, he decided, "This is what I'd like to do." The
mayor's media consultant was also Hart's, and Mike was pursuing
the connection for a campaign job when Hart suddenly became a
noncandidate. When the Houston debate took place, he volunteered
to help the Dukakis team and ended up as the driver for John Sasso,
the campaign manager. "I was a little nervous," he said. "Presidential politics seemed pretty glamorous." After telling Sasso he
wanted a campaign job, he took the bus to Boston, and hung around
the headquarters until, by chance, he started talking to the New
England coordinator, who sent him to New Hampshire to meet the
staff there. (On his first day in the state, where he was put up in
the house of a Democratic activist, he walked downstairs and saw
Bruce Babbitt sitting in the living room with his staff, reviewing
tapes of past debates.) Dukakis's New Hampshire director hired
him for the opening in Keene. Mike took the bus back to Texas,
packed his bags, ate some good Mexican food, drove to Houston to
see his girlfriend, and then set out for Cheshire County. He arrived
the day Molly Kelly was moving into the new Keene office, got out
his Rolodex, and started work.

Pete Johnson was the only comparable Republican coordinator
for the county. (Doug Kidd was a paid staff member for Robertson,
but his area encompassed nearly half the state. Dole's campaign
would finally send in a coordinator in the last weeks before the
primary. Haig and du Pont had a relatively tiny staff in the state
and no one assigned for the western portion. And the Kemp campaign, which also had a smaller paid staff in New Hampshire,
figured that a volunteer like Al Rubega was more than sufficient.)
Pete's father had been active in Colorado politics, and from the time
he held a campaign placard for a congressional candidate at age
three, Pete's goal was to go to Washington. As a student at Occi-
dental College in California, where he studied government and
economics, he was a congressional intern for a year, then worked
on a Colorado campaign after graduation in 1986, went back to
Washington for a job with the commission on the Constitution's

bicentennial, and finally decided he preferred another campaign to "pushing paper in D.C." When the Bush campaign sent him to Cheshire County in August, he was to be "temporarily" located at Kendall Lane's home. He stayed there for the remainder of the primary, turning their den into an unofficial Bush headquarters, something Kendall would occasionally—and clearly disingenuously—complain about. Kendall loved having Pete around: it gave him an excuse to stay up late at night discussing political strategy, exchanging campaign intelligence and anecdotes, and, when Jane wasn't around, smoking cigarettes again.

All six coordinators performed essentially the same tasks. They worked the lists. They visited and called the committed volunteers, handing out new assignments and spreading words of encouragement with the latest "line" and "spin" on what their campaigns were saying about the status of the race. They helped organize and staff their candidates' local appearances—or often checked in on other candidates' events to size up the competition. And, heeding the relentless directive from their bosses at state headquarters to keep adding names to their candidates' column, they searched constantly for more volunteers. In doing so, they encountered considerable disappointment. The easy pickings had been taken, and the remaining possible converts were biding their time before committing themselves. "There's a guy in Troy who's going to be a town chairman," Pete Johnson said in late September with a combination of bravado and frustration. "He just doesn't know it yet." Pete could understand someone saying he or she preferred another candidate because of some ideological fervor, but he always chafed when some of them told him they were backing Kemp "because I promised Al Rubega." That didn't seem like a good enough answer.

Some of the other coordinators began to question both the entire process of the New Hampshire primary and their own impact as field organizers on the outcome. "Coming from Wisconsin, we're lucky if we even *see* a candidate," said Mike Haas. "Here some of the people say, 'I want to see him again, I want to see him in a different setting.'" Some of the demands reflected a distortion of the way he had thought the primary was supposed to work. "They preach the gospel of grass-roots organizing," he said, "when what they really want is to be kingmakers." After an intense effort to turn out people to local Democratic caucuses that would elect delegates to the state convention—intense because the campaigns knew that the press would poll the crowd as an early measure of candidates' strength—an exhausted Mike Cook said, "It's not really grass-roots politics, but another part of the media show." By the end of the year he believed that "Michael Dukakis is going to win or lose New Hampshire, not based on how good a job Mike Cook does. People are a lot more independent of the campaigns than you think. It's hard to compete with the TV in everyone's houses."

Whatever their private doubts and aggravations, however, the thrill of the race, their single-minded pursuit of victory, their desire to do their utmost, and their gradual identification of their own success with that of their candidates always won out in the end. Despite their occasional cynicism about the New Hampshire process, all of them believed in politics as an important endeavor. And, among the core of volunteers that they had been assigned (or to whom they had been assigned), they all forged deep and lasting friendships.

As the fall progressed, the young coordinators also got to know one another. Keene is not a large city, and that long before the primary the political circles were even smaller. As a normal consequence of their duties, they bumped into one another at various functions and, being young and single, often headed to a bar together at a long day's end to talk about their shared topic of exclusive interest: politics. Their heightened sense of competition prevented them from exchanging any sensitive tactical information, but they were still bonded by a certain camaraderie. Like a small band of missionaries from different sects in a foreign land, they were emerging political operatives whose only connection with the community was their individual desire to understand and then convert it before moving on.

In late September, twelve people gathered in a function room of the Keene Public Library to discuss the presidential primary. None of them supported a candidate, nor had any of them turned out for any of the many campaign appearances that had already been held in the county. The speaker they came to hear was not a member of any campaign organization. Although the meeting included all the trappings of traditional campaign gatherings—nametags, handouts of position papers, a short speech, a question-and-answer period, and, of course, a sign-up sheet to put the names of activists into a computerized mailing list—the goal was not furthering any particular candidate's chances, but advancing a cause.

The organizer, a young woman, worked for Vote Environment, a project sponsored by a coalition of environmental and conservation groups to "demonstrate to presidential candidates how important environmental issues are to New Hampshire voters and to the entire nation." Her mission in Keene—as in other such meetings being held across the state—was to recruit and train people to attend candidates' appearances, ask them questions about environmental policy (a list of twelve sample questions was distributed), record the answers on yellow forms, and mail them to the project headquarters. She spent an hour explaining the process and leading the attendees through a series of role-playing exercises so they could learn "how to pin the candidates down with your questions."

Vote Environment was neither the first nor the only interest group to see the New Hampshire primary (and the Iowa caucuses) as a golden opportunity. With so many would-be presidents devoting so much time and intensity toward wooing a relatively small number of voters, with so much media attention focused on the opening of the election season, and with the spiraling synergy of political importance that resulted—the more effort the candidates poured into New Hampshire, the more the press accorded it coverage; the heightened coverage spurred even greater exertion by the campaigns; and so on—the primary had become a logical staging ground for organizations with a cause they wanted to bring to the attention of both the candidates and the public. Just like the campaigns, the interest groups also considered New Hampshire's small size and population as easy to manage organizationally. A modest investment of money and staff could provide a disproportionately immense amount of political leverage.

The rise of interest group and "cause" politics was relatively new in the primary's thirty-six-year history. To be sure, the 1968 Democratic race had been defined by a cause and single issue: the Vietnam War. Young college students swarmed over the state, knocking on doors and phoning voters with the message that if you didn't like the war, you should vote for Gene McCarthy. But the first major instance of an interest group using the primary to "educate" and influence the candidates and to highlight its own issue, rather than to support a particular candidate, was in 1980, when the Gun Owners of New Hampshire hosted a statewide gathering of its membership. All the presidential contenders of both parties were invited to speak. (Except for Ted Kennedy, who declined to attend, and Jimmy Carter, who sent his son to represent him, all of the candidates attended, from Jerry Brown to Lyndon Larouche, John Anderson to Ronald Reagan, and four others.) In the 1984 primary groups aligned with the nuclear freeze movement, with the push for environmental controls on acid rain, and with an interest in national security issues followed GO:NH's lead.

When the 1988 primary cycle began, every conceivable group seemed eager to get into the act. Besides Vote Environment, which in addition to dispatching recruits to candidate appearances held a candidates forum, there were the individual candidate forums, like the one Dukakis attended in Keene, devoted exclusively to long-term health care. Regional groups of the state's homebuilders' association invited candidates as well—Al Haig spoke to Cheshire County's, releasing a policy statement on housing and suggesting that the growing number of homeless people in America provided a potential growth market. People opposing the Seabrook nuclear power plant formed Search '88, mailed a questionnaire to the candidates to get their views on nuclear power, and held a press conference to announce the results. The association of real estate agents had Team '88, which, like the homebuilders' association, invited candidates to regional meetings—du Pont spoke at Keene's, promising to preserve the tax deduction on second homes. The American Association of Retired Persons (AARP) produced a large brochure outlining its own view and each candidate's position on eight issues affecting the elderly and mailed it as a "voter guide" to all of its New Hampshire members. The state's antiabortion groups held a convention in October; Kemp and Robertson were the only candidates to accept their invitation to debate. The Physicians for Social Responsibility asked each candidate to answer questions about a comprehensive test ban treaty, Star Wars, and arms control, produced a brochure on the answers it received from those who responded, and urged its supporters to ask again at public receptions. A nonpartisan group, U.S. 88: A New Road to the White House, had no single issue it wanted to promote but rather hoped to elevate the political discussion by focusing on the major policy decisions facing the next president. It organized "citizen assemblies" for role-playing games in which the participants pretended to be congressmen or persons in policymaking positions and therefore learned more about the issues. It also hosted "town meetings" for candidate debates and produced a lengthy brochure outlining the candidates' responses to questions on everything from farm credit and the budget deficit to nuclear proliferation.

None of these groups had the candidates' preeminent interest— winning in February—in mind. On the contrary, for most of them "victory" would have been to swing the entire field of candidates over to their point of view on their particular special interest. The candidates' electoral fortunes were immaterial in comparison. The campaigns understood this and, in varying degrees, resented it. Nevertheless they couldn't entirely ignore the different groups' forums, questionnaires, and "plants" in the audiences. With so much riding on the votes of so few people, deliberately snubbing even a small number of people aligned around a single issue was a risk few of the campaigns wanted to take. Besides, a number of the groups were as highly organized as the campaigns. If the candidate wouldn't come to them or answer written questionnaires, they could come to the candidates' events. Particularly during the big gap of the fall and early winter, when most of the political activists had already been recruited but the general population was still unengaged in the race, it sometimes seemed that the primary campaign was being waged in a claustrophobic room filled with people already committed exclusively to either a candidate or a cause. No one else was paying any attention.

All of the local coordinators and volunteers encountered this phenomenon. Mike Cook knew a fellow Dukakis coordinator who was trying to get the candidate to change one of his environmental positions simply to win over a handful of people. Doug Kidd and Helen Bouchie spent a Saturday manning a Robertson table at the antiabortion forum. "It was more a competition between the candidates [Robertson and Kemp] than a discussion of the issue," Doug reported. "It's unfortunate, once you start doing something like that with an issue . . . it just gets to be like a bidding procedure." Kendall Lane was invited by a local real estate agent to du Pont's speech; Kendall went out of his way to point out the number of empty seats to the *Sentinel* reporter covering the event. Dick Gephardt appeared at a meeting of the Monadnock Peace Coalition, which had two sign-up sheets at a table near the front door—one for the group's mailing list, which everyone signed, and one that the group leader said was "optional" for people who wanted to be on the candidate's mailing list. Only four of the thirty participants put their names down on it.

In early December each of the local campaigns was contacted by a group opposed to the irradiation of food (a process used to sterilize some foods and increase their shelf life). The coordinators were told that 150 to 200 people were expected to turn out for a meeting, and each campaign was invited to present its candidate's position on the issue. Pete Kujawski hurriedly phoned Simon's Senate office and had material faxed to him to prepare his presentation. Molly Kelly enlisted one of the state's leading antinuclear activists, who supported Dukakis, to join her at the event and do the speaking. Lisa Babish showed up for Babbitt. Jon Meyer stayed up all night drafting a lengthy position paper on behalf of Gore, made 150 copies of it to distribute, and rehearsed his oratory. When they all arrived they found a grand total of eighteen people (including Shelley Nelkens) waiting for them. No one signed on for a campaign.

Al Gore came to Keene in mid-November for a home reception (attended by sixteen people) and a speech at Keene State College, where he was introduced by a student who was working for Dukakis, and the audience included Lisa Babish, the Babbitt coordinator. The questions he got following the speech were about a nuclear test ban (from a member of Beyond War, reading one of the questions from Physicians for Social Responsibility), foreign policy in the Persian Gulf (from a college professor who supported Jackson), nursing home costs (from a person reading from a card prepared in advance), toxic waste (from Vote Environment's representative, also reading from a notecard), nuclear waste (from Search '88), and soil conservation (from a representative of yet another group that had mailed questionnaires to the candidates).

"I think things are going well," Tom Britton told Gore as the candidate prepared to leave.

"It turned around when you signed on," Gore said, and laughed.

"It was the bottle of Jack Daniel's," Tom joked.

Then Gore turned to Jon Meyer before getting into the car. "Pretty soon," he said, more seriously, "we've got to shift from talking to activists to talking to voters."

On a cold night in November representatives from all six Democratic campaigns found themselves loitering outside Pat Russell's house in Keene. There were fourteen in all, and they joked and laughed as they waited, feeling a little silly and ridiculous about their shared situation.

Inside the house, the mood was more somber. Fifteen local Democrats, about half of them former Biden supporters, were sitting in the living room, trying to decide whom to support for president.

They had summoned the campaign representatives to make presentations. In alphabetical order, according to the candidate's last name, each campaign group was ushered in the front door, seated on chairs in the middle of the room, allowed ten minutes to make their case, asked about three questions, and then directed to the back door, while the next campaign was invited in through the front.

Lisa Babish and Dan Burnham from the Babbitt campaign were first. Dan was nervous and, in the warmth of the crowded room, began to sweat as he spoke. He recounted why he had chosen Babbitt—the former governor's record on environmental issues and commitment to improved child care, Babbitt's life history, but most of all the personal qualities of the man, who, Dan said, had a keen intellect and appealing strength of character.

"How does he plan to deal with the military's nuclear waste?" was the first question. Dan said he didn't know. Lisa interjected that Babbitt believed nuclear waste should be stored in less populated sections of the West, rather than in the East, but the questioner interrupted that she had hoped his solution would be to stop making the waste entirely.

After a question on the deficit (Babbitt had proposed a consumption tax, which Lisa outlined in detail), another person asked what was on the group's mind about all the Democratic candidates: "How can he win?" Dan was particularly familiar with that issue. Despite his growing admiration of Babbitt, he harbored the same doubts about his candidate. Like all the other long-shot campaigns of 1988, he offered Hart's surprising meteoric rise in 1984 as the model of hope. Babbitt would do well in the Iowa caucuses and build on that in New Hampshire, he said. "He blew one debate seriously in Houston," he admitted, "but look at the press he's been getting recently." He handed out some favorable clippings. "They're all beginning to say Babbitt's the one to watch. I think he's starting to roll."

The Dukakis campaign was next. Molly Kelly entered with Charles Baker, the state director, and another staff member from the headquarters. Baker did the talking, stressing Dukakis's stand-ing in the polls in a variety of primary states, his lead in fund-raising, and his record as governor of Massachusetts. After questions about the deficit, whether Dukakis could win in Novem-ber, and his lack of Washington experience, all of which Baker answered, they were dismissed. Molly had sat silently throughout the presentation—"it felt like being in a church," she said afterward. But on the way out she invited them all to visit the Keene office. She wanted them on *her* turf at least once before they made a decision.

Mike Haas also brought along his state director for Gephardt, as well as Richard Daschbach, the campaign's leading local volunteer. Again, the principal pitch was that their candidate was best situated to win—he was leading in Iowa, had an organization in place in New Hampshire, and could appeal to southern Democrats in the multiprimaries that would follow. The questions were about his legislative priorities, whether his record in Congress matched his campaign positions, and wasn't he slipping in the Iowa polls.

Tom Britton did the talking for the Gore campaign, although for support he brought along Jon Meyer, the local coordinator, and a member of the state staff. "One of the most important issues is electability," he said, adding that Gore represented the best chance for a Democratic victory in the general election. Although he didn't say so, Tom disagreed with a number of Gore's positions, particu-larly his foreign policy. When Gore had been at Keene State College a week earlier and had been asked to defend his support for U.S. involvement in protecting the sea traffic in the Persian Gulf, Tom had shaken his head. "That answer was a bunch of shit," he had confided later. "The Monroe Doctrine is trooped out when it serves our purposes. And it's the same with freedom of the sea lanes." But tonight Tom focused on the argument he had used on himself: Gore's voting record was more liberal than his media image sug-gested. His rating by the liberal Americans for Democratic Action (ADA)—a "litmus test for Democrats," Tom said—was 90 percent, the highest of any of the candidates. "Despite being portrayed as a conservative, which serves the campaign well, he's actually in the Democratic mainstream," Tom assured them. The questions were about chemical weapons, Gore's plan for his first hundred days in office, his age, and a concern that the last Democratic president who thought he had to be "tough on defense" got America into the Vietnam War.

Chuck Weed, a local college professor (who had asked Gore the Persian Gulf question at Keene State College), made the pitch for Jackson: he was the candidate with both "vision" and a concern for the "people who need the most help." The group asked about Jackson's lack of experience in elected office, his local organization, his plans for the deficit, and, most pointedly, his electability. Weed said Jackson was doing well in the national polls once Hart and Biden had dropped out, but that, win or lose, Jackson was an important force in the party. In New Hampshire, he said, "Dukakis is a shoo-in, and I'd be happy to support him eventually. But supporting Jackson is important in this all-white state. Decent human beings should vote to reflect their conscience. There are a lot of racists out there, but I'm not one of them."

Andi Johnson didn't come to the meeting to represent Simon. She was in an angry and aggravated mood, and she thought it better to send two people from the state headquarters. Simon was on a bit of a media roll himself, but the campaign had yet to install phones in the Keene office, which constantly frustrated Andi. ("I don't like the solitude," she complained.) She couldn't take advantage of the favorable press by working the phones. Worse in her mind, she thought about ten of the people in Pat Russell's living room were already leaning toward Simon, and the notion that they were going through this review process thoroughly miffed her. "We need the help *now*," she said. Her surrogates handed out a recent poll showing Simon closing in on Dukakis in New Hampshire and stressed their candidate's integrity. They were asked about Simon's position on nuclear power, the Nuclear Regulatory Commission, and his electability and then were shown the door.

The interrogations had taken two hours, but the group still had a lot of business to transact, although they were unsure how to proceed. "Let's eliminate some of them tonight, and then bring back the *candidates* we want," one suggested. "We're in a position to have them come." They went around the room, each person offering thoughts about individual candidates and the status of the race or general thoughts about moderates and liberals. Pat Russell wondered whether they should start a movement to draft New York's Mario Cuomo, who, it was reported, was considering a run for the presidency in spite of his public professions of disinterest.

"Do we feel any closer [to a decision]?" one person asked after the first go-round. They agreed they weren't.

"We need a process," another suggested. "Should we consider them in terms of purists, electability, money?"

Another general discussion ensued, which only reached a conclusion that, as one person stated it, "all of them have an electability flaw."

After forty-five minutes they decided to try to eliminate some candidates. Jackson was the first suggestion. Others mentioned Gore and Dukakis, but several people wouldn't agree to drop those two. "I feel uncomfortable eliminating Jackson," another said, so they switched tactics. Whom were they most interested in inviting to speak?

Gore, Simon, and Dukakis topped the list. Babbitt, they agreed, didn't have a chance. Gephardt, they thought, was focusing too narrowly on trade issues. Jackson wasn't mentioned again; he had been dropped implicitly.

They discussed Cuomo again, even New Jersey Senator Bill Bradley, another prominent Democrat much discussed in the press but not in the race, until one participant closed the door: "If they haven't got the guts to run . . ." She let the thought trail off and complete itself. "Maybe they only seem better because they're not running."

Three and a half hours after the start of the evening, the group settled on extending three invitations: Gore, Simon, and Dukakis. As things would turn out, however, the three candidates who eventually would show up in Pat Russell's living room before the primary were Simon, Dukakis, and Babbitt. Regardless of their intentions to choose as a bloc, each participant would ultimately decide on his or her own. And despite the hoops they made the campaigns jump through on their behalf, more than half of them ended up voting in the primary but doing no work for the candidate they supported.

Kendall Lane was feeling like the mid-October weather: generally sunny and bright, but with occasional dreary periods and sudden plummets into chilliness. The Bush campaign seemed to be doing well in New Hampshire. The vice president was now an official candidate and only a few weeks earlier had attended a picnic at the home of Congressman Judd Gregg in Greenfield, New Hampshire, just over the Cheshire County line in neighboring Hillsborough County. More than three thousand Republicans, many of them from Kendall's area, had shown up—a massive crowd by New Hampshire standards. The quarterly campaign financial statements had just been released, and as they reviewed them at a weekly "Freedom Fighters" meeting, Bush's core supporters found two things that pleased them immensely.

According to the disclosures, Dole had outspent Bush in New Hampshire up to this point. Previously the "Freedom Fighters" had speculated that the absence of any visible Dole grass-roots effort in the state meant his campaign was saving its money for a last-minute media blitz, just before the primary. The news that he had been spending more than Bush was taken as a sign that Dole's campaign was squandering money with nothing to show for it, rather than hording it strategically. Dole himself had been in Keene earlier in the month, and Kendall, always anxious for political intelligence on the opposition, had sent someone to the breakfast reception to give him a report: sixty people—a decent crowd, but still nothing to fret over too much.

The other bit of good news in the financial reports was that Kemp's campaign was in debt. With its candidate still barely a blip in the public opinion polls, Kemp's campaign—the only other possible threat the "Freedom Fighters" perceived in New Hampshire—appeared to be losing, rather than gaining, ground. There were even rumors that Kemp might tread water until the turn of the year, when he could collect federal matching funds, then pay off his debts and depart from the race.

Although Kendall's general outlook was optimistic, even occasionally overconfident, his fall campaign was not without its problems. The voter lists had been completely updated, and chairmen had been named in every town (although Kendall and Jane had to name themselves as chairs of a few smaller towns, where no locals could be found)—organizational successes that only the Bush campaign could claim among the Republicans in the county—but the plan to make a big splash in the media by announcing a huge steering committee went awry. The goal had been a list of 5,000 people who publicly supported the vice president, but on the eve of Bush's official declaration of candidacy, they were short by 1,400. The headquarters, which had constantly pushed its core volunteers to recruit more steering committee members, had made the task even harder by deciding to count married couples as one, rather than two, names. And then some national staff member had bragged to *The Washington Post* that Bush would be releasing a list of 6,000 to 7,000 supporters in New Hampshire, thereby upping the ante even more.

Kendall was incensed. It was, he thought, another example of the national staff screwing things up for the people who did the real work on the front lines. The goal of 5,000 names had been a private target. Releasing a list of 3,600 would have been impressive enough to prove Bush's organizational muscle; no other campaign could match it. Now, because of the newspaper story, it would be perceived as an inability to meet expectations. "Why don't we just 'unmarry' all of our couples," Kendall argued at a "Freedom Fighters" meeting. That would get them over their initial goal but still fall short of the published number. In the end the campaign decided not to announce any list at all—making Kendall feel that his efforts throughout the summer and early fall had been for nothing. Will

Abbott, the state director, was less upset: the task had been a good exercise for his organization; although they didn't get the publicity they had initially desired, he now knew which local volunteers he could count on; and the exercise had forced a great number of people to commit themselves far in advance of their normal timetable.

Kendall's other great continuing frustration was Bush's schedule. He wanted a big public event in Cheshire County. Every time he thought he had a promise for one, it was eventually dropped from the itinerary. For Bush's postannouncement trip to the state, Kendall's cajoling won a scheduled stop at the Keene airport for a quick rally, not exactly what he desired, but better than nothing. But then the headquarters canceled the plan, on the grounds that the huge picnic in Greenfield was enough for southwestern New Hampshire for October. *They don't understand New Hampshire*, Kendall was further convinced. *Greenfield isn't Cheshire County. It doesn't count.* They promised an "Ask George Bush" event for Keene in late fall, then canceled it as well but assured an increasingly skeptical Kendall that Bush would make two stops in his area before the primary. His fond dream of displaying his candidate to his home region's public—especially for a motorcade parade around Central Square and down Main Street—was alive, but in serious condition.

Still, things were going well, and he soldiered on. His new task was a project inspired by the "Freedom Fighters," who believed that Kemp was on the ropes and might not be a candidate once primary day arrived. They were to contact Kemp supporters in their regions, be friendly, and suggest that, if something should happen, Kemp people would be more than welcome in the Bush camp. "Poor Jack, he's got problems," Kendall said, explaining the plan. "If he can't start picking up more conservatives, I think his money is going to dry up."

Kendall had assigned some of his troops to contact Kemp supporters in the county, but he saved Al Rubega for himself. Al would need special treatment, more than just a phone call. "He's the best thing Kemp's got going in this part of the state, one of the few areas where Kemp is doing well and has any effort," Kendall said. "I wouldn't ask him to jump ship—he wouldn't do that. I just want to indicate to him that, rather than going to some off-the-wall campaign like Kirkpatrick [Jeane Kirkpatrick was considering a bid at the time] or Robertson, there's a place for him here. We'd find a home for him."

Kendall stopped in at the Cheshire County Attorney's Office in the courthouse and asked for Al; he was in trial at the moment, so Kendall asked that Al give him a call. When Al telephoned that afternoon Kendall mentioned only that he wanted to see Al personally sometime soon to talk about the campaign.

That evening, at a local Kemp meeting, Al heard from three of his volunteers that they had been contacted by the Bush campaign, inviting them to switch sides now, or later if Kemp dropped out. They all thought it was funny—and a little perplexing. "If they've got a healthy organization, they'd be better off working with the people they've got or getting new people rather than wasting their time trying to recruit people committed to other candidates," Al said. "It seems to me that's a misdirected way to go. Maybe they think if they're doing that well, other people will be persuaded to go on over to them. I think that's kind of a laugh." He put it out of his mind, thinking it the work of some inexperienced and overzealous Bush supporter merely working off the lists of the county Republican committee.

If any candidate was going to drop out, Al believed it would be Robertson or Haig. He wished they would; their supporters would most likely turn to Kemp. But the notion of Kemp quitting was unthinkable. "I suppose anything's possible," he said. "Maybe he jaywalked forty years ago and they'll put that all over the papers. But I haven't caught the slightest, whispering, inkling hint that anything like that will happen. Not in the least."

Al had his own organizational headaches to contend with. The voter lists his county group was supposed to update with correct addresses and phone numbers and any additional registrations weren't getting completed. He was going to take a day off from

work and do the rest himself. Kemp was coming to Keene in November, and a proposed schedule needed to be worked out. A door-
to-door canvass was set for early December. Gun Owners of New
Hampshire was planning another presidential forum for February,
and Al was in charge of trying to get commitments from all of the
candidates. Court was in session, and Al had his hands full with
prosecutions. And Mary had been telling him that "everything is
meetings, we're never home together anymore."

With his mind on so many activities, Al didn't associate Kendall's
conversation with the reports from his fellow "Kempers." Besides,
he thought of the Bush offensive, "they must figure I'm a lost
cause."

October 28 was an important day for the Republican race. The first
debate among the full field of candidates was to be held—in Houston, like the first Democratic debate in the summer—and televised
nationally. The activists in Cheshire County looked forward to the
event with a mixture of excitement and nervousness. At last the
candidates, not just the organizations, would be tested head to head.

Al Rubega was upbeat in the morning. Jeane Kirkpatrick had
recently announced that she was not running for president, joining
Paul Laxalt and Pat Buchanan in the list of potential threats to
Kemp's conservative base that were now eliminated. If Robertson
and Haig would do the same—and Al believed they still might—
Kemp's chances would be further enhanced. Judith Kemp, the
candidate's daughter, and an organizer at state headquarters were
finishing the Cheshire County voting lists; Al wouldn't have to take
a day off from his job. He had considered calling a Kemp meeting
for the debate but decided instead to watch it at home with Mary,
which made them both happy. Before work, Al finished drafting a
letter to *The Keene Sentinel*, responding to an anti-NRA cartoon
that had run the night before. He was feeling good and feisty.

The debate, he thought, was a great opportunity for Kemp. "He's
been out there on the stump, sharpening his message so he's more
to the point than he once was," Al said. Bush, on the other hand,

hadn't been campaigning as much and might be out of practice. In addition, Bush "sounds like Mr. Rogers," Al said. "You know: 'It's a lovely day in the neighborhood.'" He predicted the debate would contrast Kemp with Bush the same way televised congressional hearings had contrasted Lieutenant Colonel Oliver North with Supreme Court nominee Robert Bork. North had come across forcefully on television, and Bork hadn't, so, according to Al, "even though the same people were against them both, North 'won' his hearings and Bork 'lost' his."

He hoped the debate would expose something more. Dole and Bush "have shifted with the political winds," he said. "When it was politically fashionable to be antigun and protax, they were. Then it became fashionable to be progun and antitax, and they shifted again." Consistency, steadfastness and political courage were important to Al, and he believed Kemp exemplified those qualities. Kemp had never wavered from his support of the gun lobby, had "taught Reagan Reaganomics," and had opposed the 1982 tax bill that Dole and Bush (and even Reagan) had favored. Dole, Bush, and du Pont were all campaigning now on platforms more conservative than their past records. Al appreciated their conversions, but suspected it had more to do with the political success of true-believer Reagan than their own convictions. "The thing I like about Jack is that he tries to change the fashions to suit him, rather than changing himself to suit the fashions," he said. "That's the difference between a leader and a follower. His task tonight is to show it's a three-man race—Kemp, Bush, and Dole—let people know him and his beliefs."

Kendall Lane was more nervous about the upcoming debate. His candidate was the front-runner and had more to lose than gain. Kendall's schedule called for him to be at a hospital board meeting, a city council committee meeting, and a League of Women Voters mayoral debate, but he was going to skip all three. The Bush town chairmen were gathering at his home to hear from Ron Kaufman, the northeast director of the campaign, and then watch the event together. That took priority for his time.

But in the afternoon Kendall had time for another important campaign matter. He walked over to the courthouse to meet with Al.

It didn't occur to Al that the topic was going to be a shift to the Bush campaign until Kendall sat on the chair across from him and started talking.

"I wanted to tell you that, just in case there's a money problem or staff problems in Washington with the Kemp campaign—well, we're hoping you wouldn't go to Dole's campaign," Kendall said.

"You got that right," Al answered.

"We've heard that Dole would get you."

"I don't know who would have that idea."

"I just want you to know that, if for any reason Kemp had to pull out, we hope the vice president would be your second choice."

Al smiled and nodded. "That's very nice of you. I assume the same would apply if the unthinkable happened to the vice president's campaign."

Kendall nodded, and they switched topics to something they both felt more comfortable talking about: how theirs were the only two Republican organizations in the county and how poorly run the Dole campaign seemed to be.

When they shook hands and Kendall departed, both believed they had received commitments. Kendall felt sure Al would move to Bush if Kemp was out of the picture, and if Al had the impression the reverse were true, well, the vice president wasn't in danger of dropping out—it was a good trade. Al felt the same way about Kendall. Neither candidate was going to be gone before the primary, he thought, but "you can't start too soon to build bridges for after the primary. If Kemp wins, it will be a bitter pill for some Bush people to swallow."

Kendall's debate party was held in his house's attached barn, which he and Jane had converted into a large recreation room, complete with a bar, the picture of them with the vice president, and a poster and the New Hampshire stanchion from the 1984 Republican convention. It was now the principal meeting place for the Bush campaign in Cheshire County.

Pete Johnson began with a short business meeting. He explained to the twenty town chairmen that the next project was going to be phone banks—calling registered Republicans and Independents from central locations to "ID" them according to codes ranging from GB1 (a committed Bush supporter) to GB6 (anybody but Bush), with intermediate codes for "leaners," undecideds, and those leaning toward or supporting another candidate. Using the voter lists the campaign had updated, a professional phone bank company outside New Hampshire had already made sixty thousand calls to the state, but now the local organizations were going to take over for their own regions.

"We need to know what's going on out there, intelligence on the other campaigns," Kendall added as an extra task. As an example, he said he had been called the night before by the du Pont campaign. He had kept the caller on the line long enough to find out where she was calling from (Washington) and to hear the entire pitch. Just that afternoon Jane had been called by a Dole supporter in Manchester, asking if she'd be willing to organize Keene for the Dole campaign—further proof, Kendall said, that Dole's organization was far behind Bush in forming local support groups.

"What do you all hear?" he asked his chairmen. Their responses ranged from comments about Bush being blamed for seemingly everything, including the recent stock market crash, to thirdhand anecdotes about local Robertson events, to the question, "A lot of my friends say Bush is a wimp. How do we respond?"

Ron Kaufman, an intense man and seasoned political operative whose current mission in life was to assure a Bush victory in New Hampshire, paced in front of the television set and delivered a short pep talk.

"Things are going much better here than we ever dreamed, and much better than the media perception," he said. The combined organizations of Governor Sununu and Congressman Gregg provided a solid base for Bush; the *Manchester Union-Leader* appeared to have no clear favorite among the conservative candidates to mount a serious challenge (the paper would later endorse du Pont); the steering committee had nearly five thousand members; and no other campaign in the state seemed anywhere near Bush's in the size or skill of its group of volunteers. Things looked good in Iowa, where Bush had won the caucuses in 1980, he said, but "New Hampshire is more important to us." Regardless of what happened in Iowa, he assured them, "if we win New Hampshire, we win the nomination."

The debate would not be crucial, he said—it was being carried on public television, not a major network, so even if Bush stumbled a little, there would not be an immediate analysis of it by the well-known anchors to make things worse. He suggested they consider calling the local radio talk shows the next day to say how well their candidate had done.

When the show came on, Kendall leaned on the bar and watched intently. Jane sat on a couch by the woodstove; the chairmen were on folding chairs. Kaufman kept pacing. Pete Johnson stood behind the bar, chain-smoking, and Kendall occasionally looked at Pete's cigarettes hungrily. The tone in the Republican debate was immediately more combative than the Democratic debate had been, with several of the candidates directly challenging Bush on a number of issues.

Halfway through the debate Kaufman went to the kitchen, called the campaign's control center in Houston, and talked for a few minutes.

"They say it's four-nothing Bush," he announced.

"But it's still the fifth inning," Kendall cautioned.

At that moment du Pont opened a direct assault, saying, "The problem of the Bush candidacy is where he would lead America. So far we haven't seen any leadership." Like some in the debate audience, a few of the people watching the Lanes' TV booed and hissed. Bush responded sarcastically. "Pierre, let me help you out with some of this," he said, calling du Pont's proposal to restructure Social Security a "nutty idea."

The people in Kendall's room broke into applause. Kaufman slapped his hand on the bar. "Not bad for a wimp," he crowed.

Kendall's tension evaporated only when the debate ended. "The vice president was the most comfortable, the most self-assured," he said in relief. "His body English was good. He was"—and Kendall paused before saying the word—"presidential."

Most of the political pundits agreed with Kendall's assessment. By defending himself so forcefully, Bush was seen as the principal beneficiary of the debate. Robertson, most analysts said, had been treated as deferentially by his opponents as had Jackson by his fellow Democratic candidates, but he had come across calmly and smoothly and thus had gained a little. Dole got mixed reviews; Haig was mentioned only in terms of his snide attacks on Bush; and Kemp, although some columnists wrote that he had been articulate on conservative issues, seemed almost forgotten in the postmortems. The predebate political question had been about Bush—how would he handle his first test of fire from his contenders?—and thus the postdebate coverage concentrated on the answer.

The confrontational exchange with du Pont (who was declared the only "loser" of the evening) dominated the television news' reporting of the event. That was a big disappointment to Al. Watching the entire debate with Mary, he had been elated about Kemp's performance. "I thought he did great," he said afterward. "He gave two minutes' worth of well-reasoned answers to every question." He admitted that Bush had done well but believed that Kemp, as a challenger, would get the most credit. When he watched and read the later news accounts, he was shocked at the nearly exclusive replaying of the du Pont-Bush moment. "I guess the du Pont attack made better viewing," he said dejectedly. The boost of publicity he had anticipated for his candidate never arrived.

Such a discrepancy between what they saw with their own eyes and what they saw later on television was something a number of the local activists experienced during the campaign. Dan Burnham and Tom Britton had attended a Democratic debate (hosted by U.S.

88) in November—an evening in which Gore, Babbitt, and Dukakis spent most of their time dealing with substantive issues and generally agreeing with one another while directing their fire on the Republicans. In the final minutes, however, Babbitt directly challenged Dukakis on his fiscal policies, and Dukakis responded testily. The news reports focused on the brief conflict. Dan and Tom both felt they were reading and seeing reports of a different event. "I guess these debates are going to have to get a little more down and dirty, or nobody's going to pay any attention," Tom said.

Buoyed by the debate and his sense of Bush's commanding lead in New Hampshire, Kendall went on a three-week vacation to Hawaii with Jane in late November. In 1980, when he was a Bush supporter but not intensely involved in the campaign, they had gone away in the weeks immediately preceding the primary, returning only in time to vote. This time such an absence near the big day was unthinkable. Even as he relaxed in the Pacific sun, Kendall made calls almost daily back to New Hampshire, checking with Pete Johnson on whether the phone bank work was proceeding and with Will Abbott on the campaign in general. He gave out Bush pins and bumper stickers to people in Hawaiian bars. When the second Republican debate was televised he watched the CNN highlights (Bush had defended himself well again) before going out to dinner, then rushed back to his room to watch the whole thing broadcast on NBC (five hours after the live debate, because of the time difference in Hawaii).

Upon his return, things were looking even rosier. According to the phone bank tallies, "it's either undecided or us," he declared. "As far as I can tell, Dole has abandoned western New Hampshire." The state campaign was feeling confident enough to reassign some of its coordinators to Vermont (Pete Johnson's territory was expanded to encompass their areas), and Kendall was talking about getting more than 50 percent of the vote in Cheshire County. At a "Freedom Fighters" meeting they discussed the possibility that Robertson might finish second to Bush in the state, with Dole a

distant third. Kemp, Kendall said, was "on a slow boat to nowhere."
Even in Cheshire County, where Kemp had the second-strongest
organization, Kendall no longer perceived much of a threat to
Bush's lead. He called a couple from Winchester he had seen at
the county picnic wearing Kemp hats (not knowing they were also
pledged to Robertson and Dole as well). They told him they might
be interested in joining Bush. "Kemp people are wavering," he
reported. "Their only loyalty is to Al Rubega."

His personal goals for the campaign from the beginning had been
"to help George Bush win New Hampshire, be a delegate at the
national convention, and have dinner in the White House." Learning that both he and Jane had been placed on the list of possible
delegates, and with the confident outlook of the race in the state,
Kendall felt he was already on the verge of realizing two-thirds of
his dream.

He began lobbying immediately for two Bush visits between January 1 and the primary and got a commitment for a visit in January.
He suggested another "Ask George Bush" event to turn out three
thousand people—and, of course, pushed again for his motorcade
parade across the county. Kendall was scheduled to become president of the local YMCA in early February, but he moved the in-
stallation until the end of the month. An all-day hearing by the
state's employment security appeal board, of which he was chairman, was proposed for February 12, just four days before the primary, and he ordered it postponed. He wanted all his decks cleared.
Bush came to Concord in late December to file his candidacy papers, and the Lanes went to swell the turnout. Kendall was standing
in the crowd near Bush during a press conference, and a Secret
Service agent blocking his view even moved at Kendall's request.

Near the end of the year he was given a date for Bush's next
Keene visit: January 17. At first he was pleased. Then he realized
two things. That was the day after a Republican debate in Hanover,
New Hampshire, which he wanted to attend. Preparing for a Keene
event the next day might keep him at home. Keene State College
wouldn't be back in session, and "all those warm bodies won't be

available to do the work," he said. "I'm getting amazingly practical about this whole operation. The idealism is long gone. Now it's gotta be who can I get to do the work today." The second shoe fell. Bush could be in Keene in the morning and until two o'clock, he was told. January 17 was a Sunday. "What the hell do you do with the vice president on a Sunday morning except go to church?" he raged. "We need him here when we can do something productive with him."

Jack Kemp's private plane taxied up to the small terminal at Keene's airport on a cold November morning. Al and Mary Rubega and a dozen local supporters walked out to greet him. Their homemade banner fluttered against the wire fence near the tarmac.

"Al, you look like . . . Al Capone in that hat," Kemp said when his top supporter stepped forward wearing a felt fedora and long overcoat.

The candidate shook hands with the other supporters (including the Winchester couple who, by now, were pledged to four of the six Republican campaigns) and answered some questions from a radio reporter. Meanwhile Al took aside the two national staff members traveling with Kemp—Roger Stone, a senior political adviser, and John Buckley, the national press secretary—to discuss a problem. Paul Young, the state director, had ordered a last-minute change in the day's schedule, and Al disagreed with the decision. Young had promised an interview with a Peterborough radio station for the same time Al had set a tour of downtown Winchester, a good forty minutes west of Peterborough. Young had told the Winchester people that their tour was off, setting off a flurry of calls and complaints to Al.

"You told *me* to arrange the day, and now I get set up," Al told the top staff. "We've *got* to go to Winchester. You can't blow it off like this."

They said they'd talk about it later, but Al wanted a decision immediately. When everyone was in the car, Al, the driver, raised the issue with Kemp directly.

"Al, we can't embarrass you," Kemp said. "We'll go to Winchester if you think it's important."

Al felt vindicated. "It was kind of nice to have him stand by me like that," he said later. Young, however, didn't appreciate having the snafu taken up with Kemp.

The first event, at Jaffrey's town hall, was a disappointment. Al kicked himself when he saw the tiny crowd—fewer than twenty people, including Pete Johnson, the Bush coordinator. Al had been busy at work and had left the details of each event to other people. Now he wished he hadn't. The day was off to a rocky start, and they were already nearly forty-five minutes behind schedule. The first major snow of the season was forecast. Slower driving would make it even harder to make up time.

Kemp had spoken and taken only two questions when a staff member whispered to Al and nudged him forward.

"I've been told to say we can take just one more question," Al said apologetically. The small crowd groaned.

"Well, let me take a couple more," Kemp answered. "This is my microphone. I paid for it."

During the next four questions, Stone kept looking at his watch and whispering to Al. If this was Al's schedule, apparently Al was going to have to bear the brunt of keeping to it. Stone egged him forward again, feeding him into a grinder Stone wasn't willing to enter.

"Just one more question please, so we can get you something to eat before Franklin Pierce [the next event]," Al said.

"Al," Kemp snapped. "I'll skip part of lunch to answer these people's questions." He took three more, giving long answers as if to prove who was in charge.

Lunch turned into a short walk-through of a nearby cafe—a photograph of it would run in the next day's *Sentinel*—and sandwiches in the car as they drove to Franklin Pierce College for a speech to the student body.

By the time they headed over a winding road from the college to Winchester, a wet, greasy snow was falling. No one was on Main

Street to greet the small entourage when they arrived late. Finally a local supporter showed up. Al put Kemp in his charge, gallantly gave his hat and coat to Judith Kemp, the candidate's daughter, and rushed off to find the staff members. Kemp followed his new guide on a two-block walk of Winchester's downtown, chatting briefly with some merchants, looking over an Ollie North video-cassette in a small store, and meeting, at most, twelve voters.

Al was flushed when he picked up the Kemps at the end of the tour. The staffers had called Peterborough and, after listening to the station's complaints, promised to be there at four o'clock. It was already three fifty-five, and the weather was steadily deteriorating.

Over icy roads they retraced their route east. The car was silent. The staff members kept looking at their watches and grimacing.

After the interview, on the way back to Keene, where Al had been promised that a group of Keene State College students would be gathered to meet the candidate, despite the delays, the mood inside the car relaxed. The schedule was so completely blown by this time that it didn't matter to worry about it. Mary had been moved to the lead car with Al and the Kemps; the staff conferred in the following car. Judith Kemp mentioned how pretty the woods looked in the snow.

"Yeah," Al said from the driver's seat. "It's good snow for tracking deer." He planned to go out tomorrow, Veteran's Day and a holiday from work.

"How can you hunt them?" Judith asked.

"It's easy," Al answered. "Mary used to think the same way until she went out."

"You go, too?" Judith asked Mary in amazement.

They talked some more about hunting, firearms, their families, football, and other noncampaign topics. It was a memorable drive for the Rubegas. "They're real regular people," Al said later of Kemp and his daughter. "Spending that kind of time with him, you see him kind of relaxed—it's really neat. Sort of like neighbors."

Only five students were there when the motorcade arrived in

Keene. Kemp spent five minutes shaking their hands and promised to return another time to speak to a larger group.

The staff considered the day pretty much a waste. "Try to keep it geographically central next time," Stone advised Al sternly on the way to the airport.

"To reach our key towns outside of Keene, you've got to suffer some travel time," Al answered, adding, "The day *I* had planned would have gone like clockwork."

Buckley broke the tension. Leaning forward to the front seat, he smiled impishly and said: "Al, just one question. Are you packing [a gun]?" They all laughed.

The best that Paul Young could say about the trip a few days later was that "Al learned you can't delegate things so much, you have to ride herd on everything." Cheshire County was low on the campaign's priorities of where to concentrate their efforts in New Hampshire, and despite Kemp's promise to the Keene students, Young said he didn't care if they never returned before the primary.

Al, as chronically optimistic as his candidate, took a more positive view. The crowds had been disappointing, he admitted, but the *Sentinel* story about the day had carried a Winchester dateline and devoted a lot of its coverage to the people Kemp met on Main Street. "It's a key town for us," he said. "If each one of the twelve people he met talks to twelve more people, it could help. And if we can say, 'Kemp's one of the only candidates to come to Winchester,' it might be significant."

He was feeling harried by his various commitments—to work, to the campaign, and to GO:NH. (The night of Kemp's visit, he and Mary had driven to Concord for a Gun Owners meeting, fighting an increasingly fierce snowstorm over and back and not getting home until past midnight. The next morning he was out in the woods tracking deer at dawn.) "Sometimes I feel remiss," he said. "I feel like I'm not doing enough for the Kemp campaign. Then I feel I'm not doing enough for guns. I've got a lot of irons in the

fire. Just about each one could be full time." Trials were still under
way, which meant Al went to sleep and woke up thinking about
them. In late November he won two convictions on theft. "They
walked out the proper door of the courtroom," Al said, "the one that
leads directly to a jail cell—and without 'public relations' [his term
for personal recognizance] bail." But the Christmas season was just
around the corner, and Al didn't like jury trials near Christmas:
"Juries won't convict."

Al had learned another lesson from Kemp's last visit. "I'm learning to be less deferential to the headquarters in asking for things,"
he said in December. "It's my first campaign at this level, and now
I know that the only way to get things accomplished is to *do* them
and keep after them." One of the things he kept after was a date
for Kemp to return to Keene State College. An event was finally
scheduled but was canceled at the last possible moment under
circumstances that left the suspicion that perhaps Young had never
intended it to happen in the first place.

The sun was shining on Saturday morning, December 5, but the
temperature was only in the low twenties and not rising. A fierce
north wind made the cold even more bitter. Al's Kemp banner, tied
between two trees on the south side of the town common on Keene's
Central Square, bulged and billowed like a spinnaker sail from the
breeze at its back. Al was "Kemping."

"Give me a 'J'!" he shouted into a microphone from the common's
bandstand.

"J!" cried the forty-odd people huddled below him, raising the
placards that Al and Mary had painted.

"I can't hear you," Al chided them. *"Give me an 'A'!"* And he led
them through the letters until they had chanted Jack Kemp's name
into the coarse wind.

A woman sang "America," and Al took the microphone again.
"Make sure you hand out those pamphlets to nonbelievers who walk
by," he told the crowd. The singer began another patriotic ballad.

Both Al and the audience were disappointed: Al, because he had hoped for a larger turnout to this Kemp rally; the audience, because about half of them had shown up only because they had read in the *Sentinel* that Arnold Schwarzenegger, the beefy movie star, was expected to attend and declare his support of Kemp. The campaign was staging rallies across the state, many of them featuring celebrity supporters, prior to an afternoon of door-to-door canvassing. Schwarzenegger had canceled at the last minute.

The Saturday morning traffic on the rotary around Central Square circled unmolested, people in their cars occasionally gawking at the small rally in the center. Shoppers hurrying along the sidewalks politely but briskly accepted the pamphlets being thrust at them by the "believers." When the rally concluded, Al was left with nine people willing to canvass—Mary Rubega, two Keene State College students, a neighbor of Al's from Sullivan, a supporter from Massachusetts, and Dr. David Ridge and his three sons. Ridge, whose zeal and energy equaled Al's for the Kemp effort, had already covered most of Keene in the previous week, so the canvassers departed for some outlying towns.

"Let's just put the literature in the doors," Mary suggested when they reached West Swanzey to begin the door-to-door work.

"We've got to *talk* to them," Al said, climbing out of their car and striding toward the first house.

"Al loves this kind of stuff," she confided as he walked away. "For me, it's like going to the dentist. At each door I keep hoping no one's home."

Mary got her wish more often than not this Saturday. As she and Al worked opposite sides of the residential street, a vast majority of the knocks they made at the front doors went unanswered.

At the few doors where someone was at home, Al would introduce himself politely, shake the person's hand, and ask, "Have you heard of Jack Kemp? Do you support him?" Regardless of the response, he would leave a brochure, a leaflet, a card to send into the headquarters, and a bumper sticker. In an hour's worth of walking and knocking, he found only eight people at home in the neighborhoods he covered. Just one had heard of Kemp.

"Sure, I know who Jack Kemp is," the man told Al. "Wasn't he the quarterback for the Buffalo Bills?"

In Winchester, the next town south, Al had his spiel perfected, saying it quickly and easily, never forcing the people he encountered to do much more than answer his few questions, shake his hand, and accept his offerings. To his brief speech he added that Kemp was "the only candidate who's actually visited Winchester," forgetting that Robertson had been there in the summer. Of the fifteen voters he met, one said of Kemp, "He's good," and one said simply, "Yeah," when Al asked him if he supported Kemp. Whether they were sincere or just wanted to shorten the disruption of whatever else they were doing was hard to tell. One woman spoke only Polish.

His troops were getting tired and cold, but Al pushed them on to Rindge, another targeted town a half hour away, for a quick foray in the dwindling light of the raw winter afternoon. They worked even more briskly. "Hello, I'm Jack Kemp—ah, Al Rubega, supporting Jack Kemp," Al said at one of the three contacts he made. At her last stop of the day, the young woman from Keene State College riding with the Rubegas finally located an avid Kemp supporter, someone who was happy to be reached by the campaign and promised to help out. The victory warmed the car on the long drive back in the darkness.

At the end of the year Al was busy as ever. The governor had appointed him to a new job, head of the division within the state insurance department that oversaw sales of stocks and securities, and Al was cleaning up his final cases at the county attorney's office and boning up for his new position. He had spent innumerable evenings handing out Kemp leaflets in Keene and preparing an information sheet comparing the records of Kemp, Dole, and Bush on gun issues, for distribution in the state's gun shops. He drafted a letter on the same issue—signed by himself, a gun shop owner prominent in the NRA, and the president of a large gun manufacturer in New Hampshire—to be sent to everyone in the state with a hunting license.

By his calculation, the race stood the same way the Cheshire County Republican Committee was split—about half for Bush, about half for Kemp ("but more committed," he said), and very little for anyone else. Dole, he predicted, would beat Bush in Iowa, seriously wounding the vice president politically. "The uncommitteds won't go for Dole, and neither will Bush's soft supporters," he said. "The more I see of him [Dole], the less I like him. He equivocates on everything. That goes against my grain, personally. Secretary of state, maybe, but not president." Kemp would be the likely beneficiary of Al's scenario: boosted by the demise of Robertson, which Al still believed was imminent, and with the door opened by the Dole-Bush finish in Iowa, Kemp would rocket to the lead in New Hampshire. His troops were ready and waiting for the ignition.

The GO:NH candidate forum was just around the corner. Al already had commitments from Kemp, Dole, and Haig and a "very likely" from Bush to attend; the others were either still considering it or saying that their Iowa schedule might preclude an appearance.

To those campaigns that talked of schedule conflicts, he said, "Your candidate's social agenda isn't important. What's important is the [gun] issue, and if your candidate agrees, he's going to make it his business to be there. That's the way our constituents feel." He would point out that more than two hundred national media representatives were expected to cover the forum, so "Iowa's not an excuse. Iowa has a lot of gun owners, too, and any candidate who stays away may find that out the hard way."

10

SOFTBALL, HARDBALL

Doug Kidd's emotional roller-coaster ride of the summer continued through the fall and early winter, propelling him over peaks of optimism and down through troughs of doubt at speeds that constantly challenged his temperament's normal equilibrium.

This was his first campaign, and everything was new to him. Sometimes campaigning seemed like a game, fun to play and surprisingly easy to master. The next moment politics showed itself to be a merciless endeavor, capable of inflicting pain, doubt, and anguish, and difficult to comprehend. It could be joyous; it could be ruthless. It could be demanding; and it could be tedious. It wasn't at all what he had expected.

At a softball tournament in late September in Manchester, pitting the campaigns against one another, Doug walked up to bat in the first game against the Kemp forces. He hadn't played softball in six years and hoped he wouldn't embarrass himself. *Heavenly Father, just let me hit it*, he thought before the first pitch. He swung and hit the ball out of the park.

"Hallelujah!" he said as he rounded the bases.

Al Rubega, wearing a cap and T-shirt he had emblazoned with the Kemp logo, stood in the field, watching forlornly as the Robertson team went on to a 27–1 victory. "Yeah," he muttered each time another home run sailed over the fence, "but we'll still win the election."

Robertson's team won the tournament, beating Simon's 17–2, Gore's, in the championship then, 4–2. In a straw poll at a Republican gathering in Iowa the week before, Robertson had also come out on top. Doug thought the campaign was on the move.

The softball championship pennant was hanging on a side wall of the auditorium in Manchester three days later, when Robertson officially announced his candidacy to a throng of 1,500 New Hampshire supporters. It was a long but glorious day for Doug. He spent twelve hours decorating the auditorium, arranged for Helen Bouchie and some of his other volunteers to sit in special seats near the candidate during the evening's proceedings, helped pull the ropes that released a flood of balloons at the end of Robertson's speech, distributed and collected the donation envelopes that were a standard feature of Robertson events, and rejoiced that Allison, who rose several times to applaud in the middle of the candidate's speech, seemed so excited about the campaign. His first meal of the day was a cheeseburger at eleven P.M., and after arriving home at one A.M., he was back up at five o'clock to return to Manchester to help shuttle the candidate and campaign entourage to the airport.

The announcement week, however, was not without its troubles for Doug. Robertson had resigned his ministry, a move that Doug recognized as politically necessary and yet found disquieting. Part of him understood and accepted the reasons: Robertson, as the candidate often said, was running for president of the United States, not pastor of America; giving up his religious title served to make that point clearer. But another part of Doug resented the notion that the very thing he most admired in Robertson—the man's service to church and Christ—was being shunted to the background for the sake of politics.

Several days later the news was filled with the revelation in *The Wall Street Journal* that Robertson's first child had been conceived out of wedlock, a fact that had been concealed by listing a false date of marriage in Robertson's autobiography.

Doug's first reaction was anger and disbelief. "It kind of knocked me back, because of my expectations of the man," he said. "But then I realized there were things in my own life I haven't shared with anybody except in confessing them to God, and I got to thinking, This is crazy. Why should that stuff be aired? This kind of muckraking is uncalled for—it happened thirty-three years ago, BC [before Robertson's conversion]. They're not dwelling on the fact that he married the woman and raised a fine family. That doesn't get reported."

As he checked in with his volunteers, Doug discovered they felt the same way. The notion that a person's life before being "born again" is irrelevant was central to their belief, and although they had been unaware of the facts about Robertson's first child, they knew through reading his books that he had led a wild and raucous youth until his conversion to Christ. The supporters were angry at the press, not their candidate.

"I told you this would happen," Helen Bouchie told Doug. "I told you the press wouldn't give him a break."

Once his initial shock and annoyance subsided, however, Doug decided the dark cloud had a silver lining. "At the announcement, people were almost worshiping Pat instead of focusing on what his real meaning is, what he stands for," he said. "Now maybe the focus is back where it should be."

The Houston debate was not only Doug's first chance to see his candidate next to the rest of the Republican field, it was one of his few opportunities to see Robertson on television—he and Allison didn't have a set in their home, and they watched the debate at the home of some other supporters. "I've seen Pat do better in person, so I was a little disappointed," he said afterward, but overall he thought the night was a success. Robertson, he said, had established himself as a "member" of the field, had talked positively instead of joining the others piling onto Bush, and "I just loved how at ease he was with the camera; I think that had a tremendous impact on the viewers."

He woke up the next morning thinking, *Can Pat beat a man like George Bush, who's held so many distinguished positions?* Doug decided it was possible. "What's interesting is that Bush and his campaign talk a lot about the positions he's held rather than the results of the things he's done in those positions," he said. "Pat has always talked about his accomplishments and results. I think that's a significant difference that people are listening to hear."

Robertson's next trip to the state, in late October, seemed to affirm Doug's judgment. The campaign had decided it was time to begin expanding beyond its church base. Events now included not only the standard receptions for volunteers and church clubs, but also things like stops at small diners and Main Street walks to meet the general public and speeches to groups outside Robertson's natural constituency—a mix, Doug called it, of "Christian and mainline campaign stumping." With the announcement and debate behind him, Robertson was now "a fuller candidate in the eyes of people," Doug said. "They didn't expect him to be so well informed."

Many people also commented that they liked the way Robertson had stood his ground against the media barrage over the revelation about his first child. Hart and Biden had allowed the media to drive them out of the race, these people felt; Robertson had shown more courage by comparison. At a small television station in southern New Hampshire, Doug watched through a studio window as Robertson was interviewed by a young woman reporter who apparently felt the same way.

"You have beautiful blue eyes," she told the candidate after the interview, and Robertson blushed. "You're so calm and so sweet. But you know what else—you've got a set of balls." Robertson's face dropped in astonishment. He finally mustered a mild, "thank you," as a response. Doug and the other staff members were howling in the next room.

"Did you *hear* that?" Robertson exclaimed when they got in the car, laughing along with the others. "No one *ever* said that to me before."

For the rest of the day, as they would approach the next event, one of the aides would say to Robertson, "You've got such beautiful blue eyes. You're so sweet . . ." Everyone in the car would finish the lines in unison.

A month and a half later, two weeks before Christmas, Robertson came to Keene for the evening. The campaign had gone through yet another reshuffling. Too many things had been falling between the cracks in New Hampshire. Supplies weren't arriving on schedule; the data base wasn't growing as fast as they wanted; expense checks were delayed. Doug's territory had been expanded to include the northern half of the state, doubling his time on the road and away from home. He had received $2,100 in long overdue payment for mileage only after discussing the problem directly with the candidate. Despite having a long list of registered Democrats on the campaign data base (about 20 percent of the names they had collected in 1987) who said they supported Robertson, the deadline for getting them reregistered to vote in the Republican primary had come and gone without any organized push to get the job done. A plan devised by the New Hampshire office had languished without action at the national headquarters until it was too late. A management committee of six top supporters was now installed to keep on top of such things.

The attempt to reach a new audience was also more formalized. Meldrim Thomson, a former three-term governor and arch-conservative, had joined the Robertson cause and was playing an active role in decision-making, including bringing on some of his former campaign workers to direct events. They had more experience in politics than Doug and many of his colleagues, but they also brought a harder edge to the campaign than Doug had been used to.

"We need to be careful not to have two separate campaigns," Doug said at the time, somewhat worried that the base of Christian fundamentalists was being forgotten in the drive for expansion. An audiocassette of a Robertson speech, outlining what his first acts would be as president, was being distributed to 150,000 Republican households in the state. It was not only filled with right-wing ideology—"what I'm going to do with the commies," Doug called it—but had a harsh tone that Doug thought differed significantly from Robertson's earlier pronouncements.

Thomson accompanied Robertson on the Keene visit in mid-December, introducing the candidate by saying he supported Robertson for two reasons: "he's antitax and anticommunist." At a public reception in the Ramada Inn, nearly two hundred people—many of whom Doug had never seen or contacted before—showed up to hear Robertson say essentially the same things that were in the cassettes. Robertson also boasted of how well he was doing in other states, mentioning the Iowa straw poll and the fact that "George Bush had a breakfast in South Dakota the other day, and a hundred people attended; I had thousands at mine."

The couple from Winchester who had greeted Jack Kemp at the airport in November, who were on Dole's list of supporters, and who had given Kendall Lane the impression that they were considering Bush, sat in the front row wearing Robertson pins. Never leaving anything to chance when the opposition was concerned, Kendall had dispatched an informant to the event. The size of the crowd and the large number of donations it generated (almost $10,000) forced him to reassess Robertson's potential as a threat to Bush. Jean Sowers, the member of Beyond War who had "crashed" Al Rubega's Kemp reception in the summer, was in the audience and asked the last question of the night.

"You say you're prolife, but your support for the contras [in Nicaragua] and SDI [the Star Wars defense system] are profoundly antilife, and don't have much to do with the teachings of Jesus," she said. "They have more to do with fear."

As Kemp had before him, Robertson turned the challenge to his own advantage with the rest of the crowd, some of whom murmured soft boos at Sowers. He quoted the Apostle Paul's letter to the Romans ("But if thou do that which is evil, be afraid; for he beareth not the sword in vain: for he is the minister of God, a revenger to execute wrath upon him that doeth evil"), Patrick Henry, Abraham

Lincoln, and finally General John Stark, whose statement in the Revolutionary War, "Live free, or die," was the motto on New Hampshire license plates. "I respect your pacifist point of view," he said, "but we face great consequences when we lie down in front of tyranny. And my beliefs are *not* antithetical to the teachings of Jesus." The audience rose in thunderous applause.

As Robertson and Thomson shook people's hands—"I don't consider it a good campaign day unless I shake 1,500 hands," Thomson had advised—Doug collected donation envelopes (many filled with checks for $200 to $1,000) and chatted with a few of his early volunteers.

"Didn't you love it when he spoke the Word?" he said, referring to Robertson's use of biblical verses. "I want a president who knows the Word. He doesn't have to speak it all the time, but he should be informed by it."

He told them he wished Robertson referred more often to his religious background, "but that makes some people nervous." The newer, right-wing conservative speech was "a little farther to the right than I am, actually," he said, "but it seems to get people excited—and probably gets some people upset."

11

A GRINCH STEALS CHRISTMAS

Andi Johnson looked out the window of the school bus shuttling her from downtown Manchester to the campus of St. Anselm College, where the New Hampshire Democratic party was staging a convention on November 21, 1987. The weather outside, though sunny, was bitter. The temperature struggled but failed to reach above freezing; a howling northwest wind drove the windchill below zero. As the bus turned to enter the campus, Andi's idle gaze snapped to attention.

About two dozen people stood on the corner, wrapped in heavy clothing, leaning into the cruel wind and clutching cardboard placards: "We the People Want HART for President." They were part of a contingent of sixty people, most from colleges in Massachusetts, who were launching a "Draft Hart" movement.

"I almost agree with them," Andi said when she saw the signs. "If I weren't such a good Democrat, I'd probably be out there myself."

She touched the Simon button on her coat lapel. "Some people call our campaign 'Revenge of the Nerds,'" she said. "But after Hart and Biden, I'm happy with a nerd."

The convention itself had virtually no official party business to transact, other than a few issues forums in the morning that were well attended but were hardly the reason one thousand Democrats were sacrificing their Saturday. All six presidential candidates were to speak in the afternoon, and the national political press corps would be there as well to cover the event, with an eye toward handicapping the New Hampshire race. The campaigns had gone to elaborate lengths at local caucuses in October to elect their own supporters as delegates, knowing that the media would find it irresistible to use each candidate's delegate strength as yet another early gauge of his potential.

Eleanor Labrie, the retired schoolteacher who had met her first candidate when Dick Gephardt showed up at her front door in the spring, had dragged several friends and neighbors to her ward's caucus so they could vote for her as a delegate and send her to the first political convention of her lifetime. It was also the first convention for Molly Kelly, a delegate for Dukakis. Dan Burnham had covered conventions as a reporter for *The Wall Street Journal*, but today he was attending in a different role: as a delegate and Babbitt supporter. Tom Britton and Andi, by virtue of their party positions, were automatic delegates and now accustomed to statewide political gatherings, although as Hart volunteers four years earlier, both had gone to their first convention when the Democrats put on a similar display of presidential candidates.

Though officially discouraged by the state party, the urge by the individual campaigns to turn the caucuses and convention into public shows of strength for the benefit of the media (and to build their own organizational morale) resulted in considerable rivalry among the camps. At the caucus in Keene in October, Molly had intervened to prevent a near fistfight between two students over how the Keene State College delegate selection should proceed. Each combatant believed the other was trying to adjust the rules to sway the results in the opposing candidate's favor. The night before the convention, staff workers from each campaign flooded the St. Anselm gymnasium at an appointed hour, jostling for prime locations for their banners and posters. A Dukakis worker had even rented a "cherry picker" to allow him to reach otherwise unreachable spots in the rafters, causing competitors to grumble about the "Dukakis machine."

Mike Cook, the Keene area Dukakis coordinator, assisted in decorating the hall until three A.M. Saturday, drove back to Keene for a few hours' sleep, then returned early in the morning to organize the campaign's rush of the gymnasium doors. The state party had decided not to open the convention hall (where lunch would be served and the candidates would speak) until noon. But by ten o'clock Mike was standing in the harsh cold with a herd of Dukakis supporters near the front doors; other campaigns were doing the same thing. Seeking whatever advantage they could, they all wanted choice tables near the speaking podium and the camera locations for better exposure. When the doors finally opened the partisans stampeded in like settlers seeking homesites in the Oklahoma land rush.

Each candidate's introduction was greeted by cheering, sign waving, and noise making from his supporters. Each campaign strove to outdo the others in its hoopla. The Babbitt group was equipped with walkie-talkies to coordinate a parade across the gymnasium floor, and the Simon and Gore campaigns, poorly represented by official delegates, secretly opened some doors to allow nondelegate supporters, poised outside, to surge into the convention when their candidates' names were announced. ("What did we *do* [at the convention], except make a lot of noise?" Eleanor Labrie said afterward.)

Compared to the competitive maneuverings and exertions that preceded it, the speaking program was relatively anticlimactic. The candidates, unlike their partisans, studiously avoided any direct comparisons with their opponents, focusing their remarks instead on criticizing Republicans. Jackson, the only candidate without any visible, organized effort on the convention floor, was the only candidate whose speech was received enthusiastically by the entire crowd. The others, both because their oratory was tepid compared with Jackson's soaring rhetoric and because of the competitive aura in the audience, were applauded only by their committed supporters.

Press accounts of the event the next day paid more attention to Jackson's address and the appearance of the "Draft Hart" volunteers than to the elaborate machinations of all the other campaigns.

On her way out of the convention, Andi was approached by an old friend from the Hart 1984 campaign. He was toting a Hart placard and wearing a Hart button.

"Wouldn't you rather be doing this?" he said, offering his sign.

"Oh, God," she said. "Don't even tempt me."

In the early morning of December 15, before she went to work, Andi turned on the television for the morning news. A Boston station announced that Gary Hart was in New Hampshire and, according to unnamed sources, was to make a surprise announcement at noon: he was reentering the presidential race.

No, I didn't hear that, Andi told herself, and departed.

In midmorning her office phone rang. It was Will Fay, the political reporter for *The Keene Sentinel*, working on a story about local reaction to the possibility of Hart's reemergence.

"So what do you think?" he asked.

"He can't be doing this," she answered.

A few minutes later Simon's state headquarters was on the line. They wanted to know if she was going back to Hart, and she quickly reassured them she wasn't.

Her private thoughts were less clear. "If the issue is honesty and integrity, Paul Simon is the candidate. I'm comfortable with him," she confided. "But on the issues, no one is better than Gary Hart. On military reform, foreign policy, economics, no one is more knowledgeable. No one has worked harder for the presidency than Gary Hart. He's still the best.

"Part of me says, 'Go with Gary,' but a stronger part says, 'No.' My conscience says, 'Go for it, go for it,' but the other part says,

'Shut up.' It would ruin my credibility—Hart, Biden, Simon, and then Hart again? I can't do it."

Tom Britton heard the news of the impending announcement on his car radio on the way to work. Gore's office called him at the office, and he answered their question before they asked him: he was staying with Gore. Hart was "a good candidate and would be a good president," he said later, but at this stage of the campaign, coming back would be impossible. "The Republicans and the press will just tear him apart. Gore is the next step past Hart. To win, a Democrat has to be like Hart—well versed on a variety of issues, like defense—but without the baggage. But in the next debates, those others better be pretty goddamned well prepared."

Hart filed his candidacy papers at noon, spoke on the state house steps to a wild crowd, and left to campaign in southern New Hampshire. Nearly a hundred reporters—the largest media crowd the state had seen since May, when the Donna Rice scandal had brought out a swarm in pursuit of the story—trailed in his wake, speculating on what Hart's unexpected decision had done to the Democratic race.

Andi spent the night on the phone and watching the news reports dominated by Hart's announcement. The Simon headquarters called to double-check whether she was still on board. She talked twice with her boyfriend in Massachusetts, whom she had met four years ago on the Hart campaign. He was excited about the development, ready to join the reincarnated Hart effort, and thought Andi should feel the same way. *That's easy for him to do*, she thought. *His credibility isn't on the line.* The disagreement would lead them to break off their relationship before Christmas.

She went on about her business for Simon in the following weeks. The office was now functioning, and Andi spent her evenings and weekends there. She had used her own money to pay for installing cable television so she could watch the constant political news on C-SPAN and CNN while she worked. Her coffee maker was plugged in near the TV set and was always in use. ("I can't deal with decaf," she told a volunteer who suggested switching brands.)

Simon came to Keene for an evening reception at Pat Russell's home. In an unscheduled half hour before the event, Andi brought him to the local office and put him to work on the telephone, calling potential supporters from cards she handed him out of her file box.

But Andi could not escape Hart's presence. The political news seemed to be exclusively about him. The only time the other Democrats got mentioned, it seemed, was in reports that measured the effect on their standings of Hart's reentry. The emerging consensus was that the publicity about Hart was hindering a lot of the other lesser-known candidates from getting the attention they needed to move forward. Polls in Iowa suggested that Simon in particular was being damaged by this phenomenon.

At a meeting of Simon volunteers in Keene, the frustrations broke out into the open. Andi—who was leading the meeting but known by the others as a former Hart partisan—was caught in the middle. They were discussing what they should be saying to voters in their phone banks.

"What do we do about Hart supporters?" a woman asked.

"Leave them alone," Andi counseled. "You won't be able to move them."

"It's obvious he's a wimp," the woman persisted. "If he backed down in the race, he'd back down to Gorbachev, wouldn't he? Can't we say that?"

"I'm not going to say anything," Andi repeated.

"Why can't we go after him?" another woman said, and the group murmured in support. "What do we do?"

Andi was reddening. Her loyalty to Simon was being tacitly challenged. "Let them vote for Hart," she said. "I'd rather go after Dukakis. His supporters are soft supporters. Hart's are solid; they're not going to be swayed."

A few days later, as if to answer the unspoken question of the meeting, a letter signed by Andi appeared in the *Sentinel*.

Now that the shock has worn off, I am still a very strong supporter of Sen. Paul Simon.

In my four years with Sen. Hart, I am still proud to have been a supporter, associated with his campaign. I believe his approach to solving problems is admirable.

However, Sen. Simon's approach to issues, some novel and some tried and true, are comparable and also refreshingly clear and succinct. His honesty and integrity stand above all other candidates in this race. And, in my many conversations with voters, honesty and integrity are the key issues in 1988. . . .

At times we tend to attract to controversy. But, when all is said and done, my heart is with Paul Simon.

Whether she consciously intended to make a heart/Hart pun, Andi's feelings about the new complication in the Democratic race were deeply mixed and highly charged emotionally. Near Christmas she invited all the young coordinators from the Democratic campaigns to a party at her house in Dublin. By now even she believed that Hart, regardless of her views of his positions on the issues, had become a spoiler in the race. Several earlier Hart supporters had abandoned their second choices to rejoin the rejuvenated campaign, and whether the voters would eventually do the same, it seemed clear that the media's focus on Hart was coming at the expense of the other candidates, especially Simon, and therefore hurting them at a critical juncture.

"Want to play some darts?" she asked the coordinators as they arrived for the party, and she laughed nervously.

She led them to a back room and tossed the first salvo of darts toward the wall as hard as she could. The target was a picture of "Gary."

12

THE SHORT YEAR

For the volunteers and campaign workers in Cheshire County, the new year arrived with an explosive suddenness. As much as they had been anticipating it, 1988 was upon them and sweeping them toward February 16 as if by surprise. To the public at large, the primary would signal the start of the presidential race. But to the small universe of activists and campaign staffers, it would be the culmination of a year or more's labor. More than that, as the insiders knew from past campaigns, the New Hampshire primary might be the nation's first, but for some candidates and campaigns it was also their last; a poor showing in New Hampshire has ended its share of candidacies. *Only six weeks to go!* It was a shout, a roar in their minds' ears, that could not be shaken from their thoughts.

Jon Meyer, Mike Haas, and Mike Cook, the coordinators for the Gore, Gephardt, and Dukakis campaigns, respectively, returned from brief holiday visits to their homes (in Ohio, Wisconsin, and Texas) on Saturday, January 2, and were immediately confronted with the accelerated pace of events. Al Gore, Sr., the former senator and the candidate's father, was coming to Keene on Monday and Tuesday; Tipper Gore, wife of the candidate, would be in town the next weekend. Gephardt was scheduled to campaign in Keene on

Tuesday—a tour of a nursing home and the official opening of the local headquarters. Dukakis was due on the same evening for a reception at Pat Russell's home.

In the first month and a half of 1988, the various presidential candidates would make a total of seventeen visits to the county, a number equal to the visits in the last four months of 1987 and nearly a third of the grand total of fifty-nine for the 1987–88 campaign. "Next year" was here, and it contained only forty-seven days. The pressure was on.

Molly Kelly was nervous about the Russell reception. The state headquarters staff had arranged it without even checking with the Keene office. They had Pat's offer (from the group that had interrogated the campaigns in November) in their files, and they wanted an early evening crowd event to "warm up" Dukakis prior to an important speech in Nashua. The hastily scheduled Keene reception, they thought, could kill two birds with one stone. Molly and Mike Cook were told to send out at least three hundred invitations.

Molly knew firsthand the size of Pat's house. She had sat in the living room just over a month earlier, when fewer than twenty people had made it seem claustrophobic. A crowd of fifty would fill the house, and that, Molly knew, was about the limit that Pat expected. Overflowing a room at Keene State College was one thing; there were always larger spaces to move into. But this was someone's *home*. And not just anyone's. Pat Russell was one of the state's two Democratic National Committee members and a leader of the county party, a "club" in Molly's mind that still considered her unwelcome in its circle. More than that, Pat had been one of Biden's first supporters in the state and had not forgotten the Dukakis campaign's role in Biden's demise. Jamming her house with people wasn't going to impress her or help bring her into Dukakis's camp, it would more likely make her angry.

But when Molly explained the situation to the state headquarters, they were unmoved. To them a big turnout was more important. This was not intended as a courtship call for one person or even a small group. Those days were long over. Excitement, momentum: those were the new watchwords. Crowd building was the new priority. Pat's feelings were Molly's problem—and, they made clear, Molly's responsibility. She was ordered to mail out the three hundred invitations and make the follow-up calls, but not let Pat know about it. "She's not going to like this," Molly advised, but dutifully followed her instructions.

The night of January 5 was a crystalline New Hampshire winter evening, the kind of night when you can see every star in the sky and wish they gave off heat rather than just light. The temperature hovered around zero. An hour before Dukakis was due to arrive, more than one hundred people were packed into the Russell home. They stood shoulder to shoulder in the kitchen, the dining room, the living room, and the den. They spilled into the hallway, the stairs to the second story, and a few rooms upstairs. More than a dozen shivered outside, clamoring for entry. Some sat in cars on the street.

Pat Russell was livid. She had been sandbagged: expected to be hostess for someone else's party; her home trampled by people, many of whom she didn't even know; her offer for a small reception turned into a public rally—like going away for a weekend and returning to find your teenaged daughter putting on a wild party. She was making no secret of her anger.

Dukakis finally arrived and was wedged into a doorway in the center of the house, where he spoke as loudly as possible so the throng could hear him. He answered a few questions, tried to shake everyone's hand, and was ushered out. The campaign hierarchy was thrilled by the turnout. Dukakis had been "pumped up" by the crush of people and was driven to Nashua, where he reportedly gave an uncharacteristically rousing speech.

As the candidate and staff were leaving the Russell home, Ray Buckley, the headquarters staff member who had arranged the event and given Molly her strict instructions, took Mike Cook and Molly aside.

"Pat's really upset about this," he told them as if they weren't already painfully aware of it. "You're going to have to take the fall."

While the crowd dispersed, the two sought out Pat, apologized for the overflow, accepted responsibility for everything, and took the brunt of Pat's simmering anger.

Molly, always sensitive about her role as the campaign's ambassador to the community and concerned about what the clique of local Democrats thought about her, felt that whatever progress she had made in that regard over the last year had been obliterated in one night.

A few weeks later Pat Russell endorsed Bruce Babbitt for president.

At the first "Freedom Fighters" meeting of 1988, Kendall Lane sensed a change in the mood of Bush's top staff in New Hampshire. On the surface everyone was upbeat. The *Boston Globe* had released a poll the day before showing the vice president with a commanding lead in New Hampshire: Bush, 41 percent; Dole, 23; Kemp, 10; the others in single digits. (The numbers on the Democratic side were: Dukakis, 40 percent; Hart, 18; Simon, 14; Jackson, 9; Gephardt, 3; Gore, 3; Babbitt, 2.) Dole still had no visible organization in the state, and as Bush's "Freedom Fighters" walked through each county's thirty-day plan for the end of the primary campaign— schedules for statewide canvasses, phone banks, mailings, putting up yard signs, visits by the candidate and his extended family— they were confident that no other Republican campaign had an organization capable of such an ambitious grass-roots program.

Yet Kendall perceived a subtle shift in the way Will Abbott, the state director, and Ron Kaufman, the northeast coordinator, were acting. There was a new tone in their voices, an undercurrent of urgency, even a little panic. They seemed "jumpy," Kendall said later that day. Abbott was suddenly obsessed with getting lawn signs out immediately, now that they were allowed under state law. Kaufman had insisted at the last minute that each county's plan be put in writing, so they could be more thoroughly reviewed by the headquarters. "Maybe it's the jitters," Kendall said. "There's an

240 GRASS ROOTS

awful feeling that there's one more thing you've got to do to make the difference."

The tension, like some sort of low-voltage charge, coursed through the rest of the group. Kendall's nerves were already a little frayed by the unspoken but palpable anxiety when the meeting agenda turned to two bits of particularly bad news. Bush's advance schedule no longer included a Keene stop on January 17, and the slate of the campaign's New Hampshire delegates and alternates for the national convention did not have Kendall's name on it. He was no longer nervous. He was bitter.

"I'm sitting out in the cold lookin' in again," he said. Many of the proposed delegates were elected officials and prominent party leaders who "haven't done any of the work but have prominent positions," he complained. Jane Lane, at least, was slated as an alternate delegate, and Ron Kaufman promised to arrange for Kendall to have a staff-type position in Dallas that would allow him access to the convention floor and the inner workings of the campaign's command. Kendall would still be going to the convention, although not in the delegate's role that had been his dream. But Cheshire County had been stiffed on yet another Bush visit.

It's going to be a rainy day in hell before I go to another "Freedom Fighters" meeting, Kendall told himself on his drive back to Keene.

But he was just blowing off steam. If there was one thing he detested on a campaign, it was a prima donna. Bush's organization had its share—a few were now going to be delegates to the national convention. Kendall wasn't about to join their ranks. He was a team player who argued his case in the private councils and then, win or lose, abided by the final decisions. Besides, one of the reasons he was a "Freedom Fighter" was his desire to be an insider. So the only meeting he would miss before the primary was on an icy Monday morning in mid-January, when he left early for Concord and slipped off the roads into snowbanks three times before deciding to turn around. Safely back at his office, he immediately called the state headquarters, asking Will Abbott for a complete fill-in on what had transpired.

―――――

Like a January thaw, when winter's frigid grip momentarily relaxes and the weather turns balmy enough to make even hardened New Englanders hope against all experience and the cruel facts of the calendar that perhaps spring is imminent, Dan Burnham's normally bleak view of Babbitt's chances brightened in early 1988. From the moment in a nationally televised debate in December when Babbitt had literally stood up in support of new taxes and challenged his opponents to join him, the former governor's press coverage had steadily improved. His media image had been transformed—from an unknown whose hapless television persona destined him to perpetual obscurity to a straight-talking, deep-thinking, courageous public figure whose willingness to confront thorny issues like taxes and Social Security entitlements separated him from the pack. Babbitt was still considered a long-shot candidate, but his glowing reviews from columnists and commentators suggested that he might just be the dark horse in the race. (This phenomenon is not unusual in American politics. Often the more remote a candidate's chances appear, particularly if he is witty and proposing policies that are popularly unpalatable, the better his press treatment becomes.)

Dan's support of Babbitt, which was flowering steadily into deep personal admiration for the man, had never been predicated on "electability" to begin with. Babbitt's intelligence, his self-deprecating sense of humor, and his public record of grappling with tough policy choices—the very things the recent spate of media attention was focusing on—were the attraction. As an avid reader and follower of the news, and as a former reporter himself, Dan was more than normally attuned to the switch in coverage of his candidate. Polls in Iowa and New Hampshire still showed Babbitt in the lower range of single digits, far behind nearly everyone else. But Dan believed (or perhaps *hoped* so hard that it transfigured into belief) that Babbitt's new media attention was reaching a critical mass large enough to begin moving public opinion.

The December debate, followed by a nationally televised interview with Marvin Kalb in January (which Dan attended in Cambridge, Massachusetts), and another Democratic debate in Iowa had gone well for Babbitt. *Newsweek* and *New York* magazines came out with favorable pieces, which Dan added to the thick collection of clippings that he carried with him at all times, like good-luck talismans. An economics report on the *Today* show singled out Babbitt as the only presidential candidate with forthright solutions to the deficit; NBC aired a piece saying Babbitt might provide the surprise of the campaign in Iowa. The phones at Babbitt headquarters in Concord were now ringing with unsolicited calls from people offering to help out.

"*Something*," Dan said of it all, "is happening."

In truth, virtually all of the campaigns were experiencing similar surges in interest from previously unengaged New Hampshire citizens. Huge percentages of the voters being contacted by the campaign phone banks still said they were undecided about the race, but the turn of the calendar had markedly expanded the circle of people starting to pay attention and make their choices. In addition to the heavier media coverage of the race, several campaigns were now running commercials on television, further raising their own visibility and heightening the sense that a campaign was under way.

"We were doing loads of grass-roots stuff for a long, long time— and I think we had a pretty good organization doing it," Paul Young, Kemp's state director, said in early January. "But he'd walk into a crowd of people, and maybe 20 percent would know who Jack Kemp was. Now, after being on TV [Kemp was running a heavy schedule of early advertising], we go to a public event and 80 percent of the people come up and talk to him: 'Hey, Jack, how ya doin?' or 'You're great, you're great.' It's amazing, the change in people coming up to him. I'm becoming more and more convinced that New Hampshire has become more of a media, a TV state."

Robertson ran a half-hour television program on some local stations, ending with an appeal for support, and within minutes the phones at his headquarters were busy with incoming calls. Simon's appearance on *Saturday Night Live* with Paul Simon, the song-writer and singing star of the same name, was one of the main topics of conversation at a reception the candidate attended a few days later in Keene. Gephardt's office opening in Keene in early January drew sixty people—not a throng, to be sure, but a significant enough jump in interest to make Mike Haas not mind that his car had died again and his Visa card was about to be revoked.

The partisans interpreted these signs as evidence of progress for their own campaigns, proof that *their* candidate was moving forward, rather than as a rising tide of statewide concentration on the upcoming primary that was lifting and carrying all of the campaign boats, a function of the calendar as natural and regular as the phases of the moon. Something, as Dan believed, *was* happening, but not necessarily what he, or his counterparts on the other campaigns, thought.

Dan's mood was also affected by Lisa Babish, the staff coordinator assigned to the Monadnock Region. Her indomitable optimism was infectious. She worked monstrous hours and constantly asked her volunteers for greater effort, but she made it seem like fun. Dan found Lisa's devotion to her job touching (one morning he discovered her sleeping in her car after she had driven all night to reach Keene), and it inspired in him a sense of youthfulness he had not anticipated. He treated her like a combination of daughter and compatriot—and would happily do anything she requested.

If someone had suggested to him a year earlier that in late January 1988 he would be marching behind a candidate through a college campus to the tune of "On Wisconsin," carrying a placard and growing hoarse from chanting at a rally, Dan would have dismissed the idea. He was almost sixty years old, he would have said; his college years and collegiate enthusiasms were far behind him. But on Sunday, January 24, when the Babbitt campaign staged a raucous rally for their candidate before a Democratic debate and then marched behind Babbitt to the auditorium, with Lisa Babish leading the troops in cheers through a small megaphone, Dan was lumbering along, grinning like an undergraduate on the way to a homecoming game and arguing with a policeman who tried to move him out of the roadway.

A week earlier, at a gathering for Democrats hosted by all the campaigns in Peterborough, Dan had spoken on behalf of the Babbitt campaign, saying how much Babbitt had "matured" as a candidate and how the "citizen process of the primary is working" by allowing the voters to see lesser-known competitors firsthand, which would accrue to Babbitt's benefit. If Babbitt could finish in the top three in Iowa (and Dan had a news clipping that mentioned a poll showing Babbitt moving up in Iowa), he said, then a further surprise in New Hampshire was likely.

He felt the same way after the debate. The campaign—life— seemed full of possibilities. Dan felt young again. Babbitt could win. Spring might come early.

Governor Sununu, Congressman Gregg, Will Abbott, and Andrew Card, a top Bush campaign staff member, were all at Kendall Lane's home the second week of January, when the Cheshire County town chairmen for Bush met to go over the final plans for the primary. The presence of such top brass at a local meeting was a clear signal of the critical importance of New Hampshire for the Bush campaign, a political truth underscored by a poll of Iowa voters released by the *Boston Globe* the same week. According to the poll, Dole (44 percent) had as wide a lead over Bush (29 percent) in Iowa as Bush held over Dole in New Hampshire; Robertson, Kemp, Haig, and du Pont were each under 10 percent. If Bush was going to stop a Dole surge after the Iowa caucuses, it would have to be in the Granite State. (The Democratic poll results from Iowa were Hart, 34 percent; Simon, 16; Gephardt, 15; Dukakis, 13; Jackson, 7; Babbitt, 2; and Gore, 1.)

The vice president would be going all out in New Hampshire, the group was told. He would be in the state twenty-five days between the first of the year and the primary; television and radio commercials were being prepared to saturate the airways in the final four weeks; a series of mailings to Republican and Independent households were going out to ensure that every possible voter was "touched" at least three times before the vote; canvasses and phone banks would be stepped up. John Bush, the candidate's nephew, was in charge of an extensive program to deliver lawn signs and larger street signs to local organizations and help get them placed in strategic locations. He arrived at the end of the meeting with Cheshire County's quota of three hundred signs.

"You are the frosting on the cake," the governor told the local chairmen. "Your telephoning, mailing, and contacts can make the difference." He urged them to search out people who might be out of state on the voting day ("or in nursing homes," Kendall added) and could vote by absentee ballot. Each county, he said, could "pick up a quick two hundred votes—a couple of thousand statewide" that way.

"This is the best political organization ever assembled in New Hampshire," he assured them. "Don't let the tension get to you."

Card said he had an important announcement. The vice president's first stop after the Iowa caucuses would be a rally at the Keene airport. The event would be especially significant, he said. After winning the Iowa caucuses in 1980, Bush had first come to Keene with "the Big Mo" but ended up losing New Hampshire to Ronald Reagan. This time Bush would be arriving after *losing* Iowa. He said it matter-of-factly, but the gravity of the scenario he described fell like a weight on the forty volunteers, whose chatty cheerfulness had suddenly been hushed.

"We want to double the crowd he had in 1980," Will Abbott said. The event would be designed to prove that Bush was unshaken by the Iowa results and to make the historical point that New Hampshire, not Iowa, chose presidents.

"This will set the tone for the rest of the campaign," Card said. "I guarantee you that the stop in Keene will be on national television. We've got to have an enthusiastic crowd."

Kendall stepped forward. "I want eight hundred people there, so start thinking now how to get people to come. They won't do it just because the paper says he's coming, *you've* got to motivate them."

This was going to be Cheshire County's big moment. And, at long last, his.

The Dole campaign came haltingly to life in the Monadnock Region in mid-January. The candidate had made four trips to the area in 1987, attracting decent-size crowds but leaving almost no organizational tracks behind him. Campaign committees had been established for Keene and Cheshire County in late 1987, including a number of prominent local Republicans in their ranks, but for all intents and purposes they existed more as a list in the state headquarters than as functioning groups.

Dole's principal supporters in Keene—and, in essence, the only ones trying to do any organizational work—were Barbara and Malcolm "Mac" MacKenzie and Janet Shawn. Mac MacKenzie had served with Dole in the 10th Mountain Division during World War II, and he and his wife were longtime friends of the Doles. When Dole came to Keene State College for an appearance just before the 1980 primary, as part of his ill-fated candidacy, the MacKenzies had constituted a significant portion of the audience of roughly ten people who showed up in the large auditorium. The memory of that event (and Dole's vote—fifteen in Keene, thirty-eight in the county, for 0.4 percent of the total, the same as his percentage statewide) was seared in their minds eight years later. They were not particularly experienced or active in politics, but they knew that Dole's latest campaign, despite his high poll showings nationally and in Iowa, was far behind at the grass-roots level in Cheshire County, and the state headquarters didn't seem able to correct it. They were doing everything they could think of for Dole: they often drove cars for his appearances; attended events even in other parts of the state; helped organize a "Dole Patrol" (comprised of other 10th Mountain Division veterans) that showed up at ski slopes around the state wearing special vests advertising their candidate; and painted elaborate signs for the campaign (Mac was a sign maker). But for the basics of local organizing, they relied on the state headquarters, which seemed either uninterested in, or incapable of, assistance.

Janet Shawn had been a volunteer in several campaigns in Massachusetts—enough to know that nothing was happening for Dole in Cheshire County—yet since she and her husband had only moved to Keene in the summer of 1984, she didn't know the community well enough to carry the campaign on her shoulders. Every time the state headquarters gave her a new task, she would explain that to them. It was as if she were talking to a blank wall. The next time something needed to be done, they would call Janet or the MacKenzies. "We're like three soldiers trying to fight a war," she said in early January.

When Elizabeth Dole, the candidate's wife, was scheduled to be in the county for a day and a half near the end of the month, a number of things went wrong. The advance person dispatched by the campaign alienated many of the people involved—insisting, for instance, on plastering a quaint historical museum that was to be the site of a small reception with garish balloons and posters and being rude to the museum curator and volunteers.

"Little Miss Balloons and Posters," Janet called the advance woman. "If you asked her to do an event in a cathedral, she'd bring in those posters and she'd hang those balloons all over the sacred altar. I wanted to punch her out. If I ever see her again, I will." For another reception fliers and an announcement in the *Sentinel* carried different times, both of them erroneous. Told to turn out crowds, Janet was left to her own devices. Seeking advice and help from the local Republican Women's Club, she called Jane Lane—the second time that Jane, Bush's county chairman, had been contacted by the Dole campaign a year after she had publicly endorsed the vice president.

One of the county commissioners, a Dole supporter and member of the campaign's state steering committee, learned by sheer accident that Mrs. Dole would be in the region and had an open evening. No one from the headquarters had bothered to let him know about it. He hastily arranged a reception for her in his hometown of Rindge and in three days' time turned out a crowd of 150.

This wasn't the first instance that Dole's schedule was set as much by happenstance as by careful planning from his headquarters. In October 1987 Dole attended a reception in West Chesterfield because his office had received a letter from a couple there asking him to come. The *Sentinel* made quite a big deal about the incident, editorializing that it proved again how open the New Hampshire primary was to citizen involvement (and overlooking the other fact, that it also proved how bereft Dole's statewide campaign apparently was in coming up with its own plan for what it wanted to do with its candidate). For the remainder of the primary campaign, whenever the paper would occasionally refer to the event, quote the couple who had hosted it as prominent Dole supporters in the region, or recount how they were now being invited to important Dole gatherings in the state, Janet and the MacKenzies would grind their teeth. They needed people to make phone calls, go through lists, and help find volunteers, not go to cocktail parties. The person named by the state campaign as the Chesterfield chairman would often ask the same couple for information about Dole's plans because no one from the headquarters ever called him.

At the end of January, however, a young coordinator—Steve Price, a student at Columbia University's law school—arrived on the scene. An insurance office was found with some empty rooms for a local headquarters and phone bank. The place began to buzz with activity.

Barbara MacKenzie and Janet were there every day—answering the phones, calling in a growing list of volunteers, bringing food for the troops, and typing up the daily tally sheets—happy that something was finally happening.

The crowd outside the stately Hanover Inn, on the campus of Dartmouth College, was loud and unruly. *"Bush is a wimp!"* shouted a large group of young people carrying Kemp signs. A phalanx of television cameras, waiting for the motorcades to deliver the Re-

publican candidates for another debate, turned to record the commotion, which prompted the Kemp supporters to lean across the
police barricades and chant even louder: *"Bush is a wimp! Bush
is a wimp!"*

A platoon of young Bush partisans was aligned on the other side
of the street. Realizing that they were in the wrong position—that
is, out of the cameras' view—they surged across the pavement,
knocking down barricades as they advanced, their Bush placards
thrust forward like battle flags in a military charge. They pushed
into the Kemp crowd to grab their own share of the limelight. *"Bush
in '88! Bush in '88!"* they screamed to the same beat as the
Kempers, trying to drown out their opposition. The combatants
were shouting and shoving in a free-for-all as the police tried to
maintain a semblance of order when another candidate's limousine
wheeled up and stopped near the throng.

Kendall Lane and Al Rubega had been standing in the neutral
zone, chatting amiably, before the Bush attack engulfed them.

"I don't need to get involved in *this*," Kendall said, and walked
off.

"Me neither," Al said. He and Mary waded through the melee
toward the auditorium. (An account of the incident in *The Keene
Sentinel* the next Monday implied, both Al and Kendall believed,
that the two of them had been part of the intercampaign tussle.
"Al and I have known each other long before we got involved in
presidential politics," Kendall complained. "And we're going to
know each other long afterward. We're not going to argue over this.
We're going to have some interesting discussions when it's all over.
I'm going to be quick to tell him about the amnesty program after
the convention, and I'm sure he'll qualify." Kendall was also peeved
by an implication in the article that he had paid a hundred dollars
for each of his debate tickets; tickets indeed had been sold for that
amount, but as an insider, he had gotten his for free.)

Inside the auditorium Kendall was presented with a windfall.
Governor Sununu had decided to watch the debate with the campaign's high command in the vice president's holding room, where

they could monitor the televised debate on a TV screen and prepare the campaign's postdebate "spin" for the hundreds of political reporters who were watching on television sets in an adjacent hall. Kendall was given the governor's front-row seat in the auditorium.

Throughout the debate, as he sat only several feet from the field of candidates, Kendall often found himself paying little attention to what was being said and focusing instead on the differences between what he saw and what he imagined was being shown on television. "Off camera, a lot of things go on," he said afterward. "The candidates signaled to each other and the moderator [John Chancellor of NBC]. It wasn't as free-flowing as it seemed. And the *makeup*. It doesn't show up on TV, but I could see it on all of them." He noticed small things: Bush had the reddest tie; Bush and Chancellor were the only ones wearing blue shirts; Bush and Kemp had loafers on their feet. During a break in the action, Bush leaned forward and nodded an acknowledgment to Kendall and the other Bush supporters in the front row. "Did you see me on TV?" Kendall asked several people the next day.

Bush was once again the focus of several verbal assaults in the debate. Robertson and Haig, citing a Bush brochure about a recent arms control agreement with the Soviet Union that said nuclear warheads (rather than just missiles, as they contended) would be destroyed, claimed the vice president didn't even understand the details of a treaty he supported. Dole's recent rise in the national and Iowa polls also made him a target; several other candidates said Dole wasn't firm enough against taxes.

On their way out of the auditorium, Kendall and Al ran into each other again.

"What did you think?" Al asked.

"I thought du Pont talked too damn much. Sometimes when he talks about Social Security, he sounds like an accountant—like Jimmy Carter. And Robertson didn't come across at all," Kendall answered. Haig had shown more of a sense of humor than Kendall had expected.

Al agreed. He thought Kemp had won the debate. "He stayed

clean, and didn't kidney-punch Bush like everyone else," Al said. "I think people are getting tired of it."

They talked about Al's new job, state politics, and their expectations of the primary.

"It looks like Kemp is moving some in the polls," Kendall said. "I wonder at whose expense?"

"Bush," Al replied confidently.

"Maybe Robertson," Kendall said wistfully.

The Lanes went on to a reception for Bush supporters near Hanover, where Kendall was filled in about the details of the Robertson-Haig-Bush dispute on the arms control treaty. The staff had been on the phone to Washington while the debate was in progress to make sure their candidate hadn't made a costly mistake. Bush was technically correct, Kendall was informed: although the missiles would be destroyed, as Robertson and Haig had contended, the warheads would be dismantled and the nuclear material retired from both countries' military arsenals. Getting such a quick explanation was "one of the nice things about being on the inside of the campaign," Kendall said later. He passed on the information to some of his volunteers and to a local reporter in the next few days.

The vice president arrived at the reception and circulated through the crowd.

"Sorry I'm the one you had to stare at for two hours," Kendall told him as they shook hands.

Bush laughed. "I was glad to see at least one friendly face," he said, and moved on.

The Rubegas were late getting to Kemp's postdebate reception. Al had lingered outside the auditorium, handing out Kemp buttons from a brown paper bag he had with him and joining with some college students in a "We back Jack" chant. He and Mary had trouble finding the reception site, finally locating it by spotting a restaurant surrounded by cars with Kemp bumper stickers and arriving just as the candidate's motorcade was pulling out.

They trailed the motorcade to the airport in Lebanon, New Hampshire. As Kemp and his family waited to board their private plane, the Rubegas were the only nonstaff members at the airport and so had a chance to talk again with the candidate.

Kemp, pleased with the way the debate had gone, was happy that Al had shown up. Al's boyish enthusiasm and obvious devotion to Kemp and Kemp's candidacy—his relationship to the congressman often seemed like that of a younger brother: familiar and jocular, yet reverential—always appeared to give Kemp a lift.

"You did a good job tonight," Al said.

Kemp thanked him and asked how he thought things were going in New Hampshire.

"No place to go but up," Al answered, and in the way he said it and the way Kemp knew Al, it was clear that Al's words were an expression of optimism for the future, not doubt about the present.

The next afternoon, a Sunday, the Rubegas and Dr. Ridge and one of Ridge's sons went door to door in Jaffrey distributing more than six hundred Kemp brochures until it was dark.

The job that Doug Kidd had thought a year earlier would be his first one without any stress wasn't turning out that way. The better Robertson did in other states (Bush had held him back in a party caucus in Michigan only by changing the rules; Robertson won a straw poll in Hawaii handily; reports of an "invisible army" of supporters in Iowa were surfacing), the more the pressure seemed to be cranked up in New Hampshire. The data base in mid-January stood at 35,000 possible Robertson supporters—not only far short of their goal, but also, the campaign feared, filled with a good number of names of people who had been willing to sign a petition calling for Robertson to run and yet who might not actually be intending to vote for him.

Doug's characteristic equanimity and good humor were unruffled. "We've got to leave *some* room for miracles," he said of the data base being short of the magic number of 55,000. But since the turn of the year his campaign job had become "very stressful," he admitted. His hours had become even longer, his evenings away from Allison more frequent, and his expense checks more tardy again.

Meldrim Thomson was also a growing problem. The ex-governor had a statewide reputation for an explosive temper and a habit of demanding that things be done exactly his way, and he brought both with him as he installed himself at Robertson's state headquarters. He insisted on signing off on every decision, however minor, and as a result, Doug felt, things were once more falling through the cracks. Thomson preferred to have Doug in the office every day. Doug thought his time was better spent covering his large territory in person, making sure his volunteers were happy and busy and getting them the materials they needed to move the campaign forward. "My allegiance is to the people in the field," he explained. "He [Thomson] keeps pulling me off them."

One day Thomson reached him by phone while Doug was on the road.

"Why aren't you here?" Thomson demanded.

"Because I'm *working*," Doug answered.

On a Friday a few days later Thomson learned that Doug had made a decision without seeking Thomson's approval. He flew into a rage, and informed Doug that he was fired. Doug stayed home that weekend, stewing about it, but reported back to work on Monday. The national staff had moved in again (Doug wasn't the only one having problems with Thomson), reshuffled things at the headquarters, and put Doug back in the field. They didn't want to lose Doug—in fact, they were asking him to consider relocating to a southern state after the primary for some later contests.

Doug thought the Republican debate in Hanover, which he watched on television at a fellow supporter's home, had not been a good one for Robertson. His candidate had started out on the offensive with Bush over the arms control treaty but had then seemed too "laid back" for the remainder. "It was a missed opportunity," Doug said.

Still, he was optimistic. Despite polls showing Robertson far behind, Doug was predicting a second-place finish in Iowa.

"Then it will be Dole versus Robertson in New Hampshire?" he
was asked. He nodded and smiled.

"And then," he said, "it's just Pat."

In late January Kendall Lane was given the word that Bush's airport
rally in Keene the day after the Iowa caucuses had been pulled off
the schedule, and a series of home receptions for Barbara Bush in
three Cheshire County towns were also now canceled. The League
of Women Voters was planning a Republican debate in the week
between Iowa's caucuses and New Hampshire's primary, and the
campaign was rejuggling the schedule to accommodate it.

Kendall was incensed. "It's a hell of a lot more important for him
to meet people than to do another damn debate," he sputtered.
"The news media thinks debates are more important—they hate
the idea of going out and following him around when he's meeting
people, so they'd crucify him if he didn't go to the debate. For us
in the field, who have an organization, it's a hell of a lot more
important to have him here than on a TV someplace."

Some recent polls had shown Bush slipping a little in New Hampshire, still well ahead of Dole in second place. But Kemp, whose
campaign had unleashed a series of television ads attacking both
Bush and Dole about taxes and Social Security, seemed to be creeping up in his third-place slot. Bush and Dole, meanwhile, were
involved in a nasty fight in the news—Dole raising questions about
Bush's role in the Iran-contra scandal, Bush's campaign making
statements that Dole's "meanness" as a vice presidential candidate
in 1976 had caused the Republican defeat to Jimmy Carter and
encouraging reporters to investigate Mrs. Dole's personal finances.

Kendall's network of informers had reported on the problems
surrounding Mrs. Dole's visit to the county, and he still believed
that Kemp could be the principal threat to Bush, particularly in
Cheshire County because of Al Rubega's efforts. "Dole will get some
support because of the media, but no organized help," Kendall said.
"He won't get people motivated. Al will. We will."

The latest cancellations were a big blow to Kendall's plans. They crystallized the frustrations he had harbored for more than a year. "The vice president hasn't had enough opportunities to be with people in New Hampshire, to answer their questions," he complained. "He's had *none* here. The Ramada event [in the spring of 1987] was a closed event. People are asking, 'When do *we* get to hear the vice president?' "

The events he had planned for Bush and Bush's wife would have been "all we needed," he said. "We'd have been in great shape. Now we get nothing. We're out in the cold. Once again, Cheshire County is the lowest priority and the first one to get cut in a political campaign. We've got all these people geared up and ready to go, an organization in place, and now we're going to sit here and look at each other because we've got no candidate and nothing to do."

A hostess for one of the receptions for Mrs. Bush was threatening to resign from the campaign because of the cancellation. Kendall's other volunteers were equally, if not so dramatically, disappointed. He made an appeal to Governor Sununu to intercede on his behalf with the national staff but was finally told the decision was final.

"It sure makes it tough to win an election," Kendall said when he heard the news.

The repeated letdowns about Bush's schedule, the vagaries of the recent polls, and the rising level of tension within the campaign as the Iowa and New Hampshire contests quickly approached had put Kendall on edge and shaken his confidence.

"In the legislature, I always liked to count my votes ahead of time, before we went in," he said. "I want to count our Bush votes *now*. I'm not real big on surprises. Sometimes I wake up in the middle of the night and think: What happens if we lose Iowa and then lose New Hampshire? All this for nothing. Nothing."

13

MEDIA CIRCUS

There has always been a touch of carnival to New Hampshire's presidential primary. If politicians recognized from its inception in 1952 that a victory in the Granite State's early contest was worth millions of dollars in free advertising from the national media, the state itself just as quickly realized that hosting the first primary did more than confer upon New Hampshire immense political leverage. It was also good business.

Tourism is the state's second-largest industry. An influx of candidates, campaign staffs, and political reporters provides a quadrennial infusion of commerce for hoteliers, restaurateurs, printers, advertising outlets, and car rental franchises that has been estimated to reach more than ten million dollars per primary. More important, although harder to estimate in dollars, is the public relations bonanza from the intense media coverage. Each time a network correspondent concludes a report in front of the seemingly obligatory quaint backdrop of a covered bridge or picturesque town hall, each time a photograph appears in America's newspapers and magazines showing a candidate attending a lumberjack contest in the mountainous North Country or eating pancakes at a maple syrup stand, New Hampshire as a *product* has received a national endorsement that money literally could not buy.

The grass-roots volunteers do not consider themselves unofficial emissaries of the Chamber of Commerce; helping the local tourist trade is not their motivation. But even the most novice volunteer soon comes to understand the symbiosis between campaigns and media: without the political prominence the candidates give to the primary, the press would not be so obsessed with the activities in New Hampshire; absent the certainty that the primary's buildup and outcome would be the principal political story in the nation at the start of every quadrennium, the candidates would measure New Hampshire by its few dozen delegates, the New England equivalent of, say, North Dakota.

And just as the local organizers are fueled by faith in the ultimate effect on the final vote of their painstaking and quiet work in the trenches, of the power of person-to-person "retail" campaigning, they also become acutely aware that media coverage of the campaign creates its own political reality—the "wholesale" campaign—defining events and influencing voters in greater numbers and perhaps even more profoundly than any intimate candidate reception or campaign canvass could ever hope. The primary race that began with a candidate standing in someone's living room gradually evolves into a contest waged on the TV sets in the state's (and nation's) living rooms.

Among the primary's many rituals is a bit of theater required of the state's politically active citizens, a part in a sideshow that shifts gradually as the vote nears. When Bruce Babbitt shared breakfast with a dozen voters in Dan Burnham's home in March 1987, those voters were Babbitt's principal audience and swaying them his principal political objective. Nevertheless, even that far before the primary, a television crew, news photographer, and newspaper reporter hovered around the scene. Like performers, the candidate and participants had to pretend that they weren't being recorded, interacting as if the media eye were not open and watching them. During the Cheshire County Democrats' Octoberfest, as Al Gore was speaking, a camera crew from a Boston television station arrived, barging in on the crowd, noisily setting up its equipment, turning on harsh lights, and walking through the group to get footage both in front of and behind the candidate. All the while both Gore and the audience studiously avoided paying attention to the distraction. In any other setting the crew's behavior would have seemed outrageously arrogant and rude, prompting angry stares and disrupting the proceedings. But in a political environment where the media are as necessary as air, the crew could act as if it were more important than the small cluster of activists, or even as important as the orating candidate, because, in truth, it probably was.

By the time the calendar turns it pages to the election year, the media show assumes even larger proportions. A candidate's appearance is covered not just by a local reporter and, perhaps, a solitary camera crew, but by a herd: the local press, regional reporters and TV crews, and representatives of national newspapers and the networks. The political objective is no longer the courtship of a few activists, or even the audience sitting in an auditorium—although campaigns clearly hope to convert those in attendance into supporters. The principal audience now is a larger pool of citizens: those who will be voting but, for reasons varying from lethargy to busy schedules, will never see a candidate face to face and will therefore cast their ballots based on what they read in the paper, hear on the radio, or, most probably, see on the tube. The news media move to the pivot point of the campaign, introducing the candidate to the new audience he must meet to succeed, much as the activists did the introductions in earlier months when the scale of the audience was tinier.

The grass-roots activists are now bit players in the show. In one sense their role has been diminished. Forced to choose between offering a car ride to a potential supporter or a national reporter, a candidate's campaign will easily decide in favor of the press. The organizational work that not only proceeds but intensifies in the final months is still given a high priority, but not top priority. Building an organization, it turns out, is not an end in itself, not the final measure of success or even, in a media age, the most effective or efficient way to win votes. The early organizational efforts are undertaken to build a small base of support, to impress the political pundits eager for early measurements of candidate strength, and to recruit the troops necessary for the final task of locating the much larger number of voters who have been influenced by the previous night's news broadcast or commercial.

And so, as the carnival atmosphere overtakes the primary, the activists are awash in it. Up to this point what was going on in the media was an important backdrop against which they worked on the local level. Suddenly the activists are merely part of the media show's backdrop. Their role may be proportionately smaller, but the show has moved from the county fairs of the provinces to the national big top. They are now part of something that has grown much bigger, much more gripping, much more fast-paced, and seemingly much more important than what they have been accustomed to in the early stages. Their roles are also now more complex. They work the booths as barkers and ticket takers, they assist the star performers just inside the white perimeter of the spotlight, and, preserving their initial function, they are still part of the audience that decides which act will be the most successful.

In the meantime, while the memory of when the show was all theirs during the "old days" only a few months ago is warm and touching, the bright lights and raucous excitement quicken their pulse. This is the big time.

The first major media invasion of Cheshire County in the 1988 primary season occurred when Gary Hart, Part II, arrived on the snowy morning of January 20 for a campaign day in Keene. As Hart spent the first few hours making the rounds of the cafes and sidewalks of Main Street and Central Square, a contingent of twenty reporters and cameramen closely monitored his every encounter. They moved with Hart by foot through the downtown, clustered around him like some sort of circular centipede whose head was in its center. No one having breakfast or walking to work that morning in downtown Keene was safe.

At Jean's Pastry Shop, the first stop, Hart walked in as unobtrusively as possible for someone trailing a small mob of cameras, microphones, and notebooks behind him. He sat at the counter, sipped a cup of coffee, and munched a doughnut in silence, while the reporting crew stood at a respectful distance and watched silently. At last Hart began talking to the man sitting next to him. The cameras immediately leaned in for pictures of the exchange. As soon as Hart stood and moved to briefly greet the other patrons, the reporters swooped in behind him to get the first man's name and a recounting of the conversation. (They had talked about the problems of running a small business.)

Hart left the cafe and circled Central Square, stopping at another restaurant, pausing to shake the hands of a few pedestrians, and chatting with store owners who had come to their front doors to see what all the commotion was about. By the time Hart had walked two blocks, reporters were strung out in his wake, double-teaming the people he had met as if they were interviewing accident victims: "What's your name? How does it feel?"

In Timoleon's Restaurant, where the summer before Pete du Pont had received a private lecture on the promise of America that was now part of his standard stump speech, a reporter who had recently covered du Pont learned that this was where it had all started. He rushed to the kitchen for an interview. "Are you *the* Lindy Chakalos?" he asked the cook/owner. "Pete du Pont's been talking about you all over Iowa!"

While Hart had yet another doughnut and cup of coffee with some voters, Len Fleischer walked in. Len, a child psychologist in his late thirties, had been a Hart volunteer in the 1984 primary and had come that morning specifically to talk to the candidate. Before Hart had dropped out of the race in the spring of 1987, Len had already decided to support someone else. Hart's attitude after the 1984 primary, particularly his refusal to drop out of the race after Walter Mondale had bounced back in later primaries, had disappointed Len. Over the last nine months he had conducted one of the most avid personal searches for a candidate of anyone in the county. He had hunted down Dick Gephardt on the streets of Keene for the chance to ask him a few questions; he had attended local speeches and receptions for all the other Democratic contenders whenever they were in the region; he had scoured the news for information about the campaigns; and he had watched all the debates. He was still undecided, except for his belief that Gary Hart should not be president and should not have reentered the race. "I don't care about his affairs," he said, "I don't like the arrogance, the self-importance, the posturing, lying, and denying." For reasons that probably can only be understood in terms of the personal connection that New Hampshire activists develop toward their candidates, Len, as a former Hart partisan, felt compelled to deliver his message of disenchantment personally.

Hart was moving along the restaurant's counter, shaking the patrons' hands. "You've got a lot of guts, hang in there," a diner had just told him when he turned to see Len standing in his path, waiting nervously for the opportunity to speak.

"I worked for you and voted for you in eighty-four," Len said, now standing face to face with the smiling candidate. "But I just can't do it this time."

Hart's smile went wan. A clot of reporters was forming around them. Notebooks were opening. Len's hands were shaking.

"What you're doing is divisive to the party, with everybody looking into your private life," Len continued. "You're giving fodder to the Republicans, and they'd jump all over you in the election. It's making a mockery of the process."

"But what if the voters disagree?" Hart said. The reporting crowd was growing. Len wasn't moving.

"It still deflects you from discussing the issues."

"I can't help what the press does," Hart answered. "I talk about the issues, but I can't control the press."

"But it's hurting the party," Len insisted.

"I've worked hard for the Democratic party for twenty-five years. I will show I have a better chance of getting Independent and Republican voters as time goes on," Hart replied.

Len was unmoved. "I still can't support you," he said, shaking his head.

"I understand that. But we'd be in a bad situation if an—incident—can drive someone out of politics, and that's never been made an issue before. I almost had a *duty* to get back in and let the people decide. But if people want to continue criticizing my personal life, I can't help that. It's a form of blackmail, and I won't be blackmailed. I have a comprehensive worldview that's not represented by the other candidates. I've met with more world leaders. I've written a book about military reform. It's not that I say the others don't have ideas on issues, but I've spent ten years articulating an integrated policy on education, trade, military reform. I've gone *beyond* those other candidates."

"I'm sorry," Len said, clearly still not convinced. "But good luck." He reached out, and the two shook hands.

Hart moved past, but the reporters stayed. A few minutes later Hart walked back to leave a tip at his table. He had to squeeze behind the press cluster to get by. They ignored him as he passed through them; they were talking to Len and scribbling furiously in their notebooks.

At a local shopping mall a few hours later, where Hart ambled through the stores, bought a book, and had lunch, Valerie Britton saw the man to whom she and her husband had been so devoted from 1984 through the debacle of the Donna Rice scandal in May 1987. She approached Hart, tentatively, introduced herself, said she had supported him in the past, wished him luck, shook his hand, and hurried off.

Later she wished she had said more. "I wanted him to know I had waited as long as I could," she said. "I wanted to say: 'I waited and waited for a 'Draft Hart' movement to start; people said it wouldn't, but I kept waiting. I even left my bumper sticker on longer than *Tom* did.' I wanted him to know I hung in there as long as I could. But now I'm committed to Gore."

———

A crowd of four hundred filled the lecture hall at Keene State College when Hart spoke that evening. Hundreds more—including some of the coordinators for the other Democratic candidates—were turned away by the fire marshal. Inside, the audience consisted primarily of college students, even the two who had helped Al Rubega canvass for Jack Kemp a few weeks earlier. The reporting contingent had now swelled to more than fifty. A story had broken earlier in the day about financial irregularities in Hart's campaign during 1986–87—a whiff of another potential scandal that brought out a media swarm.

Also in the audience, in the second row, were Andi Johnson and Georgina "Jo" Robinson, a member of Hart's original core of supporters in Keene now backing Gore. Jo, a short, grandmotherly woman, was clutching a blue satin pillow, shaped like a heart, which she had made for "Gary."

Hart's speech was a dry recitation of his positions on the issues (he said he wished he had a blackboard to assist him in detailing his plans on reducing the deficit), markedly at odds with the rousing oratory he had employed during his appearance at the Cheshire County Democratic dinner the March before, when he was the leading candidate for the nomination and, many thought, the presidency. In the earlier speech, his cadences and rhetoric had been designed to elicit regular bursts of applause and to stir excitement. This night, however, it was as if he deliberately did not want the crowd to clap—and they didn't, until he concluded his twenty-seven-minute address. Rather, it seemed, he had a point to prove, similar to the one he had tried to make to Len Fleischer: *he* was the candidate with a comprehensive worldview and integrated policy proposals to back them up; he was not the tabloid candidate, but the position-paper candidate; he wanted to be remembered as the candidate of specific programs, not sexual antics. His campaign, he said, was unconventional. It would rely not on paid consultants and slick commercials, but on the power of new ideas and grassroots volunteers. In many ways it could have been a speech of Hart's from early 1984.

Andi passed a note to Jo during Hart's remarks: "Tempting, huh? I just can't! Too many responsibilities with Simon camp! I don't drop my responsibilities."

Immediately after the speech the two of them slipped through a side door, allowed passage past a Secret Service agent, and were ushered into Hart's holding room.

Jo, who didn't support as much as adopt candidates, gave Hart a hug and presented her satin pillow. "Use it however you want," she said, kindly. "Maybe you can sell it to raise money for the campaign."

Andi's encounter was briefer, but as emotional. They shook hands. Her whole body trembled. Her normally pale face blushed crimson. "Good luck," she blurted, and rushed out into the hallway.

A Hart campaign worker, someone they both knew from 1984, asked them for help in Cheshire County.

"Gary's my friend," Jo said. "I'll help in the ways I can. Al Gore is a good young man who would be great as vice president on the ticket. He doesn't seem to be going anywhere, but I guess I'll stick with him."

"Gary's great, he has all the answers," Andi said. "It's tempting. But I can't go from Gary Hart to Joe Biden to Paul Simon and then back to Gary."

On her way to the car she refastened her Simon button—a small gold pin in the shape of a bow tie—which she had removed in deference to her former candidate. Within a half hour she was at the Simon office calling voters.

"I talked some people out of Hart tonight," she reported later in the evening. "'Sure he's got great ideas,' I tell them, 'but he's got no support in Washington and wouldn't be able to get anything through Congress.' It works pretty well."

Tom Britton didn't try to see Hart when the candidate was in Keene, although he attended the Democratic debate at the University of New Hampshire a week later, where, he admitted, he still thought Hart's position on U.S. policy in the Persian Gulf was correct and

Gore's wrong—and he was glad when Hart made a point of it with Gore during the debate.

"Hart must be going crazy," he said afterward. "He's got some specific programs, but no one's listening. The only press he gets is: Can a man who's committed adultery be elected president of the United States?"

Gore, who had pulled out of the Iowa contest completely, was now downplaying his efforts in New Hampshire as well, concentrating instead on the southern primaries that would follow. The strategy, Tom said, was "either the worst ever conceived or the most brilliant—we won't know until Super Tuesday." Gore had originally promised an all-out effort in New Hampshire, and Tom was a little bothered by the shift, but not nearly to the extent of the Concord group that had endorsed Gore en masse. They were in near open rebellion over their lessening importance to the campaign, grumbling to both the staff and the press.

Tom was more philosophical. He had been saving a few fingers' depth of his Jack Daniel's to drink as a victory toast on primary night. Now, he said, "I'll take a modest triumph. My expectations aren't too high. I'd have taken third before. I hate to drop to fourth. If he gets double figures, that will be all right." The new strategy might work in the long run, and he was on board.

"Gore," he said, "only comes to New Hampshire now to pick up an endorsement or get his picture on TV."

Kendall Lane is the kind of person who reads more than one newspaper—*The Keene Sentinel, Manchester Union-Leader*, and *Boston Globe*—and who watches television principally for its news—from the local and national evening news to late night news, from the Sunday talk shows to programs like *Nightline*. Involved as he is in many civic and political groups, he is accustomed to being interviewed by reporters and has a healthy respect for the power of the press in shaping public opinion, particularly in political races.

As the primary campaign proceeded, however, he became even more of a "news junkie." What the media were reporting or how the press would handle a prospective campaign tactic was a constant topic at the weekly "Freedom Fighters" meetings. Kendall enjoyed being on the inside: knowing beforehand what was going to happen and then watching as it filtered out through the press into the public domain. He had a TV set in his converted barn/recreation room, his kitchen, his den, and his bedroom, and when he was home at least one of them was invariably on and tuned to a news program, particularly to C-SPAN, whose unedited broadcasts of political events and speeches had become something of an addiction for Kendall. (He had expanded his cable coverage during the campaign specifically to receive it.) He and Jane did not throw away their newspapers after they read them; they kept them stacked in chronological piles in the den and from time to time went through them again, cutting out the clippings about the campaign. By mid-January the stacks stood like pillars in the small room, a political archaeology in layers as deep as the spring of 1987 awaiting further study.

On the night of January 25, as soon as the network news was over, Kendall's phone began ringing from friends and fellow Bush supporters: What did he think about the Bush-Dan Rather argument? Kendall didn't know what they were talking about. He normally watched NBC's news and had missed the live Bush interview on CBS. He finally found someone who had taped the show and had a cassette rushed over to his house. He was stunned by what he saw.

The interview, which followed a lengthy report investigating Bush's role in the sale of arms to Iran, was unprecedented in its acrimony. The two men interrupted each other repeatedly, often angrily. Bush claimed that CBS had misrepresented the purpose of the interview; instead of covering a range of topics, as he said he had been promised, the sole topic was the Iran-contra scandal and an attempt to impugn his integrity. At one point Rather told the vice president that he had "made us [the United States] hypocrites in the face of the world." At another Bush mentioned the much publicized incident in 1987 when Rather had stormed off the set, creating seven minutes of dead air space during a broadcast. "It's not fair to judge my whole career by a rehash on Iran," the vice president argued. "How would you like it if I judged your career by those seven minutes?" The interview also ended abruptly, when Rather, saying they were out of time, cut Bush off in midsentence.

"I was less offended by Rather than pleased with the vice president for standing up to him," Kendall said, although "both looked a little ridiculous when they were both talking at the same time."

He called the Concord campaign headquarters, which gave him the CBS telephone number, and tried all night and the next morning to call and complain. The line was always busy; so many Bush supporters were doing the same thing.

"It sure got people stirred up," Kendall said.

The incident was the top political story for several days, dominating the front pages of newspapers and replaying constantly on television. A consensus emerged among political observers that Bush—who earlier in a debate in Iowa had used the same tactic of attacking the news media for harping on the Iran-contra issue and questioning his actual role in it—had gained from the exchange. His "wimp image" was being transformed by the fights he was picking.

Kendall's own troops seemed galvanized by it, more willing than ever to help the campaign. Cautious as always, Kendall took advantage of the spurt in energy but was unsure of the interview's long-term effect. It did, however, deepen one of his beliefs.

"The closing confirmed my opinion of the news media," he said. "You can't fight 'em, because they always get the last word."

"Welcome, New Hampshire and firearms owners, to history in the making." Al Rubega quieted the crowd of 1,500 at the New Hampshire Highway Hotel ballroom in Concord. The Gun Owners of New Hampshire Presidential Forum was officially under way.

When he looked out at the audience from the dais, Al squinted his eyes, occasionally shielding them with one hand, like an Indian scout. On risers at the back of the room stood about two dozen television cameras, part of a media presence of more than one hundred people. For someone at the podium who was unaccustomed to the bright lights the cameras required, the blindingly harsh glare could make you feel a little like a suspect being interrogated in a police station.

Al's two passions—guns and politics—were intersecting at this moment. Sitting on the front platform on both sides of the podium, behind placards Al had printed by hand, was the entire Republican field of presidential candidates—Vice President Bush, Pat Robertson, Senator Robert Dole, General Al Haig, former governor Pete du Pont, and Congressman Jack Kemp. (No Democratic candidates had accepted GO:NH's invitation.) The crowd itself was friendly turf for Al. They were members of his gun association, fellow Americans who believed as fiercely as he did in the Second Amendment. Most were dressed casually. Some wore camouflage jackets and caps, as if they would be leaving the forum to go hunting; they had been the favorites for the TV crews getting scene-setting footage prior to the program. A few—like a man from the Exeter Rod and Gun Club wearing an ascot and a Bush button; his wife had gold jewelry and a Laura Ashley dress—were attired more formally.

But the army of national and local media in the rear were, in Al's mind, more enemy than friend. With a few exceptions he considered them representatives of a liberal media bias against the right to bear arms. They were not here, he knew, out of an interest in the issue, but because of the candidates (who were here both because of the issue's supporters *and* the media attention to the event).

When Al, using his prerogative as GO:NH's president and emcee of the evening, pulled out an opening speech from his suit jacket pocket, his words were meant for his three audiences—candidates, gun owners, and reporters. He had planned to have the speech memorized, like a summation to a jury, but all the commotion surrounding the event's preparations had consumed his practice time. Instead he read from his text, looking up occasionally and blinking in the media's gaze.

All through history, brave men and women have had to fight and bleed and die so you and I could stand here tonight. Thanks to their sacrifice, you and I can say what we please, do what we want; we can shoot and we can hunt, and our loved ones can feel secure in our homes and on the streets here, where we all have the right to keep and bear arms.

American soil in 212 years has never suffered the boot of conquering foreign soldier. The freedoms we have lost, we haven't lost on battlefields to soldiers with rifles and bayonets. We've lost them in courtrooms, in statehouses and in legislatures to lawyers and to politicians using nothing more than pens and paper.

They fought so that what they won from wolves wouldn't be nibbled away by *rats!*

The crowd rose for a roaring, standing ovation. Al was just warming up. He urged everyone in the audience to remember to vote, or else they would "profane the memory of those who died for our rights."

Let's leave here committed to do everything we can to put in the White House a candidate committed to preserve, protect and defend the precious rights and freedoms to keep and bear arms for ourselves and our children. Go out and make the voice of honest, law-abiding firearms owners heard in New Hampshire and all across America.

The next president of the United States is here tonight, just as he was in 1980 [at the first GO:NH Presidential Forum]. In 1980, the only candidate foolish enough to think that he could afford to ignore the ideas and the votes of honest, law-abiding firearms owners was Senator Kennedy. [The crowd booed loudly.] This year, it seems to have spread.

Al read off the names of the Democratic candidates who had been invited but had declined to show up, pausing for boos after each one. Dukakis's name prompted the longest and loudest. ("That was fun, that was *so* much fun," Al said later. "I told myself, Say it [Dukakis's name] again, and I almost did, just for the sheer enjoyment of it, but I decided not to push it. They might revoke my permit in Massachusetts.")

Whatever nervousness Al felt at being the only one on the stage with his party's constellation of candidates, surrounded by Secret Service, a huge crowd, and the nation's media, he showed only in small ways. He forgot Pat Robertson's name in introducing the candidates, until someone reminded him. He had the audience stand for a prayer, which he led, then had them sit, only to call them to their feet immediately again to follow him in the Pledge of Allegiance.

Finally the candidates got their turns. Each of them made opening statements about their devotion to the Second Amendment. Al's seat was next to Bush and Robertson, and during the speeches he talked briefly with each one. Bush wanted to make sure of the speaking order, and Al showed him the list.

"Do you want to be called 'Reverend' or 'Pat'?" Al asked Robertson quietly.

"I'm not a reverend anymore. 'Mister' or 'Pat' is fine," the candidate said.

But when Robertson's turn was next, Al, looking at his list, forgot and introduced him as "Reverend Robertson."

When he sat down Robertson looked pointedly at a Kemp sticker on the table near Al, picked it up, and then threw it back down.

Al asked each candidate to publicly answer questions on several gun control issues. Then he allowed them each a closing statement.

For weeks afterward Al would be angry about the closings. All six candidates used their time to talk about other issues. Robertson said, "There's no dispute tonight on guns, but here's some differences among us," and talked about the recent nuclear arms treaty and the "eastern liberal establishment." Du Pont took a pledge against taxes and the oil import fee. Bush criticized the Sandinista

government in Nicaragua, named his prominent supporters in the
state, and praised President Reagan. Haig said he was a true conservative who believed "the best government is the least government." Dole objected to Kemp's ads attacking him, told some jokes,
and said, "I'm the only one of us with a record; and it's not a criminal
record, either." Kemp, the last speaker, said, "Records are for the
past, and leadership is looking forward to the future," going on to
talk about tax cuts and extending the "Reagan revolution" into the
1990s.

Despite Mary's and other friends' assurances that the evening
had been a great success and his speech had been powerful, Al
was uncharacteristically disconsolate afterward. "They didn't stay
on the issue," he said glumly. "By the time they got to their closing statements, they all made a crack to the effect, 'We all know
where we stand on the Second Amendment, now let me tell you
about——.' That really pissed me off."

He was particularly disappointed in Kemp for not sticking to the
issue. "He had the most to say," Al complained. "When he said,
'Let's forget the record; the record's the past,' I almost fell out of
my chair. He's got a record that's absolutely without a blemish,
absolutely sterling. It's fabulous as far as the issue's concerned. He
let Dole get up there and say, 'Look at the record, look at the record.'
That SOB voted *against* us in 1982, and Kemp let him get away
with it."

Al blamed himself for letting the evening lose what he thought
the focus should be. "I probably should have made a stronger statement at the start," he said. An NRA representative consoled him
that even professional newsmen couldn't keep a good politician
constricted to one issue, which only prompted a new worry for Al.

"After the opening statements, the press stopped listening," he
complained. "A hostile press could use it against GO:NH that we
couldn't keep them on the issue."

The coverage of the event cheered him somewhat. Bush's display
of a tiny gun (to make a point about the problem of metal detectors

in airports), Dole's showing of his lifetime NRA membership card, and Kemp's quote, "My idea of gun control is a *steady aim*," made their way into most of the news clips. The notion that gun owners were a powerful voting group, Al noted, was an underlying premise in many of the stories.

Yet months after the primary Al would consider the evening the low point, rather than the pinnacle, of his primary season. He wished he had insisted on a few minutes with Kemp privately beforehand to convince him to emphasize his record on gun issues more forcefully and exclusively. He wished he had made time to memorize his impassioned speech. The fact that he had shared the national spotlight for an evening with the Republican candidates for president was inconsequential compared to his personal feeling that he had failed to keep six men—whose careers at the time, like all politicians', were built on talking about the issues *they* wanted to discuss—from speaking solely about *his* issue.

Whenever he wanted to review the night and consider what he might have done differently, he could put a cassette in his videotape player. Among the expensive high-tech equipment of the national networks, Mary had set up their home video camera to record the whole event.

14

THE PERSONAL TOUCH

"If they're chatty, go with it. But we're not a hard-sell campaign, and we'll never be a hard-sell campaign." Lisa Babish was giving instructions to a dozen volunteers who had gathered in a local bank office for a "Babbitt Work Night" in late January. Some of them would be making calls to voters (literally a "phone bank" this evening), and Lisa was making sure they understood the procedures.

Letters had already gone out to all the registered Democrats in one of the larger towns in the Monadnock Region, signed by eight supporters in the town who outlined their reasons for backing Babbitt. The night's calls would concentrate on the same town. Lisa handed the volunteers computer sheets that had all the town's Democrats listed with their phone numbers and addresses. She told the callers to ask each voter if he or she had received the letter— a friendly way to open the conversation before getting to the real purpose of the call. "Have you made up your mind yet on who you support?" they were to ask next, using a three-numeral system to record the response: a Babbitt voter would be a "1," an undecided a "2," a supporter of another candidate a "3." A "2" was to be asked if there were any particular issues he or she was especially interested in; they would get a letter in a few days with a Babbitt position paper on that issue and would be called again later to see if any progress had been made.

Another group of volunteers was sent to a separate room, where letters to yet another area town were waiting to be folded, stuffed in envelopes along with two recent favorable articles about Babbitt, sealed, and then hand-addressed. A third group included a woman who was signing personal letters to voters in her own town; she would hand it to a volunteer, who would fold the letter and hand it to a third, whose job was to stuff it in a prepared envelope and lick it closed. A fourth would attach the stamp.

Dan Burnham was put to work calling identified supporters to enlist them for an upcoming door-to-door canvass. He was now a full-time volunteer for the campaign, putting in nearly as many hours as Lisa was. Everywhere he went he carried a large legal briefcase filled with Babbitt position papers, speeches, and favorable press clippings. One of his tasks was to recruit the local letter writers, sit down with them to discuss what they would like to say about the candidate, help them draft the letter, edit it, and get copies made and then signed. He was also making phone bank calls every night and participating in canvasses—even outside of the region— every weekend.

If the New Hampshire primary were more like the Miss America Pageant and gave out a "Miss Congeniality" award to one of the campaigns, Babbitt's would have won it in 1988. In an atmosphere of rivalry among each party's campaigns that intensified each day as the primary approached, Babbitt's group was nevertheless always spoken of kindly by members of competing campaigns, even in private, off-the-record conversations when the sharp knives of gossip normally were unsheathed. Unquestionably, part of this was because the other Democrats didn't perceive Babbitt as much of a threat to their candidates—he was still languishing in single digits in the polls, despite his "press roll" of mid-January. But part of it, too, was because, like the supporters of all the other candidates, Babbitt's seemed to reflect the personality and style of the man they supported: they were articulate, hardworking, and intensely earnest about the issues they considered important, but they tended not to take themselves too seriously.

This night Lisa doled out a few dollops of hope—a front-page story about Babbitt in *The New York Times* and some poll numbers that indicated he might be climbing toward 10 percent in New Hampshire—and sent her troops into action. They joked and laughed as they worked. In the mailing room one person on envelope duty asked if anyone wanted to switch jobs after an hour. "My tongue has broken down," he said. Lisa had lost her voice during the rally outside the Democratic debate at the University of New Hampshire, and when she spoke it sounded very low and breathy. "I look forward to your calls now," Dan said. "They're quite a thrill for an old man."

Doris Haddock, a seventy-eight-year-old woman from Dan's town of Dublin, was their premier telephoner. She had become involved in the campaign only "because I owed Dan a favor," she explained. She had not been drawn to Babbitt initially—she didn't agree with his plan to change Social Security and other entitlement programs, her husband opposed Babbitt's tax proposal, and neither of them had been impressed with what they had seen of the candidate on television. But Dan had taken her to the Democratic convention and arranged for her to meet Babbitt personally afterward.

"I thought he was wonderful," she said. "If I hadn't met him, I wouldn't be that enthusiastic." Since then Doris had spent her evenings calling voters from her home, stuffing envelopes and writing letters, and, when Dan would pick her up, coming to work nights.

"It's quite fun," she said of her new activity. Working for a candidate was "like going to a horse race—it's not nearly as much fun if you don't have a bet on it."

Doris looked up after one of her calls.

"I just had a man who hasn't decided who to vote for, but he said he's against taxes and doesn't want anyone messing with Social Security," she said, smiling impishly at Lisa.

Lisa thought for a second and then smiled back: "I'd put him down as a '3.' "

Virtually all of the campaigns had phone banks operating by late January. They varied in the number of people a campaign could enlist for the tedious, time-consuming, and repetitive work, and their ranking systems were not identical. Bush's had an elaborate code that recorded nuances ranging from outright support for Bush to leaning for Bush, from undecided to leaning toward another, specified candidate, and from support of someone else to "anyone but Bush"; others, like Babbitt's, only went from "1" to "3." But the objective was universal: spread some positive information about the candidate, identify supporters who would be contacted again on voting day, locate people who needed more information, find those who were beyond hope and eliminate them from future contacts, and report each night's tally to the state headquarters, where the master lists were kept and where the results were monitored as indices of what the voting public was thinking.

Phones don't recognize local or state boundaries, and some campaigns (like du Pont's) employed paid, out-of-state firms to do their work. In Minnesota the Dukakis campaign had a large pool of volunteers anxious to help out, and for several weeks they went to phone banks in their state and dialed long distance to talk to Cheshire County voters. Most campaigns, however, relied on their local volunteers to make local calls—from their homes, from the local offices, or from donated spaces that had multiple phones (real estate and insurance offices were popular in the evenings for Republicans; union halls for Democrats).

"I *hate* this." Mary Rubega put down the receiver on the phone. The Kemp campaign was borrowing the lines at a local electrical contractor's office for a phone bank. Only the Rubegas, Dr. David Ridge, and a Keene State College student had shown up.

"Keep calling," Dr. Ridge told her. "It really helps."

"I still hate it," Mary replied, and dialed another number.

Sometimes the conversations at phone banks seemed like one of Bob Newhart's comedy routines. Al was having one of those evenings.

"Hello, is Mr. or Mrs. ———— there? . . . Yes, Becky, that's very nice. . . . Well, Becky, do you think I could talk to one of your parents? . . ."

Another call. "Hello, Mr. ————. I'm Al Rubega, and I'm a volunteer for Jack Kemp. I was wondering . . . Oh, I see."

Another. "Okay, but you're only *leaning* toward the vice president, is that right? Okay, do you have any questions I could answer about Jack Kemp? . . . All right, thank you anyway."

Another. "Gary Hart? . . ."

And another. "What about your husband? Is he sticking by your side?" Al had found a Kemp supporter. "Oh, I'm very sorry to hear that." The man was dead several years; the list was wrong again. (Virtually every volunteer in every campaign encountered a similar situation, asking to talk to someone who, if they were going to vote, would have to be buried in Cook County, Illinois, not Cheshire County, New Hampshire.)

"That makes a total of *two* votes for Dole in Cheshire County," Al said defiantly, putting down the receiver from another call. Mary was standing behind him, rubbing his shoulders as he hunched over the telephone and marked his tally sheet.

"Did you tell her when she gets up on February 16 to put her finger out the window and see which way the wind is blowing?" she joked with him.

"You know, I don't mind the Dole votes; it doesn't displease me at all," Dr. Ridge said from the desk nearby. Like Al, he didn't believe Dole was a threat in Cheshire County. "It's Bush I'm after," he said, and went back to work.

Ridge had a friendly but insistent style on the phone. He often free-lanced off the script the campaign had provided them.

"What is your primary concern?" he asked one voter. "What is it you're looking for in a Republican candidate? Would you say that the value of your dollar is important? Holding down taxes and spending? Having an option to do what you want as far as your retirement is concerned? I feel Jack Kemp addresses those issues. Look at his track record. You know, Dole and Bush are only *talking* like conservatives, but if you go back eight years, they're taxers and spenders, whereas Jack Kemp has been a conservative all his life. He's from the middle class. He's got consistency, and that's what we need."

To another caller: "You don't think you'll even be voting?! I'll tell you, you go down and vote on February 16 and vote for Jack Kemp."

Excluding the wrong numbers, the no-answers, the Democrats mistakenly on their lists, the young children, and the dearly departed, the four volunteers made fifty contacts with voters that night, locating seven Kemp supporters, roughly the same number for Bush, a few less for Dole.

"Everybody's undecided," Mary said as she looked over their totals. She seemed forlorn about their evening's effort.

"That's good," Al said confidently. "Kemp's got the best TV ads to reach them."

Mary picked up the thread of hope her husband offered. "The press has been saying everyone's for Bush, everyone's for Bush," she said. "But they're really undecided."

"Yeah," Al replied. "And when Bush loses in Iowa . . ."

A poll of New Hampshire voters by the *Boston Globe* in early January found that almost half of them said they had met at least one candidate or had direct contact from one of the campaigns. If the Monadnock Region was any guide, that statistic seems off on two counts.

First, a much smaller percentage actually meets a candidate. During all of 1987 and the first two months of 1988, the thirteen Republican and Democratic candidates made a combined fifty-nine visits to the region. Some people who met or heard the candidates firsthand could not vote (most high school audiences, plus a high percentage of the college crowds, an extremely large number of whom were either unregistered or registered in other states); some met more than one candidate (Len Fleischer, for instance, saw each of the Democrats); and some saw the same candidate, or even several candidates, more than one time (most of the activists, who constituted the bulk of the crowds in 1987). Taking that into account against the total crowds at the various events, a defensible estimate is possible: about 4,000 people in the county, or 22 percent of the 17,724 who voted on February 16. Compared with other states, with the possible exception of Iowa, that 22 percent is still phenomenally high. In most of the later primaries less than one percent of the voters could probably say they'd met the man they were supporting for president. But it still means that, despite the myths of the New Hampshire primary, a vast majority of the voters base their decisions on something other than a personal experience with a candidate.

Second, it's hard to believe, however, that only half of the voters had a direct contact with one of the campaigns. With all of the phone banks, canvasses, letters, and other mailings carried on by thirteen campaigns, it would be a wonder that *any* registered voter escaped contact.

On one night in late January, four separate Democratic campaigns were independently making phone calls to Swanzey, a small town south of Keene that turned out 545 Democratic votes. By the end of the primary enough people in the county were complaining about being bombarded by campaign calls and canvassers that *The Keene Sentinel* was prompted to do a story about it. Mike Cook, the Dukakis coordinator, looked over an evening's tally sheets in early February and announced these results: 10 percent "1" for his candidate, followed next by 5 percent who were angry at being called again. One night the Simon office got a telephone call; it was a Dukakis volunteer, asking in innocent earnestness if they had decided whom they would be voting for.

The mailings were even more prodigious than the phone calls. According to the state directors of the campaigns, major mailings

from the state headquarters totaled at least 1,021,000 pieces by the
Democrats and 1,780,250 from the Republicans. In 1988 there were
586,592 registered voters in the state.

Most of the campaigns made at least one statewide mailing to all
the registered voters in their party; several did more than one (the
Bush campaign, for instance, did five). In addition, some did spe-
cialized mailings. Kemp's sent targeted pieces to 10,000 holders of
New Hampshire hunting licenses and to 40,000 Republican recip-
ients of Social Security; Dole's sent an endorsement letter from
Senator Warren Rudman, the candidate's principal sponsor in the
state, to 70,000 people on Rudman's campaign list and several
pieces to the 250 resident veterans of the 10th Mountain Division;
Dukakis's did two mailings to every "1," "2," and "3" (supporters,
leaners, and undecideds) identified by their phone banks, including
letters from hocky star Bobby Orr, basketball star Kevin McHale,
and former Speaker of the House Tip O'Neill, a message about the
candidate's opposition to the Seabrook nuclear power plant to 4,000
antinuclear activists, a letter from the candidate's mother, Euterpe,
to targeted senior citizens, and special pieces to members of the
teachers', steelworkers', and government workers' unions; Babbitt's
did a mailing to 5,000 environmentalists; Simon's mailed to 11,000
members of the National Education Association; Gore's mailed to
every owner of a satellite dish for their television set (he had sponsored legislation they favored).

Even those numbers were incomplete. They didn't include the
monthly newsletters many of the campaigns published for their
identified supporters, the personal letters from town supporters to
their neighbors (like Babbitt's and other campaigns'), or the short
notes, often accompanied by a position paper, that phone bank
volunteers and door-to-door canvassers were encouraged to send
to follow up their contacts. And, of course, they did not include the
thousands of front-door, campaign-to-voter contacts made by the
canvassers themselves.

Each campaign viewed New Hampshire as the entry gate to the
kingdom of presidential success. Based on their study of past pri-

maries, they discovered several possible keys to the kingdom: intimate candidate appearances, courtship of activists, and high-visibility public events like walking down Main Streets or visiting cafes to meet voters ("retail" politics); slick radio and television commercials, media interviews, and events designed solely for the evening news ("wholesale" politics); direct mail, phone banks, canvasses, placards and signs, and word-of-mouth from neighbor to neighbor ("organization" politics). But which one was *the* key? Different primaries over the last thirty-six years suggested different answers. With the stakes so high, no campaign wanted to take the chance of not turning one of the keys. It might just be the one that unlocked the door. So they used the entire ring.

In spite of this deluge—some might say because of it—the mass of voters seemed to be responding slowly and confusedly. Even as the calendar turned to February, with voting day only a few weeks away, all the phone banks and canvasses of all the campaigns were reporting one universal fact: most of the voters, from 65 to 75 percent on most of the tally sheets, said they were still undecided on how they would vote.

Public opinion polls that were being published recorded a different level of undecideds—usually below 10 percent. But pollsters did not ask, "Who *will* you vote for?" They asked, "If the primary was *today*, who would you vote for?" Their purpose, they will tell you, was to take a "snapshot" of the electorate's mood in the present, not to predict an outcome weeks or even days in advance, and they tried to elicit a decision from a voter who might not, in truth, have decisively made up his or her mind. A "leaner" in a campaign's telephone list might come out as a "supporter" in a poll. (Of course, a voter who had already decided on a candidate might also, out of politeness or a desire for secrecy, tell a volunteer calling on behalf of another candidate that he or she was undecided, rather than break worse news to the volunteer.)

Nevertheless, whatever the discrepancy between the polls and the campaign tallies, it was clear that a great number of voters either still remained truly undecided or had only loosely attached themselves to a candidate, and it had the same impact on all the volunteers who had been working for more than a year on a campaign. It baffled them—how could these other people not have made up their minds, how could they still seem in no rush to decide, how could they not discern what to the volunteers seemed major distinctions between the candidates? . . . Why weren't they as excited and as obsessed with this as the volunteers were? Some responses to the phone bank and canvass questions—one voter said he was choosing between Simon and Robertson, another between Hart and Bush—only added to the bewilderment.

The number of undecideds also worried the volunteers and workers. Having expended so much effort for so long, how could so many other people seem so unaffected by it all? Was what they had been doing, were doing, were going to do in the next few weeks, as Kendall Lane's nightmare kept saying, *all for nothing?*

But it also gave them hope, particularly for those whose candidate seemed at the bottom of the pack. With such a large number of voters seemingly still to be persuaded, anything could happen. The primary—and the presidency—was still up for grabs.

The hope, and the worry, drove them on even harder. There were many possible keys to the kingdom. They, in fact, might even be one of them.

Dan Burnham parked his car on a residential street in Keene, rummaged in the backseat, moving the large briefcase he called his "portable Babbitt office," grabbed an armful of campaign fliers, and started down the street. A small stack of index cards, each one listing a Democratic household in the neighborhood, was in the pocket of his flannel jacket. A dark blue stocking cap warmed his head; he had on thick winter boots. It was January 30, a sunny but cold Saturday.

He knocked on the first door on his list and waited patiently for a man to answer. It was Len Fleischer, whom Dan did not know.

"Hi," Dan said. "I'm here for Governor Bruce Babbitt. We like him because he's"—he stumbled briefly for a word—"neat!" He handed Len a pamphlet.

"I kind of like him, too," Len replied. "How's it going?"

"Great."

"Getting a good reaction?"

"Yeah!... Well, I guess I'm being dishonest. But no one's thrown me out or sent their dog after me yet."

Dan walked down the steps and headed for the next house on his cards. "I guess," he confided, "you can't say you want someone to be president because he's *neat*." He made a mental note to himself not to use the word again.

Dan had been canvassing for Babbitt every weekend for the last few weeks, but he wasn't convinced it was a good method to win over voters. "I'm more likely to read something in the mail, myself," he said. Going directly to someone's home seemed overly intrusive to him, like being a snoopy reporter from one of the gossipy tabloids instead of a former writer for *The Wall Street Journal*. He was often as uncomfortable and awkward in the exchanges as the people confronted by a stranger at their front door. In his mind a canvass was a labor-intensive business of marginal political profit. He had learned from experience, for instance, that the canvass lists were often inaccurate, sending him to houses in search of Democrats who had long since moved somewhere else.

But Babbitt's principal obstacle in the race was proving his electoral viability, Dan thought. At least if voters saw some volunteers for Babbitt, they wouldn't think he was totally a lost cause. And, Dan said wryly, using volunteers instead of the mail saved the campaign twenty-two cents per pamphlet.

Dan was only two houses away when two women knocked on Len Fleischer's door. They were from Massachusetts, supporters of Dukakis and helping in that campaign's canvass, its fourth of the primary. With the primary only seventeen days away, many campaigns had taken to the streets of Cheshire County—six, in fact: Babbitt, Dukakis, Jackson, Gore, Gephardt, and Simon. If you were a registered Democrat this particular Saturday, you could count on a lot of business at your front door.

Going door to door on a Saturday morning brought a person into contact with a lot of people who had things other than politics on their minds. Dan encountered people returning from the grocery store; a man polishing the chrome on his car; a woman still in her nightie, holding the morning's wash; and a husband trying to usher five kids into a station wagon to go to the movies. Many weren't home. Several sent their children to the door and didn't want to be bothered by salesmen of any kind.

Susan Crotto, a schoolteacher who was canvassing in tandem with Dan, came back from a house where she had been talking for some time—an uncommon occurrence for most canvassers. Dan asked what issues the woman had been interested in. None, Susan replied. The woman had just made some peanut brittle, had given some to Susan, and then explained the recipe. This was Susan's first political experience, and she was alternately bemused and discouraged by the responses she was getting. Many of the voters she managed to involve in a conversation reminded her of the principal of her school: he said he had narrowed his choice down to Bush, Dole, Hart, or Dukakis. "You figure it out," she said.

Dan ran into a pair of Dukakis canvassers arriving at a street he had just finished.

"Don't bother with this street," he told them. "They all say they're for Babbitt."

They laughed with him.

"And that house," he said, pointing to a house across the street. "Don't go there. The guy's got a mean German shepherd."

Over the span of the morning, Dan turned his canvass into more than a quest for Babbitt votes. He was becoming intrigued by what motivated, or didn't motivate, the voters. His original plan of taking on the primary as an intellectual pursuit, a project, was coming back to the fore.

"All of them seem to have good ideas," one woman told him when he asked her why she was still undecided. "No one stands out as a front-runner. I liked Dukakis at first, but he's seemed to slip back lately."

"Will the results of Iowa make a big difference to you?"

"That's right," she said. "New Hampshire is waiting to hear from Iowa."

"If I've heard that once, I've heard it five hundred times," Dan said later. He was pinning a lot of his Babbitt hopes on a good showing in Iowa.

A woman came to her kitchen screen door, which she refused to unlock.

"I'm with Babbitt," Dan assured her. He held up his pamphlet—carefully, as if to show her his intentions were nonviolent—and placed it on the doorstep. "Will you read this?"

"Sure," she answered. "Someone was just here for Mr. Jackson."

"Well, there's some Dukakis people around, too," Dan said.

"I just can't make up my mind," the woman confided.

"Would you mind telling me why?"

"There's just too many of them."

"Waiting for what happens in Iowa?" Dan thought he had discovered a trend.

"Not necessarily," she said. "I'm just tired of all the debates and TV commercials."

At many doors where no one was home, Dan found leaflets from Jackson, Dukakis, Simon, or one of the other campaigns already squeezed into the storm-door jamb. He would insert Babbitt's into the growing stack and move on.

"I guess you've had your fill of political brochures today," he told one resident. "I'm with Jacks— ah, Babbitt."

On another street corner he saw a black woman already talking with a homeowner at the next house on the list. "I'm not sure of the protocol on this," he admitted, and he waited on the sidewalk for his turn.

"Who are you with?" the woman asked when she left the house.

"Babbitt," Dan answered. "Is that guy for Jackson?" He motioned to the house.

"No, he likes some things about Jackson, but he's undecided. Give him a try."

A Dukakis canvasser walked by and joined the impromptu Democratic caucus. "I've done mine," he said. "I'm going home. Maybe they'll vote for *someone*." Two more young men sauntered up the street—Mormons going door to door for their church.

By the end of the day Dan had altered his short speech, as well as his view about the effectiveness of the canvass.

"Have you been canvassed too many times today?" he would ask a resident.

"Yes," was the customary response.

"I'll just give you this from Governor Babbitt and get out of your hair. I'm sorry to bother you."

Back at Pat Russell's house, going over the day's tallies, he and Susan marked down three Babbitt supporters as their catch of the day. Susan was downbeat from the results. Ron Russell, Pat's husband and a political veteran, told her a story from the 1984 primary to try to cheer her up. During the voting, he said, he had manned a table at one Keene ward for Walter Mondale, matching the names of the people who showed up at the polls with the campaign's list of confirmed supporters (if a supporter didn't show up, the campaign would call the person and urge them to get to the polls before they closed). He was sitting next to a Hart worker doing the same thing. Mondale's organization had 158 names on its list of supporters in the ward; Hart's had 24. When the ballots were counted, Hart had received more than 200 votes; Mondale got 175.

"You never know for sure what's going to happen," Ron concluded. "The organization doesn't account for everything."

Dan had decided that, with all the other Democrats going door to door, the importance of the day's work for Babbitt had been to avoid being conspicuous by its absence. If no one had been swayed *to* Babbitt, at least they wouldn't decide *against* him for lack of trying.

As for the voters themselves, they were still a mystery to Dan. "It's like dumping chum into the ocean when you're tuna fishing," he said. "You put it out on the water and watch it sink, but you're never sure if the tuna are going to eat it."

Molly Kelly shuttled constantly from the Dukakis office to the canvass headquarters to the phone bank rooms, trying to make sure everything was going smoothly, keeping the volunteers (eighty had arrived from Massachusetts for this big weekend of work) happy by thanking them and making sure they had sodas and sandwiches when they wanted them. She called her daughter, Rachel, from one of her stops to make sure her eleven-year-old was okay. Justin, one of her teenaged sons, tracked her down on Main Street and asked for money. Zach, the oldest, had a basketball game; Molly was sorry she would miss it.

Mike Cook had put two older women to work writing "personal" letters of thanks to the volunteers over Molly's name. He provided the scripts for them to copy. After three hours they were finished and were putting the letters in envelopes when Molly came by to check on them. She looked down at the letters, looked up with a start, and then quickly ruffled through the pages.

"I'll do this," she said kindly to the women, and assigned them to another task. Then she took the letters into another room and tossed them in a wastebasket. Following Mike's scrawled script, the women had signed "Moly Kell" to each letter.

Rachel showed up, and Molly took her over to the phone bank offices. Rachel wanted to help. She now knew Dukakis's positions on the issues well enough to sit down with the adult volunteers and make calls. In her struggle to balance her family, work, and campaign obligations, Molly had arrived at a partial solution. Family life had slowly merged into the campaign. Rachel enjoyed her volunteer work, Zach had become the inhouse expert on what the media was reporting, and Justin simply liked hanging out wherever the action was. Molly was planning to use a week of vacation time for the final push before the primary.

"Getting local volunteers is getting tougher," Molly said. "There's so much to do, and I keep asking them for so much, when I go to the grocery store I think people see me and head for the back door."

She had been having fantasies recently about Saturday mornings. "I dream of waking up and having nothing to do," she said wistfully. "Maybe go cross-country skiing or watch a basketball game. Instead . . ." She looked at the melee around her. "And when I get home, I'm shampooing rugs at midnight."

Compared with most of the other Democratic campaigns in the county, Gephardt's had a small contingent of regular volunteers. Mike Haas, the young coordinator from Wisconsin, had to be creative in getting the most from his smaller numbers. He dubbed them "Team Gephardt," reflecting his sports background, and plastered his small office on Main Street with hand-lettered posters of exhortations ("Only ____Days to Game Time" was one, "What Have We Accomplished *Today*?" another), the kind that might be found on the walls of a football team's locker room. Quotes of the day—from Gephardt, volunteers, philosophers, and Bruce Springsteen, a personal hero of Mike's—were put up each morning on the front door.

He was good at finding the right approach to get a volunteer to help. "I can't say no when he asks," said Karen Greer, one of the small core group. "He can look so sad, it would be like beating a puppy."

When Mike was short of troops he simply went out and did the work himself. On a snowy afternoon in early February he was working Washington Street in Keene, finishing off a ward that had not been reached in an earlier canvass. His aging Buick had broken down again, forcing him to sleep several nights in the office. His Visa card credit was beyond its limit, and he was waiting for an expense check so he could get the car fixed.

The sky was darkening, but he trudged on up the sidewalk. Many of the voters he contacted said they still hadn't made up their minds. "It's early yet," one woman told him, expressing a sense of campaign time totally out of sync with Mike's. He thought the game was in its final seconds.

Night arrived, and Mike headed back through the accumulating snow to his office. Volunteers would be arriving soon to start another round of phone calls.

"I sincerely hope," he said as he walked, "that I don't already personally know everyone voting for Gephardt."

Dan Melanson was back in his old neighborhood. He was twenty-nine now, but fifteen years ago he had lived here in West Keene. These streets had been part of his paper route. It was the first weekend in February and bitterly cold—minus eighteen degrees on Sunday morning, with a brisk north wind blowing wisps from the high snowbanks that stung like darts when they hit his face. Dan had never before been remotely interested in politics; he hadn't even voted in past elections. Today he was braving the cold to go door to door for Gary Hart.

Dan had become a volunteer for Gary Hart's renewed campaign in an indirect way. Paige Crowley, a twenty-five-year-old from Washington, D.C., had recently been sent as the campaign's co-ordinator for the region. She was a family friend of the Harts—her stepfather, Joseph Tydings, Jr., had been a U.S. senator from Maryland—and had offered to help after Hart rejoined the race in December. When she had arrived in Cheshire County in January, just in time to organize Hart's day-long visit to Keene, she had found few local people willing to volunteer. Calling from the lists of Hart's supporters in 1984 and early 1987, Paige soon learned that most of them had either committed themselves to other candidates or, if they were still undecided, were cool toward Hart's reentry. Making matters more difficult, the place the campaign had located for her to serve as both a temporary home and an office was a cabin, donated by a supporter, at the end of a dirt road in the backwoods of rural Winchester. It would be a nice spot to get away for some winter solitude, but it was not the best place for coming into contact with political activists. Dan Melanson lived next door. He was, he would admit later, a little smitten when he first met his new neighbor Paige, a diminutive, waiflike woman with dark hair, vivid blue eyes, and a warm personality that mixed intelligence with idealism. Dan was impressed by her enthusiasm for Hart and moved by her difficult situation, being dropped at the last minute in such alien territory. For the next month, despite no previous political inclinations, he did anything he could to help her—and thus her candidate. When the Hart campaign staged its canvass, manned predominantly by out-of-state college students, Dan was one of only a few local residents to take part. He volunteered quickly for his former neighborhood.

Canvassers in Cheshire County during the primary campaign normally encountered residents who were polite but curt when they came to the front door. A few would be chatty. Most, however, would listen to the campaign spiel silently and a bit impatiently, offering little in either encouragement or discouragement except a hand to accept the obligatory leaflet and a quick closing of the door. They weren't exactly unfriendly—Mike Cook, for instance, noticed that the tallies from canvasses usually showed twice the percentage of "1" designations as phone banks of the same neighborhood. He figured some people would simply say they supported your candidate in order to get you moving without offending you. But, being Yankees or perhaps just tired of being bothered, they were rarely talkative.

What Dan experienced on his canvass, therefore, was unprecedented in two ways: the people wanted to talk, and they were openly hostile to his candidate.

"Do you have any thoughts about Gary Hart?" he asked at one house after his opening explanation of why he was standing at the woman's kitchen door.

"He's unstable," the woman answered heatedly. "If you don't have your personal life in order, you can't run the country." Dan tried to talk about the thick booklet in his hands, containing several speeches on policy positions Hart had made in the last year. She interrupted him to say that she was from Colorado, had volunteered for Hart in his Senate campaigns, but would not even consider voting for Hart this time.

Across the street Dan introduced himself to an elderly woman, reminding her that he'd once lived a few doors away and delivered her newspaper, and started his speech about Hart.

"Oh, don't *talk* to me about that man," she exclaimed. "I wouldn't vote for him if he was the only candidate on the ballot. It's one thing to be disillusioned by a president *after* he gets in the White House, but I don't want to *start* the process disillusioned." She talked at length about the Donna Rice affair.

"His family's one hundred percent behind him now," Dan offered, a bit of information Paige had told him, which he thought might slow down the woman's tirade.

"Oh, get off it," the woman replied. "She's just there hoping to get to the White House, too. Otherwise she'd be asking for alimony. I'm old-fashioned enough to still believe in morality."

"Have a good day," Dan finally said after more of a lecture. Back on the street, he mentioned that the same woman used to keep his baseballs if he hit them into her yard.

The Hart campaign's canvass scale went from "1" to "4," and as Dan went house to house he quickly became accustomed to writing down "4" once his doorstep conversation was completed. There were a few variations of his string of rejections.

"What do you think of Gary Hart?" he asked one man.

"No comment."

"So it would be—unprofitable of me to leave this booklet with some information about him?"

"Unprofitable."

"I guess he's a '4,' " Dan said back on the street.

"Oh, *no*," another woman said when she heard Hart's name. "This is a bad time." She reached hurriedly for the booklet, said "thank you," and closed the door.

Dan was almost relieved. "I don't mind a '4' if it's that way: polite," he said.

Not everyone was totally against Hart, although Dan reaped no "1" responses from his old neighborhood. Most people weren't home. One man called Hart "gutsy" for getting back into the race.

Another said he didn't intend to vote. "I'm sorry to hear that," Dan said. "Of course, I didn't last time." An elderly woman said she wouldn't be needing the extra booklet Dan offered for her husband, who was listed as a Democrat; he had been dead for three years.

As canvasses go, Hart's was one of the best organized and thorough, and the thirty-five volunteers who participated over the weekend were dedicated enough to brave the chill of the streets and the heat of the doorsteps to cover all of Keene. After the first day one volunteer from Massachusetts returned to the canvass headquarters nearly frozen. He had gone to ninety doors, he said. Only nine people were home; half of them were "4," and none was a "1." He drove the two hours home to Boston that night and returned the next morning.

Over the two days the Hart canvassers knocked on 3,993 doors in Keene. Of those, 2,378 homes had no one home, or the people listed on the canvass cards had moved. Sixty-eight voters said they intended to support Hart; 349 were adamantly against him.

The Bush campaign was canvassing the same weekend, the only extensive Republican canvass in Cheshire County in 1988. Their technique was slightly different. Rather than using cards that specifically identified households with residents registered in their party, they concentrated on neighborhoods with the highest percentage of Republicans, went to every house in those areas, gave out a Bush tabloid targeted for New Hampshire (it was designed to look like *USA Today*), made their pitch, and moved on without recording the responses for later follow-ups. In campaign parlance this is called a "lit drop." Fourteen volunteers were dispatched from the Lane home.

Both Kendall and Jane Lane did not like this kind of work. "I have to steel myself each time," Jane said. "I don't care for phoning, either, but I'd rather do that than go door to door. It's effective, though." Both of them had done it in their own campaigns—Kendall for the state legislature and city council, Jane for the county commission.

In an afternoon's canvassing Kendall covered two neighborhoods. Only four people were home, one of them a Democrat.

"There's a growing interest in this area for Babbitt," Dan Burnham reported on the first weekend of February. He had been finishing off a few neighborhoods in Keene that had not been reached in the earlier canvass. The town of Troy was the next target, and the handful of "Babbitteers" had gathered again at Pat Russell's house.

"More and more people are saying, 'He's our man,'" Dan said. "But I don't think he has a chance in hell if he doesn't beat Simon in Iowa. No matter how much people like him, I don't think they'll want to throw away their vote."

Lisa Babish was going through the mail.

"Oh, my God!" she shouted, holding up a postcard. "It's from our lit drop last week. Somebody filled out a request for information! This is the first time this has happened."

Eleanor Labrie was sitting in the Gephardt office on an afternoon in early February. She was drafting letters for Gephardt supporters to send to the *Sentinel*, letters of her own urging friends to back her candidate, letters for Mike Haas to send to volunteers, and letters following up phone bank calls.

"If I see the words *honesty and integrity* much more," she said in exasperation. Before she retired Eleanor had taught English, writing, and public speaking. "This is not exactly creative writing," she said of her new duties.

Mike Haas had a script he wanted her to follow. She looked up from her work at one point to ask: "Does it have to say, 'I hope you will join me, Norm D'Amours [a former congressman], and a *growing* number of New Hampshire voters'? Can't I say a *horde* of New Hampshire voters, or a *host* of New Hampshire voters?"

"Be creative, I don't care," Mike answered. Eleanor smiled and started another letter.

Molly Kelly came into the Dukakis office, where Mike Cook was going over the latest phone bank and canvass tallies.

"We *own* Hinsdale," he said, looking at the results from that town.

The statistics cheered Molly, who had been disquieted by an encounter a few minutes earlier on Main Street. She told Mike about it.

She had run into a man she had been slowly cultivating to become a volunteer. Just two days before, he had agreed to help out at the polls on primary day; he had even convinced his wife to register to vote, so she could cast a ballot for Dukakis. But *The Keene Sentinel*, as part of a series leading toward the primary, had run a story and a chart outlining the candidates' positions on a range of social issues. On abortion it listed Dukakis as being prochoice and in favor of federal funding for abortions sought by poor women.

Seeing Molly on the sidewalk, the man had accosted her. He was prochoice, too, he said, but against federal funding. He informed her he could no longer support Dukakis and walked off.

Mike shook his head. His persona as the inhouse cynic who believed in the power of television advertising, the necessity of the mechanics of organizing, and the absurdity of voters whose support pivoted on narrow issues was now well established. A week earlier, accompanying an environmental official from Massachusetts who had been sent as a Dukakis surrogate to Cheshire County, Mike had sat in on a long talk between the official and Shelley Nelkens. Shelley kept harping on the Price-Anderson bill before Congress. "I thought Price-Anderson was an accounting firm," he said later. As a Texan, Mike believed the value of an oil import fee was an article of political faith, but a day earlier, on the phone to a potential supporter, he had painstakingly explained why Dukakis's position opposing the fee was the "correct" view.

"I just don't understand it," Molly said of the man she had just met on the street. "I mean, I wouldn't be for Dukakis unless he *did* support federal funding."

Mike shook his head again and went back to his tally sheets.

———

Tom and Valerie Britton were spending a Sunday afternoon at the Gore office on Central Square. Jon Meyer, the county coordinator, was sitting behind his Macintosh computer (it was his sister's, and he had brought it back from his home after the holidays). Allyson, the Brittons' young daughter, sat in a corner, occupying herself by blowing bubbles from a small bottle of soap. Tom and Valerie went through the voting lists of Troy, their hometown, and some nearby towns, searching for names of people they knew. When they found one Jon would type in the name, change the salutation on a form letter on his computer screen, punch a button, and a letter would spit out from his printer.

Tom or Valerie would sign the letter, adding a handwritten post-script. "Senator Gore is a young, great, experienced leader who knows where the country needs to head in the '80's and '90's," Tom wrote on one. "I hope you'll vote for him on February 16th."

Valerie scanned the lists, which included notations from a recent phone bank. "Jackson?" she said when she came to the name of a friend. She showed it to Tom.

"No, that can't be right," he said.

"That's what it says."

"I'll call him tonight," Tom promised.

The day before, Tom had been canvassing door to door. One man had said he was deciding between Gore and Simon. Sensing an opening, Tom had said Simon was too liberal and therefore un-electable. As an example, he'd cited their differences on U.S. policy in the Persian Gulf. "We're in there," Tom had told the man. "We can't pull out now."

The man had seemed to perk up and asked about Nicaragua.

"Can you believe it? I had to defend Al for *not* supporting the contras," Tom recounted. "I finally had to say at least he's the only one to approve humanitarian aid. It's not everything, but it's closer."

The Bush campaign still had a few communities in the county without town chairmen, so Pete Johnson and Kendall and Jane Lane decided to devote an evening to the task.

They looked over the lists of prospects for each town and decided who should make the first call—often Pete, who would introduce himself on the phone as Bush's coordinator in the region. If he couldn't close the deal, they would wait a half hour while they worked on another town. After enough time had elapsed, Jane, the campaign's county chairman, or Kendall would call back. Sometimes all three would have called before the night was over.

"They didn't realize we were in the same room, using the same phone," Kendall said. "It worked pretty well."

The Kemp group was holding a meeting at the home of Dr. David Ridge, and they were brainstorming for more ways to "get the name out," as Al Rubega called it. Each person was asked for ideas.

One woman suggested putting up leaflets on the bulletin boards near the exits of grocery stores. "I always wear my button when I go shopping," she added. "You can start a lot of conversations while you stand in the checkout line."

Dr. Ridge said that when he was at a traffic light, particularly the long one at Central Square, and the vehicle in front of him had two people in it, he often got out and took a leaflet to hand through the window to the passenger. His chiropractic patients also usually got an earful about Kemp as part of their treatments.

Al urged each volunteer to write letters to the *Sentinel*. Mary said that on her way to and from school each day, she took different back roads and put Kemp brochures in the newspaper's delivery boxes. "It's not as good as going door to door," she said, "but it's better than nothing."

That reminded Al. "We need to canvass another town this weekend," he said.

Mary rolled her eyes. "We've got company coming," she told her husband.

"We'll just tell them we're all going 'Kemping,' " he answered. "They helped us at the street fair, they can help again."

Mary frowned and turned to the whole group: "Once when they

came, we left for a meeting and told them to lock the door when they left."

Mike Cook said he had come up with a "breakthrough." Using a special felt-tip pen and a professional photocopier, he could take one handwritten letter and make multiple reproductions of it, all of which looked like originals.

The Dukakis campaign was sending these "personal" letters to all the "1" (supporters) and "2" (leaners) designations on its list in the county, urging them to remember to vote on primary day.

Molly had been given a quota of one thousand. She allowed Mike to make copies of an unsigned letter but insisted on writing her name on each one herself. She wasn't taking any more chances on the spelling.

By late January the "Sign Wars" had begun. And in the battle for choice spots to display a candidate's name, David Ridge of the Kemp campaign was the Luke Skywalker of Cheshire County. His resources were comparatively meager, matched against those of many of the other campaigns—Kemp's campaign was running short of money, and Cheshire County was not one of its priorities—but he made the most of what was at hand.

Early on cold mornings he would head out in his Ford station wagon, equipped with cardboard signs, wooden stakes, a hammer and nails, a staple gun, a sledgehammer, and a bucket of water. Finding a good spot near a busy intersection or along a heavily traveled road, he would get out, pound an indentation in the frozen ground, place a sign stake in it, and pour some water around the stake, waiting until it was anchored in ice. Other campaigns stuck their signs in snowbanks, but this seemed too impermanent to Dr. Ridge.

Putting signs along public rights-of-way was technically against the law—locations on private property, with the owner's permission, were supposed to be the only places where political signs were allowed, and only during a prescribed period before the vote—but virtually everyone did it. State highway crews occasionally took down violating signs (one crew caught Dr. Ridge in the act of erecting a sign at a particularly desirable traffic island and warned him off), but signs would crop up the next day like midwinter weeds. Theft, even from legal locations, was a chronic problem. Kendall Lane and Janet Shawn each had a Bush and Dole sign, respectively, stolen from their front yards in the night. Most of the campaigns privately suspected their opponents; it turned out some high school students were competing to see who could collect the most.

Like a trapper checking his lines, Dr. Ridge regularly patroled his sign route, replacing missing or damaged ones when they needed it. As the primary approached, and his supplies were running thin, he often took down his most prized signs in the evening and put them back up the next morning.

One of his coups was a giant Kemp sign, a legal one, near the entrance of Keene's most popular grocery store. All the other campaigns were envious of its strategic location. Asked how he managed to get first dibs, Dr. Ridge would just grin slyly. "I went through channels," he said.

Signs were everywhere. Andi Johnson started with a small Simon sign on the side of a barn adjacent to her house, located on a main highway in Dublin. The closer February 16 came, the larger the sign seemed to become; she finished with one that was nearly four by six feet.

Campaigns that had offices in downtown Keene filled what window space they had with posters facing outward, and they scoured Main Street for merchants who would let them put signs in the display windows. The Dole campaign made its first presence known in the county with signs along the highway, including bumper stickers attached to the back of "No Passing" and "Yield" signs.

Doug Kidd found a religious group in western New Hampshire that wanted to help. He put its members to work making hundreds of wooden stakes and attaching them to Robertson signs and turned them loose along the roadsides. What Dr. Ridge accomplished with strategic placement, they countered with overwhelming numbers. No road was too remote. Even trees (also technically off limits) became signposts.

Some signs had people as stakes. Starting in February, Mike Haas, the Gephardt coordinator, began going to high-traffic intersections during morning and evening commuting times, where he would stand like a hitchhiker, holding up a placard instead of a thumb, searching for votes instead of a ride.

Several of the campaigns staged what was called a "honk and wave." Their favorite locale was Central Square. Volunteers would stand along the rotary bearing placards that urged motorists, "Honk If You Support ———." When someone hit the horn the volunteers would wave in return.

The Dukakis campaign tried one on a Saturday in early February. "Honk If You Like Mike Dukakis," read the first signs. Not much noise was generated, so the signs were simplified: "Honk for Dukakis." Still not much reaction. Mike Cook got in his car and began circling the Central Square, leaning on his horn, hoping it would catch on. Finally a volunteer edited the signs once more: "Honk!"

Jon Meyer watched the scene from his window in Gore's second-story office. The failed Dukakis "honk and wave" gave him an idea. He went into his supply room, worked on a placard, and walked down the stairs to stand next to his competitors.

As cars passed, Jon held up his sign—"Don't Honk If You Like Al Gore"—and smiled contentedly at the silence.

Kendall Lane was writing furiously on a piece of paper late one night in his den. The other campaigns' signs were getting on his nerves. As early as December he and his town chairmen had gone through an elaborate process to locate people who would allow them to place the limited number of Bush signs assigned to the county on their lawns and office yards. And they had waited patiently for

the legal window to open for putting up signs. Now the Bush name
seemed lost in the forest of signs that lined the rights-of-way. He
was writing a letter to the *Sentinel* (which he planned to have
someone else sign and send) attacking the other candidates.

"It said if their supporters don't understand the law and can't
obey the law, what can we expect from the candidates?" he said
the next morning. "I'd really written this vicious attack on them.
But the more I thought about it, the more I thought: Do I want to
do this?"

He talked it over with Pete Johnson, who was still living in the
Lane house. "Finally we decided the hell with it," Kendall said.
"Let's get *our* signs up!"

He and Pete loaded Kendall's car with some extra Bush signs
and headed for the major highways around Keene, sticking them
in snowbanks near the other campaigns' signs.

Shortly after midnight, as Kendall was placing a Bush sign in a
snowbank along a highway south of town, a state trooper pulled
over.

"What do you think *you're* doing?" he asked. Kendall was a city
councillor and prominent lawyer, and the trooper knew him.

Kendall looked up, shrugged his shoulders, and confessed. "Putting up campaign signs," he said sheepishly.

The trooper raised his eyebrows, as if Kendall were some wayward
but harmless teenager, laughed a little, and drove on.

"I've had my eye on this place for some time," Dr. Ridge said one
morning, a week before the primary, as he pulled his car into a
parking lot near the bottom of Main Street. He stopped near a huge
barn that overlooked the street's intersection with two highways.
It had once been part of the Lane family homestead in Keene,
adjacent to the house (now a real estate office) where the Lanes'
American flag had been unfurled to welcome President Gerald Ford
to Keene during the 1976 primary. The barn was now a warehouse
for a Keene business, and Dr. Ridge had spent part of the previous
day talking to the owner.

He pulled a ladder out of the back of his station wagon, stuck his staple gun in his back pocket, and climbed up the side of the barn, high enough, he said, to make sure no vandal could reach his spot.

He was cradling a bundle in his arms, and he struggled as he slowly unwrapped it and stapled it to the clapboards. It was one of the Kemp banners Al Rubega had made last summer.

15

IOWA

Another damn Robertson sign. Kendall Lane couldn't believe how many dotted Route 9, the highway he traveled every Monday morning to his weekly "Freedom Fighters" meeting in Concord. The signs were a minor irritation, like the rising winter sun he had to squint into on his hour drive east. He was used to the sun's glare: it had become part of his routine since the Bush group had first gathered in March 1986, nearly two years ago. The Robertson signs, however, were a fresh annoyance. They hadn't even been there last week. Now, on the morning of February 8, 1988, the day of the caucuses in Iowa, they stared back at Kendall at every turn in the twisting highway.

"Novices," Kendall muttered when he saw another Robertson sign nailed illegally to a pine tree. "They don't know what they're doing." There had even been instances, he had heard from other Bush partisans, of Robertson supporters putting up signs in the night next to Bush signs on private property, where only the Bush campaign had permission to erect campaign signs. The very idea offended him.

Kendall's February so far had followed the familiar pattern of optimism and aggravation of the preceding months. At last week's "Freedom Fighters" meeting they had sat around the room speculating on who would be second to Bush in New Hampshire. Some had said Dole, and some, like Kendall, thought Kemp was the most likely runner-up. None had doubted that Bush's lead was impregnable. The mood had been jocular, confident. "Dole doesn't have enough presence in the state," Kendall had opined. "He's got no mechanism for turning out the vote. Bad weather on primary day would kill him."

The only sour note for Kendall at the meeting had been yet another change in the schedule of appearances. After all his complaints about the campaign ignoring Cheshire County, the receptions for Barbara Bush had been put back on track. But the campaign had rejected Kendall's request that Mrs. Bush attend a banquet planned for the same day by the county's Republican women, and some local receptions for Neil Bush, the candidate's son, had been canceled. Worse, Kendall had been informed that Bush would be in Keene on February 9, but only for a small—and private—reception at an insurance company. No rally, no parade, no chance for the public to see and hear Kendall's candidate. The same old story, just like Bush's visit to Keene last April.

"From April 16 until February 16, he has not made a single trip to Keene," Kendall had complained to Will Abbott, the state campaign director. "Now he's going to make a trip to Keene, and he's going to the Grange [the National Grange Mutual Insurance Company], which is a closed event; Grange people only. Which means he comes in here, and the public, the undecideds, and even those kind of supporting him who need to get at least some payback for supporting him are being shut out. They are being told, 'You are not going to see him, not going to have access to him. You're not important enough. Keene is not important enough for him to make a showing here.'" Will Abbott's explanation—that a crowd of four hundred at the insurance company was as good as four hundred people at a public event, that there wasn't time for anything more elaborate, and that local Bush supporters would be invited to a big statewide event the night of the primary—did not satisfy Kendall. "They've had *months* to get him here," he said. "It's not my fault, it's their fault that they waited for the last week. But it is going to be *my* fault if he doesn't win here."

Driving to Concord on this morning, Kendall let his mind drift west to Iowa, where the caucuses would be held that night. *Iowa*. Another irritation. "I hate this idea of only a week between Iowa and New Hampshire," he said.

Not many years ago the Iowa caucuses had been relatively obscure in the quest for the presidency. Citizens do not vote directly for candidates at them. They gather in the evening—often in private homes—to select precinct representatives to their party's convention later in the year. The convention then elects delegates to the national convention. Sometimes the representatives selected at the caucuses are pledged to presidential candidates; sometimes not. Unlike the primaries, where the ballots are secret and final, caucus participants often are asked to declare their candidate preference openly and in some instances (if their candidate doesn't get a certain percentage required to be "viable") are even allowed to change their minds after the initial division of the room. Being several steps removed from a direct vote, the caucuses had been little regarded and little noticed by national political journalists during many elections. But after 1976, when Jimmy Carter gave Iowa a high priority in his steady march to the White House and used his finish there (his campaign declared him the winner, even though "uncommitted" placed first) to establish him as a legitimate contender, the caucuses were given serious attention by candidates and media alike.

In 1980 Bush had won the Republican caucuses in Iowa and vaulted to political prominence as the principal opponent of Ronald Reagan. At that time the caucuses were more than a month before the New Hampshire primary, and the Reagan campaign skillfully used the interval to regain its footing, culminating in a famous debate between Bush and Reagan in Nashua, New Hampshire, where Reagan grabbed a microphone ("I paid for this microphone!" he exclaimed) and the momentum he needed to win. By 1984 the time between the caucuses and primary had been cut to eight days.

Walter Mondale won the caucuses, but Gary Hart's surprising second-place finish propelled Hart to national attention as the chief alternative to the former vice president, a surge that Mondale did not have time to combat in one week. Hart won in New Hampshire, and the term the *Iowa bounce* entered political jargon.

The Iowa bounce was on Kendall's mind this morning. Dole was expected to win in Iowa. No one doubted that. The question for Kendall and other Bush supporters in New Hampshire was what impact a win in Iowa would have on Dole's standing in the Granite State. "What I don't know is where the marginal voters will go," Kendall said. "What is the potential? Will Bush people at the last minute suddenly become Dole people? Will the uncommitteds move entirely to Dole, with no percentage to Bush, and hurt us that way?" In Cheshire County, at least, he didn't perceive much of a threat. Dole's campaign had only recently shown any signs of life, still far behind Bush and even Kemp in Kendall's estimation. A few days ago he had been called by a Dole volunteer. Kendall kept the person on the line long enough to learn about the Dole phone bank and the location of the new Dole office in Keene. He considered sending a college student to the office to check out the operation but decided against it. Instead Kendall occasionally drove past the office and scanned the parking lot in the rear to gauge how many people were working. It worried him a little, but then again even the dormant Haig campaign had mustered enough last-minute energy to put up a few road signs.

He put them all in the same category, like the pair of Robertson placards around the next bend in the road, the change of schedule, and the Iowa caucuses: irritations, the kind that flared and made a person edgy the closer you got to the primary. "I wish we could vote right now," he said as he drove.

Ron Kaufman was pacing in the front of the room while the "Freedom Fighters," now about forty people, settled onto their seats. His first announcement quieted them immediately. Bush, he said, would finish *third* tonight in Iowa, behind not just Dole, but Robertson as well. Kendall had just sat down with a cup of coffee and a doughnut. He looked around the room and saw a number of shaken faces. It might even be a distant third, Kaufman added. The breezy confidence that had marked "Freedom Fighters" meetings for two years evaporated in a matter of seconds.

During last week's meeting, when they had discussed the "spin" they would put on Dole's expected win in Iowa, Kaufman had refused even to entertain the notion of anything less than a strong second-place finish for Bush in Iowa. Now he was telling them the vice president, who had won Iowa over Ronald Reagan in 1980, was going to be beaten by a senator and a preacher. "Pray for a Dukakis victory tonight in Iowa," he advised the stunned group. "Maybe the media here will focus on that, but the next forty-eight hours will be a horrid time in the news for the vice president."

The new "spin" the core supporters were to use when they talked to reporters or their volunteers, once the results from Iowa were in, was that Robertson's strong showing in Iowa would help Bush. Republicans frightened by the prospect of Robertson winning the nomination would turn to Bush to stop the televangelist. As for Dole's win, they were to remind people that he was from a midwestern state and therefore had the same advantages in Iowa that Dukakis had in New Hampshire. "Iowa picks corn, but New Hampshire picks presidents." That was to be their "line."

With Kaufman's bad news out of the way, clearing the air like a bolt of lightning, the "Freedom Fighters" went through their business agenda with grim but renewed determination—the schedule for the last week, a big canvass the final weekend, election day plans for each region, details on getting out the vote, and the themes of the week: "Through thick and thin, Ronald Reagan has trusted only one man to stand by him—George Bush"; and "New Hampshire Picks Presidents."

On his drive back to Keene, Kendall struggled to find a silver lining in the new cloud over his dreams. With New Hampshire now more important than ever for Bush's candidacy, maybe at least the campaign would finally pay more attention to Cheshire County, he thought. He would call Will Abbott to lobby again for having Barbara Bush attend the Keene banquet on February 11 and suggest that they organize a straw poll for the event. His organization could stack the event by buying most of the tickets to show the vice president's flag. He would notify his volunteers about what to expect tonight and steel them for greater exertions in the next week—being on the "inside" had its advantages. He would redouble his efforts to get a crowd to turn out near Bush's appearance tomorrow at the Keene insurance company to cheer when the limousine pulled up. And he would drive past the Dole office for another check on the parking lot.

But first he had to get back to Keene. All the way home the Robertson signs glistened in the sun, mocking him at every turn.

The other campaigns in Cheshire County kept themselves busy during the day as they waited anxiously to learn if the caucus-goers in Iowa would reshuffle the primary deck.

Jon Meyer, the Gore coordinator, was making his own placards because the headquarters had cut back on supplies. Following his strategy to concentrate on the South, Gore had pulled his resources out of Iowa some time ago and was scaling back in New Hampshire. "I think they've declared Cheshire County as part of Iowa," Jon said sarcastically as he worked.

Janet Shawn was recuperating from a hectic weekend for the Dole campaign. Seven college students had been in the county to help on the phone banks, and she and Barbara MacKenzie had been in charge of feeding them and the local volunteers. *The Keene Sentinel* had endorsed Dole among the Republicans (and Dukakis for the Democrats), and she was making hundreds of photocopies of the endorsement to mail to voters in the county.

Molly Kelly was also recovering from the weekend. A contingent of college volunteers from Syracuse University had been in Keene, and they had invaded her apartment to shower each morning. She and Mike Cook were lining up volunteers for primary day—seventy people were already signed up—and on this day Len Fleischer

agreed to assist the Dukakis effort. Molly's daughter, Rachel, was
bringing in some of her friends to stuff and lick envelopes after
school. The state campaign director got all the local offices on a
conference call to tell them that Dukakis would be finishing third
in Iowa, not as high as Molly had hoped, but high enough to return
confidently to his home turf in New England.

Eleanor Labrie composed her own leaflet outlining Gephardt's
positions on issues affecting elderly people: "DO YOU CARE ABOUT
MEDICARE, SOCIAL SECURITY, NURSING HOME COSTS? AARP HAS THE
QUESTIONS. DICK GEPHARDT HAS THE ANSWERS." Mike Haas
planned to distribute them at senior centers and evening bingo
games. "Team Gephardt" was scheduled to gather at a supporter's
home in the evening to watch the Iowa results.

Evening arrived. Andi Johnson was at Simon's office making phone
calls. Pete Kujawski, the coordinator, was celebrating his twenty-
third birthday by addressing GOTV (get out the vote) postcards to
identified Simon supporters, filling in the location and hours of
each person's polling place. As they labored, Andi and Pete watched
C-SPAN on the television. It was carrying a live broadcast of a
Democratic caucus in one precinct of Des Moines, Iowa. When the
caucus tallied its first results, Andi put down the phone: Simon,
76 supporters; Babbitt, 63; Jackson, 49; Dukakis, 47 (Andi and
Pete hooted at Dukakis's total); uncommitted, 19; Gephardt, 17;
Gore, 0; Hart, 0.

"Gephardt didn't even make the threshold to be viable!" Pete
shouted with joy. Iowa was supposed to be a race between Simon
and Gephardt, but in the caucus being broadcast it didn't appear
that way. Andi broke open a bottle of Absolut vodka and poured
herself a victory glass.

A few minutes later, when the caucus allowed those who had
supported "nonviable" candidates or had declared themselves uncommitted to align themselves with other candidates, the results
shifted. Gephardt's supporters, striving to block Simon, had shifted
to Babbitt, who was now the winner of this one caucus.

"I think you'd better come down here. We may be in for a big upset," Pat Russell told Dan Burnham on the phone. She was watching the same caucus on C-SPAN. Dan didn't have a cable hookup, so she knew he didn't know about Babbitt's remarkable showing in Des Moines's 67th precinct.

Dan rushed to his car and headed from Dublin to Keene. *Maybe*, he thought, *something is happening. He's going to do much better than we thought.*

Doug Kidd was teaching an evening business course at Keene State College and wasn't able to follow the Iowa results on television. He was hoping for good news from Iowa, but when someone called him out of the class for a telephone call it was Allison on the line. Her grandmother had just been taken to the hospital, and she needed Doug to drive her there.

Listening to the radio on the way, he heard that Robertson had pulled off an upset, finishing second to Dole in the Republican caucuses, the miracle he had been awaiting.

He and Allison spent the night at the hospital, where her grandmother died in the early morning. They arrived home at 7:30 A.M. Doug showered and headed to work. Robertson's "invisible army" was heading to New Hampshire.

Al Rubega watched television at home with Mary and was disappointed with the Iowa results: Dole, 37 percent; Robertson, 25; Bush, 19; Kemp, 11; du Pont, 7; uncommitted, 1; Haig, 0. But Al was still optimistic.

"If Bush is fatally wounded [as one television commentator had said], Kemp can win New Hampshire," he said. "Dole has no organization, and Bush's soft supporters may go to Kemp, not Dole. It would astonish me if Robertson did as well in New Hampshire—absolutely astonish me."

Kendall Lane didn't bother staying up with the television. He already knew there wouldn't be anything for him on the network specials from Iowa. He had been up early in the morning to go to the "Freedom Fighters" meeting and spent the afternoon and early evening bracing his volunteers for the bad news.

Tomorrow would be long enough. The vice president was coming to Keene, and Kendall was planning another evening of phone bank work. The next seven days would make or break Bush's chances. Kendall figured he should get some sleep to prepare for the last assault.

Before the final results were in, he turned off the TV and headed to bed. The old nightmare returned. *What if we lose Iowa and then lose New Hampshire? All this for nothing. All for nothing.*

"Team Gephardt" was glued to the set in the small apartment of Karen Greer, a friend of Eleanor Labrie's whom Eleanor had brought into the Gephardt campaign. They ate chili and talked nervously as the C-SPAN coverage of the one Des Moines caucus ended and network coverage with the statewide results commenced.

Eleanor was writing postcard reminders to Gephardt supporters when the networks declared her candidate the winner of the Democratic caucuses: Gephardt, 27 percent; Simon, 24; Dukakis, 21; Jackson, 11; Babbitt, 9; uncommitted, 6; Hart, 1; Gore, 1. The Des Moines caucus had been an unrepresentative gathering.

Mike Haas called the apartment from a town outside Cheshire County, where he had been sent to help set up a Gephardt appearance the next day. Everyone took turns talking to him excitedly about Gephardt's chances in New Hampshire, now that he would be coming in as the Iowa victor.

"Make sure someone's in the office tomorrow morning," Mike said. "A lot of people will be calling." Eleanor volunteered for the task.

Dan Burnham had not yet reached Pat Russell's house when the radio news came on with the Iowa results. The hope that Pat's account of the C-SPAN caucus had ignited was quickly extinguished. Babbitt, according to the radio report, was in fifth place and single digits.

It's over, Dan thought. Without a bounce from Iowa Babbitt didn't have a prayer in New Hampshire. The media would write him off in their rush to cover the "hot" candidates from Iowa. All those undecided voters would be either unaware of his candidacy because of the abrupt absence of Babbitt coverage or unwilling to waste their vote on someone so seemingly far back in the pack. From the very start Babbitt's strategy had relied on pulling off a surprise in Iowa and building on it in New Hampshire—the Carter model from 1976—and he had put virtually all his time and resources in those two states, hoping to beat the long-shot odds. Fifth place and single digits were not enough.

It's over. Dan knew it, and from his recent talks with the campaign staff and Babbitt himself, he knew they must feel the same way. The stark reality of it, the necessity to face the political facts, brought back Dan's old reportorial objectivity, which his unexpected devotion, enthusiasm, and hope had overwhelmed for the last few months. The only question in Dan's mind was whether Babbitt should drop out of the race now, before the primary, perhaps throw his support behind Dukakis and hope for a cabinet position if Dukakis became president, or continue competing against the odds in New Hampshire, take another beating, and then end the campaign.

Dan stopped only briefly at the Russell house. His dejection was written on his face when he arrived and when, after watching the network specials for a few minutes, he left for home. There was still a week left before the first primary. No American had yet cast an actual ballot in a voting booth. But as he drove to Dublin in the winter darkness, Dan had only one thought on his mind. *It's over.*

16

FINAL FRENZY

In her dream, Eleanor Labrie saw a golden plate resting under two feet of clear water. A spigot dropped more water into the basin. Suddenly the name *Gephardt* flashed across the golden plate. "It was," she would say later, "a beautiful moment."

Eleanor was up early the morning after Gephardt's win in Iowa. She had promised Mike Haas, the coordinator young enough to be her grandson, that she would open the campaign office and answer the phone, and forty years of teaching school had made Eleanor a woman who took her assignments seriously. Other members of "Team Gephardt" had planned to hold signs on the streets of Keene during the morning commuting time, but they had celebrated the Iowa results too late into the night; all but one slept too long to make it.

Some campaign activities—like the cold-morning "honk and wave" or door-to-door canvassing—were off limits for Eleanor. A lung condition made them out of the question. Simply climbing the two flights of stairs to the Gephardt office was a challenge, leaving her short of breath for a long time afterward. Just as meeting Gephardt at the front door of her house had been an unintended consequence of his brief door-to-door photo opportunity the previous spring, Eleanor's campaign work was having an unexpected effect on her health: her doctor had told her during a recent checkup that the daily ascent to her volunteer desk had left her lungs in their best shape in years. With Gephardt's victory and her beautiful dream still fresh in her mind, Eleanor climbed the steps more easily than ever the morning of February 9.

Sure enough, as soon as she reached the office the phone rang. It was Will Fay, the political reporter from the *Sentinel*, working on a story about local reaction to the Iowa results. "I'm very happy indeed," she told him. "In New Hampshire, he's [Gephardt] going to need a lot of help, and this is going to be the first step of help. I think people are going to recognize his name and realize he's achieved something already." (In the stories that afternoon, Andi Johnson would be quoted saying Simon's second-place finish was a strong showing. Dan Burnham said he was "deeply disappointed" by Babbitt's totals, fearing the "momentum is gone" but arguing that the Iowa caucuses "do not give a true reflection of the American public." On the Republican side, Allison Kidd spoke for her husband, who was already on the road: "As we would say, 'Hallelujah!' Pat has gone from being a media nonentity to being a force to be reckoned with." Jane Lane said the Iowa results were what the Bush campaign had expected. "New Hampshire chooses presidents, Iowa doesn't," said Pete Johnson, the Bush coordinator.)

Eleanor had a busy day. After manning the phones in the morning, she went to a local senior citizens center and distributed the fliers she had made about Gephardt's positions on Social Security and other issues. The candidate was scheduled to come to Cheshire County later in the week, and arrangements for an event in the town of Alstead had to be made. "I wish he'd do something in Keene," she said. (Gephardt's schedule called for him to arrive late, spend the night at a Keene motel, and then go to the event north of the city, on his way up the Connecticut River valley.) "The people are so *ready* for him now, and they weren't before. Instead, he'll sleep late and go to Alstead."

Kendall Lane passed out Bush buttons and stickers as employees of the National Grange Mutual Insurance Company filed past on their way to the cafeteria, where the vice president was about to appear. Like Eleanor Labrie, Kendall had spent the morning answering phone calls. His, however, had a much different tone. Town chairmen, many of them a little panicky after Bush's humiliation in Iowa, wanted to know what to do now. "It's a fight," Kendall said. They were going to have to work harder than ever. "By this weekend, we'll either be back and winning or have lost."

The vice president himself seemed somewhat stunned by the previous night's results. His speech to the crowd of 350 was flat and listless—no one applauded until he finished and Kendall, standing on the sidelines, started them clapping. Bush struggled to find new phrases to jump-start his faltering campaign. "I'm one of you," he told his New Hampshire audience, borrowing intact the line that Dole had used successfully with his fellow midwesterners in Iowa. Much of what Bush said echoed the theme offered by the "Freedom Fighters" that week: for eight years he had "stood by President Reagan" through the good times and the bad. The look on the faces of Bush's aides was uniformly grim.

"Iowa hasn't been doing this long enough to know how to pick presidents," Kendall told the vice president, trying to cheer up his candidate in the holding room after the speech.

"They're off to a good start, though," Bush said without smiling.

John Croteau, another volunteer in the room and one of Bush's key supporters in the county during the ill-fated 1980 primary, reminded Bush that eight years ago New Hampshire had reversed Iowa's verdict. Instead of brightening Bush, it seemed to bring back memories of his loss in 1980, when the "Big Mo" he had carried into Keene had quickly disappeared by the time of the vote. Bush told them he was changing his schedule to devote more time to the state in the final week.

"*Now* they understand how important New Hampshire is," Kendall said afterward. He had talked with the campaign staff, lobbying again for Mrs. Bush to attend the county Republican dinner on Thursday night. Haig and Robertson were rumored to be considering an appearance. Dole was now definitely scheduled to speak during the cocktail hour, and Kendall wanted to "show our strength in his face." The Bush campaign was buying every ticket it could find.

Kendall had arranged for a small crowd of supporters to gather in front of the insurance building for an impromptu rally when Bush left. But the motorcade departed from the rear, and as the limousine pulled out only the Lanes and a few people were nearby. They clapped and waved. Bush, alone in the back of his car, saw them at the last minute. He managed a wan smile and finally gave them a thumbs-up as his limo swept down the back street.

"It's going to be a real fight," Kendall said.

"Hi, I'm calling from the George Bush campaign, and I hope you'll be voting on February 16 in the primary and will support George Bush. Have you considered voting for the vice president? . . . Well, time is getting short. I hope you'll pay attention to the issues and consider George Bush." Kendall and five other volunteers were at a phone bank Tuesday evening, calling the names on their "1" and undecided lists.

They weren't pleased with the responses they were getting. Most people said they were still undecided. Some had moved from undecided to Dole; one, according to the list they kept, had journeyed over the last month from leaning toward to Bush, to undecided, to definitely not Bush.

"Are you getting *any* Bush supporters?" Jane asked Kendall during the phoning. "I'm either getting 'anyone but Bush' or undecided. I can't stand the rejection."

John Croteau was in the midst of a string of depressing calls. "How can they still be undecided?" he asked after one conversation. "I've had *my* mind made up for eight years." Unlike Kendall, who preferred calls to strangers, John said he preferred calling people he knew in town. "If they know me," John said, "at least they *say* they're supporting Bush to make me feel better."

Kendall had watched the evening news, where Dole had talked about momentum. "Oh, please say you've got the 'Big Mo,' please say it," Kendall said he had urged the television set. Robertson had come on, complaining that the New Hampshire primary was "closed" compared with Iowa, because it didn't allow Democrats to cross over for Republicans. "You S.O.B.!" Kendall had exclaimed. "If it had been an honest primary in Iowa, you'd have gotten 5,000 votes instead of 20,000."

John Croteau hung up the receiver after another unfriendly call. The man had angrily told John that he had switched from favorable toward Bush to undecided.

"Well, we've got to pick up on that so we can deal with it," Kendall said. "I don't know *how* we're going to deal with it, but we're going to have to."

"It didn't help to get him out of the shower," said John.

Wednesday, February 10, was blustery and cold. Bruce Babbitt arrived at the Keene airport in the late morning in one of two private planes with his wife, Hattie, two national staff members, three reporters, and a crew from the CBS show *48 Hours*. (As part of its strategy to be as accommodating as possible to the media, the Babbitt campaign had offered CBS more access than the other campaigns, and thus Babbitt's every movement from the night of the Iowa caucuses until Wednesday night was being chronicled by the network. Campaigns still in the thick of the race would be less likely to allow reporters and cameras around them in unguarded moments—it would be too risky—but Babbitt's had almost nothing to lose at this point and wanted any publicity it could get. The *48 Hours* piece, however, would not be broadcast until the night of the primary, too late to affect any New Hampshire voter, and its focus would be on the pathos surrounding the end of a presidential campaign. On the bumpy approach to Keene's airport, Leslie Stahl, the CBS correspondent sitting across from Babbitt in the small four-seater, threw up on the floor.)

The Babbitt campaign was in the midst of a kind of poignant

schizophrenia not uncommon for political campaigns about to go under. Babbitt's fifth-place finish in Iowa had sealed his political fate. No one, from the candidate down through the ranks to the volunteers, now expected him to fare any better in New Hampshire. The media had already written him off entirely. Like Gore, Jackson, Kemp, Haig, and du Pont, Babbitt had virtually disappeared from news reports on the primary. What scant coverage he was being accorded was, like the CBS story that would appear later, predicated on his hopeless situation, or it speculated on how quickly after the primary he might drop out of the race. At the same time, however, Babbitt and his troops seemed energized by his plight, as if they had been freed from the tense competition surrounding the other campaigns. The test they now faced was not how many votes they might garner on February 16, but how bravely they could make it through the next week. The end was near, and for many of the Babbitt partisans their candidate was about to be martyred for telling politically unpopular truths. Standing by him at this hour was their own badge of courage. "There's a deep sense of realism that he's not going to do very well," Dan Burnham said as he waited for the planes to land. "But there's also this remarkable ebullience."

Dan had traveled to Manchester the night before for a rally welcoming Babbitt back to New Hampshire. The crowd had been as wildly raucous as it might have been if Babbitt had won the caucuses. "Who would have thought a year ago," Babbitt joked with his supporters, "that I would be coming into New Hampshire having defeated Gary Hart in Iowa." Standing next to Dan in the audience, Lisa Babish had become teary-eyed while she applauded and laughed. Later, after talking to the headquarters staff—"What will we tell Lisa?" had been the state director's first thought when the Iowa results started coming in—she took Dan aside to dispense the last dollop of hope she could find. "If he comes in fourth [in New Hampshire]," she said, "he might consider running again in 1992."

Dan's Wednesday started at 4:30 A.M., long before dawn, when he went out to his workshop to make more Babbitt signs. Some dust had spit from his saw and lodged in his eye. Struggling in the dark, he had placed a large coffee urn (to be used later at Babbitt's last reception in Cheshire County) on top of his car while he opened a door; it had slipped and spilled over him. Nevertheless, he had manned a "honk and wave" at the bottom of Main Street for an hour before going to a doctor. Now he was going to be a driver in the small motorcade into town. "You were really great last night," he told Babbitt when the candidate climbed out of the plane. "You showed a lot of class." There was a short catch in his voice, and his smile was stoical.

The first stop was Lindy's Diner, where Babbitt mingled with the patrons as a cluster of thirty supporters gathered outside. Lisa Babish had her small megaphone, and as Dan handed out signs she led the partisans in chants of "Yea, Babbitt; Yea, Babbitt!" Her voice was failing her again. Everyone was wearing mittens or gloves; when they clapped, the noise sounded muffled and polite.

The crowd walked with Babbitt up Main Street to a senior meals site. Dan lurched up the median strip, holding his sign high and pointing to his candidate on the sidewalk whenever he caught the eye of a passing motorist. One van honked. After Babbitt and his wife toured the meals center, he spoke briefly to his admirers clustered on the front steps. "Every door you knock on, every phone call you make, is a statement about all of us together as Americans," he said. "It's a statement about our future, about change, about challenge. I'm grateful, and America will be different for our efforts."

At a Headstart center Babbitt posed with the children there and sang nursery rhymes with them for a photo opportunity before joining his supporters for egg-salad sandwiches, potato chips, and Dan's coffee—a political Last Supper for the Cheshire County "Babbitteers." Doris Haddock, one of the disciples, asked him what had convinced him to keep on going after Iowa.

"Ours is the politics of change, a challenge of the future versus the same old stuff," he said. "I am *a* voice for that message, but so are all of you. I'll soon be gone, but you'll stay as a voice for change.

When you get a little bit crusty, get a little bit angry, raise your voice. Touch somebody. And together, we will change the world. The press is already rolling my body into the grave and planting daisies. But we'll win. I don't know when, but we will."

Back at the airport, Dan stayed in his car as the entourage headed for the planes. Earlier he had told Babbitt, "You've built a good base of support in New Hampshire for 1992. You had a good year for a freshman." But now Dan didn't want another private moment with his candidate.

"I've already said good-bye to him too many times," he said.

The letters section of *The Keene Sentinel* was now filled with individual endorsements of the candidates from residents of the region. So many of the campaigns had organized efforts to flood the newspaper with letters that each day's edition was carrying extra pages devoted to them exclusively. Wednesday's *Sentinel* was no exception, carrying letters supporting Gephardt (from a member of "Team Gephardt"), Simon (from a friend of Andi Johnson's), Babbitt (from Susan Crotto, Dan Burnham's canvassing partner), and Kemp (from one of Al Rubega's volunteers, whose husband would have a letter saying much the same thing in the next day's paper).

Close readers of the section would not have been surprised to see Al's name at the bottom of a letter that afternoon. Although the absence of any mention of gun issues might have seemed unusual, his use of the *Sentinel* as a rhetorical foil was in keeping with the aggressive persona—so unlike his demeanor in person—that he had developed over the years in the newspaper:

> As a staunch supporter of Jack Kemp for president, I want to thank you for your editorial column of Feb. 5, endorsing Bob Dole.
>
> To my friends in the Dole campaign, I say: Here's proof positive you've made a mistake! Do you really want to vote for a fellow thought to be the best Republican by a newspaper that thinks Mike Dukakis is the best Democrat? A newspaper,

also, don't forget, that has agreed with little, if anything, that President Reagan has done in seven years.

Why not instead vote for strength, prosperity and economic security, for our senior citizens as well as for the rest of us, and vote for Jack Kemp for president?

Thursday, February 11, was Cheshire County's biggest day of the campaign to date. Half of the field—Gephardt, Robertson, Hart, Simon, Dole, and Dukakis—staged events in the region. Even New York Governor Mario Cuomo, who was not a candidate, was evident, at least in spirit: a small group of Democrats, many of them former Biden supporters and participants at Pat Russell's interrogation of the campaign staffs the previous December, met in the early morning to plan a write-in campaign for Cuomo.

An impending winter blizzard gathered force throughout the day and finally unleashed itself in the evening, dumping a foot of snow before it departed twenty-four hours later. The political climate had turned turbulent as well. The news was filled with a flurry of polls, reflecting for the first time that the results in Iowa had moved eastward and struck New Hampshire. According to the morning's *Boston Globe*, Dole had leaped from nearly twenty points behind in the Republican race to breathing down Bush's neck, perhaps even moving ahead. Kemp's late-January surge had dissipated, according to the poll; he was now just over 10 percent (down from 17 percent), with Robertson poised just behind him. In the Democratic race, Dukakis (36 percent) was still the poll's undisputed leader in New Hampshire, but Gephardt's win in Iowa had catapulted him from statistical insignificance to second place (18 percent) overnight. Simon (12 percent) was in third; Hart was plummeting, joining Jackson, Gore, and Babbitt in single digits. Polls by other news organizations—and it now seemed that every newspaper and television network was conducting polls and reporting them daily—reflected essentially the same, dramatically changed atmosphere.

———

Eleanor Labrie was at the Keene airport Thursday morning to greet Gephardt. (He had changed plans; rather than coming to Keene the night before to rest, he had campaigned in other parts of the state). "Team Gephardt"—about ten people in total—was there in full strength. Richard Daschbach brought along his plaid jacket, which Gephardt had worn when he'd visited a maple syrup stand a year earlier. Daschbach offered it again to his candidate. "You win some, you lose some," he said when Gephardt, wearing a dark business suit, demurred from donning the lumberjack coat. "It's probably better for him to look a little more respectable now, anyway."

Eleanor snapped a few pictures of Gephardt with her Polaroid and followed the motorcade—now a lengthy caravan of cars holding staff members, Secret Service, and a horde of media—to a woodworking shop in Alstead, where she had to huff up and down several flights of stairs simply for the chance to see Gephardt pose for the media near some wooden beams and answer a few questions before departing.

Her lungs had improved, but her back was stiff from hunching over the table in the campaign office, writing letters to potential voters. "Only one more day of letters," she said, grimacing. After that the mail would deliver them too late for the primary. The motorcade snaked away, and she drove back to her writing assignment.

Tom Britton didn't have a candidate in the region that day. Al Gore wasn't even in New Hampshire. "He's outflanking everybody," Tom said. Gore had been in New Hampshire the week before the caucuses, when all the other candidates were in Iowa. Now he was campaigning in Mississippi and North Carolina, states in the next group of primaries. His campaign was deliberately downplaying Gore's chances in New Hampshire: if he did better than expected, he could claim some momentum toward the other states; if he stayed in single digits, he could say that the real test of his electoral strength was yet to come, on "Super Tuesday," and therefore he shouldn't be written off by the press.

Such maneuvering—called "playing the expectations game"—has become a common tactic in the early part of the presidential race, when the judgment of the handicappers in the media is as crucial to a candidate's success as the actual tallies in the early contests. Ever since President Johnson (in the 1968 primary) and Edmund Muskie (in 1972) got the most votes but were declared the "losers" in New Hampshire because they hadn't matched the pundits' predictions, campaigns have strived to publicly minimize their own expectations while ballooning their opponents'. Gore's was simply the most extreme example in the primary's history.

"This is either going to be the greatest strategy in twenty years or a bust," Tom said of Gore's absence. "We have the lowest expectations of any of the candidates, which is great—unless we fulfill it." Tom was still hoping Gore would reach double digits, which he said "would be enough for a good story in the *Dallas Times Herald* [a paper in Texas, one of the "Super Tuesday" states]. If he can hold the line after New Hampshire, he'll come out smelling like a rose. If not, he's through."

As chairman of the county Democratic party, Tom was interviewed by a local radio station about the results in Iowa and the likely outcome in New Hampshire. He used his time on the air to discuss the weaknesses of Gore's competitors. "The big winner in Iowa," he told the reporter, hoping to play on the belief among some political observers that New Hampshire voters resented the attention given to the caucuses, "might have been the guy who wasn't in it."

When Pat Robertson pulled into the parking lot at Monadnock Fabricators in Rindge that afternoon, he was trailed by a long motorcade, including a huge bus carrying about fifty reporters—evidence that he and his "invisible army" were now considered a serious factor in the Republican race. The crowds he had been attracting since Iowa were larger and more enthusiastic, and his day was a regular part of each night's campaign coverage, but not all of the new attention was helpful. When he told an antiabortion audience in Concord that the founder of Planned Parenthood was once a proponent of genocide, the statement created a small firestorm in the press. Reporters were also now pestering him with questions about pronouncements he had made in previous religious broadcasts and writings. Did he still believe, one reporter asked him, referring to a book Robertson had written in 1984, that the Antichrist was alive in the world? Another reporter asked if he was willing to disavow his statement several years earlier that only Christians should be trusted in government. The harder Robertson tried to expand his appeal by focusing on traditional conservative issues, the more the press seemed interested in either exploring his more flamboyant opinions of the past or writing about his down-pedaling of religion now that he was a presidential contender.

The portrayal of Robertson as some sort of religious kook masquerading as a mainstream candidate was doubly bothersome to Doug Kidd. He didn't like the media perception that an evangelical or charismatic Christian might be dangerous in the White House, nor, as he had felt for some time, did he think Robertson should seemingly back away from his church base. But today Doug had other problems on his hands.

The explosive growth of Robertson's entourage since Iowa was creating logistical nightmares for the campaign, straining its manpower and making even more things fall through the organizational cracks. For four days Doug had been planning for Robertson to stop by the company of another supporter, after the tour in Rindge. For some reason, however, the stop was not on Robertson's schedule. The staff (concerned that they were already running an hour late) and the Secret Service (who do not appreciate last-minute changes to the route of a candidate they are protecting) wanted to blow off the extra event. Doug was adamant. When the motorcade arrived he huddled with Kerry Moody and a Secret Service agent, convinced them to go with him to the stop he had planned, and left without even getting to see his candidate.

The complications were a headache, but by the end of the day Doug was satisfied. Robertson had made the added stop, spoken to several large crowds in the region (including, Doug reported, some previous Kemp supporters), and escaped the region before the blizzard finally hit. With only a few days left before the primary, Doug felt the Iowa miracle was about to repeat itself in his home state.

As Gary Hart toured downtown Peterborough on Thursday afternoon, Dan Melanson and Paige Crowley, Hart's young coordinator for the region, served as unofficial advance staff for the candidate. They would lead Hart into stores, introduce him to voters, push the clot of reporters and cameramen out of the way on the sidewalks, hand out the thick book of Hart's speeches to anyone who would take them, and try to preserve some semblance of order to the general disturbance of it all. This was Dan's first experience with the multifooted "campaignapede."

When Hart tried to turn into a stationery store, Dan directed him instead toward a small group of people across the street. "It must be tough having all these people telling you where to go," he said to Hart's wife, Lee.

At the Peterborough Library, Hart spoke briefly with three voters in the lobby, including Bruce Anderson, still unaligned with any candidate. Anderson, the most courted Democrat in the county in 1987, had undertaken an extensive project proposing the conversion of the Seabrook nuclear power plant to natural gas and had dropped his earlier plans to become active in a presidential campaign. He shook hands with Hart, wished him luck, and after Hart left told some friends he thought Hart should drop out of the race.

"The sex thing isn't a problem anymore," Dan reported as he led the milling entourage up the street. "There are a lot of people who would like to vote for him. The big problem is most of them think that Hart can't win. The more I can talk with them [to convince them otherwise], the better."

Snow started falling when evening arrived. A crowd of 150 sat in the Elks Lodge in Keene to hear Paul Simon make his final pitch for their votes. Andi Johnson sat near the front, leading the clapping whenever Simon paused after making a point. The long hours at work and on the campaign—she was putting in fifty to sixty hours a week at the Simon office, in addition to her forty hours at her job—were taking a toll on her: her face was haggard with exhaustion, her eyes a little glazed, her blond hair frizzing at the ends.

A letter of hers had appeared in that afternoon's *Sentinel,* under the headline DUKAKIS: NOT FOR ME. It was a personal response to the newspaper's endorsement of Dukakis the week before:

> I beg to differ. Michael Dukakis is *not* my choice for president. And, while it is against my principles to speak out against another Democrat, I cannot let this one go.
>
> We have been seeing Mike Dukakis in our local media market for more than 12 years now. I am not enthralled with the prospect of having him as our president.
>
> . . . Mike Dukakis does not have 36 years of experience as an elected official. Mike Dukakis' honesty and integrity have been brought into question time and time again. Will Mike Dukakis hire John Sasso as his chief aide? And what about the others who have been involved in his campaign's dirty tricks?
>
> . . . I support Paul Simon for president. Please vote for Paul Simon.

Simon told the crowd that the race in New Hampshire was between himself and Gephardt for second place. (He and Gephardt were dueling with each other in their statements and their commercials, virtually excluding the front-running Dukakis from their crossfire.) To prove his point he recited the results of two new polls an aide handed him in midspeech, as if it were an important news flash. In the first, Dukakis had 33 percent; Gephardt, 16; Simon, 15. In the second, Simon was in second, three points ahead of Gephardt. The partisans applauded at the numbers.

Simon mentioned Andi's name at the end of his speech, thanking her for her help in the campaign. Some of the young volunteers whooped and chanted, *"Andi! Andi!"* She blushed and smiled at the attention, then hurried out the door in order to get to the next reception, in Rindge, before Simon arrived.

Gary Hart's campaign was holding a public forum in a building next to the Elks Lodge. To help build a crowd they waited for Simon's event to end and stationed volunteers near the doors to entice some of the people departing from Simon's speech to walk across the street to hear Hart.

"If the voters of New Hampshire want [my] message to be heard beyond New Hampshire, then I have to get some votes here," he told the ninety people in the room. "I have to get more votes than the polls are showing." He went on to attack Dukakis, Simon, and Gephardt as representatives of the "old" Democratic party, without new solutions to America's problems.

Sitting in the audience was Jo Robinson, a volunteer from his 1984 and early 1987 campaigns whose new candidate, Gore, had all but abandoned New Hampshire. In her lap was another heart-shaped satin pillow. This one was red, to match the blue one she had given "Gary" in January.

Earlier in the week, Kendall Lane had believed Thursday's Lincoln Day dinner, hosted by the Cheshire County Republican Women's Club, would be a pivotal event in the final days of the campaign. The wives of Kemp and du Pont had suddenly accepted invitations to attend, as had Mr. and Mrs. Haig and Mr. and Mrs. Dole. Kendall had used that information to leverage the Bush campaign into tentatively agreeing to dispatch Mrs. Bush, who was scheduled to be in the county for some afternoon receptions in three smaller towns in the county.

"It's funny how all of sudden this dinner has taken on such importance," he said on Tuesday. "Last week we couldn't *give* tickets away. Now everyone wants to come."

Kendall and his volunteers, many of them officers in the county's Republican party structure, invested considerable time and effort in preparing for the dinner—buying as many tickets as possible to make the crowd a sea of Bush buttons and planning to assure that the Bush presence would be unmistakable in the way the hall was decorated and the dinner seating assigned. As the week progressed and the daily news reported Bush's lead disappearing in New Hampshire, Kendall became more and more obsessed about the dinner: it would be the last chance until the primary to demonstrate his organization's superior strength. He was leaving nothing to chance.

So when the evening finally arrived, Kendall was in a testy mood. A combination of events had thrown a monkey wrench into his plans. Mrs. Bush was not going to make it—in fact had even canceled her appearances at the three afternoon receptions. Scrambling to recover from the Iowa disaster, the Bush campaign had hurriedly scheduled an "Ask George Bush" in another part of the state, which they were filming for later broadcast on Boston television. Barbara Bush had been sent to an event in Louisiana to fill in for the vice president, who was fighting for his political survival in New Hampshire and couldn't be spared to fulfill the commitment in the South made earlier, when the Granite State had seemed such a sure win. One of Bush's daughters was sent to Cheshire County in Mrs. Bush's stead. Governor Sununu and Congressman Gregg, Bush's biggest guns in New Hampshire whom Kendall had also planned on having at the dinner to bolster the campaign's showing, were now absent as well; they were at the "Ask George Bush" taping with their candidate. Haig had canceled, too. He was preparing to quit the race the next morning and to endorse Dole. The heavy snow prevented Mrs. du Pont and Mrs. Kemp from coming. This left the Doles as the only "headliners" in attendance.

The disappointment from all the changes, the growing tension within the Bush campaign that New Hampshire—and possibly the nomination—was slipping away, and the fact that Dole, not Bush, was seemingly giving Cheshire County the due that Kendall thought it deserved, had rubbed Kendall's already raw nerve ends into a frazzle. While Dole spoke to the several hundred Republicans during the cocktail hour, Kendall stood in the rear, sullenly nursing a drink.

Dole gave his standard stump speech, pointedly emphasizing that he had a "record, not a résumé," that he had "come up the hard way," and joking: "I've been asked about a Dole and Dole ticket, but I don't want to be vice president." More than half of the crowd standing in the room were wearing Bush buttons, followed in numbers by Kemp supporters. Dole, apparently used to more enthusiastic audiences following his Iowa victory, seemed somewhat disconcerted by the lack of response he was getting. He searched the crowd for friendly faces.

"I'll tell you one thing," he said at one point, "the 10th Mountain Division will lead the march on my inaugural. How many of us are left, Mac?"

"About two hundred," answered Mac MacKenzie, standing with a small group of people wearing Dole buttons. Mac was also wearing a sports jacket with the division's insignia on its breast pocket.

"Who's in charge here?" Kendall whispered fiercely to the woman, a Bush supporter, running the event.

"I am," she said.

"Well, how long is he [Dole] going to be allowed to speak?"

She snaked her way up to a spot in front of the platform, caught Dole's eye, and started tapping her watch. Dole kept speaking.

"That's it. Your time's up," she interrupted him.

"I didn't realize we had a time limit," Dole said into the microphone.

"You're the only candidate who got to speak," she said loudly.

"I'm the only candidate *here*," he replied testily. Dole finished his remarks, mingled briefly, and departed.

The MacKenzies and other Dole supporters were outraged. "It was incredibly rude," Barbara said of her candidate's treatment. Even some Bush and Kemp partisans felt compelled to seek out Dole to apologize before he left.

The charged, competitive atmosphere of the cocktail party was exacerbated when the crowd moved to the dining hall. The Dole contingent immediately saw all the tables near the front reserved for the Bush campaign, with large Bush signs adorning the tables and on the walls. The only places left for Dole's supporters were at the far rear of the huge hall, "Siberia," as one disgruntled volunteer muttered. Steve Price, the young Dole coordinator, was sent back to the campaign office. He returned, after Dr. David Ridge had given the invocation, with a few Dole signs and placed them on the wall at the back, next to a "Please Place Silverware in Chute" marker.

The speaking program was anticlimactic, filled mostly with apologies from the campaign's surrogates that the scheduled speakers were somewhere else.

Al Rubega had arrived after the cocktail party. (He was wearing an NRA tie clasp; Kendall's had the vice presidential seal and Bush's signature on it.) Surveying the tables, he decided that his feeling that the Republican race in Cheshire County was between Kemp and Bush was confirmed by the number of buttons and signs he saw in the crowd. One incident, however, disquieted him. The couple from Winchester he considered central members of Kemp's organization (they had attended several local meetings and had greeted Kemp at the airport during Kemp's last visit) didn't have any campaign buttons, and when Al offered them some with Kemp's logo, they mysteriously declined. He suspected something was amiss but wasn't sure what. He didn't know they had signed on to virtually every Republican campaign, which was why that night they were the only people at the dinner unwilling to publicly align themselves by sporting any paraphernalia.

The dinner ended, and the crowd quickly dispersed to hurry home in the storm. Dole's supporters, still angry at the way they and their candidate had been treated, left more galvanized and close-knit than their previously loose organization could ever have hoped.

The fierce blizzard was causing many campaigns to switch their schedules for Friday. Molly Kelly was worried that Dukakis, who was supposed to campaign in Keene in the morning before heading north to Claremont, would have to cancel. After talking with the headquarters, however, the campaign decided to fly the governor to Keene Thursday night. He stayed in a motel and at seven A.M. was at a restaurant to speak to 150 supporters.

Molly led him through the crowd, introducing him to his local volunteers, and then stood at the side, eyeing the audience anxiously as her candidate spoke. He warned them not to let the polls make them overconfident. The polls had called him invincible in a gubernatorial race in 1978, he said, and yet he had lost. He compared himself to the Boston Red Sox, a baseball team noted for its ability to blow big leads.

School had been canceled because of the storm, and Molly's three children were at the breakfast event, helping their mother. Making a point about education, Dukakis turned to eleven-year-old Rachel—by now one of his most ardent admirers and hardest-working volunteers in the county—and asked her if she wanted to be a teacher.

"No," she answered quickly. "I want to be an astronaut."

"This town isn't big enough for the two of us." A Jackson supporter was on the phone with Mike Haas, the Gephardt coordinator, late Friday morning. Mike had called a local radio station to report that, despite the blizzard, Gephardt's office was still open; it got translated on the air that Gephardt was having a party on Main Street. "Meet us on Central Square, if you dare," the caller told Mike. "We're challenging the other campaigns, too."

Volunteers and coordinators from the Jackson, Simon, Gephardt, and Gore offices squared off at high noon on the common in Keene's center and settled their differences with snowballs.

Mike Haas's troops captured the gazebo, claiming it as the "moral high ground." Jon Meyer, leading Gore's contingent, launched an attack of "single warhead" snowballs. The others played capture the flag with their opponents' campaign placards in the snowbanks. They had fun for an hour.

The Dukakis campaign had declined the challenge, further solidifying the competing campaigns' view that it was a joyless machine. At late night bull sessions in Keene bars, from which Dukakis operatives were typically absent, the others often griped about Dukakis's advantages in money, proximity, and seemingly unending supply of Massachusetts volunteers; they referred to his campaign as the "Imperial Army." The group on the common concluded their gambol by peppering the windows of the "Imperial Army's" fortress overlooking Central Square and then went back to work.

The state Democratic party held a dinner Friday night in Manchester, and all the candidates attended to give speeches. Andi Johnson was there with Jo Robinson, Tom and Valerie Britton, Bruce Anderson, and Pat Russell. The drive in the snow took her two hours from Dublin, twice the normal time.

"I'm playing hardball now," she said of her constant work on the phones for Simon. "I'm working on Babbitt and Jackson supporters to help dump Gephardt. I tell them Simon's the only national candidate out there. Babbitt won't make it, and Jackson's going to the convention anyway—we need their vote to get Gephardt out of the race. It's working." Hart, once the object of her undivided admiration, was now just another impediment to Simon's chances. "I think he should drop out *now*," she said. "Give it up—for his own good. He's in a real nosedive."

She was outraged when, after the speeches, she watched Bruce Anderson—whom she had supported for governor two years earlier and had lobbied heavily on Hart's, Biden's, and then Simon's behalf—walk up to Babbitt and promise his vote on Tuesday. (A year earlier, during their ride together in Babbitt One, Bruce had sidestepped making a commitment to Babbitt on the grounds that he wasn't sure Babbitt was electable. Ironically, now that Babbitt had proven the assessment correct, it was the unelectability that suddenly brought Bruce on board. Despite Andi's efforts, he had been leaning heavily toward Dukakis. "Dukakis doesn't need my vote, he's going to win anyway," Bruce said of his last-minute decision, made that very evening. He felt sorry for Babbitt and didn't want to see him humiliated in New Hampshire.)

Running into Pat Russell, another Babbitt supporter Andi had once thought would go for Simon, only further ignited Andi's competitive ire. "If you have any conscience at all, when you go into the booth on Tuesday, you'll vote for Simon," she told Pat. "That's all I'm going to say."

Dole was back in Cheshire County on Saturday, which meant that in the last month he had been in the region as many times as Bush had throughout the entire campaign. Large crowds greeted him in Jaffrey and Peterborough. Haig was now part of the campaign's traveling show, urging former Haig supporters (there weren't many) to vote for Dole. Donald Rumsfeld, a former defense secretary who a year ago was pondering a run for the presidency himself, was also in tow to voice his endorsement. (Bush's campaign countered this movement of prominent endorsements for Dole in two ways: making sure photographers were invited to the vice president's weekly lunch with President Reagan on Wednesday and flying Barry Goldwater to New Hampshire the day before the primary to throw his support behind Bush. Ads attacking Dole—saying he had "straddled" on issues like taxes and an oil import fee—were also now filling New Hampshire's airwaves.) The speculation in the press was that Dole's post-Iowa bounce had overtaken Bush; even his own pollster was reportedly calling Dole "Mr. President."

While the senator was answering questions from the expanded press corps trailing him, Janet Shawn was pressed into service to retype his speech in Jaffrey's high school. She couldn't figure out the machines at the school offices and instead used a black marker to emphasize the changes the staff wanted made in the remarks.

As it turned out, Dole didn't use the prepared text anyway. Relying on off-the-cuff remarks to the friendly crowd of two hundred, he mocked Bush's recent theft of Dole's "I'm one of you" slogan for New Hampshire. "Geography doesn't make that determination," he said. "It's what you've done, where you've been in your life. I told Mac [he pointed to Mac MacKenzie in the crowd] our old division has to make one more march—that's down Pennsylvania Avenue when I'm inaugurated president."

On their way out, the Doles spied the MacKenzies behind the crush of reporters. The candidate reached across a camera crew to shake Mac's hand. Mrs. Dole, noticing the MacKenzies' "Dole Patrol" vests, remembered what she would be doing later in the day. "We're going skiing today, right?" she said to Barbara.

On Saturday the Robertson campaign organized small caravans of vehicles, with Robertson signs taped to their doors, that drove around communities all over the state in the morning and then converged on Concord for a giant caravan in the afternoon, followed by a rally of 1,500 screaming supporters. The invisible army was becoming visible.

At five P.M. the combined vehicles formed a line two miles long on the turnpike between Concord and Manchester. Doug Kidd was sitting in his car in the caravan, which had come to a stop at a toll booth. (The state of New Hampshire made about $500 in tolls from the caravan that evening.)

He looked out his window into the twilight and saw a campaign motorcade—puny in comparison with the volunteer caravan— going the other way on the turnpike. Doug chuckled when he saw who was in the limousine, being treated to car after car with "Robertson for President" on their sides. It was Vice President Bush.

Her letter writing complete, Eleanor Labrie sat on an easy chair in her home Saturday night and knitted while she watched the final, preprimary Democratic debate on television. Four Gephardt volunteers and Mike Haas were splayed around the TV set. With her white hair and knitting, and with the younger people at her feet on the floor, Eleanor looked like a great-aunt baby-sitting her brood rather than one of the more competitive members of "Team Gephardt."

Like the Republican race, the Democratic campaign had grown more acrimonious in the final days, and this debate reflected the new tone. Gore demanded an apology from Gephardt for published remarks of Gephardt's campaign manager calling Gore a "phony, two-bit bastard."

"I can't *stand* that man," Eleanor said of Gore while her candidate offered an apology. Gephardt then criticized Simon's recent set of ads, which focused on several issues where Gephardt had changed positions. "Humph," Eleanor grunted as Simon said they could differ on issues but do it respectfully, "*he's* [Simon] a fine one to trust."

When Hart started in on Dukakis for not having an energy policy, and Babbitt joined in by asking Dukakis for a budget plan, one of the supporters in Eleanor's living room shouted, "Get him!"

"They're all a little tired," Eleanor said, commenting on the free-for-all on and around her set.

And so the evening proceeded, a fight among the candidates and the bleacher catcalls from the living room. "Oh, God, he's dreaming again. I'm tired of his dreams," Eleanor said as Simon made his closing remarks with his now standard refrain, "There are no limits on our dreams." Dukakis started to relate the story of his father and mother immigrating to America, and Karen Greer groaned, "Here we go again." When Hart gave his closing, one person called out, "Where's the beef?" Gephardt's remarks were greeted by cheers. Jackson was the last to speak, appealing to Democratic principles and saying, "I'd rather have Roosevelt in the wheelchair than Reagan on the horse." Eleanor nodded as Jackson spoke. "He's good tonight," she said.

The debate went off the air, and Gephardt's Cheshire County group turned their attention to the pizza that had just arrived. Eleanor, the hostess, restored a sense of decorum as she passed out plates and napkins.

"That," she said with teacherlike authority, "was the first entertaining debate I've watched."

Andi Johnson watched the debate in a hotel function room in central New Hampshire. *The Washington Post* was having a "focus group" of sample Democrats in New Hampshire view the debate on television and then give their reactions, as a measure of the event's probable impact on voters. Andi had been selected as one of the participants.

"Paul was a voice of reason," she said of her reaction to the debate. She also took the opportunity, she reported later, to "slam-dunk Dukakis a couple of times."

The last presidential candidate to visit Cheshire County in the campaign of 1988 was Jesse Jackson, whose rousing speech to five hundred people at the Keene Junior High School late Saturday night was the rhetorical equivalent of a fireworks finale to the season.

The Jackson campaign had begun organizing in Cheshire County in the fall of 1987. His core group of about ten people included several professors and students from Keene State College, a minister, a woman who was trying to establish a local Green Party, another who described herself as an "aging hippie," and a hospital administrator who came to meetings in a business suit. Jackson's two appearances in the region during 1987 had been well attended, although a good number of people in the audience supported other Democrats and showed up mostly for the excitement of hearing him speak. Two canvasses—manned by busloads of college students from Massachusetts campuses—had been carried out, and an office was opened in December. Like the rest of New Hampshire (which has a black population of less than one-half of one percent), Cheshire County is virtually all white, but its liberal voting record (Jackson had received 8.7 percent of the Democratic vote in 1984, his highest of any county and significantly better than his 5.3 percent of the statewide tally) made it a targeted region for the campaign.

A month before the primary, Michael Terry, a twenty-five-year-old from Colorado, was sent to Keene as the campaign's coordinator.

Although roughly the same age as the other campaigns' coordinators in the county, Michael's personal history was markedly different from his fellow coordinators'. Issue-oriented, grass-roots
organizing, not electoral politics, was his lifeblood. He had worked
in homeless shelters in Denver and in the movement to provide
sanctuary to Central Americans. He had lived briefly in Nicaragua,
and he had organized demonstrations to throw representatives of
the CIA off a college campus in Boulder, Colorado. In 1986 he was
among a small group of protesters who crossed a bombing range
in Nevada on camouflaged bicycles in an attempt to reach a nuclear
testing site, hoping their presence would stop the tests. He had
been caught by military police in helicopters, who arrested him at
gunpoint, and he had spent twenty-one days in jail for his offense.

This was Michael's first political campaign—and the first activity
in some time, he said, "when I don't expect to be roughed up by
the cops." The 1984 presidential campaign between Reagan and
Mondale had "disgusted" him, he said: "We were asked to choose
between one white, male, capitalist imperialist and another." Jackson, he said, was the only candidate in the 1988 race who wanted
to dramatically change America's role in the world and its treatment
of its own poor. He didn't consider his new job as real grass-roots
organizing. "Here, I'm a stranger calling people, getting them to
do things they don't have any say in; we, the 'outside experts,' have
decided it should be done," versus having the people decide themselves what actions to take. It was "slash-and-burn politics," he
said. "We'll leave, and there will be nothing [of an organization]
left behind." No one was being "empowered." Compared with his
previous organizing efforts, he felt lonely and isolated.

Cheshire County, with the lowest unemployment rate in New
Hampshire, which itself had the lowest rate in the nation, was, in
his mind, "suburban America, and it's hard to organize a *real* political movement in the suburbs. Jackson is enfranchising a lot of
disenfranchised people—blacks in the South, people like me—but
that's not happening here. Other places have poor people, activist
people [involved in the campaign]; here they're organized like the

Elks Club. Most of our support is from the intellectual community."

Michael was going to be gone on primary day: he was scheduled to stand trial in Denver for throwing blood on the walls of a U.S. senator's office as part of a protest against the contra war in Nicaragua. Two weeks later he faced another trial, for blockading the entrance to the Rocky Flats nuclear facility.

Jackson was an hour late arriving in Keene Saturday night. Part of his motorcade had gotten lost on its way over from the debate in Manchester. The crowd was entertained during the wait by a woman singing songs—"This Land Is Your Land," "We Are the Rainbow People," and seven more ballads with political messages. Chuck Weed, a Keene State College professor and leading local volunteer on the campaign, finally introduced Jackson as "the only presidential candidate who stayed above the fray [in the debate] and kept the focus on the most important target: getting rid of the Reagan revolution."

Jackson's speech went on for an hour and ranged from his call to end "economic violence" in America to stories from the civil rights movement of the 1960s, from solving the problems of the Third World without the use of military force to dismissing the political wisdom that he was unelectable. "You *need* Jesse Jackson for your president," he said. "We who are the dreamers cannot let the dream busters take our country. It's time for a change. We, the people, can win."

The crowd—nearly as large as his total vote in the county four years earlier—cheered wildly.

Sunday was the Republicans' turn for a final debate. Kendall Lane was late arriving in Manchester for the postdebate Bush rally. For the last two days he and Jane had been shepherding around Cheshire County about twenty volunteers. Nearly all of them were from Washington, where they worked either in the vice president's campaign headquarters or in the federal bureaucracy, part of a last-minute infusion of five hundred Bush workers into New Hampshire; since Wednesday one busload a day was arriving from the nation's capital. During the day they were dispatched to the smaller towns around Keene to leaflet door to door. "We're trying to let people know the Bush campaign is alive and well," Kendall said. "We haven't folded our tent yet." Evenings the troops worked the phones. At night they slept at the Lanes' home, using spare couches and sleeping bags unrolled across any available floor space. Walking through his house at night had become a hazardous navigation around bodies; mornings were scrambles for coffee cups and lines at the bathroom doors. "I've lost control of my own house," Kendall said of the encampment. "Then again, every campaign is out of control now."

By many accounts Dole was now as much the front-runner in New Hampshire as Bush, and he was therefore more of a target from the other candidates in the debate than the vice president. At one point du Pont pulled out a piece of paper which he had signed as a "pledge" against raising taxes (a political tradition among gubernatorial candidates in New Hampshire), handed it to Dole, and challenged the senator to sign it on the spot. Dole, nonplussed by the stunt, stumbled to make a joke about it but refused to sign. Robertson made the startling announcement that the Soviet Union had SS-4 and SS-5 missiles stationed in Cuba and pointed at the United States, a claim that would create a two-day furor in the press when he could not substantiate it.

Kendall had to listen to the debate on his car radio while he drove from his afternoon canvassing to Manchester. The auditorium for the rally had been closed by the fire marshal when Kendall arrived—the place was already filled to capacity with as many out-of-state volunteers as New Hampshire supporters—but he negotiated with the Secret Service to let him and Jane in by a side door.

"I want to win New Hampshire, and with this kind of enthusiasm, we *will* win New Hampshire," Bush said in concluding his short speech to the throng. Campaign staff members tugged on some ropes to release hundreds of balloons resting in a net near the auditorium ceiling. At first the net resisted opening, and the aides tugged more frantically on the lines. The band was playing; the cameras were rolling; the candidate was waiting. Finally the net gave way, and the crowd roared. The balloons—red, white, and blue—cascaded toward the floor. Kendall bounced them back into the air as they enveloped him. He pulled a small American flag from the back pocket of his jeans and waved it to the music's beat.

Tom Britton had to drive to Concord Sunday night for his last chance to see Al Gore in New Hampshire. It was a small crowd that gathered, filled mostly by the twenty-two Concord activists who had been the first to support Gore and then grumbled for the last few months as the campaign scaled down its New Hampshire effort.

"Years from now, your grandchildren will read in amazement about these times," Gore said. "In the election of 1988, something began to change. The New Hampshire primary was a surprise—someone finished better than anyone expected, won on 'Super Tuesday' and then won the election and provided new leadership. When your grandchildren ask you about it, then you can say, 'I was with President Gore *early on.*' "

It was the scenario for which Tom was still saving some of the Jack Daniel's that Gore had sent him last summer. He and Valerie, in return, had a gift for their candidate: a T-shirt proclaiming "I Survived the New Hampshire Primary." Valerie gave Gore a hug and kiss. Tom shook his hand and said, "Give 'em hell in the South."

The Bush "Freedom Fighters" were tired but nonetheless somewhat upbeat when they met for the last time on Monday, February 15. Governor Sununu welcomed Rich Bond, who had run the Bush effort in Iowa, by saying, "Thanks for the stunning performance in Iowa, to give us the chance for revenge here." The group was told that Bush's harsh ads attacking Dole, the vice president's willingness to cast aside his customary aloof style and throw himself into the "see me, touch me, feel me" events Sununu had hastily arranged (Bush had driven a snow plow during the blizzard and made other candidate-to-person appearances that were on every evening's news), the strong local organizations, and the debate (particularly Dole's refusal to sign the tax "pledge") had stopped Dole's post-Iowa momentum. By their estimation, based on their own polling and phone bank tallies, Bush would beat Dole, 32 percent to 30 percent, on Tuesday.

Kendall Lane wasn't sure about those numbers. He suspected that telling volunteers that your campaign was ahead, but just barely, might be the best way to prevent them from being either overconfident or dejected and therefore get the most out of them in the final twenty-four hours. "I just don't know what's going to happen," he said later in the day. And for someone whose guiding principle was "I'm not real big on surprises," not knowing what's about to happen, not having his votes counted ahead of time, was the political equivalent of hell. "We should have had the election six weeks ago," he said wistfully.

In addition to the influx of out-of-state volunteers, the campaign had arranged to get more signs for the local organizations. Six thousand had been flown in early Monday. Kendall loaded his car with three hundred of them before he left for Keene.

Drivers going to work in Keene Monday morning were greeted by representatives from several campaigns. Dan Burnham was at one intersection with a Babbitt sign. Dr. David Ridge was caught by a highway crew while he was trying again to plant a Kemp placard at a key intersection. Standing at a corner with a Gore sign, Jon Meyer heard a honk from a passing car and looked up to see Mike Haas, driving his recently repaired Buick, behind the wheel. An hour later Jon returned the favor and honked when he passed Mike, who was holding a Gephardt sign.

Last week's blizzard, and intermittent snows since, had strained the snow-removal capacity of the city's street crews. At the head of Main Street, where it emptied into Central Square, a huge pile of snow rested between the lanes. The pile—a small mountain about ten feet high, towering over the intersection—had quickly been appropriated by the presidential campaigns. Partisans had scaled its slopes in the last few days, leaving signs planted behind them when they left as proof of their claims. Placards for Bush, Dole, Robertson, Kemp (handmade, with an American flag painted on it), Dukakis, Simon, Jackson, Babbitt, Gephardt, and Hart—even one for an obscure airline pilot who said he wanted to be president—formed the treeline near its summit.

At noon Monday a number of volunteers gathered at the pile's base for what turned into a multicandidate "honk and wave" to greet the lunchtime traffic downtown. Jon Meyer held a Gore sign. Paige Crowley was there for Hart. Her hopes for Hart—battered by his showing in Iowa, recent poll reports, and an encounter with a reporter after Sunday's debate: "Your guy did great," he said. "Is he dropping out?"—were being kept alive by the fact that an advertisement in the *Sentinel*, offering free rides to the polls from the Hart campaign, had prompted one person to call and say he was voting for Hart. Her mother had sent her a clipping from *The Washington Post* that reported favorably on Hart's final event in Keene, which Paige had set up. This was her first real campaign, and although she had been in it only a month, she was exhausted from the long hours. A car with some young men drove by, and they noticed Paige standing with her sign. "Hey, Hart supporter!" one of them shouted from the window. "You must be Donna Rice's sister!"

A caravan of cars started circling the rotary around the common. They had Dukakis signs on their doors, Dukakis bumper stickers on their fronts and backs, and, undoubtedly somewhat counterproductively for the other motorists who were being stalled in traffic while the honking motorcade passed, Massachusetts license plates.

Andi Johnson and Pete Kujawski showed up bearing Simon standards. Andi was even more bleary-eyed. She had been in the office until two A.M., slept a few hours, gone to work, traveled to Keene for this lunch-hour campaign duty, and would be going back to her job when it was over, before another long night working the phones. Tomorrow she planned to take the day off and devote it exclusively to the campaign.

"There's more movement away from Gephardt to Simon," she reportedly confidently. The press was getting ready to eliminate from consideration whichever one finished third in New Hampshire. Andi thought it would be Gephardt.

She surveyed the snow mountain behind her. Her gaze finally rested on a battered and torn Hart sign, left behind moments before by Paige Crowley, and she sighed with an expression of pitying condescension. "Poor Gary," she said.

The Dole campaign office buzzed with activity in the early evening. Steve Price, the coordinator, took a handful of the core supporters into a small room to go over the primary day plans while the other volunteers kept phoning. He had a beeper on his belt, in case the state headquarters needed to reach him quickly and couldn't get through on the busy lines. His voice burned with intensity.

"We've got to pump these people up [in the other room]," he said. "They're tired and exhausted."

The campaign's plan for the primary was the most elaborate of any of the Republican organizations, second only to Dukakis's among both parties. Like most of the campaigns, they would have people holding signs at each of the polling places. "It helps, as ridiculous as it may sound," he told the group. "It makes our supporters and leaners confident." In addition to the volunteers outside the voting places, however, Price was assigning people to sit with voting lists inside the polls. When a voter was given a ballot, his or her name was called out by the precinct moderator before the voter entered a booth. The poll watchers were to check off the name against their list; at 5:30 P.M. each Dole precinct captain was to go over the lists, match them against the names of supporters previously identified in the phone banks, and then call any likely Dole voter who hadn't yet shown up. Special teams, called "hunters" by Steve, would be standing by to drive to the voter's house and take him or her to the polls, if necessary. "Make sure the cars are warmed up and have snow tires," he advised the "hunters." An intricate reporting system, from polls to homes serving as Dole precinct headquarters, from the homes to the office (or rooms in a local motel that were being used for added phone lines), was to be in place.

"We've done everything we can," he assured the volunteers, who had been taking notes on yellow legal pads. "People think we're a ragtag operation. I can't but believe we'll have the best GOTV [get out the vote] in this county. We don't need to brag now. Victory is our best revenge. We're going to blow their socks off."

Al Rubega spent Monday evening at home on the phone. He and Dr. Ridge had divided up responsibilities a week ago: Dr. Ridge would lead Kemp's battle in the "sign wars," and Al would line up the volunteers to hold placards at the polling places.

Despite the constant polls in the news showing a tight Dole-Bush race in New Hampshire, Al still believed it would come down to either the vice president or Kemp. "He [Kemp] has been tremendously, tremendously underrated," Al said. He and Mary had spent the weekend "Kemping" at a sportsmen's show, where they handed out Kemp fliers Al had written, outlining the differences among the candidates on gun issues. He was encouraged by Sunday's debate, especially when Kemp had ridiculed Bush for using the phrase "Give peace a chance."

Still, a few doubts had crowded their way into his usual optimism. "If we don't do real well in this county, I'm going to feel like I screwed up," he said. "We started out real well, but by midfall I should have shifted gears and got more people involved." Instead it seemed like he, Mary, and Dr. Ridge were still doing the work instead of directing it.

As he had on the night of the Iowa caucuses, Doug Kidd was teaching his management class at Keene State College Monday night. He had lined up sign carriers and tally reporters for his towns and was looking forward to seeing the primary finally arrive. For months it had seemed as though he were practicing for a game he had never played; he was tired of practicing and eager for the game to start.

The Robertson data base was still far short of its 55,000-voter goal: about 12,000 people the campaign considered "firm" votes. But that didn't overly concern Doug. "There's an invisible army out there, and nobody's got a handle on it," he said. "Not even our campaign." On Sunday he had asked Allison and some other Robertson supporters at church if they knew of people who would be voting for Robertson but weren't on the lists. They quickly came up with a dozen. "We haven't ID'd *half* of our support," he predicted. "Names keep coming up, and we don't know who they are." He thought Dole, Bush, and Robertson would be clustered at the top of the vote, all within a few percentage points of each other.

After his class he planned to go home, pray, and try to get some sleep.

Jane Lane took a short break from the Bush campaign phone bank at a Keene real estate office. There were so many volunteers, the telephone lines couldn't handle them all. Even a cousin of the vice president's had shown up, unexpectedly, from Connecticut and was working one phone. (On Monday alone the local Bush campaign made five thousand calls in Cheshire County.)

The news that night had reported that the most recent polls now showed Dole creeping ahead in the state. The phone bank tallies were showing some improvement in Bush's standing, particularly in comparison with the last four nights, but he seemed to be trailing in Keene. Some of the out-of-state volunteers had been asking why there were so many Robertson signs on the roads. Kendall had taken refuge in his law office for a little solitude, a breather from the crush of people.

"New Hampshire," Jane said dejectedly, "may not pick the president this time."

In the Democratic campaign offices in downtown Keene, the scenes were mixed. Dukakis's office was overflowing with people as Mike Cook and Molly Kelly went over the plans for primary day, including a predawn sweep of Keene's streets to leave short notes on the front doors of identified Dukakis supporters, reminding them to vote. Ten people were crowded into Simon's tiny office, where big posters covered the walls, listing tomorrow's assignments. Andi Johnson was on the phone but also watching C-SPAN broadcast a documentary film about the history of the New Hampshire primary.

Mike Haas seemed tired and a little depressed as he shut off the lights and locked the door to Gephardt's office after nine P.M., when it was too late to make any more calls to voters without the risk of offending them by waking them up. Earlier in the day he had predicted a Dukakis-Gephardt finish in New Hampshire, with Gephardt at 25 percent. After talking to the state headquarters, he now adjusted his forecast. Dukakis would still win with about 35 percent, he said. Gephardt would hold on to second place, but at 20 percent, a lower finish.

Jon Meyer and two of his best volunteers, both girls in high school, were making a few last-minute calls. Jon had given up much hope for a strong Gore showing. The pressure was off, and tonight his style on the phones was almost giddy. "He [Gore] reminds me a lot of John Kennedy. What do you think?" he asked one voter. "President Gore—how does that sound?" he said to another. The clippings, photographs, and maps had already been taken down from the office walls, in early preparation for closing down tomorrow. What posters had once been there had already been cannibalized for signs.

Kendall Lane sat alone in his law office a block from Central Square. *All this for nothing*, his nightmare of the past weeks, was there with him.

"I'm not totally confident we're going to pull it out," he said. "I'm afraid we slipped so suddenly after Iowa and the vice president didn't start acting like a candidate until it was too late." Earlier in the evening he had bet a local banker dinner of the winner's choice that Bush, not Dole (whom the banker supported), would prevail tomorrow. But privately he thought the opposite was more likely. "I like to prepare for the worst," he said. He expected the Republican race to be "very close, within four thousand votes." Kemp, who before Iowa Kendall had thought would be second in New Hampshire, would now finish fifth, he said. "He's not even a story— you have to really search to find that Kemp's even a candidate."

The response of his town chairmen to the challenge of the last week and the flood of extra workers in the last days had cheered him. "The advantage of the Bush campaign is we have the local organizations that can put these people [from out of state] to work in the field," he said. "I suspect the Dole campaign doesn't have that ability." One of his local informants had already called to outline Dole's primary day plans in Cheshire County, including the use of poll checkers. Kendall was surprised but not particularly worried by it. He had discarded the same plan for the Bush effort in the county. The manpower required for an effective poll-checking operation could be put to better use elsewhere, he thought, and the last-minute reporting system could become too cumbersome to be worthwhile. "I doubt they [the Dole campaign] can pull it off," he said. "It's more important to call our '1's' now, emphasize how important it is to vote tomorrow, and offer them rides if they need it."

His plan called for having two people outside each polling place— one local volunteer, one from out of state—at all times. Marvin Bush, one of the vice president's sons, was going to be in Cheshire County in the morning, and Kendall would be taking him to various Keene wards and area towns. Kendall had more inside information: a television network would be coming to Marlborough, one of only a few towns in the state that had always voted for the winners of both parties in past primaries. He was sending an extra-large contingent there, so the Bush campaign would have the biggest presence when the cameras showed up.

Late in the evening Kendall headed home. The thirty-four voters of Dixville Notch, a tiny town in northern New Hampshire that attracts national attention every four years by being the first to cast and count ballots, would be voting at midnight. C-SPAN was carrying it live, and Kendall didn't want to miss it.

The house was ablaze with lights as he pulled into the driveway. Volunteers filled each room, and they were still up. *I've lost control of my own house,* he thought again. Everything, in fact, seemed out of control. Tomorrow was a complete question mark. Anything could happen. Events, not people, not even insiders, seemed to be in charge. He hated that feeling.

17

WAITING

For all of them, and for such a long time, it had seemed that February 16 would never arrive. The more they had worked toward it, focused their dreams on it, put other parts of their lives in abeyance for it, and closed in on it, the more it seemed like a mirage. It had pulled them forward but was always out of reach. No matter what they had been doing—sitting through yet another campaign meeting, stuffing envelopes, handing out brochures, building crowds for candidate appearances, reading the newspaper, watching the television news, and, finally, just living lives immersed in the detailed drudgery and enormously high stakes that simultaneously constituted a presidential campaign—a tiny clock had ticked in the backs of their minds, always ticking until it was part of their very existence, like breathing.

The clock worked backward, a mental countdown. *One year until the primary. . . . Six months to get ready. . . . Four months left. . . . Only a month to go. . . . Three weeks . . . Two weeks . . . seven days . . . Six, five, four, three, two, one . . .*

An alarm went off in their minds' clock, and they awoke as if from a yearlong dream. Now it was upon them. Primary day was no longer a mirage. It was real. It had arrived.

12:30 A.M., TUESDAY, PRIMARY DAY

Andi Johnson unlocked the door and turned on the light in her kitchen. Everything was quiet, and stillness was both unusual and unwanted in Andi's life. Posters from past campaigns hung on the walls. A corkboard near the door was covered with campaign buttons silently proclaiming the names of candidates she had once supported. The refrigerator was virtually empty. Total silence. Not even the customary welcome-home greeting from D.C., her pet cat.

She was exhausted. Her house had become a place where she collapsed late at night and showered in the morning as she started yet another marathon day of work and campaign. Her regular job was merely what she did now to pay expenses; it was necessary yet secondary. Political life—what defined her self-image—had moved from an avocation to an all-consuming passion, more important than anything else. Through campaigning she had met her boyfriend four years earlier, and through it she had lost him over a disagreement about Gary Hart a few months ago. This campaign the last twelve months had not been easy. She was ready for it to end. Knowing the primary would finally arrive, she had been pushing herself to her limits, burning reserves of energy from the adrenaline rush of competition and nervous excitement, constantly promising her tired body, *When this is over, then we'll rest.*

A few hours' sleep was what she wanted now. Primary day would be long and hard, and then, regardless of the outcome, there would be a party. She looked forward to that. But if she was going to get any rest, it had to be now.

Tired as she was, sleep at this moment was actually just another part of her primary day campaign plan. Like the fact that she had already voted by absentee ballot, in case her duties later in the day prevented her from getting back to Dublin. Like the fact that she was taking the day off from work. And like the reason the house was so quiet, without even her cat to greet her and sleep with her. D.C. wasn't around. Three weeks ago she had taken him to live with her parents until the primary was over.

2:00 *A.M.*

Standing at a window in the Dukakis for President office, Molly
Kelly looked out on Keene's Central Square. The office was on the
second floor of a corner building, providing a commanding spot
from which to watch the heart of the small city. It was a nice New
England view: a town common with an old-fashioned bandstand
gazebo, a Civil War statue, two cannons, and a large fountain made
of polished granite; a traffic rotary between the common and the
downtown storefronts; City Hall at one diagonal, the county courthouse at the other, and the stately United Church of Christ, its tall
white steeple bathed in floodlight, halfway between them; a lot of
brick, some trees, and, in the wake of last week's blizzard, an awful
lot of snow.

A long day of work was done. The hectic energy of all the Dukakis
volunteers—*What am I going to do with so many people?* Molly
had wondered early in the evening—had been channeled into necessary tasks. For the last hour and a half Molly had made charts
and lists to prepare for primary morning and the next onslaught of
people anxious for something to do. Then she had cleaned the office.
That done, she could take a few calm minutes to gaze out the
window and momentarily relax in quiet satisfaction. *Nothing more
to do. Everything tidy. Ready for morning. Nice and quiet.*

This was the kind of moment a mother particularly savored. From
her window Molly could see a little ways up Court Street. A few
blocks farther, she knew, her three children were sleeping peace-
fully in her apartment. The entire town, in fact, seemed to be asleep,
with Molly standing quietly in its living room, listening contentedly
to the gentle rhythm of its slumber.

A loud noise, a deep rumbling, interrupted Molly's reverie at the
office window. Below her, at the head of Main Street, a huge front-
end loader advanced toward the snow mountain.

Molly watched as the machine's big bucket tore a bite from the
side of the snow pile, lifted it, and turned toward a waiting dump
truck. As the snow tumbled into the truck, plywood stakes from

several campaign signs clanged against the truck bed. The bucket reached out again, bit more snow, turned, and dumped again. And again and again. Each time, more signs—Dole, Bush, Dukakis, Hart, Kemp, Gephardt, Simon, Robertson, Gore, Jackson, du Pont, Babbitt—disappeared with the snow until everything was gone: no mountain of snow, no physical evidence of the campaigns' exertions to conquer it.

The town is telling us something, Molly thought as the last loaded dump truck left and the bucket loader lurched down the street. *The town is saying to the campaigns: "It's over. Get out."*

She turned out the lights in the Dukakis office and headed home.

3:00 A.M.

Kendall Lane woke up without the alarm clock. A nervous stomach was harder to ignore than a buzzer anyway.

Bush had won Dixville Notch at midnight, beating Dole 11–6. (Kemp got 5 votes; Haig and du Pont, 2; and Robertson, 1. On the Democratic side, it was Gephardt, 4 votes; Simon, 3; and the others, 0.) Kendall had watched it on television. Immediately afterward three people had called him to make sure he was aware of the results. Maybe winning Dixville was a good omen. Then again, maybe all it meant was a five-vote lead before 150,000 other Republicans voted.

Omens didn't win elections; in Kendall's book, hard work, planning, advance information, and good organizations won them. He got out of bed and headed for the shower. He'd give his houseful of Bush workers a little more time to sleep before rousing them for their final effort.

4:30 A.M.

The morning routine was important to Doug Kidd. One thing he had quickly learned in this, his first political campaign, was that you went to bed late, got up early, and spent the rest of your day at a full sprint, with little or no time for your personal life. If you wanted some time for yourself, you had to make it, even if it required getting up in the dark.

Allison, his wife, was still asleep. She'd been understanding during the last year, when it wasn't unusual for him to return to their home in rural Stoddard well after midnight and be gone again by the next dawn. Bless her, she would often even get up and see him off. This morning he let her sleep.

Doug bowed his head and began to pray, his usual morning prayer of the last six months: *Let me speak the truth and be available to reach out to anyone the Lord puts in my path; give Brother Pat favor where he should be favored—and keep him humble. Let the Lord's will be done.*

Then he opened his Bible and began reading. He had been working his way through it, as was his custom, from front to back a few chapters a day. Today he was in one of the Apostle Paul's letters, the part of the New Testament dealing with doctrines of how the church should be organized. He vaguely wished he hadn't already moved through the Gospels last month. That was his favorite part of the Bible, especially the Book of John. That was where all the miracles took place.

5:00 *A.M.*

Sunrise was still nearly two hours away. The darkness was complicated by a soupy fog rising from the snowbanks and wafting across the road. Hunched over his steering wheel, Kendall Lane tried his high beams again. They only made the fog seem even more of an impenetrable wall. But this was his home turf, and he had the route carefully mapped in his head. He kept driving.

Kendall's car was one of three dispatched from his house after four o'clock, each one filled with signs and Bush workers and with a prearranged route covering Cheshire County. Bush might be sinking in the opinion polls, but if Kendall had his way, no one was going to get to a voting booth in his territory without encountering visual evidence that a local organization was still squarely behind the vice president.

Kendall pulled his car over and stopped. He adjusted the cap on his head, dark blue with an insignia on its crown: "Freedom Fighter; Bush Backer '88."

"The first one goes right there," he said, and pointed. A young man jumped from the backseat, scampered over, and planted one Bush sign defiantly in the snow bank, then another directly across the street.

"When they come in this morning, they'll know we've been here," Kendall said as he drove on into the fog. Within a dozen yards the local Dole headquarters had disappeared in his rearview mirror.

5:30 A.M.

Dan Burnham walked out of his house and down to the barn to feed and water his heifers. His daily farm chores were more pleasure than work, providing him the same satisfaction he had known as a boy and giving him time to reflect on whatever projects he had undertaken as a man. This morning his mind raced back to his first meeting with Babbitt.

Somewhere between then and now, Dan thought as he watered his stock, he had lost his ability for objective and detached analysis of politics. When he was a young reporter for *The Wall Street Journal* he had that ability, or even five years ago during his brief tenure as editor and publisher of the *New Hampshire Times*.

But now he wasn't so sure of his instincts. He had been through a long, emotional roller-coaster ride on the Babbitt campaign. There had been moments when he had thought, *This guy's going to make it.* Yet they had always been followed by feelings of near dejection, fears that Babbitt's candidacy was doomed, hopeless. One month Dan would believe his candidate was on the verge of a breakthrough with voters; the next he was filled with resignation that Babbitt was going to finish in New Hampshire exactly where he had started: at the back of the pack.

Dan was resigned this morning. Why, he wondered, had he ever thought the guy had a chance? *Dammit, though, he's such a good man. Such a searching mind. Such a class act. Such a great candidate once you met him face to face. He'd make a great president, if only the voters could see it.*

Heifers were easier to understand. You fed them, watered them, and took care of them until they grew up; then you replaced them. This campaign was much more complicated, an enigma with so many variables: candidate, campaign organization, the press, and, most difficult to understand, the voters. Contemplating the puzzle was a stimulating intellectual project in its own right, but Dan knew he had gotten himself much more involved than that. His attachment was no longer intellectual, it had become a personal and emotional commitment to his candidate. Babbitt had shown a lot of strength and class in the week since Iowa's profound disappointment. He deserved the same from his supporters.

Chores done, Dan headed to his car. It was time to campaign.

5:45 A.M.

Molly Kelly was pretty sure Dukakis was going to win today, but she didn't want to think it consciously, as if the thought itself might jinx him. She reminded herself to find the time somehow to vote during the day. It might come down to someone's single ballot, and after all this work she wasn't going to take any chances.

The apartment was quiet, the children still asleep. Rachel had pleaded for permission to skip school today to help the campaign. Molly had convinced her otherwise but promised all three children they could go with her to the postelection party in Manchester tonight, after Zach's basketball game.

Before she left, Molly got out some paper and wrote a short note to each child, telling them when and where each one was to meet her. Today was going to be hectic, and she wanted to be sure her family didn't get separated in the shuffle.

6:45 A.M.

A cold front was moving in from the northwest, a raw wind pushing away the fog to reveal dirty, scudding clouds. Dawn. But the temperature seemed to be dropping instead of rising with the gray, hidden sun. Outside his house, deep in the woods of Sullivan, Al Rubega started to load up his car with signs, brochures, and buttons. He was running late.

Al was dressed for the cold: lined boots, corduroy pants, a zipped sweatshirt, a down vest, and a heavy jacket. Underneath it all was a Jack Kemp T-shirt; Kemp buttons festooned his overcoat; and on his close-cropped head of hair was a baseball cap with the Kemp for President logo, one of about a dozen that Al and Mary had made last summer.

This race is going to be won by the campaign that works the hardest, Al had thought when he began volunteer work for Kemp a year earlier. Certainly no other campaign in Cheshire County had outworked him and his small cadre of Kemp supporters. The county Republican picnic in June, the street fair and Cheshire Fair last summer, the rally on Central Square on that bitterly cold Saturday in December, the canvassing and phone calling, the homemade banner and hats and signs—"Kemping" had become a mission for him, and he had pursued it with the combination of ideological fervor and boyish, optimistic exuberance that defined his character.

You don't win the match on the mat, you win it in practice months and months before. He remembered his wrestling coach preaching that. In Cheshire County—in the entire state—the only campaign that had shown more in "practice" over the last year was the Bush organization, Al believed, and now Bush had been mortally wounded in Iowa. With Bush and Dole bickering in the press, Kemp was poised to be the beneficiary. As always, Al was being positive.

He put the last of the placards—ones he and Dr. Ridge had painted when the state headquarters ran out of supplies—in the back of his car. For the rest of the day he would refer to his vehicle, an aging Subaru with more than one hundred thousand miles on it, as the "Kempmobile."

He checked the folded sheet of legal paper in his pocket, his schedule for filling in at polling places in the county today when other volunteers wouldn't be available. He was behind schedule already, but he was in good spirits as he embarked on his final mission for Kemp. He started whistling as he drove—the theme music from *Star Wars*.

7:15 A.M.

The motorcade wheeled up to the front of the elementary school in Manchester, New Hampshire, with all the self-assurance and sense of power implicit in every campaign motorcade: first a police car, then a Secret Service car, the limousine, another Secret Service car, and a van full of reporters and cameramen. As soon as it stopped, the Secret Service agents were out of their cars and around the limousine; the reporters and camera crews scrambled to position near the rear door.

Doug Kidd walked up to the curb to greet Robertson as he emerged from the limo. But before Doug could say anything, the reporters swarmed around the candidate, peppering him with more questions about his statement in the debate that the Soviet Union had missiles in Cuba.

Ignoring the reporters, Robertson followed Doug's lead toward the entrance of the school, which today was the polling place for Ward 12 in New Hampshire's largest city. As he walked, Robertson stopped briefly to shake the hands of the people lining the sidewalk with placards—supporters from the campaigns of Bush, Simon, Dole, Dukakis, and Gephardt. With each one Robertson smiled and made a little small talk while the cameras rolled. Once inside the school foyer, he turned to Doug.

"Brother," he said, "why aren't there any of *my* signs and *my* supporters out there? This isn't right." He was upset. This stop was designed as a photo opportunity—a final chance for Robertson to get on the noon and evening television news before the polls closed. So far, what had been recorded was the candidate dodging embarrassing questions and being greeted by other candidates' placards.

"Pat, I don't know," Doug answered. This part of the state wasn't his area of responsibility; he had only been assigned the duty of accompanying Robertson at the last minute. "I'll check it out with headquarters."

Three people emerged from the voting area and came directly to Robertson to say that they had just voted for him. Doug breathed a sigh of relief. *Voters aren't influenced by placards near the polls,* he thought, *but by their beliefs. Things will be just fine.*

Back outside, they ran into a scene of confusion. Paul Simon's motorcade had arrived, and the senator was in the middle of his own photo opportunity. The two candidates walked up to one another, each one ringed by agents, reporters, photographers, and aides. The two circles merged, like amoebas mating, leaving the two candidates in the center of an expanded ring, where they shook hands, exchanged pleasantries, and wished one another good luck. (This, as it turned out, was the moment that would be on that day's news.)

On their way to his limousine, Robertson asked Doug whether there would be any Robertson signs and volunteers at his next scheduled stop.

"Brother Pat, I honestly don't know," Doug said. "But I promise I'll call the office to make sure they know your concern."

"Why don't you ride with me to the next stop?"

By his expression, the tone of his voice, Robertson no longer seemed upset. To Doug he seemed worried, uncharacteristically uncertain, almost vulnerable—alone in the midst of a motorcade of strangers.

Doug moved toward the limo door, trying quickly to decipher the logistics of how he would get back to retrieve his own car. A security agent put out an arm and stopped him.

"I want him to ride with me," Robertson said. "Come on, get in."

The agent again stopped Doug, who decided it was best not to press the issue. "It's all right, Brother Pat," he said. "I think I should call the headquarters anyway."

The motorcade began to move. Doug headed for the nearest pay phone. He wanted to get back to Cheshire County so he could check on his own area's organization. He felt sure, as he had during the drive to Manchester, that Robertson would finish at least third today, maybe even second, but the foul-up with the placards and especially the final look at Brother Pat as he got into his limo had been unsettling.

Doug turned back toward the parking lot just in time to see the motorcade curl at the driveway, sweep down the street, and disappear from sight. He would not see "Brother Pat" again until the votes were counted.

7:30 *A.M.*

None of the polls in Keene or the rest of Cheshire County would open for voting until 9:00 A.M., but Andi Johnson had been at the Simon office by six o'clock. A volunteer from Jesse Jackson's headquarters a block away had stopped by to say that the results of their phone calls indicated a lot of previously undecided voters were breaking toward Simon. Andi's own calls the last week hadn't picked up even the slightest support for Gephardt. The press was waiting to write off whichever one, Gephardt or Simon, finished third today. Andi felt confident. Simon might even beat Dukakis in a few towns. In her four-year career as a political worker, her candidates had always won locally, despite how they had fared statewide. Last night, she said, had felt "like Christmas Eve and Santa's coming."

Now she was standing at the intersection of Main Street and Central Square, holding a Simon placard to take advantage of the morning traffic. The huge snow pile was gone, so if people going to work were to see her candidate's name one more time, a human being would have to be attached to the sign.

A young supporter of Gary Hart showed up, bearing not only a placard, but an armful of small booklets containing Hart's speeches on a variety of issues. As pedestrians walked by on their way to downtown jobs, he would approach and press a booklet on them. He seemed to be burning with a fanatical desire to convince them of Hart's qualifications, like some sort of proselytizer of the Apocalypse intent on saving wayward souls before the end arrived.

He's assaulting those poor people, Andi thought. Four years ago that volunteer might have been her. Today she considered him pathetic.

7:45 A.M.

At the other end of Main Street, where it intersects with two major highways, Dan Burnham stood on a small median island between two lanes.

"Come on, wave," Dan muttered under his breath to the line of cars approaching. He smiled, thrust his Babbitt placard up and down with one hand, and waved with his other hand. Most of the drivers ignored him. A few smiled. One gave him a thumbs-up signal, and Dan beamed back.

Two other Babbitt volunteers were on the other traffic islands doing the same thing. *This shows that Babbitt's not so down and out.* Of all the activities Dan had thrown himself into during the last weeks of the campaign—phoning voters to check their preferences and possibly sway them to Babbitt's cause, or canvassing door to door—this seemed the least intrusive on other people's lives, because, he said, "all you're asking for is a wave and a smile." Earlier that month, on a bitingly cold February morning, he and another volunteer had manned this same intersection in the early morning. Dan liked it when the weather was inclement. The worse the weather, the more sympathy from the driver/voters, he figured, and the more it proved the commitment of Babbitt's followers. His companion that morning had become concerned about frostbite as the wind had picked up and the windchill plummeted. She was worried because she was with Dan, and, in her words, "Dan just doesn't quit."

The lights changed, momentarily stopping traffic past Dan's outpost. He lowered his Babbitt sign for a brief rest. *Who can figure out what it is that influences a voter?* He had been chewing on that problem for some time, in fact felt he had less of an answer now than he had before he started campaigning. The image that had struck him during the Keene canvass resurfaced, and he couldn't shake it: *It's like chumming for tuna. You throw the bait out on the water and watch it sink, but you don't know for sure whether the tuna are eating it.*

The lights changed again, and the traffic started moving. Dan picked up his sign. *Come on, wave.*

8:30 A.M.

Eleanor Labrie climbed the stairs to Gephardt's office one more time. She had slept fitfully in the night and was tired when she reached the office. "I need a rest," she said, talking of more than just her morning's exercise. "It's been a draining experience."

She scanned the list showing which polls were being covered by volunteers, and saw that there wasn't an opening until eleven A.M., so she settled at her desk to take care of the phones.

Mike Haas had overslept. He rushed in, collected an armful of signs, and headed back out to deliver them to his volunteers.

9:00 A.M.

All across Cheshire County, in the five wards of Keene and in the other twenty-two towns, in churches, schools, and town halls, the first polls opened for early voters.

• Kendall Lane arrived at the Ward 4 polling place in Keene, an elementary school. A city truck was spreading sand on the driveway and parking lot in anticipation of the voters. The sand had come too late for Steve Price, the Dole coordinator, however. His car had skidded on the glazed pavement and collided with a pickup truck driven by Kendall's aunt. She had come to vote for Bush because Kendall had asked her. The police were there; a wrecker was on the way. Kendall commiserated with his aunt about the accident and chatted with a few Bush supporters already in position with their placards. He planned to vote—this was his home ward—and then meet Marvin Bush. As he waited, he overheard two volunteers—one for Dole, one for Simon—chatting while they held their signs. "If it's Dukakis and Bush [in the final election]," one said, "we can all go to sleep." Dr. David Ridge pulled up, planted a Kemp sign in a snowbank, and drove off.

• Andi Johnson was already in position outside Marlborough Elementary School, holding a Simon placard and, despite the damp coldness, wearing no overcoat and only a Simon T-shirt under her suit coat. She was not there because of any inside information about possible television coverage; Marlborough was simply a polling place she had not been able to find someone else to cover. She planned to stay there all day. She was pleasantly surprised by the lack of any Dukakis or Gephardt standard-bearers. And the large number of Bush people seemed impressive, perhaps overkill, for such a small town.

• Doug Kidd was on his way from Derry, New Hampshire, back to a polling place in Manchester. He had waited for Robertson to show up for breakfast in a Derry restaurant, but the stop had been canceled when Robertson fell woefully behind schedule. Feeling frustrated, unproductive, and anxious to get back to his own part of the state, Doug stepped more heavily on his accelerator and sped along.

• Molly Kelly was in the midst of a crowd packed into the Dukakis headquarters on Central Square. She had more volunteers—most of them from Massachusetts—than she had jobs. She decided to send some of them to shopping centers to hold signs. Gephardt and

Simon had beaten Dukakis when the tiny hamlet of Dixville Notch voted at midnight, and the Massachusetts people kept asking her whether that meant trouble for their guy. Molly wasn't sure.

• Al Rubega stopped briefly at Keene's Ward 1 polling place, just long enough to deliver a placard to a Kemp volunteer waiting for him there. He had to keep moving. He was supposed to be at the polling place in the town of Winchester when it opened.

• Barbara MacKenzie was stamping her feet to keep them warm as she stood outside the Keene Unitarian Church, which today was the Ward 2 polling place. Mac was inside, getting ready to work as a poll checker. Barbara was holding a Dole sign and wearing two Dole pins. One of them, from the 1980 campaign, had a picture of a younger-looking Dole; the year was covered over with "1988." A woman nearby with a "Draft Cuomo" sign was an acquaintance of Barbara's, and they talked amiably as they fought the morning chill.

• Dan Burnham, holding his Babbitt sign aloft, was also outside the church. The sidewalk was well shoveled, but like the cluster of supporters of the other candidates there, Dan stood to the side in the snow packed a good six inches higher than the pavement. When a voter scuttled down the middle of this gauntlet toward the polls, the sign carriers all leaned forward, dipping their placards in salute.

Now it was upon them. Yet as aware as they always had been about this day, as tightly as their every effort had focused on this moment, now that it was here it seemed as unreal as it had weeks and months earlier. Maybe more unreal.

They had not been waiting for this moment, they had been work-ing toward it, and the work had so insinuated itself into their lives and then so thoroughly overwhelmed everything else that nothing was real except the work, the campaigning. Up until this moment, they were the primary. It had been theirs, almost exclusively.

But now the primary no longer belonged to them. It was being transferred into the hands of someone else. It belonged to the voters—the people who a year ago, even a day ago, had been just names. Names on a list.

The long-awaited alchemy of transforming names into people had been achieved. Now the voters were flesh and blood. All that could be done was to watch them file past toward the sanctum of the polling booth, wait, worry, and then watch them leave.

18

FIRST IN THE NATION

At noon Molly Kelly walked from the campaign office to her ward's polling place and cast her ballot for Dukakis. It relieved her to have that out of the way. A little later at the office, however, the mood—raucous and confident during the morning—began to turn anxious. No one was concerned that Dukakis might lose the primary, but unless his margin was large enough, the press might dub him, like Johnson and Muskie in earlier primaries, a "loser" to their expectations.

The state headquarters called at three P.M. to report that, by their estimates, Dukakis was losing 4 percent of his potential vote simply because people were having trouble finding his name on the ballot. A man named David Duke (a former leader of the Ku Klux Klan) was among several fringe candidates on the ballot, and the concern was that some voters were confusing the two "Dukes." Looking out the window at some volunteers holding signs on the sidewalk, Molly winced when she saw one of her people holding a placard that read, "Vote for the Duke." She and Mike Cook huddled briefly and reworked the script workers were using in their phone calls to voters, so that they'd be instructed where Dukakis's name was located on the ballots.

When school let out, Zach and Rachel arrived to join their

mother. Molly's extended campaign family now included volunteers from far outside New Hampshire's borders. In addition to the fifty-odd supporters from Massachusetts, her crew included a young woman from the Netherlands (a student at Syracuse University), a young man from British Columbia (a Harvard student), and a Yugoslavian whose thick accent could be heard in the din from the phone bank.

"I'm fading fast," Molly told Mike in the late afternoon. She went to the bank to cash some expense drafts from the headquarters and got a quick bite to eat with two of her children. Refreshed, she returned to announce, "I want to get on the phone and sell. I have to *do* something." She and Rachel sat down to join the crew for the final push of calls from four o'clock until the polls closed at seven. The simple act of telephoning—and the fact that the people the campaign had identified as supporters uniformly reported that they planned to vote and were holding firm for Dukakis—seemed to release Molly's anxious energy.

By evening the volunteers returned, tired but upbeat. "We're going to win," was the constant refrain as the office emptied and cars started toward Manchester for the victory party.

Molly was delayed leaving Keene. She had to wait for Zach's basketball game to end. It was well past eight o'clock before she and her three kids were in the car, had picked up dinner at the local McDonald's, and were on the way to Manchester. All the way, as Molly switched radio channels for the latest results, her principal worry was that Dole would beat Bush and upstage Dukakis's victory.

When they finally arrived at the site of Dukakis's postelection party, the parking lot was already emptying out. The candidate had spoken, claimed his victory, and the mass of volunteers were heading to continue the celebration at bars across the city—places off limits to someone with three minors in tow. As they waited for Molly's boyfriend, the assistant basketball coach at the college where she worked, to arrive from his own game, Molly and her kids mingled with the few supporters left in the big hall. Reporters covering the Dukakis campaign were still in the room, finishing their stories on their portable computers. Just before leaving at eleven P.M., Molly peeked over one reporter's shoulder to see what he was writing. His story began, "No surprises here."

Tom Britton's duties as Troy town moderator kept him at the polling place in his town all day, from its opening at ten in the morning to its closing at seven P.M., and then for another hour and a half as the ballots were counted. Dukakis won Troy overwhelmingly with 110 votes, followed by Gephardt (35 votes), Simon (27), Jackson (20), Gore (15), Hart (11), and Babbitt (7). Having devoted so much of his life to the campaign over the last year, part of it to weighing the finer differences among the Democratic candidates, Tom was baffled at the way some people voted: three people wrote in Oliver North; one placed checks next to three candidates' names; one wrote in "Alf," the television alien.

At the Gore party in Nashua that night, which the candidate himself did not attend (he spoke to the crowd from a "Super Tuesday" state by a phone hooked up to the loudspeaker), Tom cocked his ear when the state director announced that Gore, with just under 7 percent of the Democratic vote and fifth place of the seven principal candidates, had done well in New Hampshire by exceeding everyone's expectations. "I kept waiting for him [the state director] to smile," he said of the announcement.

Tom decided that the few swallows of Jack Daniel's left in his bottle should be saved for "Super Tuesday." Today's New Hampshire showing somehow didn't seem to warrant a toast.

Dan Burnham thought it highly unlikely that holding a sign with his candidate's name outside a polling place would influence the vote of anyone walking by. For someone who read several newspapers a day, several magazines a month; for someone who had either personally attended or watched on television close to ten candidate debates and forums in the last year; for someone who, in the back of his car, had copies of virtually every major speech and policy paper Bruce Babbitt had released in the course of the campaign and knew their contents almost by heart—the idea that a citizen might base his vote for president of the United States on a *sign* he had just seen on the way to the ballot booth was difficult to imagine.

But on this cold morning, there Dan stood in the snow outside the Keene Unitarian Church. And he was not alone. Sign carriers for Dole, Bush, Jackson, Simon, Gore, Hart, Dukakis, Gephardt, and (the write-in effort for) Cuomo huddled against the chill with him as voters walked past; a Kemp placard had been planted in the snow by Dr. Ridge before the polls opened. None of the campaigns wanted to take the chance that this wasn't *the* key to the kingdom.

Most voters avoided all eye contact with the partisans. A few, seeing the sign of a candidate they apparently backed, might smile or wink at the volunteer holding it. Others, encountering a local volunteer they knew, would pause for a brief chat with their friend and then pass on without having given any indication what they would be doing once they got a ballot in their hands.

After five hours at his post, Dan joined some other local Babbitt supporters for a late lunch. Lisa Babish was there, looking ravaged and puffy from lack of sleep. The night before, she reported, she had driven to some towns more than an hour north of Keene to deliver voter lists and Babbitt signs to supporters. At one A.M. she had gotten lost before her last stop. The fog had been impenetrable, and she'd had to stop at every mailbox on a remote road in her search for the right house. Driving back to Keene in the heavy fog, she said, she had lurched off the road a few times and begun hallucinating that a carload of Robertson workers were following her. She hadn't arrived until three o'clock, then she'd slept for three hours and had joined Dan for the morning rush-hour "honk and wave" on Main Street. She was still wearing the Cornell sweatshirt and sweat pants she had slept in.

The group turned their lunch into a "premortem" for the loss they all expected Babbitt to suffer that day. Lisa believed Babbitt's message had been presented backward. Instead of, "I've got integ-

rity, we need to raise taxes and save our future," it should have
been, "We need to save our future, and I've got the integrity to tell
you how to do it by raising taxes," she said. Dan said he no longer
trusted his political instincts, but he had never liked Babbitt's literal
"standing up" for taxes in the debate in December. It had seemed
like a desperate stunt to him. The tax issue had moved the campaign
away from emphasizing Babbitt's gubernatorial successes in Arizona, especially his environmental record, and had allowed Dukakis
to campaign, unchallenged, as the only effective chief executive in
the race. The formats of the debates, he added, had worked against
Babbitt: rewarding pithy one-liners at the expense of reasoned argument that was Babbitt's forte.

Dan left to give a ride to the polls to an elderly Keene couple who
had responded to a Babbitt phone bank. As he pulled them up to
their polling place, the woman remarked that she'd heard Robertson
and Hart were going to win today, and that Hart was a very smart
man. Dan didn't say anything, and when they returned to his car,
he didn't ask them how they'd voted. He dropped them off at a
grocery store, as they had requested.

"Some service!" the man said when he got out.

"Oh, well," Dan muttered as he drove off.

He spent the afternoon holding a Babbitt sign outside the polls
in Peterborough, a small town where the other volunteers seemed
to know everyone coming in and out. The sun, barely visible
throughout the day, sank in the west, and the temperature dropped
even farther. Asked how he felt about the day, Dan had a one-word
reply: "Puzzled."

Doris Haddock, the campaign's "secret weapon" on the phones
and a friend of Dan's, rode with him to the postelection party in
Manchester after the local polls closed. Dan was going to the party
mainly for the chance to make sure Doris got some recognition for
her work. Babbitt had finished second to Dukakis (47 votes to 62)
in their town of Dublin, she reported. The news briefly reignited
the pilot light of hope Dan had allowed to go out since Iowa. *Who
knows what the voters think? Maybe the impossible will happen.*

They turned on the car radio. Babbitt, with 4.6 percent of the Democratic vote, had finished sixth, barely ahead of Gary Hart's 4 percent in last place.

"Stop in the Name of Love" was playing on the loudspeakers when Dan and Doris walked into the restaurant where the Babbitt party was being held. It summed up Dan's feelings about the future of Babbitt's campaign. He hoped Babbitt would pull out of the race tonight. "It's better when it's clean," he said, looking at the depressing vote tallies.

After some speeches by the campaign's state leaders, during which Dan winced when their oratory turned syrupy, Babbitt took the microphone and the crowd applauded and screamed for ten minutes. Babbitt made a joke about demanding a recount and then went on to say that the people there had not been defeated, they were part of a new movement with a new message. Dan looked disgusted and walked over to the bar.

"That left me colder than hell," he said. "I'm not part of any *movement*. I was supporting a guy I thought would be a good president."

Dan stayed for another hour, waiting for the chance to bring Doris, who was having a great time at the party, through the crowd to meet Babbitt. Finally he wedged her in through the supporters and reporters and cameras surrounding the candidate, she said a few words to Babbitt, and they left.

On the way home he and Doris talked about 1992 and how Babbitt might have a chance if he started preparing in New Hampshire immediately.

Len Fleischer stood in line to vote at the Ward 1 polling place in the morning. In his quest for a candidate to support, he had seen every Democratic candidate in person, had even confronted Gary Hart (Len's choice in 1984) to urge him to drop from the race. He had gone about making a choice deliberately, almost painstakingly: studying the candidates' positions on many issues, talking with their campaigns, and discussing the race in the evenings with

Erika, his wife, and friends. Erika, a friend of Molly Kelly's, had settled on Dukakis as her candidate several weeks ago. Len had recently made the same decision, and in the past week both had been doing volunteer work for the campaign.

But as he stood in line for a ballot, something didn't feel right to Len. He turned around, walked out of the polling place, and went home to help Erika make some more last-minute calls to identified Dukakis supporters. In midafternoon he returned to the polls, got his ballot, and went behind the curtain in the voting booth.

"I looked at Dukakis and Jackson on the ballot," he said later, "and went back and forth. I scratched my head and thought about it some more." Earlier in the week he had seen a letter in *The Keene Sentinel* from a Jackson supporter, saying how many people agreed with Jackson's positions on the issues but weren't going to vote for him. Len had read the letter aloud to Erika. In the voting booth now, he thought about the letter some more.

Len paused a little longer and then put his checkmark next to Jackson's name. "I was sure Dukakis was going to win New Hampshire," he said later. "If it was close, I might have voted for Dukakis, but he didn't need my vote."

Shelley Nelkens had met every Democratic candidate for president, some of them several times, except Jesse Jackson, and she had talked to staff members on most of the Republican campaigns. For a year her principal connection with the primary campaign had been to take advantage of New Hampshire's high political profile to press forward her own antinuclear causes—changing the Price-Anderson Act that limited legal liability for nuclear plant operators, stopping the Seabrook plant and the dumping of radioactive waste, reopening the investigation into the Three Mile Island accident, and doing something about the irradiation of food—on any candidate who would listen. "Sometimes," she had said in December, "I feel guilty that I'm just using them. But that's what they're doing: using us."

Over twelve months, her opinions of the candidates had shifted, varying with her personal reactions to a candidate's personality and her assessment of his fervor for her issues. At one point, for instance, she had found Gephardt boyishly charming and considered supporting him. Then he missed a vote in Congress (he was campaigning in Iowa) she considered important; he was out of the running. Babbitt, upon whom she had heaped such scorn in early 1987 for his television style, had endeared himself in a debate in January 1988 by making several points about the environment. Gore and Simon had each gone through cycles of piquing her interest and then disappointing her, usually because they failed to match her exacting standards on the issues she held most dear. Dukakis—she never cared for him. Jackson said the right things, but she didn't trust him as a political leader and she harbored suspicions from the 1984 campaign that he might be anti-Semitic.

In mid-January, after watching him being interviewed by Marvin Kalb on television, Shelley decided to support Gary Hart. "He was so on top of it, the most knowledgeable of the candidates," she said of Hart. "He comes across as a real *mensch*." She and Hart had had a testy exchange early in 1987, before he had dropped out, over his commitment to environmental issues. "I don't have to be a friend of his to vote for him for president," she said of it a year later. And as far as the Donna Rice affair was concerned, she said, "I don't read *People* magazine, and I don't like gossip. It's none of my business; it's his and his wife's and his family's business." She called Hart's Denver office to volunteer and was given the telephone number of the New Hampshire office.

Before starting volunteer work, however, she said she had some other work to do: trying to get a bill through the New Hampshire legislature banning food irradiation was her first priority.

The first week of February, Shelley changed her mind. "Hart's not talking about the environment at all—absolutely zilch about saving this planet," she said. She had read the booklet his revived campaign was issuing, and none of the speeches it contained said anything about environmental issues. "Everything's economics," she had complained to Hart's staff. She said she had now decided to sit out the whole thing.

Today, primary day, however, she went into the voting booth in her town of Antrim and was given a Democratic ballot. She marked the box next to Jackson's name and left. "I knew he was going to lose," she explained later. "It was a protest vote. I couldn't find anyone worth supporting."

Eleanor Labrie hung up the phone at the Gephardt office in mid-afternoon. The woman on the other end had said she still hadn't made up her mind on which candidate to vote for. Eleanor couldn't believe her ears. The primary would be over within five hours.

Karen Greer arrived from sign duty at a polling place, and she and Eleanor exchanged tales from the experience. Eleanor, who had stood outside the Ward 3 polls for a few hours, had been encouraged when a man walking by had surveyed the gauntlet of campaign signs, seen hers, and said, "Ah, Gephardt. That's the man." Karen said a Bush supporter at her polling place had complained about the federal regulations that prohibited Bush from spending more money in New Hampshire. "*I'm* standing here with a homemade sign held together with Saran Wrap," she said she told the man, "and *you're* saying Bush can't spend enough in New Hampshire." Later, when the same guy tried to convince her to swap campaign buttons for souvenirs, she had told him, "Watch out. I'm a very tired person with a big stick."

Liz Daschbach, the college-aged daughter of Richard Daschbach who, with her father, was a member of "Team Gephardt," came in with a depressing story. Two years ago, when Richard was running for the state legislature, he had asked Liz to register as a Republican so she could write in his name during the primary (and help him become both the Democratic and Republican nominee for the seat representing some small towns). Today, when she showed up to vote for Gephardt, she was told that she was a registered Republican and couldn't have a Democratic ballot. She wrote in Gephardt for president and Jackson for vice president, but her vote, which would only be counted in the Republican tallies, was wasted.

The afternoon brought a lull in activity. Only two calls came in from people seeking rides to the polls. Mike Haas, the young co-ordinator, brought a mug of hot chocolate up the two flights of stairs for Eleanor. She started to stir it with a pen. "You know you're tired," Karen said, "when you try to stir your hot chocolate with a pen."

As the evening news began on the radio, a commentator said that if Simon didn't finish second among the Democrats, he could be eliminated from the race. "I hope so," Eleanor said. "We don't need another smiling, rocking-chair type. I don't know if he is, but that's the way he impresses me. I just don't like him." At sundown she left; Eleanor didn't drive at night and needed to get her car home. Someone was scheduled to pick her up for a party at a supporter's home in the evening, once the polls closed.

Gephardt's state director called at 5:45 P.M., shortly after Eleanor departed, to talk to Mike Haas, who hung up from the exchange unnerved. An exit poll had shown Gephardt leading Simon by six-tenths of one percent, the director had said; another poll had them dead even. A few minutes earlier Mike had said he didn't know what he should be doing at this point. Now it was clear: scour for every possible vote. Six-tenths of one percent equaled a two-hundred-vote lead, he informed his group. With urgency in his voice, he instructed them to start phoning every "2" (leaner) on their lists.

One of Mike's volunteers was a high school junior who had gotten up at three o'clock in the morning to go to Manchester to appear on *Good Morning America*. She was a little punchy from lack of sleep and not having eaten all day, but on her way out to find some more phone lines she tried to kid Mike a little, get him to loosen up. "We've got to get some votes," he snapped without smiling. The office went silent. No one had ever seen Mike short-tempered before.

A few minutes later Mike put some music on his tape player. "A

little mood music," he said, trying to ease some of the tension, as
"The Impossible Dream" began playing. With that song completed,
he switched to Bruce Springsteen for a harder, more driving beat.
They were calling frantically. Karen Greer said most of the numbers
she had seemed to be disconnected. Mike was hunched over his
own phone.

"It's very close," he urged one voter. "It's between Gephardt and
Simon." A sudden fear swept over him as he hung up. "Geez," he
said. "I probably just got someone to go out to vote for Simon."

At 6:30 P.M., with only a half hour until the polls closed, Mike
switched tactics. He started calling Gephardt supporters to see if
they knew of any other people he could call to get them out to vote.
One woman suggested a friend in a remote town north of Keene,
and he hung up quickly. No listing in the phone book. He called
directory assistance and got the number, phoned the person, and
pleaded with him to vote for Gephardt. The man said he'd "contemplate" it. "I hope he doesn't contemplate it too long," Mike said,
whirling through his Rolodex for another supporter to call. Only
nineteen minutes remained before seven P.M.

At 6:46 Mike was on the line with another voter, an elderly
woman who said she had already voted for Gephardt but seemed
to want to talk a lot about the race. He hung up on her in midsentence.

Greg Martin, a local lawyer and "Team Gephardt" member,
strolled in from giving rides to the polls. His last ride had been a
woman who'd insisted she voted in Ward 5, not the ward Greg had
been told was her polling place. Sure enough, she had walked out
from the Ward 5 polls without being allowed to vote; Greg had sped
her across town to the other poll just before it was ready to close.

By 6:52 P.M. another possible voter had been located, and Mike
was begging him to hurry to the polls, telling him there were only
a few times when one vote could make the difference in an election,
and this was one of them. Finally the man agreed. Mike started
searching for another number.

"Give it up," a volunteer pleaded gently, pointing to the clock on the wall. It was 6:59.

"We should have been doing this all day," Mike lamented. "We were just *sitting* here."

The "Team Gephardt" party that night was a combination of farewell fete for Mike, their young leader whom they called "the Boss," referring to his idol, Springsteen, and tense monitoring of the television for results while Mike worked the phones for tallies from Cheshire County. Eleanor read a poem she had composed in his honor:

> *He organized, he taught us,*
> *He gave us tasks to do.*
> *We followed where he led us,*
> *His smile compelled us to.*
>
> *We canvassed, phoned, wrote letters,*
> *To keep Mike's heart content;*
> *Predawn we froze, sign wavers,*
> *To brave the element(s) . . .*

Like a coach at the end of the season, Mike gave a short speech to his troops. "Every time I go to Concord, I tell people there about the people I have here," he said. "They're jealous. In the last two months, this area has gotten a lot of respect from Concord. I've been just real pleased with everything you've done for me. Last spring, they were thinking of writing off Keene. One thing I've been happiest about, we had new people working. [Eleanor and some others smiled; he was talking about them.] Today, like every day, you did everything I asked you to do. The last half was really scary. Hopefully it will pay off. Regardless of what the results are, if you do everything you can and you put yourself on the line, it doesn't really matter. People had to remind me that at 7:05. I just wanted to say thanks to everybody. I don't know where I'm going or when I'm going, but I know I'll be back in Keene sometime."

The television reported that with 65 percent of the vote recorded, Dukakis (with 34 percent) was leading the Democrats, followed by Gephardt (21 percent) and Simon (17). Eleanor made a fist and raised it. "We aren't going to beat Dukakis, but we're going to have such a good showing. . . . Oooh!"

Cheshire County results started coming in on the phone: second in Swanzey, six votes over Simon; second in Jaffrey, twenty-five votes over Simon. The television reported a slight tightening between Simon and Gephardt, with 73 percent of the vote counted.

"It looks like it's going to come down to Keene," said Greg Martin. (Keene is one of the few large cities in New Hampshire without mechanical polls; counting its paper ballots traditionally makes it the last in the state to report its vote total.)

A local radio station brought the bad news. Simon had finished second in Keene, beating Gephardt by about 60 votes, and second in the county, ahead of Gephardt by 240 votes.

"Bah," Eleanor said. "Why does it have to be Cheshire County? It really gets me."

At ten o'clock Mike left for the statewide Gephardt party in Manchester. Despite the deficit in Cheshire County, his candidate was reportedly firmly in second place. "Team Gephardt" was happy at the statewide numbers but dispirited by their region's contribution. "At least we didn't bring him down far enough to drop him below Simon [statewide]," said Greg Martin before he drove Eleanor home.

Manchester, New Hampshire's biggest and most politically conservative city, traditionally announces the unofficial returns from its voting machines early in the evening. At seven thirty about sixteen Simon supporters were gathered around a television set at the Ramada Inn in Keene, where Andi Johnson had rented a small room to monitor the results and have a local party. When the Manchester TV station announced that with eight of the twelve Manchester wards reporting, Gephardt was beating Dukakis in the city, with Jackson a distant third and Simon fourth, a quiet panic swept through most of the group. They turned to Andi as their in-house political expert for an explanation.

"Manchester is Gephardt territory," she assured them. Things would get better. She lit another Virginia Slims cigarette from one of the three packs she would smoke that day. A half hour later she calmed them with results from four Cheshire County towns: Simon had finished second in each one.

Andi had spent most of the day outside Marlborough's elementary school, the town's polling place, with a Simon sign. During the bulk of the morning, it had been just her and about seven young Bush supporters. Marvin Bush and his wife had arrived at ten A.M. with Kendall Lane, pushing the Bush contingent to ten people in a town that produced five hundred voters.

"You guys are too young to be conservatives with closed minds," Andi told the Bush crowd.

"And you're too old not to have any common sense," Marvin Bush responded.

An older man arrived and walked toward the polls. "Good morning, how are you today?" Marvin said.

"I'm just trying to get in, past all you folks in the way," the man answered.

"How do you do. I'm Marvin Bush, the vice president's son," Marvin told a woman voter a few minutes later.

"Nice to meet you," she replied. "I met your sister the other day."

Andi knew the woman, a Republican. "Mornings are the Republican time to vote," she had confided earlier.

"Are you going to write in Paul Simon?" Andi asked cheerfully.

"I'll think about it," was the answer.

Sign holders for Dole, Jackson, and Dukakis showed up late in the morning. All of them were from out of state; Dukakis's was from the Netherlands. As the day progressed, most of the campaigns sent replacements to give the sign carriers a break from the raw weather (Bush's oversize group departed, leaving just one person behind, once a television crew had come to shoot some footage), but Andi remained until late afternoon. At one point a Dole sign left in a snowbank by his campaign's volunteer began to lean from the brisk wind. Neither Andi, who was hoping for Bush to win the Republican race (she thought he would be the easiest for the Democrats to beat in November), nor the Bush volunteer standing with her wanted to set it upright. Another gust of wind finally blew it down.

The sign carriers conversed amiably during the day, occasionally seeking shelter together in one person's car when the wind got too cold and no voters were in sight. During a school recess, they talked with the schoolchildren and polled them out of curiosity: Bush and Simon won.

At four o'clock Andi went home, showered, changed clothes, went to the office, checked on the polls in Winchester, returned to the office, and then set up her room at the Ramada to await the results.

By 8:45 P.M. the crowd had grown to more than thirty people. The group seemed more intent on having a good time than paying close attention to the election results. As Andi would announce local returns, few people listened. Her prediction at nine o'clock that Simon would finish second in Cheshire County—a profoundly significant development for Andi's sense of her organization's work—was mitigated by the television: Dukakis was giving his victory speech (they booed and hissed at his image on the screen), followed by a commentator proclaiming that Simon, clearly on his way to third place in New Hampshire, was politically "dead" (more boos and hisses). "It's okay," one Simon supporter said. "I'm not used to winning anyway."

Gary Hart's speech came on at 9:20 P.M. Andi didn't bother to watch. When Robertson's turn came on the screen, someone switched channels to the Olympics.

The group dispersed at 10:30 P.M. Andi initially said she wasn't going to drive to Manchester for the statewide postelection party. Simon had already spoken to his supporters, and it would be past midnight before she could get there. Only the hard-core political "junkies" would still be there.

But early Wednesday morning she found herself with a small group of diehard politicos in a Manchester hotel room, drinking and rehashing the primary. At three A.M., she collapsed on a chair and fell asleep.

Doug Kidd described his primary day as "frustrating and very unproductive." The mix-ups with Robertson's schedule kept compounding themselves. After waiting in vain for the candidate at a restaurant in midmorning, Doug had called the headquarters for his next assignment. Former governor Thomson directed him to another polling place to meet Robertson, but it turned out to be the wrong one. Doug waited again while no one showed up.

It was afternoon before he got back to Cheshire County, voted in Stoddard, and then started calling his volunteers to check on their progress. The campaign had set up its own system for reporting individual towns' results, but by early evening Doug realized the news media was collecting tallies more efficiently.

Doug and Allison headed for Concord, for the final rally, and en route heard on the car radio that Robertson had finished last in Manchester. *What does that mean?* he wondered. At the hotel ballroom where two hundred partisans had gathered, Doug was greeted warmly by the friends he had made during the campaign. "We did it, we did it," several of them told him—indicating not that Robertson had won or even exceeded his expectations (the news on the television screens was suggesting the opposite), but that they had actually survived this new political experience together.

The final results came in. Robertson, with 9.4 percent of the Republican total and 14,775 votes, had finished last of the five candidates. Even du Pont, bolstered by a good showing in Manchester, where the *Union-Leader*'s endorsement had carried considerable clout, had finished ahead of him.

Doug felt numb, stunned. *Where are the rest of our votes?* he asked himself. Then he thought of all the volunteers he had enlisted in the campaign, the people he had nudged into their first political involvement and encouraged over the last months with promises of an invisible army that could perform miracles. *How could I have misled them? How could I have been so misled?*

Thomson finished a speech at the podium, to which Doug paid scant notice, and Robertson stepped up to the microphone. The crowd chanted, "Go, Pat, go! Go, Pat, go!"

"Tomorrow morning, we're going to the South," Robertson announced, "and they're going to be playing in *my* backyard!" He launched into his now standard campaign speech, heavy with right-wing rhetoric. Doug stood with his arms folded and rocked back and forth on his heels, paying close attention but not applauding until Robertson switched to talk about restoring family and moral values to America. On that point Doug joined in the clapping.

With Allison and a group of friends from Cheshire County, Doug left to get something to eat at a Concord restaurant. He was still in a mild state of shock—"You look like a basket case," one of his friends told him—recoiling from the final results. "I thought we had third place locked up, thought we'd get at least 15 percent," he told Allison. "You *know* how hard we worked, and we got last. We could have done nothing and got last. How could we have come in so far down?"

The waitress serving them noticed the campaign buttons they all were wearing.

"Robertson," she said. "I voted for him today. How'd he do?"

Janet Shawn spent primary day at the Ward 4 polling place in Keene. She was wearing three badges she had made with pictures of Dole cut out of magazines. Because of the bitter cold, she stayed much of the time in her car with her Dole sign held against the front window. "All these young kids around and they send an old woman like me out here," she muttered.

Barbara and Mac MacKenzie alternated from the Ward 2 polling place and the Super 8 Motel in Keene, where the campaign had rented a few rooms to serve as an auxiliary office. Everyone was nervous and tired. ("In a few more days, I might end up with you," Barbara had told a local undertaker when he passed her on his way to vote.) Steve Price, the coordinator, paced the rooms, constantly asking Mac how he thought Dole was going to do. "He's going to win," Mac assured Steve.

In midafternoon Mac settled into the motel room with the list he had kept at the poll. It showed 125 identified Dole supporters from Ward 2 who still hadn't voted. Mac and Barbara began calling them. "The senator really needs your vote," they would say, urging the people to turn out and offering them a ride to the polls if they needed one. "I feel like I'm wasting time sitting here," Barbara said during a lull in the calls. She decided to return to the polls, where she hoped the fact that she knew so many voters might help her candidate. Mac did the same before the evening voting rush began.

At six o'clock they both returned to the motel. Barbara lay down on a bed in the room to rest. She was coming down with a bad cold. One of the workers said Dole himself had called a few minutes earlier, asking to talk to Mac.

"What did Bob have to say?" Mac asked.

"He thinks they are leading by one percent," the man answered.

"That's what he always says," Mac replied.

Kendall Lane, with Mr. and Mrs. Marvin Bush in tow, pulled up to Keene's Ward 5 polling place, a church, shortly after the voting began. Richard Daschbach, a Gephardt supporter, was standing among the various campaign volunteers in the parking lot.

"We'll see you in the general election," he told Kendall. "Any predictions of your own?"

"I absolutely don't know," Kendall said. "I go from euphoria to terror."

In Marlborough Kendall went inside to check on the expected arrival of the network television crew while Marvin talked with Andi Johnson and the large Bush contingent. Learning that the TV crew would not be arriving for an hour, Kendall shepherded his celebrity to Swanzey, where a Simon supporter loaned her gloves to Marvin's wife during their brief stand outside the town hall, and then to lunch before returning to Marlborough for a quick interview. After a short stop at the Jaffrey polls, Kendall drove his charges to Hillsborough County, where he transferred them to another volunteer.

Back in Keene he helped provide some rides to the polls for Bush supporters and then settled into the large room in his converted barn for the late afternoon. Pete Johnson, the coordinator, was stationed there, monitoring calls from the headquarters with inside information on the early network exit polls. Jane arrived from sign duty at a Keene ward, and the three of them reviewed the day.

The Dole volunteers, they all had noticed, seemed to have been dressed up in comparison with the other campaigners, apparently on instructions from their headquarters.

"Boy, did they get *that* wrong," Pete said scornfully.

Kendall agreed. "People were wondering, 'Where did all these city slickers come from?' " he said.

Jane related a conversation she had had with Dr. Ridge while the two of them, one with a Bush sign and the other with a Kemp placard, stood outside a polling place. "The Dukakis campaign had to *import* its volunteers," he had confided to her in a tone that carried heavy disapproval.

They all chuckled. It was only by chance that he hadn't noticed a lot of out-of-state Bush volunteers. "I'm glad he wasn't at one of the other polls!" Jane said.

"Like Marlborough," Kendall added.

After five P.M. Kendall stretched out on a couch and watched the television. Pete had just been told of exit polls that showed Bush leading by 5 to 8 percentage points. A reporter on the set said that the Dole campaign hoped to bring Bush down in New Hampshire. "Keep dreaming," Kendall told the television. Just past six o'clock he dozed off.

As if on cue, Kendall woke up when the network news began at seven P.M. Tom Brokaw was saying that some voting places were still open in New Hampshire, but "Vice President Bush appears to be doing very, very well."

Kendall raised a fist from his supine perch and shouted, "Way to go!"

Pete was in the kitchen, watching CBS on another set. ("We don't watch Dan Rather much around here," he had said earlier.) He shouted and rushed into the barn room. Dan Rather had just said that Bush was the New Hampshire winner.

With that, Kendall got up and joined Pete at the bar for a drink and cigarette. "Victory is sweet," he said, "when you thought you were going to lose."

The phone started ringing with jubilant calls from the town chairmen. The woman who had abruptly cut Dole off at the county Republican dinner five days earlier called and asked Kendall if he thought she could be a Bush delegate at the convention. Senator Warren Rudman, Dole's principal sponsor in New Hampshire, was on the television set explaining Dole's second-place finish. "Spin, spin, spin," Kendall mocked at the screen.

Cheshire County's results were not yet in, but the Lanes departed for Manchester, where Bush was to address a rally. On the way they heard Dukakis on the radio, giving his own victory statement for the Democrats.

Once again Kendall arrived too late for a Bush event. The fire marshal had closed the hall. This time Kendall couldn't finagle his way in, so he and Jane went to the hotel bar, where he ate potato chips (his only food since noon), downed a few Scotches, and watched Bush's speech on the bar's television. He stayed until the bar closed.

At three A.M. Wednesday, a full twenty-four hours after he had gotten up to plant Bush signs around Cheshire County, Kendall got home and went to bed. For the first night in weeks, *All this for nothing* did not trouble his slumber.

"Vote for the only candidate who came to Winchester," Al Rubega told the people filing past him Tuesday morning. The Kemp volunteer he had expected to meet in Winchester wasn't there when he arrived, so Al had shouldered a Kemp sign and taken his place next to a Bush supporter, a Dukakis volunteer, and a Robertson supporter with her child.

"Robertson came to Winchester," the mother offered quietly.

"Vote for one of the only two candidates to come to Winchester," Al said when the next group of voters passed. It didn't have the punch he was looking for. He mulled over a few variations in his mind and finally came up with a statement that hewed to the truth but was less equivocal: "Vote for Kemp—he came to Winchester."

The Bush volunteer tried to make a joke. "Are you un-Kemped?" he said to Al, eyeing his clothing.

"Are you Bush-league?" Al responded quickly.

"I guess we better not start," the Bush man decided, and it ended there.

Al's volunteer finally showed up to take over the sign duty. As Al was leaving Winchester he saw the woman who was part of the couple who had declined his Kemp buttons at the dinner the previous Thursday. The husband had told Al on the phone the night before that he couldn't work the polls because he would be working. Al's suspicions were at full alert.

"When can you work?" he asked the woman. She said she had company at home; her husband was unavailable, she said, because he was sick. Al's look told her he didn't buy the excuses. "Why aren't you wearing a Kemp button?" he persisted.

"I'm a spy," she whispered. "I go to all their meetings to hear what's going on. But I've been calling, trying to get people for Jack."

"*Right,*" Al replied, and left her.

Al's assignment this day was to be a free safety on Kemp's team, and he drove his "Kempmobile" from polling place to polling place, checking up on his teammates and filling in whenever he found a gap.

In West Swanzey he held a sign for an hour next to two Bush volunteers. One of them, a young college student wearing an expensive overcoat, long skirt, and penny loafers with shiny new pennies in them, said her name was Bunny. "I guess the stereotypes fit," he said of the WASP-y Bunny. "I just don't know if the voters see all those college kids and realize they were brought in. Frankly, though, I'm jealous. We've had to rely on working people, and it's really tough to get them out."

When his replacement arrived, he handed over his sign and said loudly, "Be nice to the Bush people. They're all going to be carrying Kemp signs next week."

At the next stop a voter walked up wearing an orange hunting vest. Al asked him if he was a member of the NRA, and when the man nodded Al said, "Here's your man," and held up his sign. A woman showed up with her dog on a leash; Al minded the dog while she voted. A Dukakis volunteer from Massachusetts told Al he had supported the governor since 1966. "I'll tell you this," Al said later, "I respect that guy a lot more than the guy that doesn't vote. At least he's active. He's out here campaigning for something he believes in, even if he is a misguided Democrat."

In the afternoon Al went to Sullivan to vote and stop at his home to make some more signs. He checked in on Dr. Ridge at a Keene poll, stopped in a small town to see Mary only long enough to give her a kiss, and moved on.

Near twilight he arrived at the East Swanzey Community House, an old stucco churchlike structure with stained-glass windows in the upper story, sitting on a knoll surrounded by pastureland and woods. The Kemp volunteer he had expected to meet wasn't there. No Kemp sign was even planted in the snow. Al shrugged, pulled a sign from his car trunk, zipped up his coat, put on his mittens, and took his stand next to the sidewalk.

The first voters to arrive, a husband and wife, took one look at his sign and lit up.

"You've got the right fellow," the wife said.

"We haven't seen enough of those around," the husband added.

Al was thrilled. It was the first time all day that passing voters hadn't smiled a kind of embarrassed smile or put their heads down as they passed. "In my heart of hearts," he confided, "I'll be surprised if Jack does worse than second, and I expect him to win. I'd be really surprised if he does worse than third. We'd be in real trouble."

In the last hour the voter traffic dwindled to a trickle. Al kept his vigil. He seemed determined to be the last man standing with a sign. The thin band between darkness and light narrowed and then extinguished as night fell. The chill deepened, and a quiet descended around the hall. "This seems like the right place for it to finish," he said in the stillness before heading home.

Kemp's postelection party was in a hotel in Nashua, and by the time Al and Mary arrived at nine o'clock, the results were all but final: Bush (37.6 percent) had won a convincing victory; Dole (28.4 percent) was second; Kemp (12.8 percent) a very distant third, followed by du Pont (10.1 percent) and Robertson (9.4). Al was in a blue funk. "I've been better, I've been worse," he grumbled when someone asked him how he was doing.

Kemp stepped up on the podium, in front of one of Al's banners, to address his faithful supporters. "Tonight we're third in New Hampshire, but we'll be first in New Orleans [at the convention]," he said. "This is not a campaign; this is a cause." He talked about the conservative wing of the Republican party, which he said was represented by Ronald Reagan and himself, and said that, despite his showing in the primary, he had "dragged Bush and Dole out of their résumés and into the issues." Al started to whoop and holler and clap and interrupted Kemp in midsentence by starting a chant of "We Back Jack." Kemp paused, saw Al, whose height made him tower over the others in the back, pointed toward him, and laughed. "It doesn't stop here, it starts tonight," he said, and Al led the crowd to cheers of "Kemp in '88!"

After the speech, Al mingled with his fellow Kemp supporters. Mary wanted to leave for home—it was already past eleven o'clock—but Al said he wouldn't leave until he had shaken Kemp's hand. He was already trying to relive the campaign, hoping to understand what had happened to his hopes. It was like the days after losing a case in court, he said, when he would lie awake nights trying to figure out what had gone wrong. "I lost a case involving a child that was killed on Route 10," he explained. "Every time I drive by the fairgrounds [the site of the accident] it still bothers me, and I begin to pick apart the case once more." He felt the same way—"crappy," in his words—tonight.

The crowd had thinned, the busboys were hauling away the trays of cheese and crackers, and the reporters were watching the Olympics on one of the television monitors, when Kemp reentered the banquet hall. Al maneuvered through the small circle of people surrounding the candidate.

"Al!" Kemp said, and hugged him. "How's Mary?" he asked, and then he turned to the people nearby. "This is the guy that did it for us.

"You were the thing," he told Al. "You never left our side, and we appreciate it." He gave Mary a hug and then moved through the crowd to the door.

Now Al was ready to go home. "*That's* the guy I came to see," he said, and went to get Mary's coat.

19

AFTERMATH

And then it was over. After a year or more of anticipation, worry, work, nervous excitement, sleepless nights, endless speculation, ceaseless preparation, emotional peaks and troughs, and the building pressure from the countdown in their minds, the big day itself had arrived and then—swiftly, yet almost anticlimactically—ended. It was as if the presidential campaign were some powerful locomotive whose momentous arrival in a small community had been elaborately planned for and much awaited. Standing on the platform, with banners and brass bands at the ready and welcoming speeches in their pockets, the grass-roots volunteers had heard the low rumble of the engines and felt the shake of the earth as the mighty train finally roared into sight. There had been tumult, a flurry of activity, a great, noise-drowning doppler clang of bells and a rush of wind . . . and it was gone. The train did not stop. Before they knew it the caboose was disappearing from view, and they were still standing at the station.

In the preceding months it had seemed that New Hampshire was the premier destination point of this campaign express. The state's name was on the lips of important men, one of whom would be the next leader of the free world. Reporters from the nation's media had been dispatched to describe what the natives were like, what they had on their minds, and how the terrain looked.

Even Cheshire County, one small county in a remote corner of the state, had been featured as if in a political travel brochure. Dick Gephardt's fliers pictured him canvassing the streets of a Keene neighborhood and tasting maple sugar in Westmoreland. George Bush's imitation of *USA Today* showed the vice president at a picnic in the region and touring a business in Walpole. Jack Kemp's leaflets included snapshots of the candidate speaking to the Keene Lions Club, answering questions at a local reception (where he had been hectored about Star Wars), and meeting with the county's citizenry (including a photo of Kemp and the woman from Winchester who was supporting all the Republicans). One of Bruce Babbitt's favorable clippings, in *New York* magazine, was printed beneath a picture of him walking toward a meeting with local environmentalists in Hancock. Handouts distributed across the state by Paul Simon's campaign had on their cover a photograph of the senator speaking at Keene's Veterans Day services. Color shots of Pete du Pont at a pig roast in Stoddard accompanied a national news magazine's story about the campaign.

Seeing themselves or their home territory in the clippings, becoming accustomed to talking with would-be presidents on a first-name basis, having their opinions quoted by national journalists, being courted for advice and assistance by big-time political operatives—it had become a habit over the last year. All the attention could warp a person's sense of his or her own importance. Even those who kept their equilibrium—and the core group in Cheshire County was notable for its lack of prima donnas—nonetheless had become used to the feeling that something pivotal was going on and they were in the thick of it.

Now it was over. The train hadn't stopped, it had passed through. Destination points with names like Minnesota, South Dakota, and the southern "Super Tuesday" states filled the newspapers and the airwaves. Candidates who only days ago were standing in New Hampshire living rooms and walking snowy New Hampshire streets could now be seen only on the television screen in front of backdrops that were no longer familiar.

A kind of "Cinderella syndrome," or the political equivalent of postpartum depression, enveloped the volunteers who had danced for a while in the nation's spotlight or had labored so long and so hard, hoping to give birth to victory. All of them were exhausted, physically and emotionally drained, as the adrenaline that had sustained them over the last weeks flushed from their systems overnight. Some collapsed into sickness, others into a foglike funk. Some tried to cling to a sense of being plugged in to the driving throb of the locomotive's engine.

But they all realized that the campaign had moved on. It was somewhere else. They were still here. And the more routine lives they had led before they were caught up in the rush of it all were waiting to be resumed.

"I'm sorry," said a recorded voice. "The number you have dialed has been disconnected."

Molly Kelly hung up the phone in her apartment. It was early Wednesday morning. Partly from habit, partly just for the chance to talk to anyone else who was still keyed up about the campaign, she had dialed the number of the Dukakis office.

Molly had taken a leave of absence from her work at Franklin Pierce College to devote herself totally to the campaign during the last week. She was expected back on the job today. Several prospective students were scheduled to visit the college on Thursday, and Molly was in charge of showing them around.

After work she stopped by the Keene campaign office. No one was there. The place was silent. Mike Cook had already left for Texas, for a few days with his family and girlfriend before being reassigned to another primary state. Paul Austin, another young political worker who had been assigned to Cheshire County for the last month, had also left Keene for an assignment in another state. The office needed cleaning, and for the next several evenings Molly went in to do the work.

She felt abandoned. "I miss it—a lot," she said a few days later. "Isn't that crazy? I think about it a lot, too: what I would have done differently, the frustration of having had to work my other job at the same time." From her home she called her volunteers to thank them for their help. "They were feeling the same way," she reported. "A little discarded, that Keene seems like a ghost town with all the empty windows [in campaign offices]. It was such an intense last few days, and then it's over. They just pull up stakes and head out. Instead, you're back where you were last summer."

The campaign had posed a series of challenges to Molly, and she felt good about the way she had responded to them all. After starting the campaign feeling painfully self-conscious about being a political novice, she had learned to trust her instincts. Managing the volunteers, figuring out ways to get them to do their tasks and be happy about it, trying to match the campaign's objectives with what she believed worked best in her community—those had been skills she felt some satisfaction in mastering. Her family and personal life had been tested. It had more than survived, it had been strengthened. Her boyfriend had been supportive, and their relationship had deepened considerably. He was becoming the father of the family and was moving in. Her children had rallied around her, merging their lives with hers in a way they hadn't expected. Rachel had matured a lot during the course of the campaign; she was more self-assured around other people now. The boys had pitched in, not merely to help their mother, but to be involved in something they thought was important. "My kids saw me as something other than just their mother, and I think they respected me for it," she said.

On the night of the primary, while she was driving back to Keene after missing Dukakis's victory speech, her mind had wandered. "I thought I should have felt better than I did," she said. "It was strange. I was thinking about going back to work and doing the laundry."

She would have liked to move on with the campaign, as Mike Cook and Paul Austin were doing, but her professional and familial responsibilities made that impossible, and she was feeling behind on both fronts.

Three days after the primary Molly got a call from the campaign headquarters in Boston. Kitty Dukakis was going to Vermont for an appearance (Vermont's primary was March 1) and would be at the Keene airport briefly; Molly was asked to meet Kitty and her staff, some of whom had been assigned to Keene on primary day. They reminisced about the New Hampshire primary, as if it were already far in their past, and then went their separate ways: Mrs. Dukakis and her staff to yet another campaign stop, Molly to her home.

"There's an abruptness that is awesome," Dan Burnham said a week after the primary. "The voters go in there and decide on Tuesday, and that's it. The staff is gone overnight. The [local] group that had been bonding is broken up. It's empty now."

Dan came down with the flu the morning after the primary. Standing in the snow and raw wind all day had taken its toll. He was sick for a week.

After two dismal showings, in Iowa and then in New Hampshire, Babbitt withdrew from the presidential race on February 18, two days after the primary. "Somebody told me, 'Bruce, you fought the good fight. You were in it right up to the beginning,' " Babbitt said. (Du Pont, a Republican, pulled out the same day.) Dan's house still contained campaign stationery, signs, and brochures; his car's backseat still held his "mobile office." He had wanted to send all his material to someone, but the campaign had vaporized too quickly. Some fellow volunteers were writing personal letters to Babbitt, expressing their admiration and condolences. Dan hadn't done it yet. "I don't know what I'd say," he explained.

Having entered the process for the sake of an intellectual exercise, just another of his many projects, Dan had been swept up in his personal attachment to a candidate and overwhelmed by conflicting moments of despair and hope. In the aftermath his initial impulses reasserted themselves. He admitted that, having devoted so much to a losing candidate, he was having trouble seeing the surviving Democratic contenders as anything other than enemies. "Your juices really get going," he said. "When you favor one guy, it automatically becomes 'He's better than the others.' When he drops out, they all fall short."

But his mind quickly refocused on "the tantalizing questions of what it takes to get someone to win the New Hampshire primary," the challenge of making sense of the process, the intriguing task of understanding the puzzle of the voters.

With the exception of a few towns—like Dublin, where Babbitt had finished second—Babbitt's results in Cheshire County had mirrored his statewide showing of about 5 percent. That disappointed Dan. "I couldn't see any indication in Keene that our efforts there paid off," he lamented.

He pieced his thoughts together the way he had been trained: by writing them down. He wrote an article for the *Sentinel*'s editorial page about why he thought only one in twenty people had voted for Babbitt. The televised debates, he argued, had been his candidate's undoing:

> Babbitt's guillotine was that string of staccato July-to-January television debates, a dozen or so, each with the same light-headed format of a round of too-quick questions and two-minute summaries. A qualified candidate was whipped by the TV camera more than by political indiscretion.
>
> Reduced to studying one-line answers and one-paragraph conclusions, are we, in our living rooms, stimulated to assay glamour over reason, machismo over humility, and quips over substance? Has the format reduced presidential debates to a level where, instead of serious consideration of great issues, all we will remember of the 1988 primary are ripostes akin to the now hallowed 1984 challenge to Sen. Gary Hart by Vice President Walter Mondale: "Where's the beef?"

Dan wrote that "an ability to use television is integral to the modern presidency," but the cumulative effect of the debates had been to obscure Babbitt's many substantive proposals. Instead, "what seemingly went to the voters' booth were two Babbitt negatives: a one-liner about standing up for fiscal integrity, and those two-minute summaries about the courage to impose a 5 percent national sales tax." (The "stand up" stunt had always bothered Dan, initially because he thought it was hokey and now, in retrospect, because he thought it was bad strategy. At the debate at the University of New Hampshire, when Babbitt had used it once again, Tom Britton, who was sitting next to Dan in the audience, said, "I think he's gone to that well too many times." Dan agreed.)

Finding reasons for Babbitt's poor showing and then writing about it satisfied Dan. Through it he proved to himself that the political instincts he had honed as a reporter had been clouded, but not lost, in his campaign immersion. Figuring out the voters, however, was not so easy. That enigma still eluded comprehension. Dan considered it almost mystically.

"How difficult it is to perceive the voters as a single entity you can get a handle on and influence," he said a month after the primary. "It's very deceptive. You're doing all this work and thinking it must be having an effect—all the voters you're talking to are very polite. It comes as a distinct shock, after all of this work, that we didn't do much better in Cheshire County than the statewide average. That really is a mystery. There are very, very few ways to get his [the voter's] attention; even fewer ways to get his empathy. There's no way of reading those fig leaves.

"I have a whole new appreciation for it. In one sense, a contempt for this guy making quick decisions the way I once did, barely knowing the candidates' names. If you look at it from the point of view of the guy trying to get at him to vote for Babbitt, it's one horrendous task, a very difficult way of doing it.

"And yet, the voter is almost sacrosanct. You can only get them in the most general ways—tease them with a good flier, say the right words, try to talk as fast as you can talk to get it all in. But there's no way you can really influence his vote. He's an island, going to make up his own mind, and there's not a thing—a canvass, phones, whatever—you can do about it."

Between Sunday and Wednesday of primary week, Andi Johnson had gotten nine hours of sleep. "I got a little burned out," she said a week later. "I didn't realize how intense I'd become until Friday, when my mind started to clear." For several nights she fell asleep at 5:30 P.M., before dinner and before the nightly news reports on the post–New Hampshire campaign.

For the Democratic party, 1987 had been an extraordinary year. Two major presidential campaigns had disintegrated. Andi had been with both of them. Gary Hart, whose 1984 campaign had lured her into politics and who had inspired in her a kind of hero worship she'd carried for four years, had, in the end, disillusioned her. She still believed he should have tried to ride out the media storm after the Donna Rice exposé. But he had quit, and "people saw Gary as a quitter," she said. She did, too. "It was a real farce when he came back," she said. She could never support him again. (Despite his last-place finishes in Iowa and New Hampshire, Hart remained in the race through the "Super Tuesday" primaries in early March. Andi thought he should have gotten the message in Iowa and dropped out before New Hampshire. "I believe he's headed toward a nervous breakdown," she said.) Biden at least had "shown a lot of character" when he pulled out to devote his time to his family and defeating the nomination of Robert Bork to the Supreme Court, she believed. In the end, her dreams of another successful primary had been reduced to "getting down to Simon, who I knew wasn't a terribly viable candidate."

"Every event was a chore," she said, looking back on her experience. "Getting people to commit was like pulling teeth. It was a very tough year." She found some solace—and took some pride—in the fact that Simon had finished second in Cheshire County. (He received 17 percent of the vote, slightly lower than his statewide average, but ahead of Gephardt's 15 percent.) "I wanted to do well because of my position as county chair [for Simon]," she explained. "I had a responsibility to deliver votes." Simon's third-place finish in the state had wounded him politically, but he remained in the race for another two months. "He's staying in too long," Andi observed in April. "He won't be a power broker at the convention."

Both the Simon and Biden organizations had disappointed her. They relied too much, she thought, on their Washington headquarters to make decisions and didn't pay enough attention to people like her in New Hampshire—a stark contrast to her experience with Hart in 1984. She now considered herself a political veteran and, as such, much of what she said reflected the transition she had gone through over the course of the campaign: her focus was on the technical, organizational mechanics of the primary, rather than on any ideological or personal fervor for a candidate. "I've seen the worst and the best of it," she said of primary campaigning. "I can do it as well as they [paid campaign staff from Washington] can do it." She planned to be involved again in 1992, "but at a higher level, at least a statewide level."

The day after the primary she went one more time to the Simon office in Keene and spent the evening packing the belongings she had donated to the cause—files, pens, a table, and other office supplies. At home she unpacked the cartons. They included her most prized possession, the symbol of her political credentials. Her collection of three-by-five-inch cards now filled three boxes—with names, addresses, phone numbers, and notations (voting histories, whether the person was a good volunteer, and so on)—of more than two thousand voters in Cheshire County.

"It'll take *weeks* to sort them all out," she said.

Doug Kidd reported for work at the Robertson headquarters in Manchester on Wednesday feeling "discouraged and in a fog." *What will I tell my people?* he wondered when he thought about Robertson's last-place finish. But when he called to thank and console them, he discovered most of them were elated. Robertson had done better in their towns than he had statewide—third in Hinsdale, Jaffrey, and Winchester; second in Dublin.

This had been Doug's first political campaign, and the same held true for virtually all of his volunteers. Almost universally they had seen positive results in their own towns from their efforts and were encouraged by it. Doug himself got out a map of the state and color-coded it to reflect Robertson's vote in each town; the regions under his responsibility uniformly outperformed the others. He felt some satisfaction from that.

Doug's volunteers also differed from their counterparts on other campaigns in the way they reacted to the primary's aftermath. Few seemed to suffer decompression from the campaign's intensity, nor did they spend a lot of time reviewing and rehashing the past year's events and the primary results. It was as if they had entered the process believing that God's will would be revealed, regardless of the outcome. If Robertson now was not going to be the Republican nominee and next president, that must be His plan. They weren't about to question it.

Doug shared some of the same feelings. But he was still interested in figuring out why the "invisible army" hadn't materialized. Having taken the campaign job to apply his business management training to a Christian endeavor, he wanted to know what had worked and what hadn't. The early Robertson phone banks hadn't, he thought, because they had started too soon and the volunteers, unaccustomed to such work in the first place, had become discouraged at the low response. An attempt to set up "executive teams" in each region had fallen by the wayside. "A traditional structure never materialized," he said. "Most of the people weren't comfortable with titles and responsibilities." The "8 × 8 in '88" program he had devised "worked in my area because I pushed it; the others didn't." Nonetheless, he thought it was a good system because, by relying on volunteers to contact people they knew, it gave them a "different point of sale."

Politically Doug believed Robertson's hard swing to the right in the final months had come across as stridency. "It seemed real *narrow*," he said. "It made a lot of people uncomfortable. He was aligned with extremist, conservative positions, away from the Christian posture, not the person of hope that someone could get next to." Robertson's statement about Soviet missiles in Cuba, for instance, had scared off a lot of potential voters, Doug thought.

In retrospect, he said, "Pat could have had more of an impact on government by building an organization rather than running himself. I expected an organized group would emerge to continue getting Christians involved in the political process. That didn't happen."

For himself, the job he had initially thought would be his first without stress had become "totally consuming" by the end. He had been forced to drop his weekly prayer meetings and had spent more time away from Allison than he liked. On the other hand, his campaign contacts had led him to a new church in Nashua that he and Allison now attended regularly. Politics, he discovered, "is not particularly dirty or evil. It's definitely manipulation—trying to get your point emphasized. Television is the most important part of it."

The campaign sent Doug to Maine for three days to help prepare for caucuses there in late February. He didn't like the work so far from home, and when he returned he declined an offer to go south for "Super Tuesday." "Allison and I prayed a lot about it," he said, "but we just weren't getting any peace." Within a week he had stopped buying newspapers to follow the campaign. He started looking for another job.

A Robertson supporter offered him sales work for a phone company, and another asked him to help set up the management of a hotel the man had just bought in Connecticut. The hotel job was a tempting offer, but when Doug went to visit he learned the hotel offered pornographic movies in the rooms. "It's difficult to promote a place I don't believe in," he said. "I turned it down and kissed the money good-bye." Instead he found temporary work developing a business plan for a chain of restaurants and malls.

———

In the days after the primary, Al Rubega was disappointed but philosophical about Kemp's third-place finish. "You do everything you can up to the time of the vote, and then you can't do anything more about it," he said. "There's not much more we could have done." The fact that Dole won Cheshire County, he said, "surprises the hell out of me. God, it surprises me a lot. They didn't have *any* organization, didn't really have any people down here. This is an unusual place, this county, much its own world."

Bush's organizational effort in the last week had impressed him. "They certainly outphoned us at the end," he said. "The more I get involved, the more I think that [campaign] signs don't mean a damn thing." His principal regret in hindsight was that the Kemp campaign hadn't sacrificed some attention to signs in favor of phone banks. He was happy, at least, that Robertson had finished last in the state.

If Kemp made mistakes in the campaign, it was in being "too much a Mr. Nice Guy," Al said, in addition to Kemp's habit of talking through the applause lines in his speeches. (Al had complained repeatedly about the latter to Kemp's staff; on primary night he had taken matters literally into his own hands and interrupted Kemp's final speech by starting chants and clapping.) The *Manchester Union-Leader*'s endorsement of du Pont had cut into Kemp's potential conservative base, and the Iowa results had not helped, but on the whole, as Al replayed the campaign in his mind, he couldn't pinpoint anything in particular that had cost Kemp the victory Al had once so confidently anticipated.

For the first few days after the primary, Al followed the campaign as closely as he could in the news. He and Mary had dinner with the Ridges and then with one of the Keene State College volunteers. Mary was selected as one of the three alternate New Hampshire delegates pledged to Kemp for the national convention in New Orleans. "I don't miss the stress; it got pretty heavy near the end," Al said. "And the constant hope that he might do well—I don't miss that."

A month later Kemp dropped out of the race, and Al, except for

hoping that Bush might eventually select Kemp as his running
mate, ceased paying much attention to the race. His energies were
refocused on his new job with state government and on gun issues.
Sarah Brady—the wife of Jim Brady, who had been wounded in
the assassination attempt on President Reagan in 1981—was bringing her gun-control campaign to New Hampshire, and Al was working furiously to make posters for the pro-gun contingent he planned
to turn out to greet her.

"We're at a turning point in history," he said. "This country is
complacent. You've never got so firm a grasp on freedom that you
can't lose it—especially if you get sloppy. We've got a tendency to
get sloppy, get lazy, and figure that because we've always had the
blessings that we've got in this country, they're a birthright that
can't be taken away from us. That's real foolish and real dangerous.
I think we can lose through neglect a lot of those rights many
people gave their lives to secure. We've lost them in little degrees
already. The country's in a lot graver danger than the majority
realizes.

"The more I get involved, the more it worries me that such a
large group doesn't get involved and vote, that it's apathetic. I'm
real scared of the way the country will drift if an opposite influence
isn't exerted. He [Kemp] exerted that influence; I think obviously
Ronald Reagan exerted it in a big way, that proper influence.

"I feel a sense of urgency, and a sense of obligation, too. People *died* to give me these rights. I haven't yet had to fight in a
war. The least I can do is get off my duff and see to it that the
right people get into office. You gotta do it. That's what it's all
about."

Kendall Lane worked in his law office the Wednesday after the
primary and then stayed up until 1:30 A.M. with Pete Johnson,
going over the results. They got out town-by-town tabulations from
past elections, compared them with 1988, and hashed over theories
about what the Bush campaign had done to pull out its victory and
why the vice president had lost Cheshire County to Dole. On Thurs-

day Kendall went to the state headquarters in Concord to lobby the staff to make sure Jane would be one of the Bush alternate delegates at the convention (she was). He, Will Abbott, and Ron Kaufman spent several hours reviewing the entire campaign. "We couldn't let go," Kendall said later. "We absolutely could *not* let go. There was this horrible void to fill. It was like graduating from high school: suddenly, everyone had split."

Pete was dispatched to Maine to prepare for the caucuses. On Friday Kendall collapsed with a cold and slept through the weekend. "A lot of health went down the drain in this campaign," he said. In the next days he wandered around asking himself, *What's next?* C-SPAN was his chief link to the presidential race now, and he followed it intently.

The local returns still bothered him. Bush had won only six towns in Cheshire County. Even Marlborough, where Kendall had dispatched extra troops on primary day, had gone to Dole (and, therefore, fell from the list of New Hampshire towns that had always voted for the primary winners). Kendall's explanation was Bush's schedule. "I predicted that if the vice president didn't come to the county, we'd lose in Keene," he said, repeating a frustration he had felt throughout the campaign. "We were so close to winning Keene and Cheshire County [three hundred votes], I keep wondering, 'Was there anything we could have done, other than more visits by the vice president, which would have turned it around?' I honestly don't know what more we could have done." Despite the fact that his county was the only one Bush did not win, Kendall was proud of his local organization. They had rallied after the debacle in Iowa, had blitzed the local towns with leaflets and signs, and had called every potential voter in the final days. Without them, he thought, Dole's margin would have been even greater. "This county," he declared, "seems time and time again to be out of step with the rest of the state."

There were many things he remembered fondly, especially being intimately involved behind the scenes in Bush's two events in Keene. He also liked making contacts with the national staff, including the Washington volunteers who had invaded his house the last five days. He enjoyed "being in the loop." At the state headquarters one day, he had noticed that Will Abbott's phone had about ten telephone numbers set up for speed dialing. One was Kendall's office; another was his home.

At the end of February Kendall and Jane flew to Florida for a vacation. Florida's primary, one of the "Super Tuesday" sweepstakes on March 8, was imminent. Kendall was struck by how different it seemed from the final days of New Hampshire's primary. By comparison there wasn't much political news on the local television and in the newspapers, an "entirely different level of intensity," he said. He stopped in to visit a few Bush campaign offices in Florida and was surprised by what he found. Each office was responsible for areas covering two hundred thousand people—a size equivalent to half of New Hampshire—and the one-on-one, grassroots organizational concentration he had become accustomed to at home was absent. "It makes me laugh," he said of way the "Super Tuesday" campaign was proceeding and the way that Bush, having regained the momentum in New Hampshire, now seemed on his way to locking up the nomination. "It just proves that New Hampshire is more important than ever."

When Kendall and Jane got home from their vacation, the first two messages on their answering machine were from Will Abbott. One asked them to help run a canvass in Bellows Falls, Vermont, about a half hour north of Keene, in preparation for the Vermont primary. The other told them where they were supposed to meet.

20

THE DEMOCRATIC COVENANT

No one knows for sure which elements of a political campaign determine the final outcome of the race—the skill and depth of the grass-roots organizations, the pervasive influence of the day-to-day press coverage, the quality and timing of campaign advertising, the political predispositions of the voters, or even some indefinable personality traits the public senses in the candidates it rejects or elects. Some say that what happens in the media, both in the news and in commercials, and especially in the crucial days before the vote, is the final determinant. Others contend that underlying conditions—the state of the economy or world events, the population's voting histories, the general "mood" of the electorate—drive an election. Most campaign professionals believe that the painstaking grass-roots organizational work can sway at most about 5 percent of the final vote—hardly a big figure, but enough, they say, to swing a close election and therefore worth the effort. Even within the circle of people who place a premium on organizational "field" work, there is constant dispute over which grass-roots activities—door-to-door canvasses, mailings, phone banks, and personal contact—are the most effective.

In the constant search for the keys to the kingdom, the results of the 1988 primary offered something for everyone. A political season generates not only winners and losers, but also a lot of statistics that campaign operatives, reporters, and political scientists love to analyze and interpret with their own theories. For Cheshire County in the 1988 New Hampshire presidential primary, the cold statistics are these:

Democrats	County Vote	Percent	Statewide
DUKAKIS	3,192	41.2	44,112/37.3%
GEPHARDT	1,161	15.0	24,513/20.7%
SIMON	1,319	17.0	21,094/17.8%
JACKSON	864	11.2	9,615/ 8.1%
GORE	430	5.5	8,400/ 7.1%
BABBITT	489	6.3	5,644/ 4.8%
HART	293	3.8	4,888/ 4.1%

Republicans	County Vote	Percent	Statewide
BUSH	3,057	32.9	52,290/38.3%
DOLE	3,358	36.2	44,797/28.9%
KEMP	1,327	14.3	20,114/13.0%
DU PONT	646	7.0	15,885/10.3%
ROBERTSON	891	9.6	14,775/ 9.5%

Some 17,725 citizens in the county cast ballots on February 16. Statewide, 284,734 registered voters participated. Of the total, 159,390 people cast Republican ballots, 125,344 cast Democratic votes; the respective turnouts were 74.3 percent for the Republicans, 71.7 percent for the Democrats.

By themselves the statistics raise more questions than they answer. Why, for instance, did Dole beat Bush in Cheshire County and in Keene, the only county and the only one of New Hampshire's thirteen cities that Bush did not win? Even Dole's most ardent local supporters and workers would admit that the Bush organization was clearly superior, not only in numbers of volunteers, but in the work it did preparing for the vote. Dole made more appearances in the region than the vice president, but one of the towns (Jaffrey) that he visited and Bush skipped was also one of the few towns in the county that Bush carried. *The Keene Sentinel* endorsed Dole (and Dukakis, the Democratic winner in the county), yet the paper has a far-from-perfect batting average in backing winning candidates. In general elections Cheshire County's voting record is consistently more liberal than the rest of the state's, and Bush's close association with President Reagan, which most political observers credited with helping the vice president form a hard base of support in New Hampshire, was probably of less benefit to him in the Keene area. Yet in the 1980 primary Reagan carried the county. That year Bush's 24.7 percent for second place in the region outperformed his statewide average, and Dole had received only thirty-eight votes, 0.4 percent, to finish seventh. Bush's last-minute ads attacking Dole in 1988 (which Dole left unanswered), his shift to campaign appearances with "common people" (compared with Dole's "presidential" style in the week after Iowa), and the solid support his organization had built for him in the preceding years have all been noted in explaining the way he held off Dole's seeming surge during the last week in New Hampshire. Without question Dole got a "bounce" from Iowa—he went from more than twenty points behind to close contention in a matter of days—but it alone was not enough to turn the primary.

Cheshire County being "liberal" would not explain why Kemp and Robertson, arch-conservatives both, performed better or at least equal in the county than they did in the rest of the state. The work of Al Rubega and Doug Kidd perhaps made the difference, especially for Kemp, who not only vanished from news coverage after Iowa, but had made his last visit to the area in early November. The efforts of a dynamo volunteer in a specific town could also be detected in a place like Hinsdale, where Robertson had the tireless Helen Bouchie and received almost twice the percentage of his county average. Conversely, Cheshire County was du Pont's worst county (7.0 percent, versus 10.3 statewide), and his total lack of a local organization may be the reason. One town, however, stood out for him in the region: Stoddard, the site of du Pont's best event of the local campaign, placed him third, closely behind Dole and Bush.

Among the Democrats, Dukakis's "Imperial Army" left no organizational stone unturned. With so many volunteers a short drive away in Massachusetts, his campaign could and did mount grassroots drives (four extensive door-to-door canvasses, for instance) to the point of redundancy. To top it off, by virtue of his governorship next door to New Hampshire, Dukakis was the best-known candidate in the field; his was the best-financed campaign; he got the endorsement of the *Sentinel*; and in the final week, his principal competitors, Simon and Gephardt, aimed their rhetorical and advertising fire on each other instead of at him. Those advantages allowed Dukakis to turn virtually every key to the kingdom the hardest. He won every town in the county and every ward in Keene and, with 41.2 percent of the vote in Cheshire County, outperformed his statewide percentage.

Cheshire County was Gephardt's third worst of New Hampshire's ten counties, yet without the publicity he received from his Iowa victory it seems likely he would have finished lower. Like Dole, Gephardt "bounced" from the caucuses, made up a lot of ground in New Hampshire in a hurry to finish second, but could not dislodge an opponent who consistently had been the front-runner in the Granite State.

Simon edged Gephardt for second place in Cheshire County (and in three others), but his percentage in the region was lower than his statewide total and his fourth worst in the state. In early December he had seemed to be on the move, both in his press coverage and organizationally. Gary Hart's reentry into the race, particularly the overwhelming media attention it received, put an end to Simon's roll. He was never able to recover it. Had Simon, not Gephardt, won in Iowa, it seems more likely than not that their order of finish in New Hampshire would have reversed as well.

Babbitt did a little better locally than he did in the state, and in some towns where he had particularly hardworking volunteers—like Dublin, the home of Dan Burnham and Doris Haddock, where he finished second—his finish was markedly superior. Given his problems with his television persona and the small vote he received, it's tempting to conclude that every single vote Babbitt received in the primary was cast by someone he had met and persuaded personally in the many months he devoted to the state.

Organization would not explain Jackson's strong showing (11.2 percent in the county, versus 8.1 statewide); perhaps the county's voting history and the presence of the "intellectual community" in the three local colleges would. Gore seemed to pay a lot of early attention to the region but disappeared in the final months; his 5.5 percent of the vote, compared with 7.1 percent statewide, might reflect that. Who knows what Hart might have done if Donna Rice had not burst into the news in the spring of 1987. In 1984 he won Cheshire County with 37 percent of the vote; four years later he got a tenth of that. Joe Biden had started well in the region. He had a good organization, opened the first local campaign office, and his last appearance, in August 1987, attracted one of the largest Democratic crowds of the year. Absent the troubles that caused him to withdraw in the fall, he might have been a contender.

In a primary where, as in late January, six different Democratic campaigns canvassed door to door on the same weekend, and where on some evenings multiple campaigns were calling voters in the same small town, it's hard to believe that the carpet-bombing organizational work was persuading any voter to an individual candidate's cause. More likely it numbed them; perhaps it even angered them. At best it helped the campaigns identify some voters that were already theirs, allowing them to make sure those voters turned out on primary day.

Despite repeated opportunities to do so, despite the media mythology surrounding the primary, most of the voters never met the candidates or heard them speak in person. And despite an even earlier-than-normal start of the campaign and the prodigious efforts of the organizations to get people to choose up sides quickly, most voters kept to their own timetable, reserving judgment until the absolute deadline to choose was upon them. Nevertheless, a com-

paratively large portion of the citizenry—a little over 20 percent in
Cheshire County in the 1988 campaign—availed themselves of the
chance to examine the would-be presidents in the flesh instead of
just on the television screen. In the subsequent primaries no other
state comes close to that number; voters there simply don't have
the opportunity. Likewise, a significantly higher proportion—more
than 70 percent—of the two parties' members voted in New Hampshire's presidential primary than in the states that followed. (Even
Iowa's caucuses in 1988 drew only 23.4 percent of the state's registered Democrats and 22.5 percent of its Republicans.)

The statistics therefore can support, or contradict, any of the
various theories. The 1988 New Hampshire primary did not settle
those disputes. Only one statistic survived unchallenged, undisputed, and unambiguous. Since both parties' eventual nominees
prevailed in New Hampshire on February 16, the primary's record
was guaranteed to be unblemished: no one wins the White House
who doesn't first win in New Hampshire.

Reviewing the primary by examining numbers, however, is simply
the mirror image of starting the process by considering the people
who will participate in it merely as disembodied names. Names on
a list. Much more transpires than turning faceless names into faceless numbers.

Something different happens in New Hampshire, something best
understood in human terms rather than statistics. It's not that New
Hampshire citizens are dramatically more civic-minded, nor is there
anything in the cold well water or the clear air of the Granite State
that breeds a higher percentage of voters. The difference is that
more people believe that their vote counts for something, that they,
individually as citizens, have a say in the course of the country. All
the attention they receive—from the candidates, the campaign organizations, the media—leads them inevitably to that conclusion.
America seems to be waiting to hear their judgment on the men
who seek to lead the nation, and being human, and American, they

are ready to register their opinion if it's asked. Transpose the first primary and all its trappings to some other state, particularly a small one, and the same would undoubtedly happen there. Deny New Hampshire its place at the starting gate of the presidential race, move it back to mid- or late spring in the midst of a bunch of other state primaries, and its turnout would likely decline; the campaigns would not be as intense and the outcome would not seem so critical.

What makes the New Hampshire primary different is not so much that it takes place in New Hampshire, but that it's first. Being first has conferred upon it disproportionate, some would say unwarranted, influence in selecting America's leaders. All that attention and influence can bring out the worst, as well as the best, in people, and a New Hampshire primary normally contains more than its share of preening, pettiness, and prima donnas. But another by-product of being first is that, in the world's oldest democracy, citizen participation reaches levels unattained anywhere else in the nation.

If New Hampshire's voters, more than their fellow citizens in other primary states, believe that what they do in the privacy of the polling booth *matters*, the volunteers at the grass roots of the state's presidential campaigns take that belief and boost it up several notches. As with the voters, whose ultimate choice seems shrouded in private mystery, how and why the volunteers decide to do what they do and support the candidate they choose is not always clear cut. In some, a sense of ideological mission can be found. In others, political involvement is just another part of community involvement—a family tradition, almost an obligation. Some volunteers have a single issue they wish to further, and they see a political campaign as the way to accomplish it. (Some hold their pet issue so dear, they decide that supporting a single candidate is contrary to their cause.) Some join out of curiosity, others because the pace and the obsession on the outcome are like addictions. For some the final outcome is all-important; for others the thrill of the chase predominates. Some simply like the attention of being courted— and, in fact, consume more campaign energy than they eventually

contribute in return. Others do it simply because they were flattered
to be asked. Some hope to advance their careers. Others just think
it's the right thing to do.

Throughout these complex and contradictory motivations, however, runs a common thread that is at the very heart of how and
why our democracy is supposed to work. It is an individual feeling
of relevance. It is the American promise, a democratic covenant
with two interlocking provisions.

First, the outcome of the vote is supposed to be relevant to the
citizen. Whether that relevance is manifested in the hope for a
patronage job, the desire for a single issue to advance, or, at the
other extreme, an altruistic belief that which candidate prevails
might bend the direction of the broad flow of history, the first
promise of participatory democracy is that your life (or perhaps your
children's lives) will somehow be affected by the final result.

The covenant's second provision is that the citizen is relevant to
the outcome. That relevance might be merely the casting of one
vote, the most minimal participation. It might be the simple registering of political disgust (such as the write-in votes in Troy for
Ollie North and "Alf") or an expression of encouragement (Len
Fleischer's vote for Jackson and Bruce Anderson's for Babbitt, after
they decided that Dukakis would win without their help). Or one
vote might decide an election (as Mike Haas contended on the
phone up to the last minute of the primary).

In the case of the grass-roots volunteers, the sense of relevance
is heightened. They feel responsible for more than their own vote.
What they do might influence a group of people, might swing a
town or a region, and through it the state and the nation. They not
only have a greater personal stake in the campaign; to them, at
least, the result has a bigger stake in their effort.

The democratic covenant doesn't distinguish among the various
reasons for voting and volunteering. It recognizes them all equally.
The founding Fathers themselves recognized that democracy was
both a lofty ideal of community and an exercise in self-interest.
What matters is the covenant's two-way bargain: the outcome is

relevant to the citizen, the citizen is relevant to the outcome. In the nation as a whole in modern times, as smaller and smaller percentages of the citizenry participate in elections, this dual relevancy of the covenant has eroded. Fewer people believe that who gets elected makes any real difference in their lives; and fewer believe that their vote or their political effort makes any real difference in the result. But in New Hampshire's presidential primary, at least, the covenant lives on.

Whatever motivated the volunteers in Cheshire County to join their campaigns and select the candidates they supported, however important or inconsequential they thought their individual efforts might be, all of them became signators of the covenant. And regardless of how their candidate eventually fared or what degree of significance they felt they had exerted on the results, each one believed in the implicit bargain that had been struck. They were more than names on a list or statistics on a tally sheet. They were full partners in the business of democracy.

Even as the presidential race moved on, away from them in both space and time, leaving them behind to take up the everyday lives they had led before signing onto the campaign, they kept some portion of it with them. They had kept the covenant.

EPILOGUE

On November 8, 1988, nearly nine months after the New Hampshire primary, the nation chose a new president. Across the country, 88.4 million citizens voted. George Bush (with 54 percent of the total) defeated Michael Dukakis (46 percent). In presidential general elections since 1952, when the primary was introduced, New Hampshire had voted Republican eight out of nine times—the sole exception was the Johnson landslide in 1964—and the 1988 returns made it nine out of ten: Bush swamped Dukakis, 64 percent to 36 percent, one of the biggest margins of the fifty states.

Cheshire County's vote—Bush 55 percent, Dukakis 45 percent—more closely paralleled the national returns. In Keene itself Bush eked out a thin margin, 4,535 votes to 4,466. Dukakis was able to carry only four towns in the county. Some 27,341 citizens (72 percent of the registered voters) cast ballots.

Eleanor Labrie spent election day at the Democratic headquarters in Keene, phoning voters on behalf of some local and statewide candidates. Her sister was visiting from Rhode Island, and Eleanor put her to work as well. Eleanor was not particularly fond of the Democrats' national ticket of Dukakis/Bentsen—"They're so blah, like malted milk," she said—but she voted for them. She was hoping that Gephardt would run again in the future.

Mike Haas, who had been Gephardt's county coordinator, was in Delaware County, Pennsylvania, where he was managing a congressional campaign. Following the primary, he had continued with Gephardt's campaign in Illinois and Michigan. After Gephardt's crushing loss in Michigan, Mike had sought solace at a Bruce Springsteen concert in Detroit; then Gephardt had pulled out of the race on March 28, Mike's birthday. The congressional campaign he managed in Pennsylvania lost on election day. Mike would later find a job in Washington, D.C., working for another congressman.

Tom Britton had planned to be at the polling place in Troy during election day, fulfilling his duties as town moderator. But, as a candidate for Cheshire County commissioner, state law prohibited him from being in charge of the ballot box. Instead he went to other towns in his district to shake hands with voters. His opponent— the incumbent and a prominent Dole supporter from the primary— won easily. A few weeks before the election Tom and Valerie had driven to Nashua for a fund-raiser for a congressional candidate. Al Gore was there, ostensibly to help the congressional race, but also to maintain a political presence in New Hampshire in preparation for the 1992 campaign. Tom spent most of his time at the event talking with Gore.

Jon Meyer, who had been Gore's coordinator in Cheshire County, was a first-year student at Columbia Law School in New York City. Having voted by absentee ballot (in Ohio), he attended his classes on election day.

Paige Crowley had stayed with the Hart campaign after the primary, traveling with the candidate as a press aide in the weeks leading up to "Super Tuesday." At the Democratic convention in Atlanta, she worked as a Hart aide. During the general election, her job was assisting the production of *The Choice*, a highly acclaimed documentary on the two presidential nominees for PBS's *Frontline* series.

Dan Melanson, who had never been interested in politics until he met Paige Crowley and volunteered for Gary Hart's rejuvenated campaign, was dissatisfied with the nominees of the two parties. As in previous elections, he decided not to vote on November 8.

Molly Kelly was working part-time for Paul McEachern, the Democratic nominee for governor (whose unsuccessful campaign in 1986 had first brought her into political involvement). She had gone to the Democratic national convention in Atlanta in July, where the Dukakis campaign had put her to work in a basement office for the week, but she had gotten a floor pass on the last night to hear Dukakis's acceptance speech. During the general election, however, her efforts focused on the gubernatorial race. (The national ticket considered New Hampshire a lost cause and expended little organizational effort there in the fall.) The local Democratic headquarters was the hangout for the party's establishment, from which Molly still felt somewhat estranged. She did most of her work from her home. McEachern, like most Democrats in the state, lost overwhelmingly, although he won in Keene. "This time," Molly said just before the election, "I feel like I know what I'm doing." In December she gave birth to a son.

Mike Cook, the Dukakis coordinator in the primary, had returned to his native Texas for the "Super Tuesday" campaign and then to Michigan for the caucuses there in late March. Feeling burned out from the presidential race, he had quit the Dukakis effort and taken a bus to Guatemala to visit a friend. On election day he was working as deputy campaign manager in Austin for a candidate for the Texas Supreme Court. There were only three people on the campaign staff because, Mike said, they were running a "total media campaign." His candidate won.

Dan Burnham was the Democratic candidate for a seat in the New Hampshire State Senate. It was a new experience for him. At one Democratic gathering, when he walked in the people stood up and applauded him. "Nobody's ever done that for me in fifty-eight years," he said. He had met with Babbitt during the summer, when Babbitt had made a brief visit to the Keene area, and they had been exchanging letters ever since. In some Babbitt offered friendly advice for Dan's candidacy. Dan focused his campaign on environmental issues; he shook more than three thousand hands; he raised and spent $18,000 (including a personal contribution of $200 from Babbitt); and he used a lot of direct-mail appeals for votes. Doris Haddock was his hardest-working volunteer. But he was buried in the Republican landslide in the state, carrying only four of thirteen towns in his district and getting just 42 percent of the vote. A few weeks later an article of his about his experience appeared in *The Keene Sentinel.*

Babbitt's county coordinator, Lisa Babish, had left New Hampshire after the primary and found work waiting tables in a restaurant in Washington, D.C. During the fall election, however, she came back to the state as campaign director for Jim Donchess, the Democratic nominee for Congress in the district covering western New Hampshire, who also lost by a wide margin. Unlike the Babbitt effort, this campaign was noted as being particularly mean and nasty. Afterward she would work briefly for someone running to be chairman of the Democratic National Committee, then for a congressman, then she would enroll in law school.

Pete Kujawski, the coordinator for Paul Simon's campaign in the county, went to work for a law firm in New York City after the primary, although he volunteered for a few weekends in a Democratic voter registration drive in the fall. He planned to go on to law school in 1989.

Andi Johnson threw herself into the general election. In addition to her regular job, she was also working part-time at a store in Keene. Nonetheless she was spending two nights a week at a campaign office in Peterborough and two nights and every weekend at the Democratic headquarters in Keene. In 1984, following her first volunteer effort for a candidate, her lingering distaste for Walter Mondale (who had eventually defeated Gary Hart for the nomination) had prompted Andi to tear Mondale's name from her Mondale/Ferraro bumper sticker, and she had written in Hart's name for president in the fall election. This year, however, even though her antipathy toward Dukakis had been equally strong, she did what she could for the entire Democratic ticket. When Bush questioned Dukakis's patriotism and devotion to the American flag, Andi defiantly hung up a flag in the local headquarters. "I take these Bush attacks personally," she said. In order to fill the ticket, she also allowed her name to be placed on the ballot for state representative. She lost by a big margin. On election day she stood outside the polls in Marlborough and Harrisville with hers and other Democrats' signs. She had already voted by absentee. Her cat was staying with her parents temporarily until after the election.

Steve Price, who came to Cheshire County for the last few weeks as Dole's coordinator, had returned to Columbia Law School after the primary, although he worked briefly in Massachusetts for Dole during "Super Tuesday" in March. In August he went to the Republican convention in New Orleans and worked on behalf of the New York State delegation. On election day in November he was in New York City, where he was the volunteer coordinator for the Bush/Quayle campaign. Following the election he landed a job in the State Department as special assistant to Ambassador Richard Burt, the strategic arms negotiator for the new administration.

Barbara and Mac MacKenzie did not get involved in the fall election, although they voted for Bush. "Someday," Barbara said, "I hope to be working for Elizabeth [Dole] in a presidential campaign."

Janet Shawn, who still believed that Dole had been correct the night of the primary when he'd said Bush had lied about his record, went to the polls November 8 wearing a handmade button that proclaimed, "I *STILL* PREFER DOLE." In the voting booth she wrote in Dole for president and Elizabeth for vice president.

Doug Kidd voted for Bush, although he said he didn't really see much difference between the Republican and Democratic nominees. He did not get involved in the general election. In April, when he was still owed expense money by the Robertson campaign, he wrote a letter to Robertson, forgave the debt, and "that ended the campaign for me," he said. He could envision working again for a candidate like Robertson, but only if the campaign was better organized to prevent the local/national problems he had witnessed in the primary. Robertson had come back to New Hampshire for a breakfast with his supporters, but Doug hadn't attended. He did, however, see Robertson on television when the former candidate returned to host *The 700 Club.* Doug watched for a while and decided that "Pat looked like he was free again."

Al Rubega had attended the Republican convention in New Orleans, where Mary was an alternate New Hampshire delegate. He had hoped that Bush would choose Kemp as his running mate but was happy with the selection of Dan Quayle, whom Al considered a "young Jack Kemp." During the convention Al handed out bumper stickers that read "Defend Firearms; Defeat Dukakis." Like the NRA, which worked tirelessly against Dukakis in the general election, Al rallied around the Bush candidacy. He sported a button that featured a picture of Dukakis with a slash through it, and he often referred to the Massachusetts governor as a "stinking liar" about firearms issues. On election day he served as Sullivan town moderator (a post he had been elected to on town meeting day in March) and therefore couldn't perform any campaign duties. Staying to count the ballots also made him too late to attend the Republican victory party in Nashua that evening. As a rising star in the NRA, he attended the group's lavish party during Bush's inaugural in Washington.

Chuck Douglas, Kemp's New Hampshire chairman, was the Republican nominee for Congress in western New Hampshire and on November 8 was elected to his first term. He replaced Judd Gregg, one of Bush's principal supporters, who was elected New Hampshire's governor, in turn replacing John Sununu, who spent the election as a national co-chairman for Bush and was on his way to becoming the White House chief of staff. (History was repeating itself. After the first New Hampshire primary in 1952, then-Governor Sherman Adams, Dwight Eisenhower's biggest supporter in the state, had taken to the campaign trail on behalf of the candidate; when Eisenhower was elected president, Adams became his chief of staff.) Will Abbott, Bush's state director in the primary, had taken a state job overseeing a program of land conservation. Ron Kaufman, who had helped engineer Bush's New Hampshire victory, masterminded several of Bush's high-profile "raids" on Massachusetts during the election—a tour of Boston harbor and the endorsement of Bush by the Boston police—and later took a job in the White House.

Pete Johnson was in charge of southern Vermont for the Bush/Quayle ticket but used the Lane home (about twenty miles from the Vermont border) as his headquarters. After the election he, too, went to work for the new administration.

Following the Democratic convention in July, when Dukakis was far ahead in the polls, Kendall Lane had spent an afternoon in the Keene Library, researching past elections. He discovered that a postconvention "bounce" normally occurred and decided that Bush still had a good chance to win. That statistic quieted the old nightmare, *All this for nothing.* At the Republican convention in August, where he was accompanying Jane, an alternate Bush delegate, Kendall had the time of his life—even though he wasn't a delegate, which had been one of his three goals from the start of the campaign. Pete Johnson, working as a sergeant at arms, provided Kendall with credentials that gave him better access to the inside of the convention hall than most delegates. His hotel was the same as Bush's, and on the first day of the convention he and Jane had run into Marvin Bush near the swimming pool and reminisced about primary day. On the night of Bush's nomination in New Orleans, he was on the convention floor, waving an American flag and feeling "a sense of vindication for two and a half years of work." In the fall the "Freedom Fighters" had started meeting again—on Wednesday mornings instead of Mondays—and Kendall was a constant participant. His biggest disappointment came near the end of the campaign, when Bush toured New England and made stops in Connecticut, Massachusetts, Vermont, and Maine, but, despite Kendall's pleading, not in Keene or anywhere else in New Hampshire. By election night, however, when he hosted a party in his converted barn, he was proud that Keene opened the first Republican headquarters in the state for the general election, that people like Al Rubega and Dr. David Ridge were working wholeheartedly for the ticket, and especially that Bush carried Cheshire County. He cheered the television set when Bush began his victory speech with the words "Thank you, New Hampshire." On May 1, 1989, the third of Kendall's goals was fulfilled. Along with other "Freedom Fighters" and core supporters from New Hampshire, he ate a meal in the White House and had his picture taken with President and Mrs. Bush.

ACKNOWLEDGMENTS

When Theodore White wrote *The Making of a President 1960*, chronicling the race between John F. Kennedy and Richard Nixon, political journalism was changed forever. For the first time readers were taken behind the scenes of a presidential campaign to watch the human drama of the struggle for national power. White's book set the mold for future campaign books, which he and others have since followed: an "inside" perspective looking over the shoulders of the candidates and their coterie of aides and advisers as they devise their strategies and play them out on the national stage.

I wanted to use this approach, but apply it to a campaign from the opposite vantage point. Rather than describing a political race from the top down, I wanted to watch from the bottom up; instead of recording a presidential contest from within the inner circle of candidates and advisers, I would report on the experiences of average citizens involved at the grass-roots level. These people, I believed, are too often forgotten in the quadrennial chronicles of electioneering. Yet their role in democracy is as important as that of a candidate and his staff—and their stories as filled with the stuff of human drama. There will never be a shortage of men (and someday women) who believe they are uniquely qualified to lead the nation, nor any shortage of consultants and political operatives whose job it is to help them. But without average citizens willing to volunteer their time on behalf of a candidate, participatory democracy becomes the business of professionals instead of the people's business.

My purpose in this project was neither to deify nor demonize New Hampshire's first-in-the-nation presidential primary. Instead, my principal interest was the individual volunteers. What prompted them to get involved in politics? How did they choose a candidate to support? What tasks did they perform—and what did they think while they performed them? How did their political involvement affect the other parts of their lives? In short, for this cross section of otherwise average citizens, what was the *experience* like at the grass-roots level of presidential politics? By telling that story, however, another emerged alongside it: the unfolding of a presidential primary, not only in the lives of individual volunteers but in the larger community around them. This secondary story, I hope, gives readers a chance to see the inner workings of New Hampshire's unique primary—from its peaks of candidate-to-voter contact and citizen activism to its valleys of pettiness and silliness—and make up their own minds on its worth. I saw my job as telling the story whole and keeping the punditry at a minimum. Too much political journalism gets it the other way around.

While the incidents reported in this book are specific to the people, the place, and the time described in it, the story reaches beyond those limits. Like Thornton Wilder's *Our Town*, which was also set in the Monadnock Region of New Hampshire, this book was meant to chronicle not just the experiences of a handful of people but, by implication at least, those of many others. The setting is the year leading up to the 1988 New Hampshire presidential primary, but much of what occurs takes place in all primaries and all campaigns. Similarly, the grass-roots volunteers in this book are real people, unique unto themselves, but their collective story is every volunteer's story.

In late 1986 I started contacting the presidential campaigns that were beginning to set up organizations for the 1988 primary in New Hampshire. With their permission I was allowed to follow the progress of their grass-roots organizations in Cheshire County from their inception. The only two conditions attached to my access were that nothing I learned from my research and interviews would be made public until after the primary in February 1988 and that I would not share any of their tactical plans with either political journalists or the other campaigns.

The local volunteers whose stories are told in this book similarly were aware of my project from the outset. For fourteen months they shared their lives with me. When they held campaign meetings, I attended with them. If they went to candidate appearances or political events—both in Cheshire County and the rest of the state—I tagged along. I accompanied them during door-to-door canvasses and sat with them when they called voters from their phone banks. In addition to several long interviews to compile biographical material and, after the primary, to review the campaign experience they had just gone through, we kept in touch on a weekly basis. Most of the conversations quoted in the preceding pages are the result of my on-site reporting; where that was not possible, they have been reconstructed through the best recollections of the participants, usually within twenty-four hours of their occurrence.

Likewise, whenever a presidential candidate crossed the border into Cheshire County, I made it my business to attend all of his public events, even if one of my subjects was not involved. (In a few instances, in fact, it was through this method that I encountered people who ended up as volunteers and, eventually, characters in this book.) For the couple of events I was unable to attend, I have relied on news accounts from *The Keene Sentinel* and/or conversations with people who were there.

During the hectic final days of the campaign, when it was logistically impossible for me to follow each character personally, I arranged for friends whose reporting abilities I respect to assist my project. In particular, on primary day I am indebted to the work of Richard Watts, Tim Clark, Ken Burns, Ernest Hebert, Bob Trebilcock, David Lord, Ralph Whitehead, Andrew Kopkind, and Dianne Kearns Duncan. My reporting crew for that day rivaled that of many major publications in size and, I think, quality. This public thank-you, however, is their only remuneration.

In the interests of full disclosure, I should point out that I am a registered Democrat, always have been, and have been involved in a variety of Democratic campaigns, both in New Hampshire and nationally—a fact that all the campaigns and the people I followed were fully aware of.

I have called Cheshire County my home for eighteen years. I experienced my first New Hampshire presidential primary as a voter in 1972. I covered the 1976 primary as a reporter for *The Keene Sentinel.* In the 1980 primary, as an aide to Governor Hugh Gallen, I assisted the campaign of President Jimmy Carter. During the 1984 race my duties as deputy national press secretary for Walter Mondale brought me constantly to New Hampshire and later across the nation in the subsequent primaries and general election. Throughout 1987 and the first half of 1988, I was unaligned with any campaign or candidate while I pursued my research on this book. In June of 1988, however, I was named national press secretary for Michael Dukakis's general election campaign—and kept intact my unblemished record of working on losing presidential campaigns.

Many people and organizations deserve my thanks. First and foremost are the volunteers and campaign workers who graciously included me in their lives for more than a year, who shared their private thoughts and hopes and dreams so unstintingly, and who patiently put up with the constant presence of me and my notebook and my tape recorder. They will always have my deepest gratitude and respect. This book is their story, not mine.

The various campaign headquarters, which uniformly gave me

their blessings to proceed, had to rely on my word that any sensitive information I came across would not appear in the thick of the campaign. Keeping my side of the bargain was the least I could do as thanks.

This project would also not have been possible without the encouragement and support of a number of people and institutions: Charlton MacVeagh, Nancy Hayden, James Ewing, David Nixon, John and Elting Morison, Walter Peterson and Franklin Pierce College, Public Policy Associates, and Marvin Kalb and Ellen Hume of the Joan Shorenstein Barone Center on the Press, Politics, and Public Policy at Harvard University. Chuck Verrill, David Stanford, and Donald Mitchell provided guidance and assistance. Will Fay, Linda Fullerton, and Tom Kearney of *The Keene Sentinel* generously shared information with me. Caleb Rick's research of voting records in past primaries was a great help. My all-star reporting crew on primary day allowed me to survive February 16, 1988, with nothing more than a bad case of bronchitis.

Finally, pursuing a dozen campaigns around Cheshire County for fourteen months, traveling with a presidential candidate for five months, and then sequestering myself in either Cambridge, Massachusetts, or the attic of our house to write this book has meant that my duties as a husband and father were too often neglected over the course of two and a half years. The pages that precede are no compensation for the time lost with our daughter, Emmy. Fortunately Dianne Kearns Duncan—besides being a sharp, temporarily retired political reporter and a helpful editor—is a remarkable woman, capable of being a marvelous mother not only to our child, but also, in many ways, to this book.

Roxbury, New Hampshire
July 1989

INDEX